# Great Power Diplomacy in the Hellenistic World

Diplomacy is a neglected aspect of Hellenistic history, despite the fact that war and peace were the major preoccupations of the rulers of the kingdoms of the time. It becomes clear that it is possible to discern a set of accepted practices which were generally followed by the kings from the time of Alexander to the approach of Rome. The republican states were less bound by such practices, and this applies above all to Rome and Carthage. By concentrating on diplomatic institutions and processes, therefore, it is possible to gain a new insight into the relations between the kingdoms.

This study investigates the making and duration of peace treaties, the purpose of so-called 'marriage alliances', and the absence of summit meetings and looks in detail at the relations between states from a diplomatic point of view, rather than only in terms of the wars they fought. The system which had emerged as a result of the personal relationships between Alexander's successors continued in operation for at least two centuries. The intervention of Rome brought in a new great power which had no similar tradition, and the Hellenistic system crumbled therefore under Roman pressure.

**John D. Grainger** was a teacher for a quarter of a century and gained his PhD from Birmingham University in 1990. He then turned to writing full-time and has published over thirty books, mainly on Hellenistic history and on modern military history.

# Great Power Diplomacy in the Hellenistic World

John D. Grainger

LONDON AND NEW YORK

First published 2017 by Routledge

2 Park Square, Milton Park, Abingdon, Oxfordshire OX14 4RN
52 Vanderbilt Avenue, New York, NY 10017

*Routledge is an imprint of the Taylor & Francis Group, an informa business*

First issued in paperback 2019

Copyright © 2017 John D. Grainger

The right of John D. Grainger to be identified as author of this work has been asserted by him in accordance with sections 77 and 78 of the Copyright, Designs and Patents Act 1988.

All rights reserved. No part of this book may be reprinted or reproduced or utilised in any form or by any electronic, mechanical, or other means, now known or hereafter invented, including photocopying and recording, or in any information storage or retrieval system, without permission in writing from the publishers.

Notice:
Product or corporate names may be trademarks or registered trademarks, and are used only for identification and explanation without intent to infringe.

*British Library Cataloguing in Publication Data*
A catalogue record for this book is available from the British Library

*Library of Congress Cataloging in Publication Data*
A catalogue record for this book has been requested

ISBN: 978-1-4724-8429-1 (hbk)
ISBN: 978-0-367-88190-0 (pbk)

Typeset in Times New Roman
by Apex CoVantage, LLC

# Contents

| | |
|---|---|
| *Abbreviations* | vii |
| Introduction: Aims and plans | 1 |
| **PART I** | |
| **Techniques and practices** | 9 |
| 1 The origins of Hellenistic diplomacy | 11 |
| 2 Royal marriages | 33 |
| 3 Cities, summits, states, envoys | 55 |
| **PART II** | |
| **Diplomacy in action – the East** | 73 |
| 4 The diplomacy of the earlier Syrian Wars (274–241) | 75 |
| 5 Aegean diplomacy: Ptolemy I to Aratos of Sikyon | 84 |
| 6 The diplomacy of Antiochos III – I: the Greek world | 103 |
| **PART III** | |
| **Diplomacy in the West** | 123 |
| 7 Ionian Sea diplomacy | 125 |
| 8 The diplomacy of Rome and Carthage – I | 144 |
| 9 The diplomacy of Rome and Carthage – II | 161 |

**PART IV**
**The collision of East and West** 175

10  The diplomacy of Antiochos III – II: the Roman crisis 177
11  The diplomacy of peacemaking (222–188) 195
12  Rome and Greece (188 – c.120) 212
13  The later Syrian Wars (195 – c.140) 231
    Conclusion 248

    *Bibliography* 251
    *Index* 255

# Abbreviations

Ager, *Interstate Arbitration* – Sheila L. Ager, *Interstate Arbitrations in the Greek World, 337–90* BC, California 1996.

Austin – M.M. Austin, *The Hellenistic World from Alexander to the Roman Conquest,* 2nd ed., Cambridge 2006.

Bagnall, *Administration* – R.S. Bagnall, *The Administration of the Ptolemaic Possessions outside Egypt,* Leiden 1976.

Bagnall and Derow – R.S. Bagnall and P. Derow, *The Hellenistic Period*, Oxford 2004.

Burstein – S.M. Burstein, *The Hellenistic Age from the Battle of Ipsus to the Death of Cleopatra VII,* Cambridge 1985.

*CAH – Cambridge Ancient History*.

Dittenberger, *Sylloge* – W. Dittenberger, *Sylloge Inscriptionum Graecarum* (3rd ed.), 1915–1924.

*FGrH* – F. Jacoby, *Fragmente der Greichischen Historiker,* Berlin and Leiden, 1923–.

Holbl, *Ptolemaic Empire* – Gunther Holbl, *A History of the Ptolemaic Empire*, London 2001.

*I. Crete* – M. Guarducci, *Inscriptiones Creticae*, Rome, 1935–1950.

*IG – Inscriptiones Graecae.*

*I. Ilion* – P. Frisch, *Die Inschriften von Ilion*, Bonn 1975.

*ISE* – L. Moretti, *Iscrizioni Storiche ellenistiche*, Florence 1965–1974.

Josephus, *AJ* – Josephus, *Antiquitates Judaicae.*

Ma, Antiochos III – John Ma, *Antiochos III and the Cities of Western Asia Minor*, Oxford 1999.

*Milet* – A. Rehm, Die Delphinion in *Milet*, Berlin 1914.

*OGIS* – W. Dittenberger, *Orientis Graeci Inscriptionem Selectae,* Leipzig 1903–1905.

Pliny, *NH* – Pliny, *Natural History.*

*RGDE* – R.K. Sherk (ed.), *Roman Documents from the Greek East,* Baltimore MD 1969.

Schmitt, *Staatsverträge* – H.H. Schmitt, *Die Staatsverträge des Altertums,* vol 3, Munich 1969.

*SEG* – *Supplementum Epigraphicum Graecum.*

Sherk – R.K. Sherk, *Rome and the Greek East to the death of Augustus,* Cambridge 1984.

*TAM* – *Tituli Asia Minoris.*

Welles, RC – C.B. Welles, *Royal Correspondence in the Hellenistic Period,* London 1934.

Will, *Histoire Politique* – E. Will, *Histoire Politique du Monde Hellenistique,* 2 vols, Nancy 1979–1982.

*ZPE* – *Zeitschrift fur Papyrologie und Epigrafik.*

# Introduction
## Aims and plans

The Hellenistic period, which is taken here to last from the death of Alexander the Great in Babylon in 323 to about 100 BC, has a political and diplomatic character all its own. Of course, many characteristics were inherited from the past – from Greece, from the Akhaimenid Empire, from pharaonic Egypt – but the eventual set of diplomatic practices was different from all of them; in addition, the several regions were distinct in their mixtures of cultures and peoples; it was not a period of uniformity. It was a time, in international political terms, which is what diplomacy deals in, of several monarchic great powers, leagues of cities, and individual cities, which took the place of the independent city states of Greece and Italy of the preceding period; in place of the Akhaimenid Empire were the great monarchies of the Seleukid, Ptolemaic, and Antigonid dynasties, who both divided up that empire and dominated the Greek peninsula; but in Greece the old cities and the new leagues of Aitolia and eventually Achaia resisted that domination; to the west this monarchic factor reached Sicily and Numidia, but again the city states still resisted and remained the norm for a time.

The three great Hellenistic monarchies existed in a state of political balance for well over a century. This was the first time there had been a political and military balance of power over the large area of the Middle East since the sixth century BC; nor was this a condition which would return until after the fall of the Roman Empire (unless one counts the duopoly of Rome and Parthia).

The Greek situation had not materially changed with the great conquests by Alexander, and the cities had, politically, relatively little influence on the new great powers; yet the kings did tend to make gestures to gain the cities' approval by affecting to promote or protect their freedom. Some of the cities of Greece, notably Athens and Sparta, still played their parts in the politics of Greece, but the real powers among the Greek cities were now the leagues, of which the Aitolian and the Achaian were the most effective, but there were also others. Yet the new monarchies overshadowed even these.

It follows from this new situation that new diplomatic practices had to develop. The former practices had involved negotiations between cities, or, less often, discussions with representatives of the Persian great king. But from about 300 BC there were several monarchies which needed to negotiate with each other, and soon there were several more polities which had to be included in the system, while

2   *Introduction*

Rome also intruded from about 200 BC. That is, the new diplomacy was worked out at the beginning of the Hellenistic period, in the years following the death of Alexander the Great, among the three great kingdoms and their predecessor, the realm of Antigonos Monophthalomos, and the emerging powers of the west did not involve themselves for a century; Rome in particular was not a player in the system, except marginally, until its second war with Macedon; it then had to fit itself into an existing diplomatic system, like several other states which had emerged in the period since the system was developed.

The sheer distances involved meant that negotiations were slow, though all the main centres – Alexandria, Antioch, Pella, Pergamon, Rome, Carthage – were within reach of the sea, which helped. The personal nature of political power in the monarchies meant that the old open, public discussion of international affairs in city assemblies largely disappeared, or at least became less important, to be replaced by discussions *in camera*, usually involving the king and a few of his advisors.

The major origin and influence on the new practices was the Macedonian kingdom as it had been under Philip II and Alexander (359–336 BC) (Chapter 1). Here were the origins of the personal monarchies which emerged from the collapse of Alexander's brief empire, but a new factor also entered, for any Macedonian diplomatic practices which can be discerned were overridden to a large extent by the crucial fact that the kings of the new kingdoms which emerged after the death of Alexander the Great all knew each other.

The relations between the great power monarchies of the Hellenistic period, therefore, had a distinctive character, curiously based on reciprocated trust, an unlikely basis but one which clearly hardened into accepted practice. This can only be explained by the original atmosphere of friendship which existed between men such as Seleukos and Ptolemy and Lysimachos and the rest, who had been subordinates and colleagues and comrades in arms in Alexander's great campaigns from Illyria to India.

At the same time, the diplomatic practices which had long existed between the cities and the city leagues continued into the new period and remained very similar to those which had existed before Philip II. Here the old public discussion survived, and the relative geographical proximity of the cities speeded the process along. It is clear that the royal practices did have a powerful effect on that situation and eventually prevailed over them, simply because of the disparity in power, but the cities nevertheless continued their old methods; this was the original Roman practice also, which was to be slowly modified by that city's need to interact with equivalent great powers, which were frequently monarchies.

So the second influence on the new diplomacy was the old Greek practice of envoys visiting another state, in a fairly informal way. The increasing institutionalisation of the monarchic system gradually compelled a change into a much more formal practice, consonant with the dignity of the kings. But the need for any power, large or small, to have diplomatic relations with a wide variety of states meant that the envoys had to adapt to each meeting. Kings might discuss primarily with other kings' envoys in private, but they would also have to contact cities and leagues in which the envoys would be expected to explain their master's policies in public.

The relationship between the monarchies and the cities, therefore, partook both of the monarchies' secrecy and of the public and open civic system. The much greater weight of the monarchies in the system reduced the effectiveness of the cities, and this was clearly one of the main reasons why the Greek cities gathered together into leagues. Single cities, even relatively powerful ones such as Athens and Sparta, were very vulnerable in this new system – both of these suffered severely from their insistence on their independence. The effective resistance of the Aitolian League to repeated pressure from Macedon is a confirmation in its way of the effectiveness of the league as a political actor, though the Achaian League tended to be a good deal less effective.

There were, because this new world was a complex of kings, cities, and leagues, plenty of opportunities for diplomacy. In that term may be included the plots and intrigues as well as the negotiations and treaties which both bound the various political entities together and at the same time often drove them apart. Diplomatic practices, therefore, included alliances, royal marriages, treaties of peace, extended negotiations, sometimes lasting for years, preparations for war, and spying and disruption. The whole amounted to a system generally accepted among the participants, though never defined (Chapters 2 and 3).

This system, as it developed, is relatively clear and can be easily traced throughout the third century BC and into the next among the states of the Greek world from the Adriatic to India. Yet at the same time a variation developed in the western Mediterranean, and when Rome became involved in Greek affairs, both civic and monarchic, the practices of both systems changed, just as the old civic diplomacy had been modified by the existence of the monarchies. The dominant powers in the west, Rome and Carthage, were city leagues, but on a much greater and more powerful scale than those in Greece; the lesser powers were unstable monarchies (as in Sicily and Epeiros), and there were numerous individual cities. Yet in detail Roman diplomatic practice was not altogether unlike that of the monarchies of the Hellenistic world – though it was perhaps even more ruthless.

For all minor powers diplomacy was an essential tool for survival. None of them was capable of defying a great power militarily for very long, though they were quite capable of taking on a rival city. Therefore persuasion, submission, or gaining a protecting alliance were the necessary means if a minor power was to stave off threats or troubles or conquest. Diplomatic contacts could also be used to extract favours or at least garner great power support for a local dispute. It behoved a great power to be very careful of the wiles of these minor powers.

The fact that the great powers were monarchies meant that their policies were subject to variation with the person and character of the kings. Some kings, such as Antiochos III and Ptolemy II, were particularly skilled in diplomacy; others, such as the Seleukid Demetrios I, were clumsy and succeeded only in making enemies. The personal nature of monarchic diplomacy, however, was not such as to force serious changes; the system could not change in the short term, even if it was subject to slow development in the long.

## 4  Introduction

No word for diplomacy existed in Latin or Greek at the time. It was not an area of expertise which was recognised as distinctive by any of the societies involved. There were no professional diplomats – though some men were sent on several diplomatic missions and may be considered to have become experts – and there was no profession which might be described as diplomacy. (At the same time there were no professionals in any of the 'professions', no professional generals, governors, or senior bureaucrats; the professional levels in these areas of operations only existed at lower levels; diplomacy was thus not distinctive in its 'amateurism'.) Nevertheless it is quite possible to detect a series of institutions, if that is not too strong a word, which we may describe as diplomatic.

In this account these are sometimes described in the several chapters, or in others they merit a separate discussion. So the question of the duration of peace treaties is discussed in Chapter 1, for this is a fundamental element which is also distinctive for the period. The practice of royal marriage is a large subject, considerably misunderstood, which is discussed separately (Chapter 2). Several other issues are grouped into a chapter where they are discussed individually (Chapter 3).

The plan of the book, therefore, is to examine the development of the system in the eastern Mediterranean and highlight its particular and distinctive practices (Chapters 1–6), then to consider the contemporary system as it operated in the western Mediterranean, where it resulted in the early Roman Empire (Chapters 7–9). The later Hellenistic practice centred on the work of Antiochos III and Philip V and their reduction of Egypt to secondary status leads to the collision of these powers with Rome (Chapters 10–12). The increasing ruthlessness and unpleasantness of the Roman actions is one of the features of this last section. A final chapter (13) is on diplomacy in the eastern Mediterranean after the first intrusion of Rome, indicating the irrelevance of Rome for much of that area.

The constraints imposed by the surviving sources will be obvious. As usual in a book on this period, the cessation of detailed source material after about 140 makes it impossible to deal in much detail with subsequent events. It remains possible to deal with the eastern Mediterranean situation until almost 100, but in the west the fall of Carthage in 146 marks an effective end of information. With the annexation of the Attalid kingdom, only thirteen years after the definitive annexation of Macedon, the domination of Rome became all too obvious, and much of the international relations were from then on conducted under this lengthening shadow; by that time Rome was not practising diplomacy as it had been known in the Hellenistic period but was exercising domination disguised as a sort of diplomacy, which had been developing as a form of international relationship during the Third War with Macedon and its preliminaries, discussed in Chapter 12. This is a very different subject.

The men whom we may describe as diplomats or envoys performed several functions in international relations. Their overall function was to initiate or continue contacts between separate political authorities – cities, kings, armies, generals – who might be in conflict. This involved a variety of distinct activities. There were the visits by the envoys or embassies of one authority to another; there were the interventions of envoys in conflicts between two other warring or arguing parties; negotiations might take some time, depending in part on the purpose of the embassy, which might be to make an alliance, to make a peace, to resolve a dispute, to browbeat, to congratulate, or some other matter. (Browbeating became the favoured Roman method, one of the reasons for avoiding the subject.)

Amid all this apparent variety and varied purposes the 'system' worked, if this is not too definitive a term. Envoys, embassies, heralds, passed between states and kings, carrying messages; negotiations were conducted over long distances and long periods of time and brought to successful conclusions; treaties were made and very largely kept; truces were made in wars amid conflict and fighting; all these may be considered as elements in Hellenistic diplomacy. These are, of course, the sorts of activities which diplomats in all ages and in all regions have undertaken. In the Hellenistic period, however, there were also particular envoy expeditions as a type of sub-diplomacy, and most of these will be ignored in this discussion, which is necessarily directed to international political affairs.

Some sets of envoys were sent out, usually by cities or temples, or even by private or semi-private groups such as the Dionysiac association of artists, essentially with the function of advertising their wares. So the manifestation of Artemis Leukophryene at Miletos in 211 generated a whole series of envoys sent by that city in all directions – we know of envoys going to Delphi, to Egypt, and to a series of cities in Asia as far as Antioch-in-Persis.[1] This was also the practice of the organisers of the great festivals. Then there were other envoys, sent by one city at the request of others who were in dispute with each other, as arbitrators. These men are usually referred to as judges, and they have been thoroughly studied already.[2]

These embassies were not really the same type of diplomacy as the envoys who travelled between kings – quite apart from often being so numerous as to be unwieldy (one set of such 'envoys' numbered 150 men, who must have been a grievous burden for the city they went to). Another type of envoy were those which were sent by cities of the kingdoms to the royal courts, usually bearing a decree of the city and a gold crown, but whose real purpose was often to persuade the king to grant some concession or privilege. These are best regarded as part of the internal mechanism of the kingdoms, for the conceit of the kingdoms was that the king and the cities were allies, though in fact, as any city soon discovered when that unspoken assumption was breached or questioned, the relationship was anything but equal. This last type, however, verges close on international relations, particularly where the relationship of the two parties is new. They will therefore be brought into the discussions as required, for the subject of diplomacy is the relationship between states; this is also part of Chapter 3's collection.

This study is not intended to be a diplomatic history of the period, though at times it might read as one, and there are obvious gaps in the coverage. However, the only way to discern methods and purposes and practices in the diplomacy of the time, in the absence of any ancient discussion on the subject, is to describe those events where diplomacy was employed – and where this is adequately described in the sources – so that these distinctive elements emerge. The following chapters, therefore, consider several political episodes over periods of time, with a strong emphasis on the diplomatic processes involved. All too often in general accounts these are omitted in favour of a quick smash-and-grab account of a war or a battle, but it is the diplomacy before, between, and after these collisions which reveals as much about the history of the places and peoples as any battle or political conquest. These are the real subject of the several chronological chapters.

A further result of the usual emphasis on warfare – which, to be sure, is in large part the result of the ancient sources – is to purvey the impression that the Hellenistic period is one of, as a recent account puts it, 'anarchy'.[3] This is a characterisation which cannot be sustained, and a survey of the diplomacy which operated will show that in fact it was a period in which major efforts were made to avoid conflict and that the diplomatic system of the Hellenistic states provided a framework within which those states could operate to resolve their disputes – that it was, in fact, the very opposite of 'anarchy', because the diplomats and the kings were men who were operating within an accepted set of rules and practices.

So far as I can discover no previous study on this subject in this period has been made. The nearest is a book by Sir Frank Adcock and D.J. Mosley.[4] The title – *Diplomacy in Ancient Greece* – is efficiently vague, but the contents are essentially those of the classics university course – Classical Greece and the Roman Republic, virtually ignoring the great monarchies – and the account of the mechanics of diplomacy, by Mosley, is essentially that practised by the Greek city states in the fifth and fourth centuries BC; these were considerably different from those of the succeeding monarchies.

There are a goodly number of general histories of the Hellenistic period now available, though diplomacy as a discrete subject tends to be lost in the detail of the description of crises or culture or warfare, or is ignored altogether.[5] It is necessary to examine what actually happened (the old Rankean cliché) before the full importance of diplomatic practice emerges. Too often a general history can only point out that 'a war began' or 'A attacked B'; in fact, such political developments were invariably preceded, accompanied, and succeeded by diplomatic engagements, and these become clear only with a close examination of events. This is what I have tried to provide in the several chapters of description.

It may be pointed out, as an additional comment, that this was a period which was analogous to the conflicts of the Bronze Age kingdoms in the same geographical region or of Europe over the past several hundred years. It was, as were those periods (there have been others), characterised by repeated, even continuous, political conflicts from minor intrigues up to general wars and constant attempts to upset or restore the balances of power between the great powers. Such periods are also characterised by vibrant cultural developments, as though the political tensions stimulated cultural creativity.

The intrigues, disputes, conflicts, and wars characterised by 'balance-of-power' periods also invariably saw the development of diplomacy as a distinctive practice, but each such period had its own particular practices and characteristic features. Among the Bronze Age great powers – Babylon, the Hittites, Egypt, Mitanni – the diplomatic method was essentially an exchange of letters and gifts between the kings, each carefully graded to convey the sender's sentiments. The delivery of royal daughters into the harems of foreign kings was one of the prime elements, and long negotiations could take place on the conditions for their future lives.[6] In European international affairs since the Italian Renaissance the most characteristic institution of diplomacy has been the ambassadors resident in foreign capital cities – 'honest men sent to lie abroad for the good of their country', as the Stuart wit Sir Henry Wotton with felicitous ambiguity put it.[7] This practice began in Italy in the fifteen century, when it was possible for the great powers in Italy – Milan, Venice, Florence, the Pope, Naples – to communicate with their ambassadors regularly and speedily, and it was taken up by the great powers of sixteenth-century Europe, even though it was more difficult for the ambassadors to communicate with their home countries with any speed. The institution was successful largely because the ambassadors could conduct provisional negotiations and could defuse contentious issues; at the same time their presence was in fact a strong indication of the constant tension and suspicion within the international political system of which they were a part. That the period of balances of power in Europe lasted for so long, being upset repeatedly – the Spanish Habsburg Empire, Louis XIV, Napoleonic France, Hitler's Nazi Empire – and then restored is an indication of the system's success, as well as, with the increasingly destructive warfare on the continent, indications of its failures.

It may also be noted that we appear to be entering into a new 'balance-of-power' period with the rise of Chinese power, the revival of Russia, the growth of India, and the integration of the European Union. There will no doubt develop a type of diplomacy suited to the new age – electronic communication rather than resident ambassadors, say – but the object will be the same, to control and manage disputes, avoid wars, but also to score points and 'diplomatic triumphs'. One must hope that, given the potential for destruction available to the present great powers, they are more successful in avoiding wars than the diplomatic systems of the past.

The regularity and repetitiveness of warfare in the Hellenistic period is also an indication that the diplomatic system developed by the Hellenistic kingdoms ultimately failed, but it must be said that they did exercise some control and that the really destructive warfare was accomplished by late arrivals in the diplomatic system – Rome, above all, but also Carthage.

## Notes

1 Austin (see 'Abbreviations' section for full information) 189, 190.
2 Ager (see 'Abbreviations' section for full information), *Interstate Arbitrations*.
3 Arthur M. Eckstein, *Mediterranean Anarchy, Interstate War and the Rise of Rome*, California 2006.
4 Sir Frank Adcock and D.J. Mosley, *Diplomacy in Ancient Greece*, London 1975.
5 Without attempting to be comprehensive, the obvious books include: Peter Green, *Alexander to Actium*, London 1990; F.W. Walbank, *The Hellenistic Age*, London 1981; R.M. Errington, *A History of the Hellenistic World, 323–30* BC, Oxford 2008; Graham Shipley, *The Greek World after Alexander, 323–30* BC, London 2000; Michael Grant, *The Hellenistic Greeks from Alexander to Cleopatra*, London 1982; C.B. Welles, *Alexander and the Hellenistic World*, Toronto 1970; the various articles in *Cambridge Ancient History*, vols. 7 and 8, 2nd ed., Cambridge 1984; in French there are Claire Preaux, *Le Monde Hellenistique, La Grece et l'Orient 323–146 av. J.-C.*, 2 vols, 2nd ed., Paris 1987–1988;

8   *Introduction*

E. Will, *Histoire Politique du Monde Hellenistique*, 2 vols, Nancy 1979–1982; Pierre Leveque, *Le monde hellenistique*, Paris 1969; J. Delorme, *Le Monde hellenistique, 323–133 avant J.-C.*, Paris 1975. Then there is what is still in many ways as good as anything more recent, W.W. Tarn, revised by G.T. Griffith, *Hellenistic Civilisation*, 3rd ed., London 1952. The exception to the 'rule' that diplomacy is ignored is Erich S. Gruen, *The Hellenistic World and the Coming of Rome*, California 1984, though he is concerned above all with Roman relations with the eastern states, not relations between those states themselves.

6   Amanda Podary, *Brotherhood of Kings: How International Relations Shaped the Ancient Near East*, Oxford 2010; Raymond Cohen and Raymond Westbrook (eds.), *Amarna Diplomacy: The Beginnings of International Relations*, Baltimore 2000.

7   Garrett Mattingly, *Renaissance Diplomacy*, London 1955.

# Part I
# Techniques and practices

# 1 The origins of Hellenistic diplomacy

The Hellenistic world was a world of kings. From Sicily to Baktria and India there were only two substantial non-monarchical polities, in Aitolia and Achaia. West of the Adriatic, of course, there were also the great republics of Rome and Carthage and the cities of Sicily and southern Italy, but none of these impinged seriously on events to the east of the Adriatic until after 200 BC. Around the Aegean and Black Seas there were many cities which claimed autonomy, but many of these became subject in one way or another to a monarchy after Alexander's time, and none had much weight diplomatically – it was usually a form of diplomacy which kept them under a monarch's thumb.

In discussing the diplomacy of this time and place, therefore, the existence and power of the kings must be the first consideration. In some cases, notably Macedon, the kingdoms were ancestral, and the dynasties only temporary; in other cases the kings and their dynasties had actually formed the kingdoms, and this process of new state creation continued throughout the period. It was not uncommon for a state to suddenly appear on the political horizon simply because a man chose to call himself a king – Cyrenaica under Magas, for example, or the various fragments of the Seleukid Empire from Asia Minor to India, all of which emerged as kingdoms.

Diplomacy was therefore largely conducted by, and in the name of, the kings. Furthermore, the formation of the Hellenistic kingdoms in large part came in the wake of the death of Alexander the Great of Macedon. The various rulers in the generation following on from Alexander's death in Babylon in 323 BC were mainly men who had been Alexander's subordinates and contemporaries. They were all well known to each other, had often grown up together, and had fought and campaigned together, both in Macedon and then in the conquest of the Persian Empire. This is personified in the reported comment of Seleukos I when he found that Ptolemy had filched part of the spoils Seleukos had expected to collect after the collapse of the kingdom of Antigonos Monophthalamos; he is said to have commented that Ptolemy was his friend, and he would not fight him.[1] There were, of course, plenty of other considerations involved in his decision not to fight, principally that Seleukos would probably be beaten and might therefore lose all his gains. But the remark sets the tone, and indeed it is reflected in the practice of diplomacy among the kings for the next century and a half and more.

The basic problem in studying diplomacy in Hellenistic times, however, is that for the people of the time it was not a concept they recognised. There were no diplomats, though there were men who travelled from one state to another as envoys or in a group as an embassy. No concept of diplomacy as such existed, and yet recognised diplomatic practices did. In such circumstances the only way to discover how diplomacy worked is to look at what the men whom we may recognise as diplomats actually did.

## Durability of treaties

The public product of diplomacy is agreements between political units – that is, treaties. A treaty regularises a situation by solving a problem. It therefore deals only with the conditions at the time it was agreed. Frequently they are agreed after wars, in which case they adjust the power between those making the treaty in the light of the results of the war. But what treaties cannot do is to prescribe for the future, though some attempted to do so. So after a time, possibly after another war, a new treaty was required. Treaties, in other words, were repeatedly required as conditions of international affairs altered. It was not always necessary that a war should take place, only that the new conditions be recognised and addressed. Hence treaties also formed alliances, or royal marriages, or agreements between kings and cities, none of which necessarily involved warfare. And, of course, one function of diplomacy, which is perhaps most prominent in the modern world, is to solve minor disputes and problems and so avoid war.

For the Hellenistic states in a few cases we can examine what took place in negotiations and so gain some idea how an agreement was reached, but more usually we have only the bare record of a treaty, or even only the presumption of a treaty. However, there is one principle which appears to operate throughout the monarchical system and which was even adopted by republican Rome in its relations with the Hellenistic monarchies. It is best elucidated by considering the longest sequence of wars the ancient world ever knew – those between the Seleukids and the Ptolemies, usually called the Syrian Wars.

The wars display a distinct and telling pattern.[2] The first war, in the late 270s, was ended by an agreement between Antiochos I and Ptolemy II – or so we may suppose, though such a treaty is not mentioned in any ancient source. Their fathers, Seleukos I and Ptolemy I, had not gone to war over Palestine and Phoenicia, which Ptolemy I had seized in 302–301, and Seleukos' comment that Ptolemy was his friend was certainly apposite, even if self-serving and propagandistic. Seleukos very noticeably simply avoided fighting; he did not accept that Ptolemy's seizure of 'Koile Syria', as it became called, was permanent or definitive. Antiochos I, who was adult at the time of the dispute, inherited the Seleukid claim to Ptolemy's Syrian territories. That Antiochos I and Ptolemy II waited until *c.*274 before fighting each other is easily explained – Antiochos had many more urgent tasks elsewhere, notably the invasion of Asia Minor by the Galatians, and Ptolemy, being the man in possession of the disputed lands, had no need to attack. Antiochos was necessarily the aggressor.

The war ceased in c.271; then there was peace until 260, when the second war broke out. That was the year after Antiochos I's death, when Ptolemy II was still king. It is the sequence of Antiochos' death followed very shortly by the outbreak of the new war which is significant.

This pattern was replicated in 246, when both Ptolemy II and Antiochos II died. The apparent occasion for war was the death of Berenike, Ptolemy II's daughter and the second wife of Antiochos II, though in fact the fighting had broken out before Ptolemy III, Berenike's brother, knew of her death. That is to say, the occasion for war was the death of Antiochos II and the accession of the new Seleukid king, Seleukos II; Berenike was one of its early casualties, but her death was not its cause. Ptolemy III's forces had a free run in this war for a time, since it coincided with a rebellion by Seleukos II's brother, and peace was made in 241 when Seleukos had recovered most of Ptolemy's conquests and felt it necessary to attend to the rebellion. The third war, however, began in 221, when Antiochos III attacked Phoenicia soon after the death of Ptolemy III and the accession of Ptolemy IV. Again both men were new kings, and Antiochos was attempting to gain renown in part because of troubles in his own kingdom, but he did not start the war until after he received the news of Ptolemy III's death. The war ended with a peace treaty, following the Seleukid defeat at Raphia, and the peace held until the death of Ptolemy IV in 205.

At that point, very significantly, the men in Alexandria who were operating as regents for the child king Ptolemy V sent out a series of envoys to Macedon, to Rome, and to Antiochos III. The man who went to Antiochos asked him to respect and maintain the treaty of 217; the other envoys were looking for allies. The Alexandrians clearly understood that the 217 treaty had expired with the death of Ptolemy IV, and they were hoping Antiochos would refrain from starting a new war. They failed in this, and the Fifth Syrian War lasted from 202 to 195, ending in a new peace treaty in which large territories, including Palestine and Phoenicia, were transferred to Antiochos; another clause was that Antiochos' daughter Kleopatra ('Syra') was to be married to Ptolemy V, by then a teenager.

The pattern continued into the next reigns. The peace of 195 remained unbroken until after the death of Ptolemy V, but even before he died he had been encouraged by members of his court to attack the Seleukid state, for by then Antiochos III had also died, in 187. The dire state of Egypt after the fifth war and the great Egyptian rebellion (which lasted until 186) had made it effectively impossible for Ptolemy to contemplate any new war in 187, but some substantial recovery by 180 made it worth contemplating.

The theory here, then, is that a peace agreement between two kings lasted until the death of one of them. So the peace of 271 lasted until the death of Antiochos I in 261; the peace of c.255 lasted until 246, when both Ptolemy II and Antiochos II died, but it was the latter's death which triggered a new war. The peace which ended the Third Syrian War was agreed in 241 and lasted through the reigns of Ptolemy III and Seleukos II, by which time the Seleukid kingdom was in too bad a state to start a new war, but Antiochos III felt free to do so after the death of Ptolemy III in 222 or 221. He was defeated, and then the peace of 217 lasted until the death of Ptolemy IV in 205. At that point Antiochos III began to negotiate an agreement with Philip V of Macedon with a view to dismembering the Ptolemaic empire. This they did from 202 onwards. On most of these occasions the death of the king did not automatically entail an end to peace – Antiochos I waited six or seven years before starting the First war, and Antiochos III three years before starting the Fifth, while Ptolemy V refused even to consider a new war (a policy for which he was eventually assassinated), but the death of the king rendered war possible without a king breaking his word.

## The power of the oath

Why this practice existed and continued is not explained, but it must be a consequence of the form which the agreement took. A treaty was an agreement between two men, the kings, and it was concluded with an exchange of oaths. This is referred to only in one case, but in such a casual manner that it was evidently normal. In 311 Antigonos Monophthalamos made peace with Ptolemy, satrap of Egypt. Antigonos had already concluded peace with Ptolemy's allies, Kassandros and Lysimachos, and Ptolemy found himself alone facing Antigonos' power. He hurriedly sent envoys to Antigonos asking to join in the new peace, and Antigonos responded by sending three envoys of his own to take Ptolemy's oath. Antigonos sent copies of the oaths which formed part of the treaty to his correspondents.[3]

This was thus the basis for the periods of peace which lasted until the death of one of the oath-sworn kings. So long as both lived the oaths held them; when one died, the other was released, as the Egyptian envoys in 205 appreciated. The origin of the practice may well have been in the personal relations of the early kings, but it clearly hardened into more than a custom in later generations. The proof of the pudding is in the eating: the proof of the theory is in the fact that no Seleukid or Ptolemaic king broke such an oath over the whole period of Hellenistic history.

An example of the form of the oath is in a treaty between Antiochos I or II and the city of Lysimacheia in Thrace. The oath of the king is incomplete in the inscription recording the treaty, but that of the envoys of the city seems to be the same: 'I swear by Zeus, Ge, Helios, Poseidon, Demeter, Apollo, Ares, Athene, Areia, and the Tauropolos, and all the other gods and goddesses, to abide by the friendship and alliance I have made with King Antiochos and his descendants'.[4]

It may appear a flimsy basis on which to build agreements, essentially a matter of honour and personal probity on the part of the kings. Yet it is essentially the same as any other diplomatic agreement, ancient or modern, all of which depend on the participants keeping their word, usually without any viable sanctions available. There were few things which angered his victims more than the repeated breaking of agreements by Adolf Hitler. Several of the Roman politicians were similarly capable of such tergiversation – see the discussion on the destruction of Macedon in Chapter 11 – but they did not blithely break their oaths. It may be concluded that the form of the oath sworn, particularly by the Hellenistic kings, was powerful enough to force them to abide by the treaties they had agreed.

The international consequence of such a diplomatic practice is that the two parties to a peace treaty could be confident that their agreement would hold for the foreseeable future. So in 217 Antiochos III, having made peace with the very young Ptolemy IV, could be confident that his kingdom would not be attacked from Egypt, and therefore he was able to mount successive campaigns into Asia Minor and Armenia and then to go on an extended expedition to the east over the next dozen years – because he knew his rear in Syria was safe. A similar reaction was shown by Antiochos IV after his own war with the Ptolemaic kingdom, the Sixth Syrian, in 170–168. Once the peace had been agreed he was also free to mount a major campaign into the east. Antiochos III did the same after his defeat by Rome in 190, though to be sure Rome showed no interest in further adventures in his direction. These kings both died on their expeditions, but the point is that they had no qualms about taking their main field armies on a two- or three-month journey away from an enemy they had cause to regard with hereditary animosity – and in no case did the Ptolemaic kings break their pledged word.

This, therefore, is a particular Hellenistic diplomatic institution, peculiar to the period. The oaths sworn by participants were similar to those used among the Greek cities in their conflicts before Alexander's time, though neither was sufficient to ensure that agreements were always kept. Detailed treaties such as those apparently organised and negotiated by these rivalrous kings notoriously contained clauses whose violation was all too easy, and it is certain that some participants had mental reservations even as they swore their oaths. Ptolemy used an awkward detail to excuse his resumption of the war against Antigonos in 310, breaking the peace he had agreed in 311.[5] No doubt other violations could be found on all sides. One main clue to a long-lasting peace, of course, is simplicity, for a complicated agreement is one which will unravel easily; it also requires that both sides trust each other. This latter circumstance clearly existed among and between the Seleukid and Ptolemaic dynasties, enforced by the kings' oaths and by the pressure of outside opinion, for a king who broke a vital – and public – oath was hardly to be trusted in other matters.

The other element which will make for treaty-continuity is for one party to be overwhelmingly powerful – as in the delays evident in starting wars in the 270s and 220s, and later in the 150s. In such a case the weaker parties have a strong interest in maintaining the peace, though the stronger party may well find it worthwhile to pick a quarrel at need – an example would be Ptolemy III's exploitation of the dynastic confusion amongst the Seleukids in 246, though in fact he had started the war before that confusion developed.

## The Macedonian effect

The origin of this practice cannot have lain with Antigonos and Seleukos and Ptolemy: Antigonos scarcely knew the others, having been employed in Asia Minor while the younger men went eastwards with Alexander. They also knew better than to trust a man who so evidently was grasping at being Alexander's real successor. But if we look further back in Macedonian history there are clues that the lifetime treaties were the practice amongst a group of kingdoms in the southern Balkans for at least a century before Alexander. This is an area and period which is even less well documented than the subsequent Hellenistic, but there are strong indications that a set of similar practices can be detected.

One of the major powers in the region in the early fourth century was Bardylis, an Illyrian king. He invaded Macedon at the accession of King Amyntas III in 393 but was driven out when Amyntas managed to call in Thessalian help. He returned to attempt a new conquest some years later. This time Amyntas gathered local support to drive the Illyrians out,[6] and there was presumably a treaty of peace between Amyntas and Bardylis, for the fighting ceased. There is, in fact, no evidence for a treaty, but Amyntas had other troubles,[7] which left him relatively vulnerable, and if Bardylis was determined to do so he could have taken further slices of Macedon for himself; hence the presumption that the two kings had made a treaty.

When Amyntas died in 370, his successor Alexander II was soon subjected to another Illyrian invasion led by Bardylis, who was bought off by a large payment. After Alexander's murder in 368 the succession went to his brother Perdikkas III, whose regent Ptolemy of Aloros had perhaps been associated with Alexander's peace agreement with Bardylis two years before. But when Perdikkas, having grown up, assassinated Ptolemy, Bardylis attacked again, with what results we do not know.[8] They fought again fairly soon, and this time the Macedonians were beaten and Perdikkas killed.[9] Bardylis was successful in annexing several areas of upland Macedon, and hostilities were presumably ended by an oath-sworn peace treaty. Bardylis invaded yet again at the accession of Philip II in 359. This time it is known that Philip sent ambassadors to discuss peace with the invader.[10] The envoys apparently had instructions to spin out the discussions until Philip was ready to meet Bardylis in battle. No doubt Bardylis had hopes of a cash payment to go away, such as had been given him earlier. The envoys did succeed in delaying matters, so that it was not until the summer of 358 that the battle took place. It was a disaster for Bardylis and resulted in a new treaty by which Philip recovered all those territories lost by Perdikkas in the previous crises.

These wars and treaties are not, it must be admitted, very well sourced, but the pattern seems to be very similar to that of Seleukid-Ptolemaic history: the death of a king (Amyntas, Ptolemy, Perdikkas) negated any treaty he had made; the accession of a new king meant that war quickly began after their deaths (in 393, 370, 368, 359/358) and led to a new treaty which lasted until one of the parties was dead.

During the year between Bardylis' invasion and Philip's victory, Philip dealt with several other problems he faced as a result of his accession. There had been another invasion of Macedon in 359, this time by the Paeonians led by their king, Agis, which came even before Bardylis' attack. Philip had at first made peace with Agis diplomatically, by promising tribute and handing over the first instalment. But then King Agis died, which of course negated the treaty, and so his successor re-opened the war. This time Philip took the initiative and led an invasion of Paeonia, where he imposed a new treaty upon Agis' successor, Lyppeius.[11]

A further instance may be detected forty years later. On Kassandros' seizure of control of Macedon he was attacked by Glaukias, king of the Taulantanii. Kassandros won the battle which followed, and the two men made a treaty, after which Glaukias turned his attention westwards.[12] He is next discovered attacking the Greek cities of the Illyrian coast,[13] while Kassandros turned his attention to the Greeks to the south. That is to say, the two rulers, having made their treaty, turned away from each other, apparently confident that they would not be attacked, just as Antiochos III and Ptolemy IV ignored each other after the peace of 217.

It appears, therefore, that the practice of respecting a treaty until one of the parties has died was, at least in part, inherited by the Hellenistic kingdoms from their Balkan predecessors.[14] And yet this is scarcely a sufficient explanation. The men who formed those new kingdoms after the defeat and death of Antigonos Monophthalamos had few memories of the Balkan past of Macedon under Philip II. Their military predecessors, Antipater and Antigonos, could have known of the practice, being of Philip's generation, but Seleukos and Ptolemy, Lysimachos and the others, were of Alexander's generation, and Alexander's diplomatic practice was based on a personal assumption of imperial supremacy. He regarded himself as the successor of Philip at home and of the Akhaimenid great kings in Asia, but he had spent only a little time in Macedon as king, and in Asia he dealt only with the great king.

The reaction in Greece and the Balkans to Philip's death in 336, however, was exactly the same as when his royal predecessors had died. At least two Balkan groups began wars, as did, a little more hesitantly, the Greeks, implying a general recognition that the treaties with Philip II had expired with him. Alexander's victories in these conflicts, and the subsequent treaties he made, left him free to invade Asia, just as the peace between Antiochos III and Ptolemy IV left the former free to conduct wars without any Egyptian threat. Macedon's enemies remained at peace until Alexander died. After the treaties he then ignored the Balkans. His own diplomatic method – in his letters to Darius III, or later in his dictatorial messages to the Greeks – was scarcely one which was adapted to keeping faith with equals.

The practices of diplomacy in the Hellenistic period, specifically those operating among and between the kings of the successor kingdoms of Alexander's empire, therefore originated in the conflicts and relationships of the generation of Alexander's immediate successors, with their memories of the practices of Philip's time in the Balkans, rather than from Alexander himself. It was in this long generation (323–280 BC), when these terrible old men – Antigonos, Seleukos, Ptolemy, Lysimachos, Kassandros – fought and intrigued their way to power and kingship, that the general and specific diplomatic practices of the Hellenistic period evolved as the means by which the rulers ordered their interrelationships.

## Greek civic influences[15]

They had also obviously inherited other practices from their Greek and Macedonian past. It was the normal practice amongst the Greek city states to send delegations of envoys to each other in order to sort out problems. To take only the very

18  *Techniques and practices*

latest period of the crisis of the Greek cities, Athens had sent a delegation of ten envoys to discuss peace with Philip more than once.[16] The kings, on the other hand, both those in Macedon and elsewhere, including the great king, tended to use just single envoys or perhaps two. Philip, for example, used the actor Artemidoros to carry a message to Athens which began the process of making peace in 346,[17] and in 344 he employed Python of Byzantion – though on this occasion a larger group from his allies also arrived in the city,[18] and he sent Alexander with Antipater and Alchimachos to Athens after the victory at Chaeroneia in 338.[19] Alexander continued this practice, sending just a single envoy, Nikanor of Stageira, to Greece in 324 with his unwelcome message that the cities should receive back their exiles.[20]

The cities' methods of diplomacy were therefore not unknown to the Macedonians, and, if the reinforcement of a period of intense experience is required, it happened to Philip II during his internment as a hostage at Thebes during the heady days of Theban power in the 360s, the time of Epameinondas and Pelopidas. These methods continued in use among the cities throughout the Hellenistic period and tended to be adopted also by Rome. The practice of sending a group of envoys was perhaps rooted in the politics of the cities, where the achievement of a diplomatic success by a single ambassador might well be translated into subversive local power; the hazards of accident and disease are other likely considerations. The single envoys – or a pair – of the monarchies are a sign, perhaps, of the greater political stability of the kingdoms.

## The rise of Antigonos Monophthalamos

The practice of the kings sending just one or two envoys, rather than a larger delegation, certainly continued through the Hellenistic period, and so it might be thought that it would be in the reigns of Alexander himself and his father Philip that this basic Hellenistic diplomatic practice began. In fact, the conditions under which Alexander's successors conducted their foreign relations were very different, and at first discussion seems to have been more or less informal, as between colleagues. Their mutual negotiations began almost as soon as Alexander was dead, and significantly they tended to ignore or bypass the regent Perdikkas for much of the time. In Macedon, Antipater faced the Greek enmity of the Lamian War – the king was dead, after all, and his treaties had lapsed; calling it a 'rebellion' would therefore be inaccurate, though it was useful for the Macedonian case. At once Antipater communicated with two of his contemporaries, Krateros, who commanded a contingent of Macedonian soldiers who were in Kilikia on their way home from Babylon, and the governor of Hellespontine Phrygia, Leonnatos.[21] The connection was by way of single messengers, of whom we have the name of just one, Hekataios,[22] who went from Antipater to Leonnatos. The three principals were contemporaries and had perhaps met and corresponded as friends and colleagues earlier. However, since Antipater proposed to give one of his daughters in marriage to Leonnatos in exchange for his help, the messenger he sent partook more of the nature of an official envoy from one power to another; perhaps this can be seen as a moment of transition from the informal messages of a group of

*The origins of Hellenistic diplomacy* 19

aristocrats to official ambassadors exchanged by kings. Intermarriage in the Macedonian aristocracy was of course normal, and this was clearly what Antipater was doing. That it developed into a royal practice later was in part an inheritance from the Macedonian past, but it was also the almost automatic response of a group of kings in search of political connections (but see Chapter 2).

The position of Antipater as regent in Macedon gave him a position from which to make such agreements. After his death (and that of the other regent, Perdikkas) the numerous satraps, fighting each other, found they had to act in the same way. It is notorious that Ptolemy in Egypt appears to have worked to make himself an independent ruler almost from the beginning, but he was not alone in this. From the beginning Antipater and his fellows adopted the diplomatic methods of the kings they had earlier served. They negotiated agreements and alliances, sent envoys, and made treaties with each other.

By 315 Antigonos Monophthalamos emerged as the main power;[23] he was surrounded by four rivals who began repeated and concerted attempts to block his progress, employing both war and diplomacy. It was a situation very like any other balance-of-power condition, in which the weaker powers repeatedly combine to bring down the greater – Antigonos was the superpower for the moment, Seleukos, Ptolemy, Lysimachos, and Kassander the lesser enemies. It was a situation guaranteed to put a premium on diplomacy. Antigonos' diplomacy was aimed at securing the others' submission; by his rivals it was aimed at organising an alliance to resist him.

Antigonos had already faced a similar situation in his conflict with Eumenes. The latter, the weaker of the two, was assiduous in attempting to form alliances with others. Several of the satraps refused to join him,[24] but once he reached Media he allied with a group of satraps of the eastern provinces, who had formed an uneasy coalition in which no one of them could claim primacy.[25] When Eumenes was defeated and killed, his allies almost all submitted to Antigonos when he sent envoys to demand it. Negotiations and exchanges of envoys were clearly required in all of these cases. Antigonos' position required that he be acknowledged as chief. In return he generally confirmed the satraps in their offices.[26]

On his return to the west late in 316 or early in 315 he drove out Seleukos from his satrapy in Babylonia.[27] Seleukos imparted his news, both of Antigonos' claims and of his power and wealth, in person to Ptolemy, with whom he took refuge. Ptolemy then sent envoys to the major western satraps to spread the news of Antigonos' wealth and power and to solicit alliances. Antigonos sent his own envoys to the same men – Lysimachos, Kassandros, and Ptolemy.[28] Here again are the two types of diplomatic purposes – one which aimed to form an alliance of equals, the other to gain acceptance of Antigonos' supremacy. The three coordinated their responses. When Antigonos reached Syria (having appropriated an imperial treasure in Kilikia, thereby making it clear that he regarded himself as the successor not only to the regents but to the kings as well), he was met by envoys from the satraps with an ultimatum. Seleukos had acted as coordinator of the alliance, and the four demanded a share in the provinces and treasure Antigonos had accumulated and that Seleukos be allowed to take up his satrapy of Babylonia again. That is, they denied Antigonos' authority as 'general over Asia'. Antigonos refused to accept this, or to negotiate; war inevitably followed.[29]

The satraps and Antigonos had thus, despite their mutual disagreements, worked out a method of diplomatic contact by means of trusted envoys, who were, as heralds had been in the Greece of the city states, clearly regarded as sacrosanct in their persons. This sacrosanctity was obviously necessary if envoys were to be able to deliver their messages in safety and carry back the replies (though they are rarely mentioned in the sources).

In the war which followed Antigonos' rejection of the ultimatum, both sides were as active diplomatically as they were militarily. Indeed, it is sometimes difficult to discern any difference between these activities. For example, Antigonos sent out several envoys during 315, Agesilaos to Cyprus to persuade the Cypriot kings to join his alliance, Idomeneus and Moschion to negotiate an alliance with the city state of Rhodes, aimed at securing the use of Rhodes' fleet, and Aristodemos of Miletos, with a large sum of money, into the Peloponnese to secure allies for Antigonos among the cities there.

The choice of these men is significant. So far as can be seen they were all Greeks, not Macedonians. Certainly Aristodemos was from Miletos, and Moschion came from Thera, though the other two, despite having Greek rather than Macedonian names, cannot be pinned down so definitively. The choice of Greeks for these missions indicated a certain delicacy in Antigonos' policy which is not always obvious in a man so arrogant and ambitious. All the objects of these missions – Cypriot kings, Rhodes, Peloponnesians – were Greek: Antigonos was being tactful.[30] Aristodemos was not successful in negotiating an agreement with Polyperchon, Antigonos' theoretical colleague in regency,[31] but he soon developed into the commander of the men he had recruited with his large treasury.

The missions to the Greek cities were assisted by the pronouncement by Antigonos that he intended to guarantee the 'freedom' of the Greeks. By this he meant that he would not impose garrisons on the cities but that he did expect contributions to his treasury in exchange for his forbearance. This was so effective a diplomatic gesture that Ptolemy copied the announcement with one of his own, and other rulers felt compelled to honour the idea in practice, if not in actual proclamations. This was one of the themes for the relationships between kings and cities for the next century and was influential enough to persuade the Roman Republic to follow suit. It also set up a pattern of diplomatic contacts which were widely recorded in inscriptions.

Antigonos and Ptolemy met in 313 at Ekregma on the border of Syria and Egypt in an unsuccessful attempt by the former to detach the latter from the satraps' alliance; Ptolemy's price was pitched too high for Antigonos to meet, no doubt deliberately so. The meeting was arranged when an envoy went from Antigonos to arrange the ransom of one of his commanders who had been captured by Ptolemy's forces. The fact that Antigonos proposed the meeting, of course, put Ptolemy on his guard, but also left Antigonos seeming to be the supplicant.[32]

A year later Antigonos and Kassandros met near the Hellespont, but again no agreement could be reached, once more probably because Kassandros required

## The origins of Hellenistic diplomacy 21

more than Antigonos would concede.[33] A year later again, Antigonos finally succeeded in bringing Kassandros and Lysimachos to agree to a peace, which left them in control of their regions (Macedon and Thrace) and Antigonos over Asia. These 'summit meetings' failed to become the normal means of conducting negotiations. It was less dangerous to send envoys, whose provisional agreements could be carefully revised later. It was also highly unusual, certainly after the time of Demetrius Poliorketes, for kings to move outside their kingdoms except in war and with an army (see Chapter 3).

We only have Antigonos' version of this peace process, in an inscription of most of a letter he sent to his city-allies, which is preserved from Skepsis near the Hellespont. The initiative supposedly came from Kassandros, who sent his brother Prepelaos to see Antigonos, giving him full negotiating powers. Prepelaos was accompanied on his journey by Aristodemos, Antigonos' active envoy, and agreement was reached when they met Antigonos. This is, of course, not necessarily to be accepted whole, since it imputed a recognition of defeat to Kassandros, who was in a strong enough position to insist on some terms Antigonos did not like, as Antigonos admitted. That is, even in Antigonos' own account the peace came about by negotiation between roughly equal powers. Prepelaos also had plenipotentiary powers from Lysimachos, which shows that he and Kassandros had coordinated their demands beforehand.[34] It appears clear enough that the terms had been negotiated first between Aristodemos and Prepelaos on their joint journey.

Antigonos may have conceded points to his opponents, but the quadruple alliance was broken, and Ptolemy and Seleukos were thus abandoned by their allies. It was thus a diplomatic triumph for Antigonos. Hearing of the agreement Ptolemy asked to be included, sending envoys to Antigonos, so reversing the sequence of the year before at Ekregma. Antigonos agreed (out of consideration for his new allies, of course) and sent envoys to Ptolemy to secure his agreement and his oath. Ptolemy sent further envoys to secure Antigonos' oath.[35] This exchange of oaths had also presumably been part of the peace agreement with Kassandros and Lysimachos.

One of the reasons for Antigonos' willingness to make peace had been the thorough trouncing of his forces in Syria by an army commanded jointly by Ptolemy and Seleukos at Gaza in 312. Seleukos had then succeeded in making a dashing cavalry ride through Syria to recover control over Babylonia and Media from Antigonos' subordinates. In the process he had gathered into his service a large number of Antigonos' (former) soldiers; along with the defeat at Gaza, this much weakened him in Asia. Seleukos was out of touch during the peace negotiations with the westerners in 311 and 310, probably far off in Iran, and Antigonos was apparently in no mood to include him in the peace terms as he had Ptolemy. So the war in the east continued. Seleukos and Antigonos continued fighting for the next three years, and Ptolemy, perhaps more sensitive to the importance of this fighting in the east than were his western allies, soon accused Antigonos of breaking the terms of the treaty – he chose to complain of Antigonos putting garrisons in Greek cities, which was one of the key promises Antigonos had said he would not do – and recommenced fighting.[36] This may well have distracted enough of Antigonos' forces to prevent him from defeating Seleukos, who in turn made peace with Antigonos in about 308; we have no details, but the pattern of events in 311 suggests one or other of them initiated contact, envoys travelled, and oaths were exchanged, the terms being that each man should hold what he had.[37] It is clear from these several agreements that the alliances were hardly agreements set in stone and, like other arrangements in similar political situations, were for convenience only.

Three diplomatic practices had therefore emerged in this period of Antigonos' grasp at hegemony. One was the ancient equivalent of the summit conference, as at Ekregma between Ptolemy and Antigonos and near the Hellespont between Antigonos and Kassandros. As it happened this was to be one of the least used of diplomatic institutions; discussions generally in the future were to be conducted between envoys, so allowing the principals to repudiate any agreement they did not like.

A second element was the proclamation of the justification for opening, or declaring war, by referring to a failure, or supposed failure, by one party to have observed the terms of the previous treaty – as by Ptolemy in 310. This in fact was an appeal to public opinion, since few autocrats ever need an excuse to go to war with a disliked or feared neighbour, or one who was already in trouble. Precisely what this 'public opinion' was is difficult to say, but it would normally include the literate and articulate inhabitants of the Greek cities and the soldiers of the various armies. Without an audience there could be little point in claiming a justification, and the idea of an appeal to the 'public', however defined or envisaged, was part of the same mindset as the peace treaties agreed on oath by the kings: without some sort of sanction (other than the gods, of course), even the least scrupulous politician could break his word with impunity.

There is, in these brief treaties, no clear indication that they were expected to last the lifetimes of the participants; in fact, however, by making accusations of bad faith and of breaking the terms, a much longer period of peace was clearly envisaged, and it may perhaps be taken to indicate that lifetime durations were already expected. This may also be concluded by the results of the peace agreed between Antigonos and Seleukos in 308. Seleukos was so confident that his agreement with Antigonos would stand that he at once set out on a prolonged campaign to the east, aiming to reduce the eastern satrapies and then to invade India. He was eventually defeated by the Indian Emperor Chandragupta Maurya, with whom he made a peace agreement. Once again, fully confident that this agreement would stand, he returned to the west.[38] Seleukos had been absent from the west on this expedition for five years, yet no attempt was made by Antigonos to disrupt their peace agreement. It would appear that Chandragupta had similarly accepted the sacrosanctity of the agreement.[39]

The cities were technically allies of these great men, and Antigonos in particular seems to have been generally scrupulous about respecting their autonomy – hence Ptolemy's accusation that he oppressed the cities was particularly hurtful. By this time Greece was the major source of mercenary soldiers, and so a good opinion among the Greek population was worthwhile. The existence of large numbers of mercenaries was also a constraint, since they were fully capable of changing sides from one employer to another. Antigonos, for example, was a notoriously disliked employer. When Seleukos reclaimed Babylon from him in 312–311, he had set off with only a small force of his own, but rapidly recruited several groups of disaffected Antigonid soldiers on the way; within a few months he had an army of over 20,000 men.[40] Later Antigonos found that Ptolemy was able to tempt his men to desert and, instead of meeting his price, resorted to punishing the deserters; quite likely they were men who had been captured by Demetrios in Cyprus, that is, former soldiers of Ptolemy.[41]

Antigonos and Seleukos did not totally trust each other, of course – but then this was normal between the kings. At the same time, it is clear that the two kings, as they had become by 305, were confident that neither would be attacked by the other. Of course, with Seleukos campaigning far in the east, there was no serious danger to Antigonos; however, Antigonos was not so constrained and was based in northern Syria for much of that time, and yet Seleukos was clearly confident that he could go to the east and not be attacked from the rear while he was there. In other words, the sanctity of the peace agreement was accepted by both men. Antigonos was old enough – he was born about 382, and lived through the bad times in Macedonia and through the triumphant ones of Philip II – to have known of this practice in and before Philip's time. It would seem he had recalled it and implemented it. Of course, Seleukos would agree to the notion, since it was in his interest at the time to do so.

The use of envoys was ubiquitous in these wars. To arrange the meeting at Ekregma Antigonos sent an envoy first, to discuss the release of captives held by Ptolemy; the suggestion of a meeting between the two principals became part of his message. The meeting with Kassandros may have been arranged by envoys from Aitolia and Boiotia who made an alliance with Antigonos just before the meeting;[42] it would be in their interests to see an end to the war in Greece. Antigonos by this time was very willing to negotiate with any of the allies, especially since meeting with them individually would clearly undermine the cohesion of their alliance; detaching one member would clearly destroy it, as had been done in 311. That peace was organised after Kassandros suggested a truce in the Greek fighting; his suggestion followed soon after Antigonos' meeting with Ptolemy at Ekregma; quite possibly it was Aristodemos who took the initiative in the later agreement as well. Antigonos' envoys thus appear to have had plenty of scope for independent initiatives.

## The Rhodian crisis

The peace agreements Antigonos had made with his four opponents eventually failed – but that is something which can be argued for almost every peace agreement. Antigonos in fact used the peace to continue his conquests, his forces by now commanded by his son Demetrios, first at Athens and parts of Greece, then Cyprus, and finally he attacked Rhodes. That he was able to do this was the result of his diplomatic achievement in breaking the opposing alliance. The principal victim at Athens (apart from the Athenians) was actually Kassandros, and at Cyprus it was Ptolemy. In other words Antigonos had also succeeded in keeping his enemies separate. It was clearly a threat to Ptolemy if Kassandros was reduced in power, just as it was a threat to Kassandros if Ptolemy was beaten, but neither of them reacted to Antigonos' conquests.

The assault on Rhodes, however, was soon seen as a threat to everyone. Had Demetrios succeeded quickly in his assault, or had the preliminary diplomatic contacts been successful in defusing the crisis, it is likely that Antigonos' victory would have evoked no more of a response from the rest than the conquests in Greece and Cyprus, but Demetrios took a year over the siege and then failed. In that period the enemy alliance began to re-form, because it was clear that it was only by their combination that Antigonos could be stopped. He had already proclaimed himself and Demetrios as kings, thereby in effect reiterating his old claim to supremacy over all the other competitors, which had begun fifteen years before with his appointment as 'general over Asia'. It had been agreed between all the rivals in the 311 peace that Alexander IV should not be permitted to reach adulthood; Kassandros accomplished the murder, only to find Antigonos taking the boy's place; he was of course followed by the others, who made themselves kings as well, so denying his claim to exclusivity. And by continuing his aggressions, Antigonos finally forced the allies to fight.

The diplomacy of the successors of Alexander may have been very personal, and so the detail is generally invisible to us, but during these great intrigues and clashes two major events, the siege of Rhodes and the re-formation of the League of Corinth, are less opaque than usual. The crisis between Antigonos and Rhodes is a classic case of a diplomatic dispute which escalated through mutual misunderstanding into open war. It also shows that Antigonos was a master diplomat who was foiled in his endeavour only by the obtuseness of his Rhodian interlocutors.

Antigonos sent Idomeneus and Moschion as his envoys to Rhodes in 315 to make an alliance with that city. This was at a time when he was developing his power at sea, building a huge navy in the ports of Phoenicia and Kilikia, for example. Rhodes appears to have been quite willing to join him at the time.[43] Ten years later, however, matters had changed. In 306 Demetrios, in command of Antigonos' fleet, launched a major offensive against the cities of Cyprus, which had become part to Ptolemy's territory a few years before. This posed a problem for the Rhodians, whose major commercial partner was Egypt, so they found themselves allied to one combatant and commercially dependent on the other. When Antigonos requested that the Rhodians honour the terms of their alliance and supply him with ships from their fleet to assist in the Cypriot campaign, the Rhodians declined and stated that it was their intention to remain neutral.[44]

The war for Cyprus was a great victory for Demetrios (and provided the political foundation for Antigonos' self-proclamation as king). Antigonos then turned him back to deal with Rhodes, having come to the conclusion that Rhodes's defiance posed a major threat to his imperial system, which in part depended on alliances with many Greek cities, alliances which were claimed to be on equal terms. If Rhodes could simply withdraw from the alliance when it was inconvenient, Antigonos' imperial system would not work. Added to that, Rhodes' defiance appears to have acted to favour Ptolemy in the Cypriot war. The city of Rhodes, which controlled the island itself, part of the mainland, and several islands between itself and Crete, did in fact hold an important strategic position within Antigonos' imperial geography[45] and could sever his communications if it chose.

While the fighting in Cyprus was still continuing, Antigonos sent a second embassy to Rhodes, asking that the city resume its alliance and again requesting that it send ships to assist him. The city refused, and Antigonos identified its trade with Egypt as a useful pressure point. He sent a commander with a small squadron to intercept Rhodian vessels trading with Egypt and confiscated their cargoes. This was, given his war with Ptolemy, a fairly reasonable action, though presumably the Rhodians did not see it as such. When the Rhodians reacted by driving Antigonos' ships away, he took it as a hostile act,[46] which of course it was, though scarcely more hostile than his attempted blockade. In form this was still no more than a minor incident, for neither party was using very much force, and Rhodes was only a very minor power at the time, though of some importance by sea.

Antigonos wanted the city back into his alliance more than he wanted to punish it for its defiance, but the city was clearly recalcitrant. Antigonos announced that Rhodes had begun the fighting, which was clearly debatable but which Rhodes quite reasonably understood to mean that he would attack. In a diplomatic move which was clearly intended to be conciliatory, the Rhodians voted honours for Antigonos and sent an embassy to him to inform him of this, but they still did not renew the alliance. They then negated any good effects of the honours by announcing that they had treaties with Ptolemy which could not be broken.[47] The city was clearly aiming to remain neutral, but to Antigonos this meant it was favouring Ptolemy. He was rightly angered by this, since he was at war with Ptolemy at the time. He could remark with some force that breaking a treaty was exactly what Rhodes had already done, but it was its treaty with him.

A failed attack on Egypt in 306 by Antigonos' army and navy after the Cypriot victory made him all the more determined to settle with Rhodes, and he sent Demetrios with the fleet and army to do so. Demetrios was met on the voyage by another embassy from Rhodes, which now agreed to resume the alliance and to fight Ptolemy after all, but this was far too late. Demetrios demanded that a hundred hostages selected from the wealthiest families in the city should be handed over to him as a pledge of Rhodian good faith and that his ships should be allowed to enter the harbours of the island. The Rhodians refused,[48] apparently without even attempting to negotiate these demands down to something they might have found acceptable. It is clear that the Rhodians were particularly inept diplomats, and that Antigonos and Demetrios between them had conducted a careful and well-thought-out method of slowly increasing the pressure on the city designed to persuade the Rhodians to return to their alliance. The Rhodians did not understand this and swung from defiance to submission in such a way that they could hardly be trusted. Of course, exerting pressure to make the city his ally was not the best way for Antigonos to succeed.

The Rhodians were sufficiently alert to the general situation, however, that they sent several sets of envoys to Demetrios hoping to avert open conflict, but without agreeing to the terms he required. Then they sent other envoys to Kassandros, Lysimachos, and Ptolemy, claiming that their fight was also on behalf of those kings.[49]

It took most of the year before a serious response came, since the kings were happy enough to see Demetrios tied up in the siege: if he was fighting Rhodes he was not attacking them. The result was a long siege of the city by Demetrios' army, famous in antiquity, in which Demetrios eventually failed to capture the city. But after the fighting was over, the agreement between the city and the king was exactly what Demetrios had offered before the fighting began: the right for his ships to enter the harbour and the surrender of a hundred hostages.[50]

The end of the fighting actually came when it became clear that Ptolemy and Kassandros were at last beginning to intervene seriously, first by sending supplies and then by sending troops.[51] An attempt by an Athenian delegation supported by envoys from other Greek cities – to the number of fifty men – failed to bring about an agreement.[52] But then Antigonos came to the conclusion that the siege had become a waste of resources and urged Demetrios to end it;[53] the arrival of a delegation from the Aitolian League (allies of Antigonos who were feeling increasingly threatened by Kassandros) brought the same message. It is not clear if the Aitolians actually mediated between the two forces, but their arrival (and perhaps the Athenians', who were also under pressure from Kassandros, hence their earlier intervention) combined with Antigonos' message, was decisive.[54] (In fact, it may be that Antigonos had instigated their intervention; both the Athenians and the Aitolians were his allies.)

The diplomatic events of the Rhodian crisis therefore demonstrate that the kings had developed a well-considered method of exerting pressure, comprising a carefully considered method of increasing the pressure on the city, but the city had not yet caught up with this new diplomatic sophistication. The Rhodians seem to have assumed that honours and fair words would be enough to stop Antigonos and that commercial connections would bring in Ptolemy; their messages to Kassandros and Lysimachos and Ptolemy that the city's war was also their war had absolutely no effect, since it was clearly an attempt at blackmail. Similarly the mass embassy of Greeks to Demetrios in the midst of the siege was conceived in the same spirit as Rhodes' earlier attempts at meaningless conciliation. The only outside intervention which affected Demetrios was that of his father, reinforced by the sensible Aitolian message, each pointing out that the Antigonid position in Greece was decaying because of Demetrios' long concentration on Rhodes. That is to say, it was the wider strategic situation which eventually operated to end the siege, not the fighting, not the threatened interventions, nor the Greek and Rhodian blackmailing messages.

## The League of Corinth

Antigonos had a meeting with Kassandros in which he made it clear that this time he required full and complete submission[55] – the same condition he had attempted to force on Seleukos in 315, on Kassandros in 313, and on Ptolemy in 306. It was apparent to Kassandros that Antigonos had not abated any of his ambition to succeed to Alexander's empire. In this ambition the possession of Macedon and the domination of Greece would have become the eventual validation. At this point

Demetrios had largely acquired domination in Greece by his conquests of Athens and Corinth, alliances with Boiotia and Aitolia, and by the enclosure of all these into a new League of Corinth, in imitation of that produced by Philip II; this was a substantial diplomatic achievement, even if Demetrios was enlisting his conquered cities.

The formation of a new league in 302 tapped into a long series of such Panhellenic organisations going back in effect to the league formed to defeat the Persian invasions. There had been several attempts to form new leagues, but almost all had been produced, like that formed by Demetrios, by a predominant power with the aim of institutionalising its power – the Athenian Empire, the Spartan domination, the King's Peace of 386, Philip II's League of Corinth – though this meant that each of the leagues soon fell apart.

These were not therefore really diplomatic achievements in themselves but were imposed by main force. Antigonos might be said to have had a sort of league in his diplomatic armoury from the time he returned from the east in 315. The proclamation of Greek freedom made the next year was a clear attempt to establish Antigonos' influence in Greece; to this the new League of Corinth was in effect a successor, and it certainly included provisions which appear to be intended to ensure that it continued in existence once Antigonos had won his war. Since he did not, the essential nature of the league was exposed as a yet another subordinate wartime alliance, and it soon vanished.

## The fall of Antigonos

This new league was too much for Kassandros. As soon as his conference with Antigonos had failed he dispatched envoys in his own name and that of Lysimachos, his neighbour and ally in Thrace, to both Ptolemy and Seleukos. The message was the same as that which Ptolemy had relayed to Kassandros and Lysimachos by way of Seleukos well over a decade before: Antigonos' ambition is to overthrow all of us.[56]

The four men, all now kings, were well scattered but formed a new alliance.[57] This could only have been done by extensive travel by their envoys, in some cases making their journeys through what was in effect enemy territory. Ptolemy in Egypt could reasonably easily communicate with Kassandros and Lysimachos in Macedon and Thrace, though their envoys would need to travel through seas dominated by Demetrios' ships. Rather more difficult would have been communicating with Seleukos, who seems to have been in Iran at the time, or even further east. Certainly his military approach to the final confrontation was from Iran and through the Armenian Mountains rather than by way of Babylonia. Antigonos and Demetrios also needed envoys to communicate with each other, the former being in Asia Minor and earlier in Syria, the latter in Greece.

The justification for the alliance and for the war the allies now conducted against Antigonos was partly in the fact that he and Kassandros had already begun fighting in Greece and that the earlier peace agreement had been breached by Antigonos' aggressions. In fact, there is no sign in the sources that any justification was made at all, which either meant that the historians did not bother with it or that the situation was so obvious that everyone understood. No attempt was evidently made among the allies to discuss the division of the spoils in the event of their victory. One must therefore assume that the alliance was strictly limited to the defeat of Antigonos and Demetrios; this was going to be difficult enough, in all conscience.[58]

The four allies appear to have treated each other as equals, each making his own military contribution to the destruction of Antigonos' empire. The victory at Ipsos in 302 lead on to an agreed distribution of Antigonos' territories, but the agreement, no doubt made after considerable negotiation, was concluded between only those allies – Kassandros, Lysimachos, and Seleukos – whose forces had taken part in the final battle. Lysimachos took the greater part, Asia Minor; Kassandros was satisfied to recover his position in Greece and to have his brother gain a kingdom in southern Asia Minor; Seleukos gained Syria – only to find, of course, that Ptolemy had taken over Palestine and Phoenicia. The result was that the four men formed approximately equal kingdoms, based on Macedon for Kassandros, Asia Minor for Lysimachos, the east for Seleukos (essentially Babylonia and Iran before north Syria was developed), and Egypt for Ptolemy.

## A new balance of power

Not surprisingly, the fourfold equality which emerged from the destruction of Antigonos only stimulated competition, which was worked out by diplomatic action, the formation of alliances, and the dispatch of envoys rather than by wars. Ptolemy and Seleukos quarrelled over their shares of Syria; Seleukos' announcement that he would not fight Ptolemy was a clever diplomatic ploy, subtly putting Ptolemy in the wrong, but was also an announcement that Seleukos was available as an ally. Within a year he concluded an alliance with Demetrios, who had saved his father's fleet and a number of fortified cities ranging from Tyre and Sidon in Syria to Athens and Corinth in Greece. Demetrios came east with his fleet, collected his mother Stratonike from Kilikia, and seized Prepelaos' Kilikian kingdom, so becoming a close neighbour of Seleukos in Syria. They then formed an alliance, a pact which included the marriage of Demetrios' daughter Stratonike with Seleukos. They quite deliberately met in a spectacular way on one of Demetrios' great ships at Rhosos, more or less on their (new) mutual boundary. The meeting was a summit conference designed to demonstrate the existence of the alliance to all possible competitors.[59]

The whole process was scarcely achieved in quite so straightforward a fashion, and the details, the marriage especially, had necessarily been arranged between envoys before Demetrios' arrival in Syria. (Perhaps the rescue of his mother had been the publicly announced cover for the voyage.) Demetrios reinforced his grip on Cyprus, Tyre, and Sidon while he was there and conducted a raid into Ptolemy's new province of Palestine as far as Samaria, so demonstrating his enmity towards Ptolemy and assuring Seleukos of the sincerity of their new alliance. The reply of the other kings, of course, was to form a rival alliance, Ptolemy with Lysimachos and Kassandros. Apart from Demetrios' raid, these alliances were sufficient to prevent any major war breaking out. They were, that is, essentially defensive in purpose, and as such were successful.

The mechanics and personnel involved in these negotiations are unknown, except for the principals' actions. The personal nature of the diplomacy in these exchanges is very evident. It took a summit meeting of Seleukos and Demetrios to ratify their alliance. Most piquant was the use Demetrios then made of his wife, Phila. She was the daughter of old Antipater and so the sister of Kassandros and Prepelaos. When Demetrios removed Kilikia from Prepelaos' rule, he sent his wife to her brother to explain the dethronement of their other brother. And meanwhile Demetrios was using their daughter Stratonike to seal his association with Seleukos by a marriage.

This episode makes it clear that the reaction of Seleukos to Ptolemy's aggression in Syria after the destruction of Antigonos' kingdom in 301 was quite consonant with the diplomatic methods developed during the previous generation, above all by Antigonos. Seleukos based his claim that Ptolemy had stolen part of the land he had been awarded on the agreement between the three allies after the victory at Ipsos to divide up Antigonos' former kingdom. They in turn based their right to do this on their joint victory over Antigonos and Demetrios at Ipsos. In this Ptolemy had taken no part, for obvious geographical reasons, though he had clearly taken part in the war. He had instead conducted a careful campaign into southern Syria, which was Antigonos' territory at the time. This was not Ptolemy's first venture into Syria: he had attempted to acquire that land at least three times before during the previous twenty years. In this he was reacting to the early experience of being attacked from Syria in 321 by the regent Perdikkas. No one can have been at all surprised at his actions in 302–301, least of all Seleukos, who had been at his side for several years and had jointly commanded the Gaza campaign. It is noticeable that Seleukos' allies in the battle showed no interest in assisting him to make good his supposed gains; therefore the alliance which had sustained them to victory had ended with the division of the conquered lands.

## Conclusions

The diplomatic institutions and practices developed in the generation since Alexander's death were thereby confirmed. There was an extensive and probably fairly continuous use of envoys, to negotiate alliances, gain intelligence, or simply to maintain contact with allies, and even – perhaps especially – with enemies. Information was at a premium, so the envoys were also researchers and spies. (Those fifty Greek envoys who went to see Demetrios at Rhodes were as much interested in the progress of the siege as in Demetrios' later intentions and in the prospects of victory for either side as in attempting to end the fighting.) Alliances were formed only after the details had been worked out by envoys and confirmed at a summit meeting – ratified – if it seemed necessary, which it rarely was. Intermarriage between the newly royal families was confirmed as an instrument of diplomacy, though as was later proved the existence of such marriages could never sustain an alliance when the rationale for it had evaporated (see Chapter 2). The alliance of Seleukos and Demetrios, for example, lasted only until, at latest, 294, when Seleukos seized control of Kilikia from Demetrios; next year his marriage to Stratonike ended in divorce, and she married his son Antiochos; both of them went off to govern Central Asia, well away from the diplomatic contacts around the eastern Mediterranean,[60] a subtly clever move in the internal diplomacy of the Seleukid family.

These are all institutions which had been developed since Antipater had opened the way for Antigonos' attempt to realise his ambitions. Out of this experimental phase came the crucial element, the practice of accepting the sanctity of treaties negotiated between kings.

When Seleukos said that Ptolemy was his friend he was perfectly serious. They had been boys together as pages at the court of Philip II and had risen to high command together during Alexander's campaign in Asia; Lysimachos was another. Kassandros, Antipater's son, was not of Alexander's fellowship, but he became a personal friend and constant ally of Lysimachos while they were both threatened by Antigonos. Antigonos himself was not part of this circle, nor was Demetrios. Antigonos was older than the others, Demetrios younger, and neither had taken part in the great campaign under Alexander. Antigonos had instead been left to fight alone – most competently – in Asia Minor. In this period of lone command he developed his ambitions and his capabilities.

The friendly relations and the shared experiences of the younger generation clearly helped them to join in their alliances against their joint enemy. It was also the foundation for the acceptance of the idea that treaties made between two kings were to remain in force until one of them died – though, as noted, this was something accepted by Antigonos as well. This picked up on the practice observed in the Balkans, where Philip II made treaties with his Balkan neighbours which lasted until one of the parties died. They would probably have claimed that it was a matter of honour to keep those agreements, as well as their duty to the gods in whose name the ratifying oaths were sworn; for whatever reason, the kings accepted the practice, and it became a crucial element in the international relations of their day and later.

It was a different matter with non-royal states. These were usually oligarchic in government at this time, with just a very few radical democracies. Such states usually conducted their diplomacy openly, discussing their moves more or less in public, but they were also subject to local opinion much more than were the kings; a perfect example is the waywardness of Rhodian responses to the successive pressures from Antigonos. So the kings could not rely on the cities maintaining their agreements in the same way as those they made with other kings. Rhodes felt able to refuse to help Antigonos when his anti-Ptolemaic policy crossed their commercial activities, even though the city was technically Antigonos' ally.

City states in preceding centuries had concluded time-limited agreements – thirty years was often a favourite; they almost invariably broke down well before their expiry date, and this was clearly expected. This was not, however, acceptable to the kings. The cities could not be trusted to abide by their agreements in the way kings could. This was clearly a problem which would need to be addressed now that the great powers were all monarchies, and since it was the kings who now had the real power, it was they who set the terms of the debate and secured a resolution which would comply with their wishes. The first generation of post-Alexander kings had therefore worked out a viable, if distinctive and unusual, diplomatic system, one which operated successfully for at least the next century and a half.

## Notes

1. Diodoros 21.1.5, but also his contemporaries.
2. I have discussed this series of wars in detail in *The Syrian Wars*, Leiden 2010; I shall not therefore provide the full references for these wars, except when it is particularly needed. I pointed out this coincidence of the wars' outbreaks and the deaths of kings on pages 89–90.
3. *OGIS* (see 'Abbreviations' section for full information) 5.
4. *I. Ilion* (see 'Abbreviations' section for full information) 45; Austin 171; Burstein (see 'Abbreviations' section for full information) 22; J.-L. Ferrary and P. Gauthier, 'Le Traite entre le roi Antiochos et Lysimacheia', *Journal des Savants* 1981, 327–345; the date of this treaty is disputed, but this is not relevant to the discussion here.
5. Diodoros 20.19.3–6.
6. Diodoros 14.92.3 and 15.19.2; Isokrates 6.46.
7. The best account of Amyntas' reign and troubles is in N.G.L. Hammond and G.T. Griffith, *A History of Macedonia*, vol. 2, Oxford 1979, 172–180; see also J.R. Ellis, *Philip II and Macedonian Imperialism*, London 1976 and George Cawkwell, *Philip of Macedon*, London 1978.
8. Polyainos 4.10.1.
9. Diodoros 16.2.4–5.
10. Diodoros 16.4.4.
11. Diodoros 16.1.4 and 4.4.
12. Diodoros 19.67.6–7.
13. Diodoros 19.70.7.
14. This is not a practice confined to the Balkans in the fourth century BC but appears in other regions, though it is only the Balkan practice which is relevant to this study; it is clearly a practice relevant to illiterate or semi-literate societies.
15. Sir Frank Adcock and D.J. Mosley, *Diplomacy in Ancient Greece*, London 1975, is the basic study here.
16. In 346: Aischines 2.18; in 344: Demosthenes 7.187.
17. Aischines 2.57.
18. Demosthenes 7.19–21.
19. Polybios 5.10.4–5; Plutarch, *Demosthenes* 22.
20. Diodoros 18.8.3; Nikanor was himself an exile; his city had been destroyed by Alexander's father in 341 (Plutarch, *Alexander* 7.3).
21. Diodoros 18.12.1.
22. Diodoros 18.14.4.
23. Richard A. Billows, *Antigonos the One-Eyed and the Creation of the Hellenistic State*, California 1990, for a comprehensive study.
24. For instance, he negotiated with Seleukos, satrap of Babylon, and Peithon satrap of Media, who refused to serve under him.
25. Diodoros 19.13.7 and 14.4–15.5.
26. Diodoros 19.48.1–5; some, of course, were killed or sacked, but a whole group from the Baktrian region were merely confirmed in office.
27. Appian, *Syrian Wars* 53; Diodoros 19.55.2–5.
28. Diodoros 19.56.3–4.

32  *Techniques and practices*

29 Diodoros 19.57.1–2.
30 Diodoros 19.57.4–5; for brief biographies of the envoys, cf. Billows, *Antigonos*, app. 3, nos. 3, 16, 56, and 75; he points out that Moschion, from the Aegean island of Thera, went to the Aegean island of Rhodes as his envoy, and later was in command of a group of mercenary soldiers from the Aegean island of Kalymna.
31 Diodoros 19.57.5 and 60.1.
32 Diodoros 19.64.8.
33 Diodoros 19.75.6; in the letter to Skepsis, Antigonos blamed 'certain men' (*OGIS* 5, lines 5–9) for the failure of the Hellespont negotiations; who these men were is not known, but it seems that there was more to the talks than a meeting of the two rulers.
34 *OGIS* 5; Billows, *Antigonos*, 131–133.
35 *OGIS* 5, lines 26–52.
36 Diodoros 20.19.3–5.
37 Billows, *Antigonos*, 146–147; J.D. Grainger, *Seleukos Nikator*, London 1991, for an attempt to locate the boundary between the two. Will, *Histoire Politique*, 1, 61–65.
38 Grainger, *Seleukos Nikator*, 109.
39 Charles Allen, *Ashoka: The Search for India's Lost Emperor*, London 2012, 51–61, discusses the various identities of Chandragupta; identifying him as an Indian mercenary in Baktria helps explain his acceptance of Macedonian practices; he and Seleukos may well have met during Alexander's Indian campaign.
40 Diodoros 19.90.1–92.5.
41 After Gaza Ptolemy sent the captured enemy soldiers into Egypt and settled them there as cleruchs (Diodoros 19.85.4); deserters: Diodoros 20.74.5–75.3.
42 Diodoros 19.77.1–4.
43 Diodoros 19.57.4, 58.6, 61.4, 62.7 and 64.5.
44 Diodoros 20.82.1.
45 For the extent of the city's territory see P.M. Fraser, *The Rhodian Peraea and Islands*, Oxford 1954.
46 Diodoros 20.82.2.
47 Ibid.
48 Diodoros 20.82.3.
49 Diodoros 20.84.1.
50 Diodoros 20.99.3.
51 Kassandros and Lysimachos: Diodoros 20.96.3; Ptolemy: Diodoros 20.96.2 and 98.1 and 7.
52 Diodoros 20.98.2.
53 Diodoros 20.99.1.
54 Diodoros 20.49.3.
55 Diodoros 20.106.1–2.
56 Diodoros 20.106.2–4.
57 Diodoros 20.106.5.
58 Schmitt (see "Abbreviations" section for full information), *Staatsverträge*, 447.
59 Plutarch, *Demetrios* 22.
60 Plutarch, *Demetrios* 38.1–9.

# 2 Royal marriages

Several particular institutions in use in diplomacy were mentioned in passing in the first chapter, and in this and the next chapter I shall examine them in more detail. The first is the problem of royal marriages, whose existence is so often assumed to imply political alliances; in the following chapter I shall consider the diplomatic relations of kings and cities and the question of arbitration, 'summit meetings', the 'recognition' of new states as they appeared, and the persons of envoys.

In a political community of hereditary monarchies such as that of the Hellenistic eastern Mediterranean, the practice of royal intermarriage has always seemed a useful politico-diplomatic tool and, for historians, a helpful guide to political alignments. Marrying a daughter or a sister to another king suggests that the two kings were friendly to the point of being allies in foreign affairs. There are sufficient cases of such marriages in the Hellenistic period to suggest that this may have been appreciated in that time as it has been in others – if that interpretation is correct. (For a list of such marriages, see Annex A to this chapter.)

## Philip II and Alexander III

The Hellenistic kings inherited the practice of intermarriage from their Macedonian royal forebears. Philip II used marriages to a succession of women to mark and confirm his military conquests, rather like a dog marking his territory, and to forge links with other kings among his neighbours. Relations with Bardylis of the Illyrians were cemented by Philip's marriage to Audata, Bardylis' daughter or granddaughter; Phila, of the royal house of Elimiotis, was his second wife; third was Philinna, probably of the noble family of the Aloadae of Thessaly; Olympias was of the Molossian royal family and was perhaps the nearest to Philip himself in terms of royal rank; Nikesipolis, a niece of Jason of Pherai in Thessaly, was his fifth wife and his second from the Thessalian nobility; Meda was a daughter of the king of the Getai; and the seventh wife, whose name is not known, was probably the daughter of a Scythian ruler; finally, and ultimately disastrously, he married the Macedonian Kleopatra, a ward of Attalos, a noble of his own court.[1]

How effective this marriage strategy was in its political aims is not at all clear. Philip tended to collect a wife after every successful military campaign which had resulted in a submission, the wife arriving as a sort of prize as part of the political settlement; this seems to have been the status of the first wife, Audata; the Getan and Scythian girls were probably given to him as a token of his victory, but their presence at his court would scarcely assist him to exert any control over their distant homelands; they were therefore reminders that he had beaten their fathers and had then made peace with them. The two Thessalians, on the other hand, Philinna and Nikesipolis, were political signals that he was allied to and gave his political support to the aristocracy of Thessaly; marriage to the niece of Jason of Pherai also implied that he would pursue Jason's policy of unifying Thessaly into a powerful state. This may well be the message of his marriage with the Macedonian Kleopatra also, perhaps a sign of his essential alliance with the Macedonian nobility. Philip was, after all, a usurper, and the king by hereditary right, Amyntas, was still alive; several of the wives, therefore, were part of his internal policy: holding on to Thessaly and Elimiotis, not stirring up trouble in Macedon.

The only one of his marriages which had any real significance in Philip's foreign policy was that with Olympias, who came as part of a treaty of alliance with her father, the king of the Molossi, not as the result of a conquest; she held a superior status at his court, as befitted her superior birth, and it was her son, Alexander, who was always seen as Philip's heir. Later, during the crisis caused by his last marriage, he gave his own daughter Kleopatra (by Olympias) to the Molossian King Alexander as a reward for the latter's ostentatious neutrality in the matter.

The first four of these women were married to him within two years of his accession to the throne, 359–357. He would thus seem to have held them in a harem. Audata, Philinna, Olympias, and Nikesipolis all bore him children, as did the last wife, Kleopatra, so the marriages were not merely ceremonial arrangements.

It seems inescapable that Philip was using his position as a victorious king to marry this sequence of women largely for political reasons. The concentration of marriages in his earliest years as king implies this also, with a wife each from Illyria and Molossia and two from Thessaly, his nearest and most dangerous neighbours. He did, of course, gain a reputation, at least amongst those who did not marry so many women, for lustfulness, and this was probably accurate. But he had plenty of opportunities in Macedon to secure women for his use if that was all he wanted, and until the end he carefully refrained from any such attachments which involved the Macedonian aristocracy; until Kleopatra the daughter of Attalos, he only married foreign women. He was thus not secure enough on his throne to risk allying with any Macedonian family (or faction) until he had ruled for twenty years – and the disaster which followed on that marriage shows that his earlier policy was correct. The foreign wives were in most cases symbols of his warlike victories and could be brandished at his Macedonians as marks of their own new power as well as his successes. But only Olympias could be considered to be the symbol of a political connection and alliance with her homeland. The rest were trophies, marks of the reduction of their homelands to subordinate status. Philip's marriages were not therefore marks of international alliances; they were trophies, or they were moves in the internal politics of his kingdom; even the marriage to Olympias was not a mark of an alliance, for the connection with Epeiros had to be reinforced later by another marriage – to ensure Epeirote neutrality in an internal problem of Macedon.

Philip's son Alexander was as keen to use marriage politically as his father had been and was equally careful to avoid choosing a Macedonian wife. He was urged to marry before setting out on his great expedition, and his refusal is usually taken as an impatient decision not to be distracted from his 'mission';[2] but it may also have been a lesson taken from his father's fate, to avoid choosing among the eligible daughters of his seniors and therefore to avoid exacerbating the rivalry amongst them.

During the next ten years he had a son by Barsine, the widow of the enemy mercenary commander Memnon of Rhodes, though it does not seem that they went through any marriage ceremony first – she may have been regarded as a prize of war, in the same way as his father's early wives.[3] His first 'legal' or official, marriage was to Roxane, the daughter of the powerful and influential Baktrian noble Oxyartes;[4] he also apparently married both Barsine, the daughter of the last Akhaimenid king, Darius III, and her mother, Parysatis, the daughter of Artaxerxes Ochos.[5] None of these women was particularly important in a Macedonian context; all three may be seen as more trophies of victory. On the other hand, the choice of these three women was clearly political in a different sense. Roxane's father could help to hold the turbulent Baktrian-Sogdian area; the two Akhaimenid women connected Alexander quite deliberately with the old imperial house, thus indicating his claim to be the heir of the last great king. The Persian and Baktrian marriages were therefore directed at the Persian and Baktrian nobilities, not at the Macedonians, in the same way as the Thessalian women, and perhaps Kleopatra, had been elements in Philip's internal policies. (For the Macedonians, however, the multiple simultaneous marriages of Philip and Alexander set a powerful precedent for the next generation.)

This consideration points to other elements in these marriages. If Alexander married Parysatis and Barsine it was because of their parentage; they were, as he would claim, his social equals (like Olympias with Philip); it was also too dangerous to allow anyone else to marry them. Their parentage gave them a royal status, and their husbands would acquire such status from them. (Barsine, the widow of the two Greek mercenary generals Mentor and Memnon, was also a royal Akhaimenid.) Hence Alexander's monopoly of them. Roxane became significant later, as the mother of his son Alexander IV, but she was at first no more than another trophy of victory, like the first Barsine.

He had sons by both the first Barsine (widow of Memnon) and Roxane, both of whom were later recognised, at least by some, as kings of Macedon: Herakles for a brief time in 309–308, Alexander IV from the moment of his birth in 323.[6] Back in Macedon, Alexander's sister, Kleopatra, was married to the Epeirote King Alexander, who was Olympias' brother, and therefore the bride's uncle. Alexander's half-sister Kynnane (daughter of Audata) had been married to Philip's nephew Amyntas; their daughter Adea, or Eurydike, eventually married Philip Arrhidaios, the son of Philip and Philinna, who was also recognised as king of Macedon for some years after Alexander's death. Adea-Eurydike was Arrhidaios' niece, so her parents were first cousins. All of these women transmitted claims to the Macedonian kingship to their husbands.

36  *Techniques and practices*

Royal marriages were therefore mainly made for political reasons, which is hardly news, though the politics were mainly internal to the kingdom, not international. The other main element was that royal daughters were expected to marry their royal equals – that is, kings. Royal sons could perhaps have a wider choice, but not much, and were generally expected to marry royal daughters. When the royal family becomes too exclusive, of course, this means incestuous marriages, such as those noted in the previous paragraph. This practice had thus begun under Philip (though it had existed in the Akhaimenid family as well).

## Choice

In the third and second centuries BC the upstart Attalid family became notorious for marrying commoners, and in fact royal daughters were rejected. No Attalid king married outside the kingdom, and Eumenes II refused the daughter of Antiochos III. Their most famous catch was Stratonike, described as the daughter of a citizen of Kyzikos, who became famous as a particularly generous and effective queen.

As it happens, Antiochos III also married a commoner, but as his second wife: Euboea, daughter of Kleoptolemos of Chalkis in Euboea. This was clearly a political gesture, made in the midst of the campaign in Greece, presumably as a signal that the king was fully committed to the Greek case against Rome – the girl had her name changed to that of her home island, emphasising the political aspect;[7] this was a marriage similar to those of Philip II with his Thessalian brides.

## Antipater

The elimination of the Macedonian Argead royal family from power, which was effective almost as soon as Alexander was confirmed dead, brought the Macedonian nobles to the fore. Almost at once they used Philip's marriage tactics. Antipater's daughter Nikaia was given to the regent Perdikkas; another daughter, Phila, went to Krateros as early as 321 as a token of their alliance; a third, Eurydike, went to Ptolemy; another was possibly offered to Leonnatos.[8] From the time of Alexander's death, therefore, Antipater was acting as a king, though in all likelihood he was actually only behaving in the traditional way of a Macedonian noble. Alexander's sister, Kleopatra, the widow of Alexander the Molossian, was locked up in Sardis to prevent her from marrying and thus lending her ancestry to a new husband. When she tried to escape, Antigonos had her killed – and then killed his murdering agents and saw to her funeral in an (unsuccessful) attempt to conceal his deed.[9]

The practice of intermarriage which had been used among Alexander's family was pursued by the Hellenistic kings. The real lesson for Philip's marriage with Olympias had been so that by linking with the Epeirote royal family (both by his marriage with Olympias and later by his daughter's marriage with Alexander of Epeiros) he had protected his western flank. The connection may not have had any other effect, since the Epeirote royal family turned its attention westwards into Italy under Alexander and later with Pyrrhos. This choice, of course, may have been more as a result of Philip's obvious power and military successes, which would deter any eastward adventures by Epeirote kings – certainly Pyrrhos was seriously interested in seizing Macedon; it may also have been emulative, which could be a sort of influence.

The legacy of royal marriages to the Hellenistic successors of Philip and Alexander therefore included the value of royal women as transmitters of a claim to a kingship; their uses as the producers of (male) successors; their potential as presents to other kings. The first of these was the reason behind the intermarriages of Alexander's sister Kleopatra and Alexander of the Molossians, and of Philip III Arrhidaios and Adea-Eurydike. This concept also surfaced later in the Ptolemaic and Seleukid dynasties.

Antipater's marriage policy was of only limited utility, for he died only three years or so after Alexander, and by that time two of his sons-in-law, Perdikkas and Krateros, were also dead, and so was his political partner, Leonnatos. The daughters were, however, still valuable and available again and were soon married to others of the successors: Phila later married Antigonos' son Demetrios, Nikaia went to Lysimachos.

## The first successors

These men were of the next generation, the contemporaries of Alexander. The survivors emerged as kings from 306 onwards, and their marriage policies became highly exclusive. Most of that generation adopted Philip's (and Alexander's) marriage policy of collecting several wives, though in their cases it was usually in succession rather than simultaneously. So Lysimachos had three wives, the daughter of Antipater (Nikaia, widow of Perdikkas), Amestris, widow of and successor to the ruler of Herakleia-Pontike, whom he married for her city and then discarded, and Arsinoe (II), daughter of Ptolemy.[10] Ptolemy himself had married a Persian lady at Alexander's behest, whom he may have retained for a time, then Antipater's daughter Eurydike, and then Berenike, who was the widowed grandniece of Antipater[11] and who arrived at his court in Eurydike's train and then supplanted her. Demetrios, the son of Antigonos, married five times: to Phila, Antipater's daughter, who had originally been married to Krateros; to Eurydike of Athens, the widow of Ophellas who had ruled Cyrene for Ptolemy I; to Deidameia of the Epeirote royal family (who had been engaged to be married to Alexander IV); to Lanassa, the daughter of Agathokles of Syracuse, who had fled from Pyrrhos of Epeiros; and finally to Ptolemais, a daughter of Ptolemy and Eurydike, Antipater's daughter, to whom he had been betrothed for over a decade while she languished ignored at Ephesos. He seems to have continued to be married to Phila during all these later marriages.[12]

Most of these were political marriages, in the sense of the women bringing to their husbands more than just status. Amestris and Lanassa both brought important strategic places with them as their dowries. The prominence of the daughters of Antipater, even, or especially, after his death, is curious. They were clearly regarded as valuable spouses because of their ancestry. They were also of a notably independent disposition. Phila was Demetrios' valuable political adviser all along, even while he was taking other wives; her sister Eurydike decamped from Ptolemy's court when he married Berenike.[13] Lanassa had been married to Pyrrhos of Epeiros but left him when he collected a couple of extra wives from the Illyrian hinterland on the same principle as Philip's collection; she took her dowry, the island of Kerkyra, with her.[14] Eurydike of Athens was both notable as Ophellas' widow (he had taken a large Athenian contingent with him on his invasion of Carthage) and was said to be a descendant of the Athenian hero Miltiades.

The exception to this multiple marriage practice was Seleukos, at least in a way. Seleukos was one of the men who were married to a large set of Persian ladies at Alexander's great ceremony at Opis in 324, but where the rest (supposedly all of them) repudiated their wives as soon as Alexander was dead, he chose to keep his wife, Apama, who was the daughter of Alexander's great enemy Spitamenes of Sogdiana.[15] Seleukos married again after her (presumed) death, in 299 BC. In the meantime his original marriage had perhaps been politically useful during his campaign to gain control over the Central Asian satrapies, including Sogdiana, though this did not happen until the marriage was nearly two decades old. This advantage cannot have been part of Seleukos' calculations as early as the marriage; we are therefore entitled to assume that he remained married to her by choice rather than political calculation.

Seleukos' second marriage, to Stratonike, the daughter of Demetrios and Phila, was a spectacularly political marriage, a symbol of the alliance of the two men in their political isolation and vulnerability. The marriage took place at a summit meeting on Demetrios' great ship in the harbour at Rhosos, on the border of the two men's territories, a deliberately well-publicized event.[16] The alliance reintroduced Demetrios into the international political system, and just to emphasise his power, the marriage took place on his own ship, just after he had, with no difficulty at all, seized control of Kilikia, which had been allocated to Kassander's brother in the recent share-out.

The high political content of this marriage was demonstrated once more eight years later, by which time the political relationship between the two kings had been severed. Seleukos had already seized Kilikia from Demetrios, but his Syrian lands were now vulnerable if Demetrios chose to attack – he certainly had the naval power to mount an invasion if he chose. There were considerable numbers of old soldiers of Antigonos and Demetrios who were settled in the new cities Seleukos had founded in Syria, and they might recall their old allegiance if Demetrios attacked.[17] Stratonike was therefore in part a symbol of Demetrios and was now a danger to her husband. Seleukos neatly solved the problem by handing her on to his son by Apama, Antiochos – still unmarried in his late 20s – giving out a story that they were in love with each other and that therefore Seleukos was being particularly self-sacrificing and generous. He sent them both off to his eastern provinces as governors, where Antiochos, as Apama's son, already had relatives. This was a region in which Antigonos had never shown any interest and where few if any of his former soldiers had settled.[18]

So the political marriage of 300 BC was succeeded by the political divorce of 292, and by another political marriage; the wife was thus not wholly repudiated, presumably also for political reasons. The presence in Syria and elsewhere in Seleukos' kingdom of settlers who might have been more loyal to Demetrios than to Seleukos in a crisis may have been the crucial consideration. (Several years later when Demetrios attempted to invade Syria, Seleukos was exceptionally careful to capture Demetrios alive rather than to kill him, then kept him in comfortable drink-sodden half-free confinement until he died; one might cite the same reason for this unusually compassionate treatment;[19] Seleukos also publicly refused a rich offer from Lysimachos to have Demetrios killed, so making good propaganda out of his refusal.) Seleukos' second marriage is generally seen as a move in international affairs, but if so it was also as much an internal matter, on the pattern of both Philip and Alexander.

All this marrying clearly required much preliminary diplomacy, and yet the permanence of most of the connections so formed was less than total, as the sequences of Stratonike's marriages to father and son and their virtual exile in Central Asia would suggest. The marital and sexual career of Demetrios implies that none of his liaisons or marriages were anything but political. In other words, these royal marriages were contrived not for permanent or even long-term alliances but more often for short-term political purposes, as implied by the multiple and brief marriages of some of these men. (Demetrios' one long-term marriage, to Antipater's daughter Phila, was notably political; she was also considerably older than he was.)

## The second generation[20]

In the following generation, the practices of royal marriages changed again. Only one of the kings who were active in the 270s had a string of wives like those among men of the previous generation. This was Pyrrhos of Epeiros, whose marital career more resembled that of Philip II than any other king. He first married Antigone, a stepdaughter of Ptolemy I, with whom he had formed a cheerful and lasting friendship, though the girl seems to have died fairly soon; later he married Lanassa, daughter of Agathokles of Syracuse, the Lord of Sicily, which brought the island of Kerkyra to him as dowry – clearly a political marriage. Pyrrhos' third and fourth wives were from the hinterland of his kingdom, to Bikenna, daughter of Bardylis of Illyria, and to a daughter of Audoleon of Paeonia, more or less simultaneously, and here no doubt he was emulating Philip most directly. The arrival of these girls drove Lanassa away, a clear sign that harems of wives had become less acceptable. Finally he married a daughter of Ptolemy Keraunos, who was briefly king in Macedon; she was the niece of his first wife.[21]

These were all primarily political unions, and Pyrrhos followed them up or accompanied them with campaigns in the Balkans (the daughters of Bardylis and Audoleon) and attempted conquests in Sicily (Lanassa) and Macedon (Keraunos' daughter). These two last regions were connected with his wives, but only briefly – like the marriages – and he clearly felt that the connections were to his advantage. The defeats he suffered in both attempted conquests were indications that a marriage was never alone sufficient to provide a man with political power; it might give him an entry into a particular area, but from then on he had to exert himself and provide leadership and governance.

Pyrrhos died in 272 in the midst of another attempted conquest which would no doubt have proved to be as temporary and as futile as his others. His contemporaries, Antiochos I, Kassandros, Ptolemy II, and Antigonos II Gonatas, were much more restrained in their policies and in their marriage politics. Clearly a great deal more thought was involved in the marriages they undertook or arranged, and perhaps they were regarded with less importance. That of Antiochos I has already been noted; he remained married to Stratonike until his death. Kassandros secured as his wife the last living daughter of Philip II, Thessaloníke, the daughter of Nikesipolis of Pherai, Jason's daughter, which presumably assisted him in holding on to the Macedonian kingship he assumed in 305; this despite his probable responsibility for the murder of Alexander IV (his wife's nephew) and his bribing of Polyperchon to murder Barsine and her son by Alexander the Great, Herakles (another of Thessalonike's nephews).[22] Kassandros was also the son of the well-respected regent Antipater, so he had as good a claim as anyone to the vacant throne of Macedon; adding Thessalonike was perhaps extra insurance; it was clearly a dynastic union. The children of Kassandros and Thessalonike inherited the Macedonian kingship without difficulty, overseen by Thessalonike, who was another of these formidable Macedonian women, though all three of her children failed to hold onto the throne once she had been murdered by the elder.[23]

In the 270s this new pattern of marriages emerged, but with a new emphasis on incest, which had been largely discarded in the pursuit of apparent political advantage. Among the Ptolemies the marriage of Ptolemy II and his sister Arsinoe II, the widow of Lysimachos and of her stepbrother Ptolemy Keraunos, provoked a mixture of horror and guffaws from the Greek public. The purpose of such marriages was to keep royal Ptolemaic women within the family – once again a matter of internal policy.[24] Ptolemy II's father had sent his daughters off to marry various rulers, but Ptolemy II did not permit his other sister Philotera to marry anyone, and from now on for over a century only one Ptolemaic woman married out of the family. The Greek horror at the sibling marriage was undoubtedly largely feigned, for this royal marriage was only the final example of the common royal practice of incestuous marriages – uncle-niece, first cousins, son and stepmother, were all recent examples; the shock expressed at Ptolemy II's marriage with his full sister Arsinoe was either politically naïve or as politically motivated as the marriage itself.[25]

Among the Seleukids the policy became somewhat different, but it eventually converged with that of the Ptolemies. The daughter of Seleukos I and Stratonike, Phila, was given in marriage to Stratonike's brother Antigonos II Gonatas, when he established himself as king in Macedon.[26] She was her husband's niece, a relationship in marriage which was the same as that of Alexander's sister and her Molossian husband; this seems not to have occasioned the same prurient comments as Ptolemy II's marriage with his sister. It was clearly a political marriage, by which Antiochos I supported Antigonos in his newly won kingship, and it also replaced the Ptolemaic-Macedonian axis which had existed earlier, when Ptolemy Keraunos was briefly king in Macedon; Keraunos was the murderer of Seleukos I, so this would be a very satisfying political *coup* by Antiochos. The connection was renewed in the next generation by the marriage of Demetrios II and Stratonike II.[27] Demetrios was the son of an uncle-niece marriage; Stratonike was Phila's niece. This was intermarriage almost as incestuous as that of the Ptolemy II.

The apparent alliance between Antiochos I and Antigonos Gonatas scarcely impinges on the history of the time. There was no point at which they can be judged to have acted in concert. The political relationship may thus have been one of benevolence and lack of hostility rather than active alliance. Both of the dynasties were repeatedly at war with the Ptolemies, and it is just possible that they cooperated; however, the only example is in the Aegean in the 250s: Antiochos II was fighting the Second Syrian War and Antigonos was fighting Ptolemy II in the Khremonideian War, but no evidence exists to demonstrate any cooperation between them, though such cooperation would certainly help to explain the difficulties Ptolemy II had in both wars. This effect would not need a direct political coordination, for, once Ptolemy was involved in one war, others of his enemies would likely take advantage of his difficulties. It may be concluded that the Seleukid-Antigonid marriages did not signal political alliances.

## Negotiations

Despite the lack of political results from royal marriages, they were nevertheless important. There were careful negotiations between the contracting parties before the bride was handed over. No case exists where we have any details of such negotiations, though they can sometimes be deduced from later events. In three instances envoys were involved. In 221 the Seleukid official Diognetos went to Pontos and escorted Laodike, daughter of King Mithradates II, to her marriage with her cousin Antiochos III.[28] If this was Diognetos' only task, earlier envoys had obviously travelled between the kings to arrange the details, for Diognetos' visit to collect the girl was only the conclusion of the negotiations. A daughter of Antiochos III and Laodike, Kleopatra (Syra), was married to Ptolemy V as part of the peace terms which ended the Fifth Syrian War in 195. Again we have information only about the end of the process of negotiation, when Eukles of Rhodes travelled to Egypt as Antiochos' envoy to make the final arrangements. Negotiations for peace had been going on for some time before this visit, and the marriage contract was part of the peace terms. Eukles' mission was to hand over the ratification and, by proxy, render and receive the oaths.[29] In an earlier example we have a notice of the start of the process, when Hekataios was sent by Antipater to Leonnatos asking for help to fight the Lamian War; Antipater promised a daughter.[30] Hekataios certainly negotiated the alliance between the two Macedonians, but Leonnatos was killed in the war; whether the marriage ever took place is not known.

Putting the three cases together, the process can be tentatively outlined. First an envoy – e.g., Hekataios – would be sent by one party to suggest the marriage but probably also had other tasks in mind, notably a political or military association, the offer of a daughter being both an inducement and an offer of trade. There followed exchanges of envoys to sort out the details, such as dowries, status, safety of the wife, for example, which might include specifically political arrangements, such as military action in support of each other. Hekataios' main task was to get Leonnatos to bring his forces to the assistance of Antipater in the Lamian War; the daughter was an extra, even an optional extra. Finally the bride would be taken to the bridegroom. This was the task of Diognetos and perhaps of Eukles, though it is of interest that Diognetos was the agent for the groom, collecting the bride, whereas Eukles was the agent for the bride's father, delivering her to her new home. The more interesting part of the process, the arguments over the details, is hidden from us by the lack of sources. The details were probably never available to any of the ancient writers; much will have been oral; only the final terms would need to be written down.

## The Cyrenaican crises

The uses to which royal marriages could be put are shown by Antiochos I's policy. He arranged the marriage of Phila and Antigonos about 277, and was clearly convinced of the policy's utility; he was also probably therefore the originator of the marriage of his daughter Apama with Magas of Cyrenaica, though he was assisted in this by the household problems left by Ptolemy I, and his purpose in this case was less peaceable.

Berenike, Ptolemy I's third wife (who was also of Antipater's family), had two children by a previous marriage. Her son, Magas, was sent by Ptolemy I to govern Cyrenaica, and Ptolemy II kept him on. Antiochos offered Magas his daughter Apama in marriage, and that marriage took place about 275. This triggered Magas' revolt against Ptolemy a little later. Magas wished to establish his independence and was supported militarily by Antiochos. This became the First Syrian War. How far this had been the intention of Antiochos I in suggesting the marriage is not known, but he must have realised that, at the least, Magas would use the prestige it gave him to shift into independence.

The Ptolemaic kingdom was to a degree weakened by this conflict, for Magas succeeded in maintaining his independence as king in Cyrene, though Antiochos cannot have regarded the war as a whole as a victory. When Magas died, leaving the rule in his kingdom to his daughter, Berenike, there was an international scramble to provide her with a husband king. At first she became betrothed to the son and heir of Ptolemy II, but Queen Apama brought in Demetrios the Fair, the son of Demetrios I and Ptolemy I's daughter Ptolemais; Berenike contrived Demetrios' murder when the latter was rash enough to allow himself to be found in Apama's bedroom. It may be that he appreciated that marrying Apama would secure him the kingship of Cyrenaica more certainly than marrying the hostile Berenike – though it is not clear if they were actually married. The ultimate victory went to Ptolemy III, whose marriage with Berenike reintegrated the Cyrenaican kingdom with the main Ptolemaic state; she took the kingdom with her into the marriage.[31]

*Royal marriages* 43

The story is embellished with curious and extravagant details of sex and passion in the best Hellenistic style, not to mention the intervention of a couple of Greek republican revolutionaries, but the whole sequence of events was primarily a power play. Demetrios was the half-brother of Antigonos II Gonatas, king of Macedon (and of Stratonike, the mother of Apama, Berenike's mother). The marriage of Apama and Magas had brought Cyrenaica to independence; the marriage of Demetrios with Berenike could maintain that independence by bringing it into a firm alliance with Antigonos Gonatas – but also the hostility of Ptolemy; Antigonos was friendly with the Seleukid kingdom, and a determined and repeated enemy of Ptolemy II. Berenike was also related to the Ptolemies through her father and grandmother, the earlier Berenike, though it was not a blood relationship. The marriage plans on all sides were politically highly charged, and once Berenike had made her choice (and it seems to have been hers), her kingdom slid into a permanent association with the Ptolemaic kingdom for the next century.[32]

This Cyrenaican crisis took place in the time of Ptolemy II, and it was he who arranged the marriage of his son with Berenike II. He was another king who clearly believed in the utility of such unions for political purposes. As part of the peace terms which ended the Second Syrian War, his daughter Berenike (III) married the Seleukid King Antiochos II. The precise political purpose in this case is unclear, but to designate it as an alliance is clearly wrong. In part, it was a grand gesture of power and prestige by Ptolemy, though Berenike was no more than a symbol of the peace. Perhaps it was hoped, in the Ptolemaic context, that her presence would disrupt the Seleukid kingdom – which did eventually happen. On the Seleukid side it is likely that the prize of a Ptolemaic princess was seen as the price Ptolemy II paid for peace; that is, Antiochos II was winning the war. The eventual result was not an alliance but the Third Syrian War, which was followed by a dynastic civil war between Laodike's two sons and the effective collapse of the Seleukid state into a condition of confusion and dismemberment which lasted for about two decades. Ptolemy II was dead by then. It is past belief that his plan was subversion by marriage; he was sufficiently ruthless himself to know that his daughter would be one of the first casualties in any civil strife over the Seleukid kingship.

The episodes of Magas and Berenike would suggest that the policy of marriage alliances and of marriages to seal peace treaties were weapons which might turn in the hands wielding them. Antiochos I's *coup* in marrying Apama to Magas produced a war which he did not win; the peace which the marriage of Berenike and Antiochos II was intended to seal produced for the Seleukids a new war and a disastrous civil war which the kingdom barely survived, while for the Ptolemies the costs of the campaign in Syria led directly to serious internal trouble in Egypt. The attempt to continue the independence of Cyrenaica by an Antigonid marriage led only to its recovery by the Ptolemies. On the other hand, the result of the Third Syrian War (246–241) was to place the Ptolemaic kingdom in superpower status with regard to its rivals, a condition which it maintained for the next two decades.

44  *Techniques and practices*

## New policies

The Ptolemaic policy on marriage changed after 246. For the next century there is only one case of a king marrying outside the Ptolemaic family – that of Ptolemy V with Antiochos III's daughter Kleopatra, who was given the surname Syra. The Ptolemaic family was reduced to royal minorities three times between 222 and 180, and by the time of Ptolemy V there were no Ptolemaic women available for him to marry. It does not seem to have occurred to the Ptolemaic rulers that a Ptolemy could marry a non-royal Egyptian or a princess from one of the several Asia Minor or Greek dynasties. Only the families of the Seleukids and the Ptolemies were by then regarded as socially suitable for marriage. It would be interesting to know at whose initiative the marriage of Kleopatra with Ptolemy V was proposed: did Antiochos offer, or did Ptolemy's regent ask? In the generation following Ptolemy V, royal marriage was again confined within the family, with his two sons being married to his daughter (simultaneously). The marriage with Kleopatra Syra must therefore be seen as a desperate genealogical measure which only took place because there were no candidates from the family left.

By contrast, the Seleukid kings were very active in marriage diplomacy despite the experience of Berenike and her son and the collapse into prolonged civil war. During the War of the Brothers (241–227) several royal marriages were concluded, partly results of the civil war. The elder of the two brothers, Seleukos II, married Laodike II, the daughter of a powerful figure in Seleukid Asia Minor, Andromachos, who commanded armies for the king. (This was near-incestuous, for Andromachos was the brother of Laodike, the wife of Antiochos II and mother of Seleukos II.[33]) The king's brother and enemy Antiochos Hierax married the daughter of Ziaelas, king of Bithynia.[34] Hierax was campaigning to make himself an independent king in Asia Minor, and this was clearly a political move to secure an alliance which would assist him, just as Seleukos' marriage with Laodike was aimed in part at securing the adhesion of another major Asia Minor family. Bithynia was at odds with the Pergamene kingdom, another competitor with the Seleukids in the region, so they could neutralise one another. Ziaelas had a traditional friendship with the Galatians, who had settled in central Anatolia, and the association would give Hierax access to recruiting Galatians into his army;[35] in addition the rival kings' sisters were married to the kings of Kappadokia and Pontos: Stratonike to Ariarathes III, Laodike to Mithradates II.[36]

The civil war between the two brothers was fought out mainly in Asia Minor, and these marriages were clearly designed to secure or maintain the support or neutrality of the non-Seleukid kings surrounding the cockpit. In the next generation the daughters of Mithradates II and Laodike, both also called Laodike, respectively married Akhaios (II), the son of Andromachos and so the brother of Seleukos II's wife,[37] and Antiochos III, Seleukos II's son (she was the bride fetched from Pontos by Diognetos.) These two sisters were therefore married to men who became enemies when Akhaios made his own bid to become king. Antiochos defeated the rebellion and executed Akhaios;[38] family sentiment clearly did not operate either to ensure Akhaios' loyalty or to defeat Antiochos' determination to destroy rebels.

This series of marriages was probably produced in part by the exigencies of the civil war, but there was also perhaps another element. The father of Andromachos and Laodike (Antiochos II's wife) was an earlier Akhaios (I). He was a wealthy Macedonian landowner in Asia Minor and so was a useful ally for the Seleukids.[39] His older daughter, Antiochis, had married Attalos I of Pergamon, the enemy of the Bithynian King Ziaelas and of Hierax.[40] These marriages among the Asia Minor dynasts, therefore, produced a network of royal connections involving all the kings from Pergamon to Antioch, and it was by such marriages that the network was being created.[41] Again this is in part political but also in part social, in that the Asia Minor families evidently regarded themselves as a distinct social caste. The Attalid kings of Pergamon were part of this group, and the practice also deflected any possible claims to the succession from outside the family.[42]

One of the main political reasons for the network was to hem in the turbulent Galatians. These, as Hierax knew, were very useful as mercenaries, but they were also a menace to all their neighbours, and even to their employers at times. Surrounding them with an alliance network was a useful defensive measure for all involved. The Galatians' main opponents had always been the Seleukids; their main friends were the kings of Bithynia, who had originally invited them into Asia Minor; Antiochos Hierax's alliance with Bithynia and the Galatians was thus unlikely to help his cause in the rest of Asia Minor. Here then is a marriage alliance which is perhaps a measure of desperation, in that Hierax did not have any other support in his war with his brother which he could count on. The Seleukid-Kappadokian connection was maintained into the next generation: the son of Ariarathes III and Stratonike, Ariarathes IV, married Antiochis, a daughter of Antiochos III.[43]

These Asia Minor marriages are convincing signs of a long-term association between the several member-families, yet they did not prevent wars between them, nor did they induce supposed allies to join in wars. Akhaios and Antiochos III fought each other, as did Akhaios and Attalos. About the only active wartime partnership was between Antiochos III and Ariarathos IV during the former's Roman war. Antiochos' supposed marriage alliances with the Pontic Kings produced no cooperation. The marriages therefore produced no political linkages; it was probably the other way about: the social linkages existed, and therefore the marriages were negotiated.

## Sibling marriages

The Ptolemaic practice of sibling marriage was not continuous in every generation.[44] That of Ptolemy II and Arsinoe II produced no children and in fact may well have been a purely formal and ceremonial (and political) arrangement. Ptolemy III married Berenike of Cyrenaica, who was no blood relation. The first sibling marriage to produce children was that of Ptolemy IV with his sister Arsinoe IV. Their son Ptolemy V, married out to Kleopatra Syra in the next generation, though their sons Ptolemy VI and VIII both married their sister Kleopatra II; after Ptolemy VIII killed her, he married his niece as a second wife.[45] It is clear that the practice of incestuous marriage was a fixed and permanent matter in the family: the only marriage out, with Syra, tends to prove the point since it took place in effect as a result of the genealogical emergency which had arisen.

The marriage of Ptolemy V and Kleopatra Syra was also another attempt to seal peace by linking the two great power royal families, but Ptolemy V was considering a new war when he was assassinated in 180.[46] The regency for his infant successor was in the hands of Kleopatra Syra. It is possible that she did not wish to attack her homeland, now ruled by her brother,[47] but it is more likely that she had her work cut out merely keeping some control over the Ptolemaic court and kingdom. Going to war would have put the generals in power in Alexandria, so marginalising the regent; she had plenty of reasons to avoid a war. There is thus no sign that the dynastic link acted to preserve peace; peace lasted for many other reasons.

Sibling marriage returned under Kleopatra Syra's children and was practised again in the generation which followed. But the Ptolemaic kings were rarely monogamous, and the royal succession went to the son of a sibling marriage only twice. This practice did, of course, avoid the need for diplomatic negotiations for a marriage, which could be expensive in treasure and politically, but it is to the point that the practice was in part designed to avoid any outside challenges to the succession. In the same way the Attalid marriages with non-royal women were a different solution to the same problem. If, as seems to have been the theory, the daughter of a king transmitted a claim to the kingship to the man she married, then it was best, from a dynastic point of view, to ensure that the daughters did not marry out of the family. The husbands – that is, the kings – could, however, father children on other women than their sister-wives, women who might be secondary wives, or concubines, or mistresses, and this increased the supply of possible royal wives in the succeeding generation. But they were then dangerous since if they married out of the family, a claimant might well appear. So it is unsurprising that, until the middle of the second century BC, only one Ptolemaic daughter – the unfortunate Berenike, wife of Antiochos II – was married out.

The second of the women married out was Kleopatra Thea, daughter of Ptolemy VI and his sister Kleopatra II. Thea was used by her father all too obviously as a diplomatic pawn in the complicated Seventh Syrian War in the 140s.[48] This was the product of a complex diplomatic intrigue (see Chapter 13). Here it is the use to which Thea was put which is at issue.

Ptolemy VI gave his eldest daughter to the Seleukid usurper Alexander I Balas in 150 as a clear mark of his political support. The troubles with Alexander's suitability and his dubious Seleukid descent were then scotched: by being given Thea as his wife he was being recognised as royal, socially equal with the Ptolemaic king. (Alexander's sister, Laodike, married Mithradates III of Pontus, which had the same legitimising effect.) Three years later Ptolemy brought his army into Syria to help Alexander against his rival Demetrios II, but when Alexander turned out to be less than cooperative Ptolemy abruptly transferred Kleopatra to Demetrios II, in what was perhaps the most blatant and cynical example of the use of a woman as a political pawn in the whole period. Both Alexander and Ptolemy were soon killed, but Thea's ancestry and marriage provided her with a strong position within the Seleukid family. When her second husband, Demetrios II, was captured by the Parthians, she asked his younger brother Antiochos VII, living in exile, to come to Syria. He successfully claimed her as his wife, and this marriage was a clear sign of Antiochos' rightful claim to the throne. The marriage took place in all probability before Demetrios was even captured; in either case she had two husbands bigamously; her mother Kleopatra II was also married to two husbands, her father and her uncle; in captivity Demetrios was provided with a Parthian wife – therefore also bigamously – with whom he had two children; it is evident that 'bigamy' as a 'crime' was not an issue.

After all Thea's husbands had died – she was accused of having contrived the killing of Demetrios II after he had escaped from captivity and had reassumed the kingship, and certainly she would give him no support, though the murder was more likely a private act by the governor of Tyre[49] – she also disposed of the kingship among her sons; the eldest was murdered by her for displaying independence; the second son, having secured the kingship, murdered her in turn, supposedly, and credibly, in self-defence.[50] Meanwhile, Demetrios' wife in Parthia was the daughter of King Mithradates I; their children were clearly in the line of Seleukid succession.[51]

Apart from the cynicism displayed by all in this, it is evident that any political content of the marriages was very short lived. Ptolemy certainly used his daughter as a political piece on the table, but Alexander did not regard himself as bound to his father-in-law's policies as a result. They were allies against Demetrios II, but Thea's marriage was only a symbol of that alliance, not its heart. Thea's later marriages owed less to her Ptolemaic ancestry and more to her position as the mother and wife of Seleukid kings and princes. Her Ptolemaic connections did not survive her father's death; none of her Ptolemaic relatives claimed a political connection through her, still less a claim on the Seleukid kingship.

Well before Thea was inserted into the Seleukid family to follow such a destructive career, that family had also adopted the Ptolemaic view of the value and exclusivity of royal daughters. They were not quite as exclusive on the subject as the Ptolemies, and some daughters were still sent off to marry out, but for two generations from the 190s the senior daughters of the kings married within the family. The most notable – and extraordinary – case is that of the eldest daughter of Antiochos III, Laodike, who was married to his eldest son Antiochos, 'the Young King', during the elder king's lifetime. This was therefore a quite deliberate dynastic choice of a sibling marriage organised by their father. The Young King died before his father, and she was then married to the second son, Seleukos IV; again, this was organised by Antiochos III; finally she married her third brother, Antiochos IV, when he arrived in Syria to assume power after Seleukos' assassination, no doubt as a precaution to secure his own doubtful legitimacy. That is, she married three brothers in succession, and she had children by all three.[52]

In the next generation three daughters were sent off to marry other kings: Nysa, daughter of Antiochos the Young King and Laodike, married Pharnakes I of Pontos[53] (the fourth marriage between these dynasties); Laodike, the daughter of Seleukos IV and Laodike, was married to King Perseus of Macedon; and Antiochis, daughter of Antiochos III, married Ariarathes IV of Kappadokia. All these royal families were already linked by earlier marriages. Then, after Perseus' defeat and imprisonment in Italy by the Romans, Laodike was sent back to Syria by the Roman conquerors.[54] (This unusual consideration would seem to imply that the Romans understood the value of these women.) There she married her brother Demetrios I, when, unlike Perseus, he escaped from Roman detention in Italy several years later.

The combination of sibling marriage and the export of daughters is a curious combination of the methods of the Ptolemies and the earlier Seleukids. Clearly the sibling marriages were a response to the theory that the eldest daughter of the king carried a claim to the throne, which had to be retained within the family. Other daughters, however, were available to be used as diplomatic weapons. And yet both Nysa and Laodike, the wife of Perseus, were eldest daughters, though Nysa's father was dead when she was married, and her marriage was arranged by her brother Seleukos IV. And Seleukos' own daughter Laodike was married off to the Macedonian king, who was extremely unlikely to attempt to seize the Seleukid kingship. Similarly, a generation later, Kleopatra Thea was the eldest daughter, but her father had two sons and a brother, so her husbands were not likely to make an attempt on the Ptolemaic kingdom – though in fact Demetrios II ultimately did just that, but failed. These exceptions may again prove the rule insofar as there was one.

The Seleukid policy of exporting daughters could be successful in creating friends and successful also in guaranteeing a supply of princesses who could be brought in as wives of later kings. It did not guarantee political support in either direction. The Pontic kings intermarried with the Seleukids for three generations, but there is no circumstance where the two kingdoms acted together; Seleukos IV almost marched to assist Mithradates II against Eumenes II of Pergamon, but the war ended before he crossed the frontier. The Kappadokian kings Ariarathes III and IV both married Seleukid princesses, and the latter did send troops to join Antiochos III (his father-in-law) in the battle at Magnesia and was punished by the Roman consul Cn. Manlius Vulso afterwards. The next king, Ariarathes V, quarrelled with Demetrios I, who instigated his dethronement; his return to the kingship three years later was a diplomatic defeat for Demetrios. Yet the two men were brothers-in-law. These alternate alliances and clashes were more likely due to the fact that the two kingdoms were geographical neighbours than to any marriage links; the marriage links had no influence.

There is also the possibility that such marriages could go drastically awry. The prime example is perhaps the havoc wrought in the Seleukid family by Kleopatra Thea, but there were also two earlier Seleukid women who were almost as disruptive, to put it no stronger. Stratonike, the daughter of Antiochos II, was married to Demetrios II of Macedon, who married a second wife; Stratonike thereupon returned to Antioch and attempted to get her nephew Seleukos II to marry her, presumably so as to return to a centre of power; she was killed because she was so disruptive.[55] Antiochis, the younger sister of Antiochos III, was married to the

Armenian King Xerxes as part of a peace agreement, but she soon murdered him and returned to her brother.[56] It is, however, no certain that they behaved in this way because of their ancestry. They were high-born women with a strong sense of their social position and a tradition of political activity; their assertiveness is as likely to be the result of personal pride as it is of their family origins.

## Conclusions

The reason for this long catalogue of royal marriages is to provide the material for an estimate of the extent to which such marriages had political effects. It is obvious, first of all, that they were above all usually contracted for political reasons. The women themselves had little or no say in the matter. The most extreme example of this is where Ptolemy VI abruptly transferred his daughter Kleopatra Thea from one husband to another, but Antiochos III had not hesitated to marry his daughter to a second of his sons when the first died young.

When all the results of these marriages are counted up, the conclusion is inescapable. The policy of royal marriages, as pursued by the Hellenistic royal families, rarely resulted in any permanent political connection and never in an active alliance. This is not to deny that the marriages had a political content when they were negotiated. The contest for Cyrenaica was clearly affected by the marriage of Magas and Apama, for Magas evidently used it to make himself an independent king. When Magas died, Apama did not turn to her Seleukid relations for assistance in securing Cyrenaican independence but to the Antigonid king in Macedon; her daughter Berenike was crucial to the independence or otherwise of the territory, and when she chose to marry Ptolemy III, this marked the union of their kingdoms. But the most spectacular dynastic out-marriages in the second century – Kleopatra Syra with Ptolemy V, Kleopatra Thea with Alexander I and Demetrios II and Antiochos VII, and Laodike with Perseus – had no such consequences. The intermarriages of the Seleukids and the Mithradatids and the Seleukids and the Ariarathids similarly did not mark alliances between those states. In the crisis of his kingdom, in the Roman war, only Ariarathes IV joined Antiochos III, and this can best be ascribed to his enmity towards Eumenes II, who was on the other side.

In almost all cases, therefore, these royal marriages can have done little more than signal the friendship of the two kings who arranged the match, a friendship which might not last much beyond the actual marriage ceremony. These were not marriage alliances in any political sense of the term, since their political content was minimal beyond the immediate occasion.

Going back into the previous (third) century, the marriage of Antiochos II and Berenike had no political effect other than to provide Ptolemy III with an excuse to invade north Syria – but he had decided to do that before he knew either of the death of Antiochos II (his brother-in-law) or of his sister Berenike and her son. The marriage of Antiochos I's sister Phila to Antigonos Gonatas may have repaired relations between the two kings (who had fought a brief war earlier), but there is no other case where they fought together, or even where they acted diplomatically in concert. There is no reason to suppose that they remained allies, though both were opposed to Ptolemy II; there was equally nothing which set them at odds. The various marriages in Asia Minor in the time of Antiochos Hierax's rebellion are interesting as a network linking the several kingdoms, but none of the kings involved actually fought in alliance with any of the others, though many fought against each other. Their intermarriage network was more a social recognition of their joint importance and their similar social rank, though their joint antipathy to the Galatians was part of this.

If the political content of these 'marriage alliances' was minimally important, the question arises as to their real purposes. I would suggest that it was a largely a matter of social prestige and royal class distinction – kings should only marry the daughters of kings. In the most extreme cases this meant that kings should only marry their royal-born sisters. Other daughters could be used to participate in the system outside the sibling marriage, though the Ptolemaic unwillingness to allow this is manifest. The main exceptions to this practice were the Attalids of Pergamon and, to some extent, the Antigonid dynasty in Macedon, but, even among the less exclusive Attalids, two of the kings, Eumenes II and Attalos II, married the daughter of Ariarathes IV of Kappadokia, Stratonike, who was in fact the granddaughter of Antiochos III. She married them serially, though everyone had a good laugh when Eumenes was thought to have died and Attalos rapidly took over his *faux*-widow, only to have to return her when Eumenes turned up alive. Among the Antigonids, Antigonus III Doson and Philip V confined their choices to Greek and Macedonian women who were of sub-royal status,[57] though Demetrios II's second wife was an Epeirote princess, and she was taken over by his cousin Antigonos III after his death. When Demetrios repudiated his first wife, the Seleukid Stratonike, there is no sign that this occasioned any resentment in the Seleukid family (except in Stratonike, of course). Perseus achieved a status-marriage with a Seleukid princess.

This negative, or rather dynastic, conclusion that there is little or no political significance in royal marriages beyond the actual moment of the marriage seems to be confirmed by the complex series of dynastic marriages during the last Seleukid generations. After Kleopatra Thea's death in 121 there was a series of marriages between Seleukid kings and Ptolemaic princesses. It is difficult, if not impossible, to discern any diplomatic content in any of the unions. Demetrios II made a fairly serious attempt to unite the two kingdoms, based in part on his marriage to Kleopatra Thea (though the trigger for his expedition towards Egypt in 128 was the promise of marriage to her sister, yet another Kleopatra), but no further effort in that direction was made. Three Seleukid kings were later married to Ptolemaic princesses, but none ever attempted to claim the Egyptian throne.[58] It seems therefore that the main reasons for the marriages were that only kings of the Seleukid dynasty were regarded by the Ptolemies as of sufficiently high social status to become husbands of their princesses – the Ptolemies themselves having the best claim, of course. This was certainly the case later in the 50s BC when Berenike V of the Ptolemaic dynasty was looking for a husband who could become king to her queen. A forlorn Seleukid (his family had finally been deposed from their rule in Syria a decade earlier) turned up and was swiftly married to Berenike, merely because he was of an exalted rank; but Berenike found him personally offensive

*Royal marriages* 51

and had him killed after only a few days – these women could be very scary. She was then persuaded to marry Archelaos, who was claimed to be a son of Mithradates VI of Pontos, the great anti-Roman campaigner (who was descended from a series of Seleukid marriages); in fact Archelaos was not royal, but the son of a Pontic general. The marriage lasted long enough for him to be killed in battle, so perhaps Berenike's standards in husbands had been adjusted to circumstances.

The final Egyptian ruler who indulged in out-marriage was Kleopatra VII, who first allowed herself to be seduced by Julius Caesar and then both seduced and married Mark Antony. Such men were no doubt of sufficient rank for her standards, but in both cases the relationships were primarily political, a means to put off any annexation of Egypt by Rome – that is, whatever their social position, it was their power which attracted her. The marriage of the last Ptolemaic ruler was thus mainly a diplomatic action, just as had been the first to the daughter of Antipater. It was, of course, only briefly successful. Kleopatra's father had planned for her to marry her brother Ptolemy XIII in the traditional way; he died before this could be carried through, and the children quarrelled. The marriage never took place.

The conclusion must be that royal marriages did not produce political alliances more than occasionally and very briefly. They may at times have provided indications of political friendship and alignment (as with the Seleukids and the Antigonids against the Ptolemies, though even this alignment – which never resulted in any joint actions – could have happened without any marriages), but no king was naïve enough to accept that the marriage of a daughter or a sister to another king was more than a social connection. The few cases of marriages which supposedly secured a peace treaty in fact did no such thing, for the lives of the kings were the only real means of maintaining the peace. One may conclude that the term 'marriage alliance' has no meaning in political terms in the Hellenistic period beyond the immediate occasion; it was no more than a social and dynastic process designed to mark a family's prestige. That, of course, was a political concept, but one mainly confined to a kingdom's internal affairs.

*Annex A* Royal intermarriages:

|        | King           | Bride                             |
| ------ | -------------- | --------------------------------- |
| 356    | Philip II      | Olympias (Epeirote)               |
| 324    | Alexander III  | Parysatis and Barsine (Akhaemenid)|
| c.300  | Demetrios I    | Deidameia (Epeirote)              |
| c.300  | Kassandros     | Thessalonike (Argead)             |
| c.300  | Agathokles     | Theoxene (Ptolemaic)              |
| c.300  | Pyrrhos        | Antigone (Ptolemaic)              |
| c.300  | Pyrrhos        | Lanassa (Syracusan)               |
| c.292  | Demetrios I    | Lanassa (Syracusan)               |
| c.260  | Mithradates II | Laodike (Seleukid)                |
| c.255  | Ariarathes III | Stratonike (Seleukid)             |
| 252    | Antiochos II   | Berenike (Ptolemaic)              |
| 250    | Ptolemy III    | Berenike (Cyrenaic)               |

*(Continued)*

|  | King | Bride |
|---|---|---|
| c.240 | Demetrios II | Stratonike (Seleukid) |
| c.235 | Demetrios II | Phthia (Epeirote) |
| c.230 | Antiochos | Hierax (daughter of Ziaelas) (Bithynian) |
| 228 | Antigonos III | Phthia (Epeirote) |
| 221 | Antiochos III | Laodike (Pontic) |
| c.218 | Akhaios | Laodike (Pontic) |
| c.212 | Arsames | Antiochis (Seleukid) |
| 195 | Ptolemy V | Kleopatra Syra (Seleukid) |
| 195 | Ariarathes IV | Antiochis (Seleukid) |
| c.190 | Prusias II | Apama (Antigonid) |
| 174 | Perseus | Laodike (Seleukid) |
| 152 | Alexander I | Kleopatra Thea (Ptolemaic) |
| 145 | Demetrios II | Kleopatra Thea (Ptolemaic) |
| 139 | Antiochos VII | Kleopatra Thea (Ptolemaic) |
| c.137 | Demetrios II | Rhodogune (Parthian) |
| c. 120 | Antiochos VIII | Tryphaina (Ptolemaic) |
| c. 114 | Antiochos IX | Selene (Ptolemaic) |

*Annex B* Sibling Royal Marriages:

| 278 | Ptolemy II to Arsinoe (siblings) |
|---|---|
| 280 | Ptolemy Keraunos to Arsinoe II (step-siblings) |
| 220 | Ptolemy IV to Arsinoe III (siblings) |
| c. 195 | Antiochos the Young King to Laodike (siblings) |
| 193 | Seleukos (IV) to Laodike (siblings) |
| 175 | Antiochos IV to Laodike (siblings) |
| 175 | Ptolemy VI to Kleopatra II (siblings) |
| 162 | Demetrios I to Laodike (siblings) |
| 145 | Ptolemy VIII to Kleopatra II (siblings) |
| c. 120 | Ptolemy IX to Kleopatra IV (siblings) |
| 115 | Ptolemy IX to Kleopatra V (siblings) |
| 80 | Ptolemy XII to Kleopatra Tryphaina (siblings) |

## Notes

1 These marriages are detailed in all books on Philip, for example J.R. Ellis, *Philip II and Macedonian Imperialism*, London 1976; George Cawkwell, *Philip of Macedon*, London 1976; N.G.L. Hammond and G.T. Griffith, *A History of Macedonia*, vol. 2, Oxford 1979.
2 Diodoros 17.16.2; Plutarch, *Demetrios* 23.5.
3 Plutarch, *Alexander* 21.7–9.
4 Ibid. 47.4; Arrian, *Anabasis* 4.19.5–6; and others.
5 Arrian, *Anabasis* 7.44.
6 Another son, Argaios, has been suggested: B.E. van Oppen de Reiter, 'Argaeus, an Illegitimate Son of Alexander the Great?', *ZPE* 287, 2013, 206–210.
7 Polybios 20.8; Livy 36.11.1–2 and 36.17.7; Plutarch, *Flamininus* 16.1–2; Appian, *Syrian Wars* 16; Diodoros 29.2.

## Royal marriages 53

8 Diodoros 18.12.1, 18.7 and 23.1; J. Seibert, *Historische Beiträge zu den dynastischen Verbindungen in hellenistischer Zeit*, Wiesbaden 1967.
9 Diodoros 20.77.3–5; John Whitehorne, *Cleopatras*, London 1994, ch. 5.
10 Helen S. Lund, *Lysimachos*, London 1992.
11 Holbl (see 'Abbreviations' section for full information), *Ptolemaic Empire*, 24.
12 Plutarch, *Demetrios* 14.1–4, 25.2, 46.4, and *Pyrrhos* 10.
13 Holbl, *Ptolemaic Empire*, 24.
14 Plutarch, *Pyrrhos* 10.5.
15 Arrian, *Anabasis* 7.4.6.
16 Plutarch, *Demetrios* 32.
17 J.D. Grainger, *The Cities of Seleukid Syria*, Oxford 1990, ch. 5.
18 Plutarch, *Demetrios* 38; Arrian, *Anabasis* 59–61.
19 Plutarch, *Demetrios* 48–52.
20 Daniel Ogden, *Polygamy, Prostitutes and Death*, London 1999, for details of the royal families.
21 Plutarch, *Pyrrhos* 6 and 9.
22 Diodoros 20.1–2 and 28.2; Justin 15.2.3–5.
23 Plutarch, *Demetrios* 36, and *Pyrrhos* 6; Justin 16.1.1–9; Diodoros 21.7.
24 S.M. Burstein, 'Arsinoe II Philadelphus, a Revisionist View', in E. Borza (ed.), *Philip II, Alexander the Great, and the Macedonian Heritage*, Washington, DC 1982, 197–212.
25 See the list of incestuous marriages in Annex B to this chapter.
26 W.W. Tarn, *Antigonos Gonatas*, Oxford 1913, 168.
27 Justin 28.1.2.
28 Polybios 5.43.1–4.
29 Livy 35.13.4.
30 Diodoros 18.11.12 and 14.4.
31 Justin 26.32–6; Polybios 10.22.3; Plutarch, *Philopoimen* 1.4.
32 A. Laronde, *Cyrene et le Libye Hellenistique*, Paris 1987, 360–361 and 379–381.
33 Polybios 4.51.4.
34 Eusebios, *Chronographia* 1.251.
35 Justin 27.2.11.
36 Diodoros 31.19; Justin 38.5.3.
37 Polybios 8.21.9.
38 Polybios 8.21.8.
39 It may be in fact that Akhaios was a younger brother of Seleukos I, or perhaps a younger son; this is largely assumed from the fact that many of his descendants bore typically royal Seleukid names, though this is perhaps a flimsy basis; however, the fact that the family moved so extensively into several royal families does imply royal acceptability.
40 Strabo 13.4.2.
41 See Richard A. Billows, *Kings and Colonists: Aspects of Macedonian Imperialism*, Leiden 1995, ch. 4, for other aspects of this.
42 For the family see R.E. Allen, *The Attalid Kingdom: A Constitutional History*, Oxford 1983, appendix 1.
43 Diodoros 19.7.
44 This issue has been considered, from an anthropological viewpoint particularly, by Sheila M. Ager, 'Familiarity Breeds: Incest in the Ptolemaic Family', *Journal of Hellenic Studies* 125, 2005, 1–34.
45 Holbl, *Ptolemaic Empire*, 194–197.
46 Diodoros 29.29; Porphyry, *FGrH* (see 'Abbreviations' section for full information) 260 F 48.
47 John D. Grainger, *The Syrian Wars*, Leiden 2010, 279–281.
48 Ibid., 334, 344–345; I *Maccabees* 10.54–58; Josephus, *AJ* (see 'Abbreviations' section for full information) 13.80–82.
49 Josephus, *AJ*, 13.268; Justin 39.1.7–9.

50 Appian, *Syrian Wars* 69.
51 On Kleopatra Thea, see Whitehorne, *Cleopatras*, ch. 12.
52 Ogden, *Polygamy, Prostitutes*, 140–142.
53 Her own uncle; the practice of sibling marriage entered the Pontic royal family when Pharnakes' brother inherited the kingship and married his sister.
54 Diodoros 31.28.
55 Josephus, *Contra Apion* 1.22.
56 Polybios 8.23; Strabo 11.14 ad 19.
57 Justin 38.1.1–4.
58 See the third genealogical table in Holbl, *Ptolemaic Empire*.

# 3 Cities, summits, states, envoys

This chapter gathers together several items concerning diplomatic practices in the Hellenistic period which can be dealt with relatively briefly. One of these practices, royal marriages, has been examined in the previous chapter because of its length, and the issue of the longevity of peace treaties has been discussed in Chapter 1. A further consideration is that, in one case discussed here – the relationship of the kings with cities – it is not entirely certain that 'diplomacy' is the right term, though messengers and envoys did get exchanged. Two other items, 'summit' meetings and the diplomatic recognition of new states, are fairly minor matters, so their consideration becomes too brief to merit chapters of their own. Finally, there is a section considering the work of the envoys.

## Kings and cities

The relations between kings and cities, while not entirely a new issue in the Hellenistic age, were central to the self-regard of the times and provided one of the more important of its legacies to the following Roman period. The policy of the pre-Alexander Macedonian kingdom was one of the main sources for the development of the relationship, but that between the Akhaimenid great king and his satraps on the one side and the cities within their empire on the other was also relevant. A variety of other factors was involved as well: the need of the new kingdoms to populate their lands with Greeks and Macedonians encouraged the establishment of new cities in the conquered lands. The kings also needed to recruit educated men for various civil tasks and soldiers for the army. There was the necessity, as it came to be seen, that the kings were well regarded by the inhabitants, or at least by the rulers, of the cities. That is, much of the relationship between kings and cities was necessarily conducted by a type of diplomacy in which the kings had to take care how they exercised their undoubted superior power.

The conquests of Philip II in Macedon included a large number of cities along the coast of the Aegean. Many of these had earlier formed themselves into the Chalkidian League, centred on the city of Olynthos. The league posed a major challenge to the integrity of the Macedonian kingdom, and Philip found only one to way cope with the problem – by destroying the league by destroying many of the cities.[1] His successors as kings in Macedon were usually less drastic – though

56  *Techniques and practices*

Alexander destroyed Thebes – but equally they were also usually in a much less difficult position – the Hellenistic cities did not threaten the existence of any kingdom. The remaining cities within Macedon retained a measure of local self-rule, but it was made quite clear that they were subject to the king's authority. Philip also transferred people, willingly or not, to new areas and planted them in new towns; again, these were all part of the kingdom and subjects of the king. This became, in essence, the pattern for the relationship between the newly established cities in the Hellenistic kingdoms.[2] The cities founded or organised by the kings – the Seleukids in particular – were automatically subject to their royal authority and do not figure in this chapter for that very reason. Their relations with their kings did have diplomatic aspects, but there was never any doubt that they were subjects.

The old established cities of Greece and Asia Minor, however, were proud and self-governing entities with long histories of independence, or at least autonomy. They were often of a considerable age, and their life continued through the Hellenistic period. Their relationship with the kings varied from permanently hostile to instantly submissive. The real diplomatic problem for the kings, therefore, was with the older cities, scattered 'like frogs round the pond' of the Mediterranean Sea. Those in Greece notoriously struggled for a century and a half to maintain their independence of the great powers, particularly with the Antigonid Macedonian kings, until finally driven to submission by Roman ruthlessness and conquest. Even then, however, the outward forms of independence and democracy continued. It was, for the Romans, easier to let them be than to meddle in the details.

The work of Kallias of Sphettos, as detailed in an honorary decree of the Athens Assembly from 270 BC,[3] gives an idea of the variety of tasks performed by envoys, especially in a fraught political situation. Kallias was first involved as a Ptolemaic mercenary commander on the island of Andros, one of the Kyklades which had become part of the Island League. This was taken over by Ptolemy I about 288 when Demetrios I was expelled from his Macedonian kingdom. Demetrios attempted to recover from this loss by invading Attika to recover control of Athens, whence he had been expelled; Kallias came across from Andros with a thousand men to assist the Athenian defence, staying out in the countryside to protect the harvest. When Demetrios arrived, Kallias used his troops 'in defence of the people', probably by now from inside the city. Ptolemy sent an envoy, Sostratos of Knidos, to intercede, and the city chose Kallias as one of its envoys to the peace conference. As an Athenian in service with Ptolemy he was in a useful position.

He returned to Ptolemaic service but was still able, or was expected, to help Athenian envoys and to work for the city, an intermediary role apparently also acceptable to Ptolemy. Four or five years after the peace, Kallias was employed by the city again to solicit assistance 'in corn and money' from Ptolemy II. Four years later he again was appointed head of a sacred embassy to attend the *Ptolemaea* festival at Delos; while there he got Ptolemy to provide ropes for the trireme of Athena for the Panathenaia. His value as an intermediary between Athens and Ptolemy earned him a post at Halikarnassos, in a position where he could assist other Athenian embassies.

Kallias therefore at various times was, while in Ptolemy's employ as a mercenary officer or as some sort of official, also employed as an envoy by his city of origin, variously as a delegate to the peace conference, to ask for relief for the straitened city, as leader of a sacred embassy to a royal festival, to ask for material help to assist the city in its own festival. Also he was expected by the city to assist other Athenian embassies and Athenian private citizens as well. For this, Kallias was, according to the decree, voted a gold crown to be awarded at the great public festival the Great Dionysia, his statue in bronze was set up in the agora, and he was provided with a special seat of honour at 'all the festivals celebrated in the city'.

These are some of the methods by which the cities, not just Athens, adapted to the overwhelming power of the monarchies, a combination of subservience, demands, joint celebrations, and armed assistance, though Athens would no doubt claim that the city was manoeuvring between overbearing great powers to maintain its independence. What the record of Kallias does not show, of course, is the policies of Ptolemy I and Ptolemy II towards what seems to be a relentless series of Athenian demands. They certainly required an Athenian response of some kind, and the repeated communications between king and city imply that the Ptolemies received it; by the reign of Ptolemy II king and city were acting within a set of parameters which were a generation old.

The agenda for the relationship of the cities with the kings had been set by Antigonos Monophthalamos in his declaration at Tyre in 314 that 'the Greeks should be free, exempt from garrisons, and autonomous'.[4] This was the founding charter of royal-civic relations, and every king had to more or less conform to this concept. Antigonos aimed by his action to secure Greek support, acquire access to the recruitment of Greek mercenaries, and reduce the need to garrison the cities, which could have swallowed up his whole army. He also expected to be paid for his forbearance: gold crowns were usually awarded by the cities. But this did become the agenda to which other kings also worked.

The means by which the kings instituted this policy varied. The Seleukids hardly had to bother for a generation, since they had contact with very few of the older cities – a few in Kilikia and, eventually, after the defeat of Lysimachos, a few in Asia Minor. The concerns of Antigonos' son Demetrios I and his grandson Antigonos II were primarily with the Greek peninsula, the old, proud, and powerful cities which had dominated Greek affairs over the previous centuries. Establishing a cordial relationship with Athens, Corinth, Thebes, or Sparta was never going to be easy, while at the same time new powers were developing, notably the two leagues in Aitolia and Achaia, which were even more awkward to deal with. The record of Kallias' actions illustrates the methods the cities could use to fend off an attack without wholly succumbing to the deliverer.

Demetrios had the advantage of a powerful navy, with which he dominated the Aegean and reached out east to Cyprus and Phoenicia and west to Kerkyra. His methods of domination, however, tended to be less than gentle, and his similar treatment of his Macedonian subjects brought his downfall in 288. His son Antigonos II then took another decade to re-establish his family's power in Macedon, by which time the country had been severely damaged by the Galatian invasions; this delayed any further attempt to re-impose his power on Greece.

As a result of the (temporary) Antigonid eclipse Ptolemy I and Ptolemy II were the men who were left to work out the ways of accommodating the sensitivities of the cities of the Aegean coasts and islands to their great power. Given that Egypt required their constant attention and the hostility of the Seleukid kings in Syria was liable to erupt in open war (as it did in 274–271, 260–252, and 246–241), it was inevitable that the Ptolemaic kings would use their fleet as their power instrument in the Aegean and that they would need to appoint a viceroy to command it and to work out that royal-civic accommodation. Ptolemy I had been able to go himself to the Aegean at times, but Ptolemy II could not: he appointed as his first viceroy a man who was perhaps chosen deliberately because he was neither Greek nor Macedonian but had been the ruler of a city, Philokles, formerly the king of Sidon.[5]

Ptolemy I had already established relations with several cities in the south-east of the Aegean, in Karia and Lykia and into Ionia. It seems to have been Philokles who, by a permanent fleet presence in the Aegean, was able to institutionalise Ptolemaic power. This is visible mainly in the appearance of records in stone at various places, and so it is incomplete, since some records will have been destroyed, and others not yet found. But those which are known give some indication of the methods used. Miletos, for example, was in Antiochos I's sphere, but was given some land by Ptolemy in 279, thereby bringing it into the Ptolemaic system;[6] the Island League of the Kyklades had been one of the instruments of Antigonos I's power, and of his son; this was taken over by Ptolemy as a going concern; Philokles summoned a meeting of the leaders of the islands at Samos in 280/279, indicating that Ptolemy II's influence was paramount by then. He appointed a series of Nesiarchs of the league, always men from outside the islands.[7] Samos was taken over as a directly ruled island and became a crucial Ptolemaic naval base,[8] and in time other bases were established at Itanos in Crete, the island of Thera, and at Methana in the Argolid.[9] From Itanos there are records which indicate that the city itself was effectively autonomous, though the presence of Ptolemaic power was no doubt a constraint.[10]

The crucial aspect of all this was that, as at Itanos, the cities ruled themselves internally, but in their foreign relations they were expected to observe the requirements of their suzerain. For most of the time this occasioned no difficulty, but it was always possible for another king to provide inducements to change sides, as apparently happened at Miletos. One result of this was that in wars the Ptolemaic grip tended to tighten, and its reach expanded. It seems to have been during the First Syrian War in the 270s that several cities in Karia, for instance, were brought into the Ptolemaic sphere, presumably to deny them to Antiochos.[11] Then in 260–259 Samos was seized by a mercenary captain, Timarchos of Miletos, who then took over Ephesos; the current Ptolemaic viceroy, Ptolemy 'the Son', was killed. The net result of the conflict which followed was that Antiochos II gained control of Miletos, but Ptolemy II regained Samos. The signal of Antiochos' local power was that he was recorded as the *stephanophoros*, the local honorary president.[12] The whole Ptolemaic system was thus vulnerable. After 246 its reach extended along the Asian coast into the north Aegean and the Thracian Chersonese. At Maroneia a Ptolemaic governor, Hippomedon of Sparta, is known.[13]

The means of control therefore were at first a matter of diplomatic persuasion, where cities were rewarded (as at Miletos). At Phaselis, as another example, considerable harbour works can be dated to the period between 300 and about 250, when Ptolemaic influence in the area was at its strongest.[14] The celebration of Ptolemy's power at Delos, the *Ptolemaea*, brought together the islands of the league, a time no doubt when issues were discussed, gifts handed over, and rewards provided. In Lykia a descendant of Ptolemy I and Lysimachos was installed at the city of Telmessos and established a four-generation local dynasty, but in the Ptolemaic interest.[15]

The policies of the Ptolemaic kings towards these old cities were therefore to leave them alone as long as they accepted the reality of Ptolemaic power, which was exercised by the presence of the Egyptian fleet and by a wide variety of institutional agreements, and by men who may be called governors – such as Kallias in Halikarnassos or Hippomedon in Thrace. Later the navy's numbers and readiness faded; Ptolemaic authority lasted, but only until it faced a series of armed challenges, at which point Ptolemy's competitors muscled in.

The Antigonid and Seleukid kings were able to overthrow the Ptolemaic protection almost totally. Antiochos III and Philip V agreed to partition the Ptolemaic empire, though the precise terms of the agreement are not known – not surprisingly since it was obviously a secret agreement.[16] Philip campaigned in Europe and Asia Minor, Antiochos in Syria. But then Philip had to face the Romans, and Antiochos was able to sweep the board in Asia Minor. He systematically campaigned along the south coast of Asia Minor, along the Aegean coast, and into the Propontis and Thrace, while Philip went down to defeat in his Roman war. Most of Antiochos' gains came from rapid submissions by cities he approached; only in one case, Korakesion, did Antiochos have to fight. He may have sent out envoys in advance, but there is no evidence of this.

Antiochos had also campaigned in western Asia Minor at least twice before for several years, at first with considerable violence to suppress the kingdom of Akhaios, but later with force being threatened mostly only as a persuasive. So between 212 and 196 there are numerous records of agreements made by Asian cities with Antiochos.[17]

The policy adapted from Antigonos' original 'charter' was therefore honoured in practice and rhetoric by most kings until the Roman blanket fell in 146. Like all bright political ideas, the devil was in the detail, and it took time for the details to emerge and to be accepted or imposed. Greek cities assumed they would have no royal overlords, but the kings assumed that the cities whose freedom and autonomy they were guaranteeing would show their gratitude by limiting their freedoms of action. Garrisons were admitted by invitation of the city governments, or at least technically so; getting them out by a similar invitation was, of course, much more difficult.

There were plenty of areas for disagreement and interpretation; that is, it was all essentially a matter of diplomacy. Over time a technique within which both sides could operate was evolved. During the early campaigns of the successors of Alexander a number of these cities suffered killing, burning, occupation, and looting; Alexander had, in effect, once again set the pattern by his sack of Thebes. This suffering is hardly surprising, given the extent of the warfare, and is part of the standard behaviour of all states in the Hellenistic period, from Rome at Carthage and Corinth in 146 to King Menander in the sack of Pataliputra in India at about the same time. Even in the midst of such events, however, diplomacy was working. Some cities avoided the worst excesses of the armies by a timely surrender, best achieved by sending a delegation of city officials to meet the approaching commander; then the city opened its gates when the army arrived, no doubt devoutly hoping that the commander had told his troops the situation and had them well in hand, so that their behaviour would be peaceable. Cities which were just a little late in their submission might suffer less than a complete sack or be subject to a heavy tribute; those which resisted were regarded as fair game for the army. So Sardis, for example, the headquarters of King Akhaios, in rebellion against Antiochos III, suffered a violent sack, much looting and destruction, because it was taken after a siege and assault;[18] Amyzon, however, which carefully surrendered in advance, suffered much less, even if it did not entirely escape trouble.[19]

Each city had to negotiate its own terms. Alexander doubled the tribute to be paid by Aspendos when that city first capitulated, then withdrew its surrender, and then finally gave in definitively.[20] Ephesos was ordered to pay its customary tribute to the temple of Artemis instead of to the king;[21] Ilion was declared free and autonomous because its citizens greeted him warmly, though after showering the city with promises and privileges, he moved on, and it was left to various successors to implement his intentions;[22] Rhodes was garrisoned by Alexander's troops but later negotiated the garrison's removal.[23] In each case a diplomatic contact was made, either at a meeting in the city between the king and the city council or in a more distant contact by means of envoys designated by both. The variety of techniques of subordination imposed by Alexander was a problem to be sorted out by later kings, made worse in the case of the cities of Asia Minor because they lay in the zone of contact and contest between the three great powers. For a time the Ptolemies were overlords of the cities as far north as Smyrna;[24] the Antigonid Kings Antigonos III and Philip V made attempts to gain control in Karia as the Ptolemaic power hollowed out.[25] The Seleukid kings pressed heavily on the cities all along the coast, and it was this pressure, exerted by Antiochos III, which was one of the causes of the conflict with Rome.[26]

In all cases some sort of diplomacy was required to make it clear just what relationship with the king each city was to have. It was, for instance, a sign of the city's subordination when a group of envoys visited the king's court to deliver a gold crown to congratulate the king on his birthday, or on some achievement; equally it was a sign of the king's authority over the city when he generously providing gifts for a new theatre or a civic charity or some other cause. Each city would be treated individually, and each would know it was effectively under the king's control. Most cities were probably content with the protection this provided and with the social stability it all implied. But the whole system was maintained by the constant movement of envoys.

A good example of the process can be seen in a group of inscriptions from Sardis. After its capture by Antiochos III the king imposed an extra tax on the city and installed a garrison, which was billeted on the citizens and in the gymnasium. The city, after suffering from this unwelcome attention for some time, sent a delegation of four men to Antiochos and asked him for relief. He granted this, and in addition provided gifts. The city responded with a decree setting up a cult for Antiochos' wife Laodike.

All this was done while the king and queen were actually in the city, and was done moreover through decrees voted by the city assembly. One of the four envoys was Metrodoros, who carried the king's reply back to the assembly: it looks very much as though Metrodoros was the *epistates*, the king's representative who kept king and city in contact. This, in other words, was a process of negotiation. Quite possibly, the process originated with the king, in order to find a way of lifting the punishments he had originally imposed. The lesson learned, the city was able to recover.[27]

A series of inscriptions from Amyzon gives an indication of the complications. The city was acquired by Antiochos in 203, after some fighting, after having had been under Ptolemaic suzerainty for several decades. Antiochos' viceroy in Asia Minor, Zeuxis, wrote to reassure the citizens that all would be well: 'we intend to take care of you . . . be of good cheer'. Antiochos himself wrote to caution the army 'concerning the sanctuary of Apollo and Artemis' – actually the Artemision, which had been damaged in the fighting – to which he appointed an *epistates*. Zeuxis reassured the Amyzonians that it remained inviolate and *asylos*. The *epistates*, Menestratos of Phokaia, earned the goodwill of the citizens 'for many demonstrations of his excellence in favour of the interests of the people'. He had written to Zeuxis and to the governor of Alinda, had recovered the Amyzonian property which was held at Alinda, and had 'repeopled' the Artemision. He was, that is, performing the duties of an *epistates* as an interface between the royal administration and the city. The city also issued decrees of thanks to an unnamed royal official, sending an embassy of four men, and to Nikomedes, 'a benefactor', to an officer in the army, and to a private citizen called Hermeias, who had, 'at his own expense', gone to the king to recover the sacred slaves of the Artemision.[28]

Matters were different at Teos, where the king himself arrived in the city with his army. It had been subject to Attalos I of Pergamon, and now Antiochos removed some of the Attalid impositions. He then asked for an embassy to be sent to him to discuss other matters. This embassy consisted of three men; a little later another embassy, of two men, took a copy of a decree of the city to the king, in which the city expressed gratitude and gave him a golden statue and a gold crown; this was followed by several more letters in the same vein. In each case envoys were sent by the city to the king and were then acknowledged by the king, who sent his own envoy with the reply.[29]

How far this was really a diplomatic matter in the sense of negotiations between autonomous powers rather than an internal political affair of the kingdom, or even an automatic bureaucratic affair, is difficult to decide. The Teos letters seem to be essentially repetitive in many ways, suggesting the city had become accustomed to subordination, but the first of them was clearly dealing with a new situation. Both Teos and Amyzon had felt the weight of Antiochos' arm, Teos by being occupied and Amyzon by a surrender which did not wholly save it from violence. The original arrangement would necessarily be organised through envoys, possibly instigated by the king. So also would any subsequent changes, either of the terms of the arrangement or of the person of the king. But as the system became established and the terms were regularly implemented – tribute paid, problems attended to, garrisons changed, honorary decrees passed, an annual gold crown presented – the actions would be automatically granted by an effectively bureaucratic action in the city assembly, never disputed. At that point they had become bureaucratic, and the autonomy of the city scarcely existed.

These examples of particular incidents at Sardis and Amyzon and Teos represent the imposition of royal authority by Antiochos III for the first time, and this must have happened with every city at some point. Every monarchy acted in much the same way, though most of these occasions are invisible to us. Once the initial exchange of envoys had taken place, the subsequent contacts were usually initiated by the cities, the occasion usually being a notable event. The city passed a decree, chose envoys, and sent them to the king with a gift, usually a gold crown. The process allowed both sides in the contact to claim that the city was autonomous and untaxed while in fact it was evident that it was paying a fee for the king's protection and to remain ungarrisoned.

This was the process used by all the monarchies, though at times it was necessary to use force – if the city changed allegiance, for example, or if it was seized by an enemy. It was also possible that the city insisted on its independence, as the greater cities around the Aegean tended to do – Sparta, Athens, and Rhodes are particular cases. Their autonomy was always limited, since they were often in alliance with one of the kings.

The Ptolemaic approach to the cities had been diplomatic in most cases, so that the Ptolemaic 'empire' consisted largely of alliances between the king and many of the cities, and these alliances could be severed. The many cities were not all essential to Ptolemy's power, which was largely naval, so that the cities away from the coast had a tendency to drift away or to be acquired by another 'empire'.

By contrast the Seleukid approach, perhaps because the cities within the kingdom came much more fully under royal control, was not really a diplomatic one but aimed at subjection. This has been seen in the examples cited earlier: Sardis, Amyzon, Teos. Under Antiochos III the process of subjugation was systematic; until in the dispute with Rome which ended in the expulsion of Seleukid power from Asia Minor, there were just two cities which were outside Antiochos III's control – or rather the dispute was over two of the cities (Lampsakos and Smyrna, and perhaps Alexandria Ilias). There was also a line of cities in the Aiolis outside Antiochos' control, but these in fact were even more tightly controlled by the Attalid king.

The processes by both kingdoms are similar, binding the cities firmly to the royal policy. This has led one student of the subject to claim that the Attalids and the cities of Aiolis formed a 'symmachy', that is, a military alliance in which a number of more or less weak states (the cities) were dominated by a single much more powerful state (the Attalid kingdom) and that the symmachy developed a series of institutions.[30] This interpretation has not been widely accepted and is discussed with something close to contempt by another student.[31] Nevertheless, the relationship between the powerful kingdom and the much less powerful cities was close and under fully royal control, and this was the method imposed by Antiochos III when he was finally able to dislodge Ptolemaic power all along the coast from Kilikia to Thrace. 'Symmachy' is perhaps the wrong term, but 'empire' comes close enough and implies just as much royal control.

This was not a diplomatic arrangement in either the Attalid or the Seleukid case. The outward form of diplomatic contact was preserved, in that the cities sent envoys to solicit royal assistance or to vouchsafe praise, always giving gifts, and the king generally handed out presents in return and granted privileges – though the value-exchange was to the king's financial advantage. But there is no doubt that the cities were less than independent; the term autonomous will do, but only so long as it implies no more than local self-government, the cities having little more control over wider affairs than in English local government but a lot less than a state of the United States.

The only true diplomacy involved in the whole process was in negotiating the terms by which the cities were to submit – that is, at the very beginning. From then on there was to be little discussion. The test, of course, came when Antiochos was threatened by an equal or greater force, namely the Roman army. When he was confronted by that army on his home territory, many of the cities he had subdued so recently gave him minimal support or abandoned him as soon as the Roman army neared them, or immediately after the defeat he suffered at Magnesia. The Romans took the hint; in the Treaty of Apamaea of 188 they instituted their war aim, to free the cities.

## Summit meetings

Hellenistic kings often negotiated on their own behalf with subordinate cities or with envoys of other kings, as with Antiochos III at Teos, but it was not a Hellenistic practice for kings to negotiate directly with each other. Such a meeting, of king with king, may be termed, using the modern journalistic phrase, a 'summit meeting', and they were very rare, all the known examples are early, and almost all are associated with either Antigonos I or Demetrios I. In some diplomatic encounters, such a meeting was actually impossible. If the king was to negotiate with a republican state he did so with an elected or appointed delegate or delegates; any terms agreed were then subject to ratification by an assembly – the Senate at Rome, or an assembly or a popular meeting in the Greek cities and leagues. In that case there was no guarantee that the terms as negotiated would be implemented. Rome, in particular, was notorious in this regard, and the ratification process was a constant source of Roman aggrandisement. Once the terms of a peace treaty were agreed by the delegates, it was customary for the Senate to modify the terms in Roman favour. The victim was then faced with the prospect of renewing the fighting or knuckling under to the new terms.

Even when a Roman consul was the official conducting the negotiations, the terms he agreed, though he was technically a head of state, could be changed by the Senate. So in 242 Q. Lutatius Catulus negotiated peace with Carthage, but the Senate increased the monetary indemnity he had named,[32] while Atilius Regulus, captured by the Carthaginians, is said to have negotiated terms which were then refused by the Senate. The Romans had no compunction in assuming that such behaviour by the Senate was to be expected.[33] In such circumstances, summit meetings were impossible. If a king agreed to a treaty with the Roman delegation which was subsequently altered by the Senate, the king would suffer a serious blow to his authority. As a result kings stood back and away from the process and themselves operated as the ratifiers, in the same way as the Senate at Rome.

In the early decades after Alexander's death, as the system of Hellenistic kingdoms was emerging from the wreckage of Alexander's rackety empire, meetings of kings (or satraps, as they originally were) did occur. This was a standard practice of Antigonos Monophthalamos. He met with Kassandros at the Hellespont in 312, with Ptolemy at Ekregma in 313,[34] and possibly with Seleukos in Mesopotamia in about 307. The practice was taken up by his son Demetrios Poliorketes, who met with Seleukos at Rhosos in 299, and with Lysimachos and Pyrrhos in Macedon.[35] It is probable that Kassandros and Lysimachos consulted together fairly often, for they certainly coordinated their opposition to Antigonos and Demetrios.

Most of these meetings were fruitless, if they were intended to produce any sort of agreement. The meeting of Demetrios with Lysimachos and Pyrrhos did stop any fighting; since all three kings then quickly left the area; probably the purpose was to agree to no more than a truce, so that they could each go off to attend to more urgent matters. The meeting of Demetrios and Seleukos in 299 produced an agreement in which Demetrios' daughter Stratonike was handed over to Seleukos as his new wife. But when Antigonos had met successively with Kassandros and then Ptolemy in 313 and 312, it was only too obvious that he was aiming to make a separate peace with one of them so as to then concentrate on the non-attender; this did not work. Later a second attempt succeeded, and significantly this time it was arranged between envoys, while the satraps later ratified it; Ptolemy asked to be included after Lysimachos and Kassandros made the original agreement.[36]

The Demetrios-Seleukos meeting at Rhosos in 299 points up the basic problem with such meetings: that they must be well prepared in advance if they are to be successful. In this case it is obvious from the speed of the meeting that detailed negotiations had already taken place, and the actual meeting at Rhosos was really a ratification. That is, the real work had already been done by envoys passing between the kings during the previous months. One of the reasons Antigonos' meetings with Kassandros and Ptolemy had failed was that he probably assumed that he could personally persuade or browbeat the others into an agreement but found he could not; he was not a natural negotiator face-to-face, even if his diplomatic skills, as in the dispute with Rhodes, were considerable.

At the conclusion of the battle to defeat Antigonos at Ipsos in 301 the three victors met to divide up their conquests. Present were Seleukos and Lysimachos as principals, but Kassandros was represented by Prepelaos, who had commanded the Macedonian forces sent to assist Lysimachos. It had hardly been possible to do much advance preparation for such a meeting since its existence depended on winning the battle, and none of these men was naïve enough to believe this was either likely, or even probable, beforehand. The result of the meeting clearly favoured Lysimachos, who had the strongest force camped on the field and was present at the meeting. The division of Antigonos' empire, however, was straightforward enough. Kassandros apparently wanted nothing for himself, and this must have been discussed with Prepelaos and Lysimachos in advance, though he did insist on a principality for his brother. Seleukos therefore could divide the Asian territories with Lysimachos, more or less on the line of the Taurus Mountains, though Seleukos also acquired some territory to the north ('Seleukid Kappadokia'). It was known that Ptolemy aimed to take southern Syria, but Seleukos could neither prevent this nor gain 'compensation' elsewhere. So this was a summit meeting which was superficially a success, in that it produced agreement amongst those present, but which actually stored up much trouble for the future, which lasted throughout the next two centuries; even in the short term, it took only a year or so for Prepelaos to be deprived of his kingdom by the defeated Demetrios, with the silent concurrence of Seleukos.

For the rest of the Hellenistic period there is no sign that any other such summit meetings took place. It was, of course, in the interest of the principals always to remain in a similar position to that of the Roman Senate or the Aitolian Assembly, standing back from the detailed discussions so as to be able to reject the terms negotiated by their agents. This is so obvious that it is surprising that any summit meeting ever took place at all. As modern examples have shown, such meetings almost invariably fail, unless they merely ratify previously negotiated agreements.

## The recognition of new states

Throughout the Hellenistic period new states, usually monarchies, appeared constantly, normally as fragments of larger kingdoms from which they had broken away. Thus the four great powers which emerged from the wreckage of Antigonos' kingdom in 301 BC – the kingdoms of Lysimachos, Kassander, Seleukos, and Ptolemy, with that of Demetrios as perhaps a fifth – had become at least a dozen by 150 BC. Some of these new states were regions which had moved into independence as a result of the incomplete conquest of the Akhaimenid Empire by Alexander. This was the origin of the string of kingdoms along the north coast of Anatolia and into Iran, which were mainly ruled by Iranian dynasties – Bithynia, Pontos, Armenia, Media Atropatene. Then there were regions such as Cyrenaica, which moved in and out of the Ptolemaic kingdom until it slid into the Roman Empire as a province; the Hasmonaean kingdom had the same relationship with Seleukids, though it achieved independence by much greater violence; the Nabataean kingdom developed in reaction to hostility from Judaea.

As these new states appeared each of them created a political problem, which may be summed up by the concept of 'recognition', or possibly 'acceptance', by the other states. In modern times this is a formal matter, indicated by an outside government which will appoint an ambassador to the new state or government – or not, if the new regime is hostile. In the Hellenistic period no such clear diplomatic process existed, but something analogous to it did take place.

The complication came from the fact that when a new kingdom claimed independence it was usually at the expense of one of the original kingdoms, and therefore the recovery of the lost territory was of primary interest to the parent kingdom, while its continued independence was of some concern to that kingdom's enemies and rivals. Before 275 BC Magas had been the governor of Cyrenaica for Ptolemy I and then Ptolemy II, but then proclaimed himself king. In that year he was presented with a new wife, Apama, the daughter of Antiochos I, Ptolemy's Seleukid rival. This was the effective recognition of his new status as an independent king by Ptolemy's enemy, but it was also an interference in Ptolemaic internal affairs by Antiochos; it was followed by a war between the greater kings. (In fact it is not altogether clear which came first, the proclamation of independence or the marriage and recognition; the combination, however, was the real issue for Ptolemy.) In the end Magas' new status was accepted internationally, that is, by Ptolemy II, no doubt at Antiochos' insistence, in the peace negotiations which ended the First Syrian War in about 271.

Twenty years later, in 255, in a similar process, but one which worked better, the marriage of Stratonike, the daughter of Antiochos II, to the self-proclaimed king of Kappadokia, Ariarathes III, brought that land into the international system as an independent state; it had originally been part of the Seleukid kingdom but had become a frontier region between the Seleukids and the invading Galatians. During the previous generation a local dynasty of Iranian lords had clearly established an authority in the new kingdom. The presentation of a daughter of Antiochos II to King Ariarathes was thus the formal recognition of the kingdom's existence and of its independence by the great power from which it had seceded. The kingdom was also a useful buffer between the Seleukid lands and the turbulent Galatians, which must have helped in the negotiations preceding the marriage.

These two examples indicate that it was the responsibility of the parent state to accept the independence and status of the new kingdom; in the case of Cyrenaica and Magas it was Ptolemy's annoyance which brought on the First Syrian War, and it was his acceptance of Magas' kingship and independence, presumably in 271 or perhaps before, which was the effective recognition.[37]

Other new kingdoms had to fight their former overlords directly to gain what Magas and Ariarathes acquired mainly by diplomacy. The usual method was for the ruler to defeat an army of the supervisory state, and then claim the title of king because of his success. So Zipoetes of Bithynia defeated one of Lysimachos' commanders in 297;[38] Mithradates of Pontos in c.280 defeated one of Seleukos I's commanders.[39] As a result they called themselves kings, at least to themselves and their subjects. Then, by issuing coins in their own names, by founding cities, usually named for themselves (Nikomedia, Prousa), and therefore doing those things which Hellenistic kings normally did, they became in fact independent. It was thus largely the passage of time which brought acceptance once the initial victory had been won; it helped if the defeated king had priorities elsewhere and that the seceding kingdom was geographically out of the way. Bithynia was a functioning kingdom from about 300, but it was only when a king's daughter married Antiochos Hierax of the Seleukid family about 230 that true recognition occurred; similarly, when another daughter of Antiochos II married the king of Pontos (some time earlier) and their daughter married Antiochos III in 221, recognition was clearly complete.

A reasonably well-documented example of the process is Baktria, which had been a Seleukid satrapy which was ruled by Antiochos I during his father's lifetime. About 255 a new satrap, Diodotos (I) took office, and stayed as governor for twenty years; by the time he died he was issuing coins in his own name, a mark of at least an ambition for independence. He still had the title of satrap, but he was to all intents an independent ruler. When he died, about 235, he was succeeded by his son, also Diodotos (II), and this man soon took the title of king, possibly after defeating a nomad invasion, perhaps after the retreat of an invading force commanded by Seleukos II, who was attempting to restore his authority in Iran.[40]

This retreat meant Sekeukos failed to impose his authority, but it was not an acceptance of Baktrian independence, still less than complete; only when Antiochos III failed in his attempt to recover full control in his eastern expedition in 208–206 could Baktria be said to be an independent kingdom – though in fact it had operated in an independent way for fifty years by that time. The decisive moment was when the Bactrian King Euthydemos, unbeaten in a long siege of Baktra made a peace with Antiochos. He sent an envoy out of the city to discuss the terms, and when they were agreed he sent out his son Demetrios with the ratification.[41] There was talk of Demetrios marrying a daughter of Antiochos, and while this did not happen, it is significant that it was at least discussed, for this was one of the normal methods of indicating recognition.[42] It does not seem that the two kings ever met face to face. Euthydemos acknowledged Antiochos' suzerainty in a vague way and in return was accepted as a fellow king, if of a subordinate status, like the king of Kappadokia. It was an effective recognition of Baktrian independence, with face-saving on both sides.

This gradual process of evolving recognition, until it was a *fait accompli*, may be contrasted with the altogether less comfortable early career of the Parthian kingdom. This was not a breakaway area but a region of the Seleukid kingdom which was conquered by outsiders, possibly from a rebellious satrap.[43] Recognition was slow in coming, depending as it did on the decisions of Seleukid kings, and perhaps the kingdom's independence was never really accepted by the Seleukids. Seleukos II's expedition to the east in c.235 was directed in part, at least, at Parthia, and Antiochos III's expedition two decades later was similarly aimed at suppressing the kingdom. Antiochos recovered part of the lost territory, but in the process he had to accord effective recognition to the Parthian king in order to secure peace.[44] Only after he was dead did the Parthian kingdom revive and was able to recover the territory it had lost to him.

In Asia Minor the principality of Pergamon shifted equally gradually into a semi-independent part of the Seleukid kingdom and then into full independence. Philetairos, the first dynast, was a former official of Lysimachos' who joined

68  *Techniques and practices*

Seleukos I on his invasion and then put Antiochos I under an obligation by recovering Seleukos' murdered body. When his successor Eumenes I defeated Antiochos in a small battle in 263, this established his formal independence. By defeating Galatian raids he confirmed his local authority, but Eumenes did not call himself king; that was left for the next ruler, Attalos I, who chose the moment when the Seleukid kingdom was involved in a civil war to claim the title. The whole process, like that in Baktria, took four decades to complete.[45]

During the century between the victory of Seleukos I and the death of Antiochos III (281–187), at least eight new kingdoms appeared in the Hellenistic state system and were granted recognition in one way or another as independent states. The methods of recognition varied, but the basic process was for the new king to demonstrate his control over his territory and its population over a period of time, preferably by defending it and them against an invasion, either by the Seleukid king or by some other enemy – or both. This generally took a minimum of two decades or so to be achieved.

At that point, it had become accepted by the other kingdoms. Perhaps it was the arrival of a new generation which had grown up with the knowledge of the existence of the new state which was decisive. The formal moment would come when a decisive political act took place whereby it was clear that the king was accepted as such – a royal marriage, say, or a peace treaty. As it happens it was normally the Seleukid kings who had to indicate the acceptance, because it was their kingdom which was shedding the peripheral areas which became the new kingdoms. There were some regions – Elymais, Persis – which probably drifted away by a process of neglect. But there were others, notably the Galatians of central Anatolia, who were detested so much that none of their neighbours ever seem to have accepted them, though their warriors were recruited as mercenaries, which must have been in part a diplomatic process, as an envoy visited the central towns of the tribes to conduct the recruitment.[46] The Galatians were difficult to deal with because they had no central authority which they themselves recognised, though the three constituent tribes were each capable of political action. On the other hand, the whole group had a long-standing alliance with Bithynia, beginning when they were invited into Asia Minor by Nikomedes I.[47]

The process of fission continued, though the energy of Antiochos III retarded it somewhat. He was successful in suppressing the Asia Minor kingdom of his cousin Akhaios, and returned Armenia from an independent kingdom to two satrapies. For a time in Egypt a breakaway section in Upper Egypt maintained an independent existence under a pair of Egyptian pharaohs, but the Ptolemaic system was just vigorous enough to suppress it.

After the defeat of Antiochos III by Rome, however, the disintegration process resumed, first in Armenia, where the satraps installed by Antiochos made themselves kings. Recognition for one of these men came in 166, when Antiochos IV defeated him, then made a treaty in which Artaxias was referred to as a king, so accepting his independence once more. (The other Armenian kingdom was well out of reach of Seleukid power by this time.) When the Maccabees revolted against Antiochos IV and his successors, it took some time before they appreciated the need for international acceptance, but by the late 160s they were in contact with Sparta and Rome. The latter accorded a neglectful recognition but failed to provide the assistance the Maccabees wanted; the Romans accorded the same negligent recognition to the Seleukid rebel Timarchos, which did him no good; both were suppressed. It was therefore seen to be necessary not just to control territory but to be able to defend it successfully. Timarchos could not; nor for a time could the Maccabees. That is, the same considerations and procedures – if that is not too strong a word for such a vague process – were still essentially operating by the 150s.

## The envoys

An envoy, or ambassador – the shorter term is best – was a man who was appointed by his master – king or city or league – to travel to another state with the object of initiating or continuing discussions. As such he will have been provided with some sort of accreditation which showed his authority, probably a letter, with servants to demonstrate his status as an important man; he took with him funds to provide for his own and his servants' needs and gifts for those with whom he had to meet. It was a mark of an especially well-regarded envoy that he refused his expenses and made the journey at his own cost. Kallias of Sphettos took his 50 minas but gave it to 'the people'; Hegesias of Lampsakos travelled to Gaul and back at his own expense; Hermeias, the man who rescued the slaves stolen from the temple at Amyzon, did so at his own expense, as the appreciative decree in his honour states.

The hard physical work of travelling, talking, negotiating, was done not by the kings (though there were exceptions) but by men who were commissioned by the kings and republics to do that work for them. They might travel alone or in groups. The royal envoys tended to go in ones and twos, whereas those from cities and republics were in larger groups. So one of the earliest envoys we know of, Hekataios, who was sent by Antipater to enlist the help of Leonnatos for help in the Lamian War, travelled alone;[48] Antigonos Monophthalamos sent Aristodemos to Greece with a large amount of money as his (very successful) envoy,[49] though by 'alone' one must realise that though they may have travelled without other envoys, they were accompanied by guards, servants, slaves, and so on. Clearly these men were well trusted by their employers.

It was, of course, dangerous to entrust a serious mission to just one man; he might die, or be killed or kidnapped, or might even defect. Travelling with a retinue did not always save them. A group of five Aitolian envoys going to negotiate at Rome, who must have had a retinue of two or three dozen followers – one of them, Alexander Isios, was the richest man in Aitolia – was captured by an Epeirote pirate.[50] It was more usual to send envoys in pairs, though singletons were still not unknown, and sometimes a pair of envoys travelled separately; two envoys of Antiochos III to Rome returned by different routes. It was not unknown for Roman envoys, who usually went in groups of three, to separate to carry out a variety of tasks.

The envoy will be an eloquent speaker, capable of speaking effectively in public, and persuasively in private, vigorous in mind and body, probably handsome in appearance – in Greece the use of Olympic winners was common. These were all qualities which were intended to prejudice his hearers in his favour (as were the gifts). In the midst of his campaign in Egypt Antiochos IV was visited by several sets of Greek envoys; he listened appreciatively to their exposition, enjoying the display of eloquence – but he ignored their proposals.[51]

The servants would include body servants such as a valet but also clerical assistants whose function would be to record the progress (or otherwise) of the negotiations, maintain the necessary record, take down a record of their speeches, and perhaps send regular reports back to the home authority.[52] If he was representing a city, the envoy might fund much of this himself out of his own resources, as already noted, though men travelling for kings were more likely to be provided with resources, not least because gifts given on behalf of a king were expected to be more lavish than an individual citizen might be expected to provide. Gifts were another matter which is rarely mentioned, simply because it was so customary. There is a silly story in Plutarch that some Roman envoys to Pyrrhos were horrified at being offered gifts, assuming they were being bribed.[53] But both before and after this other Roman envoys are known to have been given diplomatic gifts. (It is a normal diplomatic practice to this day, of course.) Plutarch's story is an invention, presumably from a Roman family involved in the embassy seeking a reputation for probity.

As an envoy a man was assured of a certain status as a privileged individual, and was protected as a sacrosanct person, just as was a herald on the battlefield. This was a practice which was, so far as can be seen, rarely violated. (The kidnapping of the Aitolian envoys to Rome was probably for money and partly perhaps to delay them. The Romans, despite their general hostility towards Aitolia, were just as annoyed as the Aitolians and insisted bluntly on their release; the Epeirote authorities complied.) It was, of course, fully understood that such men would observe the enemy and his preparations and dispositions, as did the Greek envoys who visited Demetrios in the midst of his siege at Rhodes. Indeed, one of the purposes of an envoy was precisely to operate as a spy.

The main aim of a diplomatic envoy, however, was to discuss differences between his home state and its adversary. His normal purpose would be to aim at resolving disputes, but this was not always the case, for the delivery of an ultimatum or a declaration of war was also his function. This was not always understood, as when the young M. Aemilius Lepidus delivered an ultimatum to Philip V in such a downbeat and obscure way that the king did not even realise that he had been threatened.[54]

All this is only to be expected, and is the normal practice of diplomacy in all ages. There were also occasional semi-public or public peace conferences. That at Corinth in 196 is perhaps the best known of these, but the prime example, though one that was really unique, was at Apameia-Kelainai in Phrygia in 188 at the end of the war between Rome and Antiochos III. Yet both of these were less negotiations than pronouncements by Rome of decisions already arrived at, either unilaterally or in private discussion. The reason the private peace discussions were replaced at these times by public statements and meetings was the involvement of Rome, and the Senate's determination to sort out the problems, as they were seen in Rome, of Greece and Asia Minor. What actually happened, of course, was that the assembled envoys listened to a Roman statement of the terms to be imposed with little opportunity to get any modifications accepted. So the word 'conference', with its implication of to-and-fro discussions and compromises, is not the right word – Roman *diktat* is closer. These therefore were not really diplomatic occasions, though the envoys from all the affected cities and states had to attend.

## Notes

1. N.G.L. Hammond and G.T. Griffith, *A History of Macedonia*, vol. 2, Oxford 1979, ch. 8 (by Griffith).
2. Getzel M. Cohen, *Hellenistic Settlements in Europe, the Islands, and Asia Minor*, California 1995, ch. 3.
3. Austin 55; T.L. Shear, *Kallias of Sphettos and the Revolt of Athens in 286 BC, Hesperia* Supplement 17, Princeton, NJ 1978.
4. Diodoros 19.61.1–4.
5. J. Seibert, 'Philokles Sohn des Apollodorus, König von Sidoner', *Historia* 19, 1970, 337–351; H. Hauben, 'Philocles, King of the Sidonians and General of the Ptolemies', *Studia Phoenicia* 5, 1987, 413–427.
6. *I. Milet* (see 'Abbreviations' section for full information), 123.
7. Dittenberger, *Sylloge* 1 (3), 390; Austin 256.
8. R.S. Bagnall, *The Administration of the Ptolemaic Possessions outside Egypt*, Leiden 1976, 80–88.
9. G. Holbl, *A History of the Ptolemaic Empire*, London 2001, 42–43.
10. Austin 107, 108.
11. Bagnall, *Administration*, 89–91.
12. J.D. Grainger, *The Syrian Wars*, Leiden 2010, 119–121.
13. Bagnall, *Administration*, 160–161.
14. J.D. Grainger, *The Cities of Pamphylia*, Oxford 2009.
15. M. Worrle, 'Epigraphische Forschungen zur Geschichte Lykiens, II: Ptolemaios II und Telmessos', *Chiron* 8, 1978, 83–111.
16. Polybios 3.2.8, 15.20.2; full references in Schmitt, *Staatsverträge* 3.547; numerous discussions are also listed there.
17. Ma (see 'Abbreviations' section for full information), *Antiochos III*, with an extensive 'epigraphical dossier', as an appendix.
18. Polybios 7.15–16.
19. Welles (see 'Abbreviations' section for full information), *RC*, 38; J. Ma, P. Derow, and A. Meadows, 'RC 38 (Amyzon) Reconsidered', *ZPE* 10, 1995, 71–80; see also later in the book.
20. Arrian, *Anabasis* 1.27.2–4.
21. Ibid. 1.17.9–10.
22. J.M. Cook, *The Troad*, Oxford 1973, 100–106; Cohen, *Europe*, 152–157.
23. Diodoros 18.8.1; Curtius Rufus 4.5.9; H. Hauben, 'Rhodes, Alexander and the Diadochi from 333–332 to 304', *Historia* 26, 1977, 307–339.
24. Bagnall, *Administration*.
25. F.M. Walbank, *Philip V of Macedon*, Cambridge 1940 (reprinted 1967).
26. Ma, *Antiochos III*; Sviatoslav Dmitriev, *City Government in Hellenistic and Roman Asia Minor*, Oxford 2005.

27 Ma, *Antiochos III*, documents 1–3, and pp. 61–63.
28 Ibid., documents 5–14.
29 Ibid., documents 17–19; P. Herrmann, 'Antiochos III und Teos', *Anadolu* 9, 1965, 29–159; F. Piejko, 'Antiochos III and Teos Reconsidered', *Belleten* 55, 1991, 13–69.
30 Roger B. McShane, *The Foreign Policy of the Attalids of Pergamon*, Urbana, IL 1964.
31 R.E. Allen, *The Attalid Kingdom: A Constitutional History*, Oxford 1983.
32 Polybios 1.62–63.
33 Polybios 1.31.4; Diodoros 23.12; Cassius Dio fr. 43.22; Schmitt, *Staatsverträge* 3. 483.
34 With Kassandros, Diodoros 19.75.6; with Ptolemy, Diodoros 19.64.8.
35 With Seleukos, Plutarch, *Demetrios* 32; with Lysimachos and Pyrrhos, Plutarch, *Pyrrhos* 6.
36 *OGIS* 5; Diodoros 19.105.1.
37 For both of these cases, see Chapter 3.
38 Memnon, *FGrH* 434 F 4–5.
39 Diodoros 20.111.4; Appian, *Mithradatic Wars* 9.
40 Frank L. Holt, *Thundering Zeus*, California 1999.
41 Polybios 10.49 and 11.34.1–10.
42 This marriage is too often assumed to have taken place, but Polybios is clear that it was only discussed.
43 E. Will, *Histoire Politique du Monde Hellenistique*, vol. 1, Nancy 1979, 301–312; this is, to put it mildly, a controversial area.
44 Polybios 10.28–32; Justin 41.5 and 7.
45 Allen, *Attalid Kingdom*.
46 As when Antiochos Hierax recruited them: Justin 27.2 and *Prologue* 27; *OGIS* 275, 278–280.
47 Memnon, *FGrH* 434 F 8.8.
48 Diodoros 18.14.4.
49 Diodoros 19.57.5.
50 Polybios 21.26.7–19
51 Polybios 28.19–20.
52 Of these people there is no ancient evidence; but their existence and presence is clearly to be assumed.
53 Plutarch, *Pyrrhos* 18.2–3.
54 Livy 36.16.1–2.

# Part II
# Diplomacy in action – the East

# 4 The diplomacy of the earlier Syrian Wars (274–241)

Between 300 and 100 BC the rival kingdoms founded by Ptolemy Soter son of Lagos and Seleukos Nikator son of Antiochos fought nine wars. These 'Syrian' Wars, which actually spread over all the eastern Mediterranean, have provided the vital clue to understanding one of the diplomatic practices of treaty-making and treaty-keeping which obtained in the Hellenistic period, in that they show that treaties were operative until one of the signers died, at least among the kingdoms in the eastern Mediterranean (see Chapter 1). They also, if intermittently, show a good deal about diplomatic processes, particularly as they operated in the reign of Antiochos III (223–187 BC), and this will be discussed in Chapters 6 and 9. Here it is the diplomacy employed in the first three Syrian Wars (274–271, 260–253, 246–241) which will be examined. Inevitably there is a certain overlap with Chapter 1.

## The origins of the dispute

The two founder kings Ptolemy I and Seleukos I had often cooperated in the wars against Antigonos Monophthalamos, but once he was beaten they immediately quarrelled over the allocation of the spoils from Antigonos' defunct kingdom. They had cooperated fifteen years before, when Seleukos had been driven from his Babylonian satrapy by Antigonos and had fled to Ptolemy for refuge with the information that Antigonos' ambition involved establishing himself as supreme ruler. Seleukos entered Ptolemy's service, using his familiarity with other contemporaries such as Lysimachos and Kassandros to stitch together the intermittent alliances which challenged and eventually destroyed Antigonos. He went with a small force to recover his Babylonian satrapy with Ptolemy's support in 311, after the two of them had jointly defeated the army of Antigonos' son Demetrios I at Gaza. Since then both men had prospered and they had again cooperated, if rather distantly, in overthrowing and killing Antigonos, even though, from his Egyptian base, Ptolemy could hardly operate in Asia Minor, where the decisive battle took place. He did, however, seize control of Palestine and Phoenicia during the war; this may or may not have been a distraction to Antigonos. Seleukos had provided a major portion of the allied army – cavalry and war elephants – which had defeated Antigonos, along with the armies of Kassandros and Lysimachos; he was allocated Syria and an area called 'Seleukid Kappadokia' as his portion of the spoils. Their

76   *Diplomacy in action – the East*

joint activity in the years before fully justified Seleukos' assertion that Ptolemy was his friend.

'Syria' was the name of the land from the Taurus Mountains to the Sinai desert, and Seleukos found that his gains were in fact only a small part of this territory, that part in northern Syria which Ptolemy did not want. Seleukos felt he had been cheated and was distinctly annoyed, but he was unable to do much about it. His ostentatious proclamation that he was Ptolemy's friend – which had certainly been true years before, and perhaps still was – and that he would not fight him was a clever propaganda *coup* but did not give him any territory.[1] This was the megaphone diplomacy of the time, a loud statement of his policy, which was presumably publicised widely; an earlier example had been Antigonos' proclamation that he regarded the Greek cities as free. If Seleukos' statement was designed to shame Ptolemy into surrendering southern Syria, it failed, but it may have seemed to put him in the wrong. Stories circulated that a rumour of Antigonos' approach had sent Ptolemy scuttling back to Egypt;[2] this story can only have originated after the defeat of Antigonos; its aim was again to disparage Ptolemy's contribution to the fighting. Seleukos' loud complaints may in fact have been a cover for an actual treaty between the kings, for, although they busily fortified their sections of Syria during the next two decades, and each fully understood the threat that the other posed to his part of the land, neither actually attacked the other so long as they lived, and both felt able to march off to other wars without mounting a great guard against the other. It is their willingness to ignore each other which rather implies a treaty.

At the same time, Ptolemy was by no means confident that Seleukos' proclamation truly meant what it said. He was soon allied with Kassandros and Lysimachos; isolated, Seleukos almost as quickly made an alliance with Demetrios, who still held Cyprus, Tyre and Sidon, a great fleet, Athens and Corinth, and had seized control of Kilikia. Objectively, Demetrios posed as big a threat to Seleukos' position in Syria as did Ptolemy; an isolated Seleukos could well be a target for Demetrios, and the alliance was probably aimed as much at deflecting him as it was intended to block Ptolemy. A diplomatic and military balance of power developed. It did not last long, but the major players had been clearly marked out, the essentially unsolvable nature of the conflict over control of Syria had been defined; for the next two centuries international diplomacy in the eastern Mediterranean revolved around the permanent Ptolemaic-Seleukid antagonism.

Seleukos I's proclamations that he would never fight Ptolemy I was, of course, a cover also for his recognition that if he did attack Ptolemy he would probably lose. Ptolemy I and his son Ptolemy II Philadelphos steadily developed the defensive strength of his hold on Koile Syria, on Phoenicia in particular, especially once he had gained control of Tyre, Sidon, and Cyprus from Demetrios, probably in 288. The longer the peace lasted the more difficult it was for Seleukos to contemplate any sort of invasion of the south. (So, in addition to the balance of power, there was a sort of arms race, as each king developed the fortifications of his part of the country.)

## The First War

So far as can be seen the two founders kept the peace, at least in Syria. The First Syrian War began about 274. The founder kings died in 281 (Seleukos) and 282 (Ptolemy), so in each kingdom a new king had been ruling for the past few years when the First War began. Both Antiochos I and Ptolemy II had been joint kings for several years before their fathers died, but they still had had to devote their full energies in their first years as sole kings to establishing themselves firmly in power before considering any foreign adventures. Antiochos had to fight a brief war of succession,[3] and he then campaigned for several years against the Galatians in Asia Minor, who had been introduced by the Bithynian king after careful diplomatic negotiations which protected Bithynia from Galatian ravaging but opened up the rest of Asia Minor to them.[4] Ptolemy had to contend with a possible rival within his family, Ptolemy Keraunos, who had a brief career as king in Macedon (having murdered Seleukos I when he was about to take over Macedonia)[5] before he was killed after being captured in battle by other Galatians. By 275 Antiochos had surmounted his own problems and had established an alliance with the ruler of Cyrene, Magas, another of Ptolemy II's ambitious relatives, who had been employed as Ptolemy I's viceroy. He was given Antiochos' daughter Apama as his wife,[6] a union which marked a political alliance and brought both to attack Ptolemy II's lands. Details are missing, but this achievement presupposes a preceding period of perhaps a year during which negotiations will have taken place. In 274 Magas attacked Egypt from Cyrenaica, and Antiochos attacked the Ptolemaic possessions in Syria. Again, details are unknown, but it is clear that their war was prepared for by detailed diplomatic contacts which included the negotiations for the marriage; on the other hand, the fighting was begun by Magas while Antiochos was in Asia Minor, and he was apparently taken by surprise by the beginning of the fighting. The war lasted three or four years and ended in a peace treaty in 271 involving all three kings; the result was actually something like a draw,[7] but Magas' kingship and his independence in Cyrenaica were confirmed.

The diplomatic processes in all this can only be conjectural, but some facts help to reveal what went on. Magas was Ptolemy II's half-brother and had been made governor of Cyrenaica by Ptolemy I. This happened well before 282, when Ptolemy II succeeded his father, perhaps as far back as 300. Probably it was in 275 that he married Apama, the daughter of Antiochos I and his wife Stratonike, and it was the next year that Magas began his march on Egypt. Before he got very far, a rebellion took place in his rear, or it was an invasion by native Libyans (and either could have been instigated by Ptolemy), and he had to turn back.

So the diplomatic activity was first of all a contact between Antiochos and Magas. The girl Apama was available (about fifteen years of age) by 275; her parents had been married since 292. To both men the marriage clearly signified that Magas would become at the least an independent ruler in Cyrenaica who was allied with Antiochos – he certainly took the title of king about this time, an act which marked his detachment from Egypt and perhaps his rebellion, and the marriage with Apama implied Antiochos' recognition of the independence of Cyrenaica.

78   *Diplomacy in action – the East*

It is quite possible that Antiochos did not expect to find himself at war as a result of the alliance. He was in Sardis in Asia Minor when Magas' invasion began and failed, and he had to move swiftly to Syria when Ptolemy identified the Seleukid king as being at the root of his troubles (Ptolemy II attacked Antiochos first). The treaty which ended the war restored the position in Syria as it had been at the start of the war. Considerable fighting had taken place in Syria, including a Ptolemaic invasion of Seleukid north Syria and a Seleukid invasion of the Ptolemaic south, in which fighting may have taken place to secure control of Damascus[8] – though details other than this are unknown. The one concrete result was that Magas remained independent as king in Cyrenaica.[9]

## The wider context

Given that the Syrian situation was essentially a stalemate, two consequences followed. The first was that repeated wars became inevitable as one or the other side attempted to seize an advantage which might be only momentary. The other was that both sides felt compelled to search for allies. Antiochos' alliance with Magas was one example, but it was not the only diplomatic manoeuvre of the time. Antiochos, for example, had assisted Antigonos Gonatas (his brother-in-law) to become king in Macedon and had then given him his stepdaughter Phila as his wife.[10] Macedon's weakness after a long period of ravaging by the Galatians meant it needed considerable help, above all a lengthy period of stability and peace, to allow it to recover. The Seleukid alliance helped in this by acting as a potential protection against Ptolemaic attack – Ptolemy II might be said to have a tenuous claim to that kingdom. On the other side, the alliance with Macedon protected Antiochos' Asia Minor territories against further Galatian attacks (and, of course, against any Macedonian invasion).

Ptolemy II was also very active diplomatically. He used his naval strength to reach out to new contacts. A ship or ships went through the Straits of Bosporos and Hellespont to visit the Bosporan kingdom of the Crimea, where one man was so impressed that he painted one of the ships on a fresco;[11] Timosthenes of Rhodes was sent on a similar exploratory cruise into the western Mediterranean and wrote an account of the voyage, *On the Ports*, on his return.[12] Since he had travelled in a Ptolemaic naval vessel, his mission was clearly official. Ptolemy made contact with Carthage;[13] the independence of Magas in Cyrenaica was a disturbing element, and friendly relations with Carthage could help to keep matters calm – it was a similar move to that of Antiochos with Macedon. Ptolemy's father had been a sponsor of Pyrrhos in regaining his Epeirote throne; but when his adventure into Italy and Sicily finally failed, Ptolemy II hastily contacted Rome to establish friendly relations with the winner.[14]

It is unlikely that any of this diplomatic activity was particularly useful in the direct context of the contest for Syria, and it was perhaps more in the nature of exploiting the diplomatic possibilities than a search for useful allies, but the contacts were successful in keeping the Ptolemaic government abreast of affairs in the west. One problem was that Ptolemy's two western friends, Carthage and Rome, soon fell to fighting each other, and in 264 it was necessary for Ptolemy to execute some careful diplomatic footwork when that war broke out: he had to refuse Carthage's request for a loan of two thousand talents.[15]

## The Second War

The peace established in Syria as a result of the First Syrian War lasted until the year after the death of Antiochos I (that is, until 260). The next war began when Antiochos II, who succeeded his father in 261, meddled in an internal Ptolemaic crisis. At Ephesos, a son of Ptolemy II who had been installed as the local governor rebelled. He had the support of some of his mercenaries and of the Aitolian mercenary commander Timarchos, who had made himself tyrant of Miletos and had seized the Ptolemaic island of Samos. Ptolemy 'the son' was soon eliminated by Timarchos, who thereupon for a brief time held Ephesos, Miletos, and Samos as an incipient kingdom. But then Antiochos II moved in to support the Milesians and get rid of Timarchos. In the process he seized control of Ephesos as well, but not of Samos, which had been Ptolemaic and now became so once again, except for its *peraia*, a mainland strip of territory where Antiochos had taken control.[16] Until Antiochos moved against Timarchos the whole problem had been an internal Ptolemaic one (though in the past Miletos had taken Antiochos' part); now the problem had widened and had developed a much bigger international dimension. In order for all this to have happened Antiochos had to have gained the support of the citizens of Miletos in taking the city and in removing Timarchos; there had obviously been preliminary intrigues and diplomatic contacts between the governor, the mercenaries, and Timarchos, and between the king and Timarchos' opponents in the city. And these intrigues are diplomacy just as much as the Ptolemaic naval demonstrations and goodwill visits which also took place.

This, however, is only one of several indications that such intrigues were going on. There are hints of others at Erythrai in Ionia,[17] at Lysimacheia on the Hellespont,[18] and at Arados on the Syrian coast.[19] They cumulatively suggest that, along with Ephesos and Miletos, both sides were busy in this activity, intriguing to secure local advantages, perhaps with a view to springing such prepared political mines when a new war began. This is exactly what is to be expected, of course, given the competitiveness of the situation. If diplomatic practice prevented Ptolemy II and Antiochos I from going to war openly between the peace of 271 and the death of Antiochos in 261, it is only to be expected that they would attempt to seize advantages whenever possible but carefully acting well short of going to war. They would both expect their kingdoms to be at war in the relatively near future, and so preparations for that future conflict were sensible.

The danger was that these intrigues would be seen as going too far and that they would be regarded as breaking the peace treaty. Any intrigues which became too noticeable would have to be either disavowed, since they were obviously conducted by agents, or blamed on the opponent, or could become the excuse for a war if one side was ready; it would then be made the fault of the enemy.[20] Care was clearly necessary, as was the employment of agents who understood the dangers and could be reined in if they were heading into danger. At Ephesos it was the blatant involvement of Antiochos II in taking over the city – which, until Timarchos seized it by eliminating the viceroy, had been under Ptolemy's control – which was the real spark for the war. That Antiochos moved so openly in a very sensitive Ptolemaic area suggests he was fully prepared for a wider war.

The fact that these several items of conflict came to light just after the accession of Antiochos II rather suggests that both kings were quite willing to allow the situation to worsen and both were prepared to fight, on Ptolemy II's side partly because his opponent, as a new king, could be assumed to be unprepared and partly because the treaty of 271 had expired with the death of Antiochos I. The meagre evidence for the actual fighting in the war seems to suggest that Ptolemy was able to invade north Syria and Kilikia, implying his greater immediate readiness for war.[21]

The diplomacy, of course, continued during and after the fighting, as well as before. Antiochos gained the support of Rhodes. This was unusual, for Rhodes usually supported Ptolemy, though the details of the arrangement are unknown; the evidence consists in Rhodian participation in a battle at Ephesos in 258, fighting against the Ptolemaic forces.[22] Ptolemy installed his nephew Ptolemy, son of Lysimachos, at Telmessos in Lykia[23] and installed a garrison at Xanthos nearby.[24] Both of these installations will have involved negotiations with the host cities. Ptolemy son of Lysimachos must be regarded as in some way Ptolemy II's viceroy in Lykia, where Ptolemy I had earlier exercised a powerful influence and had already installed some garrisons. The installation of a man of high rank connected with the royal family as viceroy may well have been a response by Ptolemy II to Rhodian participation in the war on Antiochos' side. At the peace which was agreed in 253, which clearly required more negotiations of some length and complexity, Antiochos held onto his gains (Miletos and Ephesos and perhaps other places) and prevented Ptolemy from acquiring any other territory.

The other item in the peace was an agreement that Berenike, Ptolemy II's daughter, was to marry Antiochos.[25] This item in particular will have required very considerable and detailed negotiations, probably more than all the territorial clauses put together. Berenike was Ptolemy's only daughter; he also had two surviving sons. (He is reported to have had children by a number of mistresses but made sure that few or none of the infants survived.)[26] Ptolemy clearly felt that he was bestowing a gift of great price in delivering his daughter to his enemy; it is not altogether certain that Antiochos was as appreciative as Ptolemy thought he should be – but then this was a diplomatic negotiation. The marriage might be thought to have given Antiochos a claim to the Ptolemaic throne as the husband of a royal princess; equally any children they had might be expected to take precedence in the succession to the Seleukid throne. All these were subjects for negotiation, but, frustratingly, we have no information about the terms of the marriage settlement, though it seems likely that Antiochos was to repudiate his existing wife, Laodike, so that any children of his marriage to Berenike would take precedence in the succession.

The political purpose of this marriage is difficult to understand. It cannot have been intended as a guarantee of peace, since that was included in the peace treaty itself, and it was the lives of the kings themselves which were the real guarantees of peace. That is, the two kings did not become allies, nor could the marriage be construed as an alliance. Nor would either ever accept the other as being in the line of succession – there can have been no question of Antiochos, as Berenike's husband, becoming Ptolemy's heir or successor. Nor could the treaty dictate to the Seleukid king who should be his successor, so any child of Berenike's would probably not succeed. Perhaps the best reason for the marriage is that Ptolemy was offering Antiochos a trophy wife, or that he was deliberately inserting a disruptive element into the Seleukid royal family – it certainly caused trouble. More cynically, it could be argued that since Ptolemy was losing the war (defeated in his invasion of Syria and at Miletos and Ephesos) he was buying peace by handing over his daughter.[27] (See Chapter 2 for an exploration of the diplomatic element in royal marriages.)

## The Third War

The peace of 253, apart from the gift of Berenike to Antiochos II, was no more successful in establishing a permanent peace than any other such agreement. It was also no less successful. It did, of course, block any direct attacks by one on the other for the immediate future. Once again, therefore, the premium focus reverted to intrigue, and in effect, to diplomatic preparations for the next war, though at the same time both kings could now switch their main efforts to other problems. Ptolemy II was considerably the older of the two kings, so Antiochos II could expect to be able to start a new war when his antagonist father-in-law died. He prepared for it by establishing political positions which could be exploited when the war began – once again, the ancient equivalent of mines planted in advance of an attack. He revived an alliance with the Cretan city of Lyttos which his father had made. The city was a close neighbour of the Ptolemaic naval base at Itanos, and the alliance could be interpreted as a threat to that base; it also gave Antiochos access to the mercenary market in Crete.[28] He expanded his control into Thrace,[29] thereby taking up a position to block any Ptolemaic move aimed at seizing the straits, where Ptolemy's exploratory expedition to the Bosporan kingdom in the Crimea had established friendly contact with Byzantion; Antiochos also established close contact with Macedon, where his relative by marriage, Antigonos II, was as anti-Ptolemy as any Seleukid and had been involved in a war with Ptolemy II in the 250s, the Khremonideian War.

Of course, all these plans went wrong, as plans do. Ptolemy II certainly died first, but only by a few months. And it was Ptolemy's mine – Berenike – which detonated first, while those laid by Antiochos did not even fizz, for his death cancelled any arrangements he might have made. Berenike and her infant son were quickly murdered, to leave the succession to the adult sons of Antiochos and Laodike, but the two boys soon quarrelled. (The murders were of course blamed on Laodike, the wronged wife; they were actually carried out by Antiochenes,[30] and Laodike lived in Ephesos or nearby, but they may have been yet another of the advance preparations, made this time by Laodike and/or her sons.)

## 82   *Diplomacy in action – the East*

The collapse of Seleukid royal authority in Syria in 246 (but not elsewhere) allowed Ptolemy III to conduct an almost violence-free campaign through north Syria, and perhaps even into Babylonia.[31] He withdrew as Seleukos II's power revived, but kept hold of the royal city of Seleukeia-in-Pieria as a souvenir – together of course with plenty of booty. A new peace treaty was made in 241, leaving Seleukos free to pursue his dynastic war against his brother, who had now claimed the royal title; this was, no doubt, much to Ptolemy III's continuing satisfaction.[32] One of the elements which may have permitted the war to begin was Ptolemy III's marriage with Berenike, the daughter of King Magas; this united Egypt with Cyrenaica and obviated any danger of a second front for Egypt in a Seleukid war.

From the point of view of this study it is the timing of the wars and the peace treaties which points to the decisive diplomatic practice of the time. The wars broke out almost as soon as one of the parties to the peace treaty died. This makes it clear that the treaties were to last only as long as both parties were alive, but when one died his adversary was free to start a new war – or to accept a new treaty, of course.

These wars were as much diplomatic contests as they were military. Indeed if the years of fighting between 274 and 241 (17) are contrasted with those when there was no active fighting (26), it might be better said that it was a diplomatic contest interrupted by bouts of fighting. The usual mixture of ploys and methods were used by both sides: minor military campaigns, local intrigues, assassinations, spying, alliances, royal marriages. These incidentals were not intended to bring about peace, any more than the wars were, but were aimed at gaining advantage, something which might only be temporary. The whole problem centred on the possession of southern Syria was actually insoluble, since if one side won and gained the territory in question, the other would strive to recover it and thereby ensure yet another war. It was a perfect setting for active diplomacy mingled with intermittent wars.

## Notes

1. Diodoros 21.1.5.
2. Diodoros 21.113.3; Ptolemy had in fact retired to winter quarters as normal; there is no evidence, apart from the story, that the rumour existed.
3. There was some undefined trouble in Syria (*OGIS* 219 = Austin 162).
4. Memnon, *FGrH* 18, F 11, 11 = Austin 159.
5. Ibid., 1–14; Appian, *Syrian Wars* 59.
6. Pausanias 1.7.3.
7. J.D. Grainger, *The Syrian Wars*, Leiden 2010, chapter 3.
8. Porphyry *FGrH* 260 F 32.8 (Eusebios, *Chronographia* 1.251); if and when this happened at Damascus is extremely unclear; I tend to think it was to be dated to the time of Antiochos III; cf. Bagnall, *Administration*, 12.
9. Holbl, *Ptolemaic Empire*, 39.
10. Diogenes Laertius VII.1.8.
11. L. Basch, 'The *Isis* of Ptolemy II Philadelphus', *The Mariner's Mirror* 71, 1985, 129–137.

## The diplomacy of the earlier Syrian Wars 83

12 P.M. Fraser, *Ptolemaic Alexandria*, vol. 1, Oxford 1972, 152.
13 N. Huss, 'Die Beziehungen zwischen Karthago und Ägypten in hellenistischer Zeit', *Ancient Society* 10, 1979, 119–137.
14 Dionysios of Halikarnassos 14.1.1–2; Livy, *Per.* XIV.
15 Appian, *Sicilian Wars* 1; this was not, of course, necessarily a gesture of support for Rome, more a gesture of neutrality.
16 This is a complex and difficult issue: cf. Grainger, *Syrian Wars*, 119–121, with references there.
17 *OGIS* 223.
18 *I. Ilion* 45.
19 At Arados a political change took place in 259, during the war and while a Ptolemaic army was campaigning in Syria and Kilikia: J.D. Grainger, *Hellenistic Phoenicia*, Oxford 1991, 55–56.
20 Transfers of blame, retaliations in advance, disclaimers of responsibility, and so on, are all too familiar in the present day, not least in the current Syrian civil war.
21 Grainger, *Syrian Wars*, 121–129.
22 Plutarch, *Moralia* 45 B; Athenaios 5.209e and 8.334a.
23 *OGIS* 55 = Austin 270.
24 *TAM* II.262.
25 Porphyry, *FGrH* 260 F 43, is an account of the transfer of the bride to her husband, with elaborate gifts.
26 Ptolemy VIII, *Hypomnemata*, *FGrH* 234 F 4; this is a list of Ptolemy II's mistresses compiled by his great-great-grandson.
27 The peace is usually seen as marking a Ptolemaic victory (e.g. Holbl, *Ptolemaic Empire*, 44), but this is very unlikely, given the lack of evidence for it; it is perhaps more likely that Ptolemy was buying peace after his lack of success.
28 *I. Crete* (see 'Abbreviations' section for full information) I, Lyttos 8.
29 Grainger, *Syrian Wars* 143–144.
30 Justin 27.1.1–2; Porphyry, *FGrH* 260, F 43; Polyainos 8.50.
31 *P. Gurob*, *FGrH* 160; *OGIS* 53 = Austin 268; Grainger, *Syrian Wars* 161–164.
32 Justin 27.2.9.

# 5 Aegean diplomacy
## Ptolemy I to Aratos of Sikyon

The conflicts between the kings of the eastern Mediterranean kingdoms largely centred on the successive wars between the Seleukids and the Ptolemies, where the main prize was Syria, but another major region of conflict, involving the Ptolemies, the Antigonids of Macedon, and the Greek states, was in and around the Aegean Sea. The immediate origin of this conflict area was in the ambitions of Antigonos Monophthalamos. He had dominated Greece, the Aegean region, and Asia Minor until his death, but he had never managed to gain full control in Greece nor any access to Macedon. His son, Demetrios Poliorketes, inherited control of his father's great fleet after the old man died in the battle at Ipsos and proceeded to seize control of Macedon for a time from 294. He instituted a great programme of army and navy expansion, clearly aiming to revive his father's dead empire.

**Ptolemaic policy in the Aegean**

Ptolemy I had intervened in the Aegean region more than once during his conflict with Antigonos and Demetrios between 315 and 288. Generally unsuccessful in these interventions, he had nevertheless established some control in Lykia, he was friendly with Rhodes, and his fleet was active inside the Aegean. Gradually the Ptolemaic involvement widened and deepened and solidified into permanence, but warfare in the Aegean was a long way from Egypt, and Ptolemy I personally was not willing to leave his main kingdom after about 300. It was hardly possible to control the movements of armies and fleets in the Aegean from Egypt, so from around the mid-290s bases were developed and viceroys employed.

A base on the island of Andros allowed him to develop intrigues aimed at destabilising the Antigonid hold on Athens; the city was successfully provoked to rebel, but once the rebellion began Ptolemy was most reluctant to render any further help to the city. When Demetrios went down to ruin in Macedon in 288 the Ptolemaic possibilities expanded further. The Kyklades Islands, in the centre of the Aegean, had been formed into an Island League under Antigonid auspices but were set adrift by Demetrios' collapse; the organisation fell into Ptolemaic hands as a going concern, and Ptolemy installed his own man as president (*nesiarchos*).[1]

All the Egyptian kings from Ptolemy I to Ptolemy VI felt it necessary to exercise some power in the Aegean area. The various temporary naval and military bases in the region used by Ptolemy I evolved under his son into a series of well-placed and permanent naval bases: at Itanos in Crete, the island of Thera, Methana in Argolis, and Samos. Ptolemy II employed a series of generals in the region as his agents to enforce his policies, who were in effect his viceroys for the Aegean area. They included Philokles of Sidon, Patroklos, and Khremonides of Athens, and there were no doubt others.

This was one element of the Ptolemaic 'empire' in the Aegean and Greece, but it was only in part a matter of direct rule. Outside the permanent naval posts the region was controlled by a series of alliances and diplomatic action organised and administered by the viceroys, and by their actions much of the Aegean came under Ptolemaic domination. This was essentially a diplomatic system. Many of the islands and the cities along the mainland coast of western Asia Minor were linked into the Ptolemaic system by individual agreements.[2] The cities were, of course, expected to pay tribute, and in exchange they were to be protected from possible enemies. In Asia this meant the Seleukid kings, but once Macedon had recovered from the Galatian raids of the 270s, the hostility of Antigonos II Gonatas in Greece and at sea had also to be countered. The arrangements with the cities were in fact rather weak, and it was not too difficult for cities to break away so long as they could find another protector. And indeed they may only be under threat from the Seleukids and the Antigonids because of their Ptolemaic connections, so it was never too difficult to persuade them to 'rebel'. If one or even several cities moved into independence or into the shelter of a rival great power, this was hardly much of a loss.

This system has been termed a thalassocracy – a sea empire – though it was somewhat looser than that term implies; it was diplomacy rather than direct control which was the primary means by which Ptolemaic power was projected into the area. Only the bases and some of the really important cities, such as Ephesos, were kept under direct control, having governors for their 'protection'.[3]

Ptolemy's competitors had linked themselves by a royal marriage when Antigonos II Gonatas married Phila, the daughter of Seleukos I and Stratonike. No doubt partly in response to this connection, Ptolemy II sent a naval expedition into the Black Sea, where he received extravagant honours at Byzantion and assisted that city in its war with local Galatians by providing food, arms, and money. In reply the Byzantines established a temple and a cult in honour of Ptolemy II.[4] Such things were the visible elements of Hellenistic Aegean diplomacy: practical assistance by the wealthy great power; religious and civic honours by the recipients. At base it was a serious matter of the exercise of power – the cult for Ptolemy II at Byzantion was a visible mark of the strength of the city's alliance with the king. These elements can also be found in other places and are marks of the success and reach of Ptolemaic diplomacy – but of course, other kings were honoured in the same way and for the same purpose.

## The Kremonideian War

Ptolemy II and his sister and eventual wife Arsinoe (II) cultivated good relations with Athens for several years. They welcomed prominent Athenians to their court, employed the former Athenian dictator Demetrios of Phaleron, provided money and food as gifts (arranged by Kallias of Sphettos – see Chapter 1).[5] Friendly contacts had also been made with King Areus of Sparta, whose military ambitions were well understood, and which could be financed relatively cheaply from Ptolemy's massive Egyptian resources.[6] Ptolemaic diplomacy was carefully designed to attract both cities, appealing to Athenian cultural pride and to the old Spartan military ethos.

These diplomatic 'campaigns' were successful in creating the atmosphere in which an alliance with Athens and Sparta was directed against Macedon. In a sense this system had been road-tested at Byzantion, and the approaches were generally tailored to the requirements and sensitivities of each city. The joint link with Ptolemy promoted a full alliance between Athens and Sparta.[7] Ptolemaic diplomacy was thus being deployed to use the two cities in the Ptolemaic contest with Macedon, but Ptolemy himself was not committed to joining in any war – not that Athens was at all reluctant, aiming to drive Macedonian occupation forces from Attika. Ptolemaic policy was thus similar to its contacts with Rome and Carthage, or Syracuse and Pyrrhos of Epeiros. These pairs were all in a precarious relationship of potential or actual conflict; it seems probable that the Ptolemaic policy was designed to gather diplomatic fruits when a fight broke out, at which point one or other of the diplomatic friends would be ditched – as in 273, when Pyrrhos was abandoned when Rome was victorious, and later when help for Carthage was refused when the Roman war broke out.

In the Khremonideian War the fighting was mainly done by Athens and Sparta, with little or no Ptolemaic involvement, and the war is quite suitably referred to by the name of the Athenian politician whose diplomacy brought about the conflict. The further diplomacy in Greece was, it seems, all Athens' work, with eminent Athenians going about securing alliances with most of the cities of the Peloponnesos.[8] But the war could not have started without Ptolemaic backing and subsidies to the two cities, and it only went on as long as it did (267–261) because of Ptolemaic resources being drip-fed to the allies. This was, in fact, a masterly Ptolemaic diplomatic performance, which embroiled Ptolemy's own enemy, Macedon, in an awkward war for almost a decade at very little cost to Ptolemy himself.

Successful Ptolemaic diplomacy was not, however, enough for its allies to actually win the war. The Macedonian army was strong enough to fend off Sparta, which fell out of the war when King Areus was killed in an attack on Corinth in 265. The Macedonian army also kept a firm grip on Attika and prevented any serious Ptolemaic land campaign from developing – Greece was really far too distant for a major Ptolemaic expedition, which would need to be carried by sea from Egypt and probably supplied from there as well. Ptolemy never seems to have committed more than a thousand or so of his soldiers to the war, though his navy was more active. It must have been obvious very quickly that a decisive victory for the allies was highly unlikely, and it seems that Ptolemy was only interested in keeping Antigonos occupied at Athenian expense. Ptolemy, in other words, left Athens to fight alone.

The death of Antiochos I in 261, just after the fighting in the Khremonideian War ended with Athens' capitulation to Antigonos, freed Ptolemy II to indulge in war with the Seleukid kingdom. This was the Second Syrian War, which was partly, possibly even largely, fought in Ionia. It was in fact intrigues in Ionia which set off the war. It seems probable – this is obscure – that Seleukid intrigues began to upset the Ptolemaic position in Miletos and then in Ephesos, the latter being one of those places which were important enough to require a governing Ptolemaic presence. Both Antiochos II and Ptolemy II were operating mainly through proxies in the Aegean area, such as Ptolemy 'the Son'. The intervention of the Aitolian mercenary Timarchos, who aimed to create a minor principality for himself, upset everybody's intentions. Diplomatic intrigues, combined with Timarchos' ambitions, eventually pulled the two kings into open war.[9] This was much the same pattern as Ptolemy's intrigues in Athens which had induced Athens and Sparta to fight Macedon, whereupon Ptolemy had sat back and let them fight. This time, however, he took advantage and spread the fighting to Syria (the Second Syrian War).

## Ptolemaic expansion

So the Khremonideian War segued into the Second Syrian War, and both were largely fought in the Aegean area. Ptolemy II gradually extended his control over more of the Aegean islands, which was essentially a diplomatic process backed up by the powerful Ptolemaic navy, with the aim of denying them to any competitors. The cities and islands of the Aegean were, of course, extremely vulnerable to such a power, but they probably fully appreciated the sea control the ships exercised; the Aegean was always liable to produce pirates if left to itself. This expansion was continued by his son Ptolemy III during the Third Syrian War (246–241) when he took control of cities on the Aegean coast of Thrace and on the Gallipoli Peninsula.[10] So the former system of diplomacy and alliances developed into a more direct rule – the informal thalassocracy had developed into a more firmly controlled empire requiring steadily increasing resources from Egypt for its maintenance. This is always a tendency with any empire, for any neighbour not under the imperial control is seen as a potential enemy. In the end the Ptolemaic state became seriously over-extended, and the system, of course, broke down.

Before that point the same tactics of gifts, bribery, the judicious expenditure of Ptolemaic tax-money, and the ever-present and obvious dispositions of the Ptolemaic navy – in short, imperial diplomacy – were displayed once more in mainland Greece. After the Khremonideian War it was hardly likely that Ptolemaic promises would be readily heeded by such local powers as Athens and Sparta, and anyway the mainland war had been won by Antigonos Gonatas, who had even succeeded in inflicting a defeat on part of the Ptolemaic Aegean fleet, though this had no effect on the general situation. In the end Macedonian power remained dominant on the Greek mainland, and the Ptolemaic fleet at sea.

Ptolemy II had taken up his father's Aegean policy and expanded it. The naval expedition which called at Byzantion went on through the straits and paid a courtesy call on the Bosporan kingdom of the Crimea.[11] In other regions the evidence is, as at Byzantion, cults and temples and statues. At Delos he founded and financed a new festival, the *Ptolemaea*, perhaps in celebration of a naval victory or maybe merely as a sign of his power;[12] his allies' attendance at the four-yearly celebration was mandatory. Delphi and Dodona received gifts, though it has to be said this was a normal practice for any serious power. A statue at Thermon, the federal centre of the Aitolian League, attests Ptolemaic diplomatic contact with that constant enemy of Macedon[13] and possibly the delivery of subsidies and an alliance. Delphi was under Aitolian control; Dodona was in Epeiros; both were friendly to, and at times allies of, Ptolemy; both were hostile to Macedon.

## Aratos

In the Peloponnesos, power shifted. Antigonos II held Corinth, Peiraios, and Chalkis in Euboia to dominate Greece. From Corinth he supported tyrants in several of the Peloponnesian cities, a policy highly popular with those tyrants, though not necessarily so with their subjects. It was not, in fact, all that different from the similar control of other cities exercised by both Seleukids and Ptolemies, though they generally eschewed tyrants. (The tyrants were generally home-grown, not imposed by Antigonos.) In effect this was an Antigonid alliance system.

Along the north coast of the Peloponnesos there had developed a league of small cities, democracies. By the 250s this Achaian League was substantial enough to provide a clear political alternative to Macedonian (or Spartan) domination in the region, and Ptolemy soon became involved. In 250 the tyrant of Sikyon, a city lying between Macedonian Corinth and the Achaian League, was overthrown by Aratos, the son of a former political leader of the city who had been murdered.

Aratos proved to be the most notable politician and diplomat in the Peloponnesos for the generation following 250 BC. He was still only twenty years old when he and a small group seized control of his native city from its tyrant.[14] A mob of exiles quickly returned, producing a situation which might have degenerated into retributive violence. Aratos showed his mettle by negotiating the accession of Sikyon to the Achaian League, so providing decisive political support for the new democratic regime.[15] The expansion of the league had generally been accomplished until then by a process which, like the accession of Sikyon, was one of persuasion and diplomacy. It was a true federation, with substantial authority left with the member cities but with foreign affairs decided at the federal level.[16]

Sikyon, even inside the league, was still disturbed by the continual conflict between the returned exiles and those who now occupied their former lands. Aratos acquired 25 talents from 'the king' (either Antigonos II of Macedon or Ptolemy II) which he used to ransom Sikyonian prisoners, thereby strengthening his political base in the city.[17] He then visited Alexandria and persuaded Ptolemy II to provide an even bigger subsidy (150 talents, forty up front, the rest in instalments), which was used to grease a solution to Sikyon's internal problems. The voyage to Egypt had been dangerous, a factor not minimised in Aratos' own telling.[18]

All this was a considerable diplomatic achievement by Aratos, showing imagination, initiative, and persuasiveness. It was also carefully operating along the groove of contemporary affairs, in particular exploiting the enmity of Antigonids and Ptolemies, and fitting into the tradition of Ptolemaic support for those Greek states who defied Macedon. Aratos' strengths were obviously diplomatic, but it was also necessary for him to be able to command troops. His seizure of Sikyon had shown his ability to conduct small swift operations in the commando style; later events showed he was much less capable in larger scale fighting.

The rapid reaction of Ptolemy II to this situation is noteworthy. He had already demonstrated a keen eye for political developments. In 273 he had sent envoys to Italy to, in effect, recognise the conquests Rome had made.[19] He and his father had been friends and allies of Pyrrhos until then, but it was clear that Pyrrhos' Ionian Sea empire was collapsing (Taras fell to Rome the next year – see Chapter 7), so Ptolemy was carefully covering his bets. Yet Ptolemy still patronised the Epeirote shrine at Dodona. He was clearly adept at being friends to all – except the rival great powers in the east. In the case of Aratos and the Achaian League, however, he had made a friend with the strength of will (like Pyrrhos) to make his own policy without reference to Egypt. This, of course, was always a danger in an alliance, one which Rome tended to avoid by insisting on subordinating treaties.

Aratos was elected general of the Achaian League in 245. He was still only twenty-six years old, in a polity in which the franchise was restricted to men over thirty, so he was clearly seen as an exceptionally capable man. He may well also have been able to persuade the members of the assembly of his plan for the expansion of the league. It had ceased to expand after the accession of Sikyon and was becoming surrounded and hemmed in by powerful neighbours who were less than willing to be persuaded to sink their identities into the league. In an attempt to break out, Aratos made an alliance with the Boiotian League, and at more or less the same time, perhaps as a distraction from this diplomacy, he led a raid into southern Aitolia. But the Aitolians were not fooled. They invaded Boiotia and defeated the forces of the league; Aratos had not been able to reach Boiotia in time to assist these new and temporary allies. The Boiotians now became Aitolian allies instead.[20]

Aratos had been successful at Sikyon in part because Corinth was at the time ruled by Alexander, the son of the old Alexandrian commander Krateros, who had been put in place by Antigonos as his governor and had then rebelled, proclaiming himself king. This meant that Antigonos could look more or less benignly on Aratos' exploits since they were partly directed against Alexander.[21] Aratos' alliance with Boiotia was aimed at, among other things, the encirclement of Alexander, who was at war not only with Antigonos and the Achaians but with Athens and Argos as well.

It is easy to explain the enmity of Antigonos, for Alexander was rebelling against him, while Athens was involved because it was more or less directly under Antigonos' control, with Macedonian garrisons in Attika, including Peiraios; Aratos made a practice of opposing tyrants, but, as was later shown, one of his main ambitions for the Achaian League was to gain control of Corinth. Aristomachos II, the tyrant of Argos, was also involved, and when the (incomplete and difficult) sources for the war are examined, it is clear that Alexander made peace with both Athens and Argos, but not with Antigonos. Antigonos' control over these cities was thus less than complete. Antigonos presumably permitted Athens to make peace, but that peace was made on the initiative of Alexander and Aristomachos in negotiations – and it was Aristomachos who insisted that Athens be included; he provided an indemnity (or 'bribe') to ensure it.[22]

## 90  Diplomacy in action – the East

It is evident that whatever had been the situation in Athens, Aristomachos of Argos acted independently, both in waging war on Alexander and in making peace with him. It was on his initiative that peace was made, leaving Antigonos at war with Alexander, and it was on his insistence that Athens was included in the peace terms. Athens later decreed thanks to Aristomachos – part of a long decree covering the whole Argive tyrant's family[23] – but we must not assume that Aristomachos acted for Athens' benefit. By including Athens in the peace he calmed the whole local situation and in fact succeeded in distancing himself from Antigonos as well as stopping the war with Alexander. He was, of course, acting mainly for his own benefit. He was also a completely independent agent, not a Macedonian puppet, as well as being a clever diplomat; this was, of course, a good example of diplomacy being used to solve an awkward difficulty.

In 248 or so, soon after he had made peace with Aristomachos, Alexander died; his rule was inherited by his widow Nikaia. Antigonos intervened and proposed that she marry his son Demetrios, which would, she presumably thought, secure her influence and position. (Demetrios was already married, to Stratonike, the daughter of Antiochos II, but she would probably be removed – another indication of the diplomatic unimportance of such marriages – but Demetrios would have become king in Corinth by marrying Nikaia.) In the pre-ceremony festivities Antigonos succeeded in first getting his men into the town, then in seizing, by an outrageous bluff, the fortress of Acrocorinth. (Altogether an original use of the concept of a marriage alliance; Nikaia is no more heard of; Stratonike's marriage lasted only a few years longer.) This action was also a type of diplomacy, one quite within the methodology of Aratos, in its lies, deceit, and bluff, with a backing of force. (Antigonos had a group of soldiers with him to take over as garrison in Acrocorinth).[24]

This brought Macedonian power back to Achaia's and Argos' doorstep with a vengeance. The network of Macedonian-supported tyrants was reactivated, notably at Argos and Megalopolis, though the example of Aristomachos' independence in the war must render such a concept rather less than total. These relationships, that is, operated successfully when one power had a strong military (or naval) presence; but like the cities on the edge of the Ptolemaic domination, they were liable to fade without such a presence. In his last years Antigonos was relatively successful in his naval and diplomatic campaign to restrict Ptolemaic power in the Aegean, using similar methods – diplomatic rather than overtly military or naval – to those of his rival: festivals at Delos, presidency of the Island League, building up a navy, the occasional victory, sometimes even a treaty of peace.[25] In the case of Achaia he had not yet faced active hostilities, but an obvious antagonism was developing, notably over Corinth once that city was back in Macedonian hands. Aratos was a friend of Ptolemy, while the Macedonian control of Corinth (and Peiraios and Chalkis) was a standing threat to, and at the same time a temptation for, the league.

Despite the defeats in Boiotia and now, in effect, at Corinth, Aratos was elected general of the Achaian League again in 243. (The Achaian constitution limited an elected *strategos* to one year in office, but there was no limit to the number of times a man might be elected.) Aratos' target was now Corinth. By a skilful clandestine penetration he led a force of four hundred men into the city and succeeded in capturing the acropolis.[26] Achaian control thus cut the Macedonian source of political support for the Peloponnesian tyrants. A string of cities then joined the league – Corinth, Epidauros, Megara, Troizen – extending the league's territory to include a substantial section of the Aegean coast.[27] Aratos had carried out his Corinthian *coup* in time of peace, but Antigonos II did not directly reply. During his term of office Aratos led a raid into Attika, ravaging the fields and capturing but then releasing Athenians. The apparent intention was to persuade Athens to rise against the Macedonian garrisons in Attika. In this the raid failed; no doubt the Athenians knew exactly who to blame for their ravaged fields,[28] and they responded with a decree appealing for contributions to a defence fund.[29] Aratos made a truce with Macedon in the winter of 241, but this did not lead to a full peace.[30] He attempted to stimulate a rising in Argos which failed through lack of local support. Aristomachos was then assassinated by two of his slaves; the complicity of Aratos in this is very likely.[31] Even this did not persuade the Argives to join the league, for Aristomachos' son Aristippos succeeded his father as tyrant of the city, evidently with plenty of local support, which presumably rallied to him in part because of Aratos' activities.

The variety of methods Aratos was using in his campaign to expand the Achaian League is impressive: clandestine military attacks, diplomatic persuasion (of the small cities south of Corinth), assassination (probably), guerrilla raids, a temporary truce, monetary subsidies from Egypt. Altogether this is a wide repertoire of diplomatic activity and it was backed up by military force. The problem, however, lay in this last, for at no time did the Achaian League, even at the height of its expansion, ever deploy serious military power. Much of this aspect of Aratos' activity was therefore bluff and was rapidly seen to be so – Argos understood it quickly, as did Athens. At the same time, his methods were also seen to be unpleasant, devious, and deceitful. He was not gaining any friends by using such methods, even if he did oversee the accession of a series of cities to the league. Not only that, but his methods showed that he could not to be trusted.

The Achaians elected Ptolemy III as *hegemon* of the league soon after the capture of Corinth.[32] It was, of course, an honorary post, but it was also a clear warning to Antigonos – though really a bluff – that the Achaians were friendly with, or allied to, Ptolemy, and that a counter-attack to recover Corinth might involve him in a new Ptolemaic war. Ptolemy may not have been very interested in a Macedonian war (he was in the midst of the Third Syrian War against Seleukos II at the time), but he was quite willing to be used in this ambiguous way. As a helpful, if indefinite, diplomatic gesture, it looks very much like Aratos' work.

Aratos and his league had therefore antagonised the two major powers in the north of Greece, Antigonos and Aitolia, as well as the league's immediate neighbours, Athens and Argos. Aitolia reacted by helping its ally Elis in the north-west Peloponnesos to expand, thus posing a threat to western Achaia. Antigonos meanwhile assisted his supporter Lydiadas to seize the tyranny of Megalopolis, a major city in Arkadia to the south of Achaia.[33] This, however, was also seen as a threat by

Sparta and was as persuasive as Aratos himself in forwarding the formation of an alliance between Achaia and Sparta. In the subsequent war Aratos lead his Achaian forces to a victory over an Aitolian raiding party at Pallene,[34] but the main target for the Aitolians seems to have been Sparta. The Achaians came off very lightly, possibly by merely showing themselves militarily alert. Antigonos' reaction to the loss of Corinth was therefore mainly diplomatic – in Achaia, in Megalopolis – and it was others, notably the Aitolians and Antigonos' own troops in Attika, who did the fighting.

Aratos resorted to diplomacy in this situation, probably because it was his preferred political activity. Abandoning the Spartan alliance, which was unpopular with the wealthy in Achaia because of King Agis' revolutionary policies of land distribution and debt cancellation, he contacted a prominent Aitolian, Pantaleon, and between them they arranged a peace.[35] Aitolia, though ambitious to expand into the Peloponnesos, was as uncomfortable at being the ally of Macedon as Achaia was with Sparta, and by detaching Aitolia from the Macedonians Aratos erected a substantial defensive screen for Achaia across the north. Aratos sent or conducted more raids into Attika and made futile attacks on the Peiraios;[36] these raids are a sure sign that his diplomacy was ineffective. He does not seem to have been able to stop these activities; possibly, having succeeded by such guerrilla methods early in his political career, he felt it necessary to go on using them; instead they made him a restless and disturbing colleague and opponent. He was liable, as in the unsuccessful attack on the Peiraios, to blame others when his schemes failed.

Neither the Athenians nor the Argives were interested in being 'liberated' by the Achaians. Aratos' raids and attacks always failed, yet the Athenians left it to the Macedonians to do the fighting. Similarly the Achaian League was advancing slowly southwards, but now it did so by capturing small cities rather than by persuasion, though this southern advance did persuade Lydiadas of Megalopolis to resign his tyranny and bring his city into the Achaian League. This took place during another of Aratos' terms as *strategos*; it would seem that his talents for diplomacy were as sharp as ever when they had the chance to work.[37] (Lydiadas was elected as *strategos* of the league alternately with Aratos for most of the next decade.) The accession of Megalopolis brought with it other cities in the neighbourhood, Tegea, Mantineia, Orchomenos, and Katyai, but these four soon pulled out and joined first Aitolia and then Sparta.

## Athens and neutrality

Aratos' policy of expansion by persuasion and raids was rather overtaken by Lydiadas' more forceful version. This meant that the league was pushing alternately against Athens when Aratos was *strategos* and against Sparta or Argos when Lydiadas was elected. They alternated in office every year between 235 and 228, though neither was successful in his chosen policy. Aratos ceased his raids into Attika after a defeat in 233, and as a result, when the new king of Macedon, Antigonos III Doson, was mired in troubles at home in 229–228, the Athenians felt able to use Aratos' diplomatic skills to persuade the Macedonian garrison commander, Diogenes – a native Athenian – to withdraw his men; one of the clauses in the agreement was that the men must be paid, and a subscription was collected among the Athenians and their neighbours to buy them out – Aratos personally is said to have contributed twenty of the 150 talents required, though one wonders where he got such a large sum; Ptolemy is the obvious ultimate source to be suspected.[38]

Contrary to what Aratos expected, however, the Athenians did not join the Achaian League after their liberation. For Athens, liberation from the Macedonians was not a prelude to enclosure within another polity. Aratos was foiled in this by his old ally, for it was the friendship of Ptolemy III that provided the Athenians with a sort of independence as an alternative. This was the moment when the policies of Ptolemy III and Aratos diverged. Ptolemy was at the height of his power in the Aegean, Macedon was weak, and the Seleukids were involved in the long dynastic dispute called the Brothers' War, a conflict Ptolemy carefully encouraged; in Greece Ptolemy's policy was designed to block any Achaian expansion north of Corinth as well as preventing the return of Macedonian control.

The change at Athens in 229/228 was the first of a series of diplomatic developments which altered the whole Aegean pattern within the next few years. At Athens it has been supposed that the result of the city's liberation was that it then pursued a policy of 'neutrality',[39] but a careful examination of the events in and about the city suggests that this interpretation needs to be modified.

Until 231 Athens had been dominated by the Macedonian garrisons in the Attikan forts, implying that Athens was under Macedonian 'protection' against the ambitions of other great powers – namely, in the Macedonian context, Ptolemy – and that it was under some degree of Macedonian control. That control appears to have been exercised lightly, for it was not in the scheme of things operated by Antigonos II, who reigned in Macedon until 239, to exercise direct control over his distant satellites, but the presence of the garrisons was certainly inhibiting. In terms of protection the enemy was Ptolemy, whose interferences in the past had resulted in considerable damage to Attika, but in the 230s, with a new king, Demetrios II, on the Macedonian throne, the situation changed. Demetrios was confronted by the joint enmity of both the Aitolian and the Achaian Leagues, by raids from beyond his northern frontier, and by Achaian raids into Attika.

The Macedonians, assisted at last by active Athenian resistance, had succeeded in holding on to Attika against Aratos' raids throughout Demetrios' reign, but the king's death early in 229 brought a crisis which blocked any Macedonian foreign policy activity for the next year and more. The removal of the Macedonian garrisons was not therefore only a result of Aratos' diplomacy but was facilitated by the paralysis in Macedon. Then a set of wars in Greece between 227 and 217 provided clear indications of the problem, which resulted for Athens by its being cast adrift from the safe Macedonian shores into a world of larger and stronger states, most of whom would be only too happy to gain control of Athens and Attika.

Athenian salvation lay in three elements. First was the refurbishment and improvement of the fortifications in Attika, the border forts and the walls protecting the city itself and the Peiraios, a task partly completed in the 230s. This was all the more necessary since the reopening of the silver mines at Laurion provided an interesting target for an enemy as well as being the source of a useful public fund – and Aratos' raids had emphasised Athenian vulnerability. The second and third elements were more closely diplomatic. The city was at risk no less from its near neighbours than from the more distant monarchies. The city's experience of the Macedonian garrisons was such that direct military help by anyone was neither wanted nor desired. Joining either of the Greek leagues was just as unwelcome; both of them had ravaged Attikan lands in the recent past, and in time of peace at that. Ptolemy, however, was not interested in imposing garrisons, but he was powerful at sea. Since it was the kings who were the real threat to Athens' independence, the answer was either to hunker down under the wing of one of them or to resort to 'the adulation of the kings, especially Ptolemy', as Polybios scornfully put it.[40]

In the event Athens did both, by accepting, and perhaps soliciting, gifts from several of the kings, signalled by lavish honours decreed for the kings and their envoys. In September 226 an associate of Antigonos III, Prytanis of Karystos, was honoured by the assembly for his work as an envoy, but there then followed a long sequence of honours for Ptolemy: in October a Ptolemaic courtier/envoy, Kastor of Alexandria, was honoured by a decree of the city;[41] two years later a new *phyle* of the city was created and called Ptolemais, and a *deme* was renamed Berenikidai after Ptolemy III's wife; a statue of the king and a cult with priests for the royal pair were set up; a festival, the *Ptolemaea*, was instituted; a new gymnasium called the Ptolemaion was paid for by Ptolemy.[42] All this was voted by the city within the years 227–224, so 'lavish' is perhaps not a sufficient description; politically it implied that Ptolemy was exercising a protectorate over the city, replacing the Macedonian occupation; Athens was thus not a neutral city among the power brokers but was clearly aligned with Ptolemy.

The main danger to Athens was Macedon, where Antigonos III Doson's accession to the kingship in 229/228 had coincided with the buying out of the Peiraios garrison. It soon became clear that he did not intend to attempt to re-establish the garrisons, though it was always a threat which he could hold over the city, and one which Ptolemy, as previous wars had shown, would be unable to prevent except by waging a distant and maritime campaign which would not threaten Macedon directly; on past form, however, Attika would suffer.

Athenian neutrality, therefore, as Polybios saw quite clearly, was only conditional, depending as it did on the distant protection of Ptolemy and on the forbearance of Macedon. Indeed it is perhaps better to describe it, not as neutrality, but as an alliance with Ptolemy. The Athenian honours for Ptolemy were a compendium of those which had been offered by many other Aegean states in the past half-century and did not require the Athenians to participate in Ptolemy's wars. The problem for this Athenian policy of Ptolemaic shelter and protection was that Ptolemaic power was becoming increasingly hollow. The Ptolemaic alliance-cum-protection lasted for only twenty years or so. In that time Athens was spared involvement in some crucial Greek events; that is, the Ptolemaic protection worked, but it unravelled from 207.

In 207 Ptolemy IV began to be seriously distracted by a great native rebellion in Upper Egypt, and when he died in 205 his successor was a child. The subsequent instability of the Egyptian government and its early involvement in a new Syrian war (the Fifth) rendered any pretence of Ptolemaic protection null for the Athenians or anyone else; the dire condition of the Ptolemaic fleet at Samos when Philip V seized it in 201[43] was only confirmation of the emptiness of the Ptolemaic power in the Aegean area, which must have been sensed by others in Greece besides the Macedonians. Not by coincidence, the forbearance of Macedon, now ruled by the ambitious and belligerent Philip V, ended.

Without Ptolemaic protection, and subject to Macedonian raids (not unlike those of Aratos), Athens' supposed neutrality policy was finished, as was its protection from Ptolemy; the city had to seek a new protector. This turned out to be Rome, the only power in the Mediterranean world now capable of facing up to Macedon. However, when Athens' quarrel with Philip developed in and after 201, the Athenians' first resort was to canvass support from Rhodes, another city which made a pretence of neutrality, but in this case more convincingly, since it was a well-armed and well-defended island. Athens also contacted Cretan cities (perhaps to investigate the hiring of Cretan mercenaries), King Attalos, and King Ptolemy V.[44] This last was the obvious protector on past form, but Egypt was now prostrate and was under attack by Antiochos III. The Pergamene king and Rhodes were clearly no more willing to fight Philip than was Athens itself. But they did point out that their Italian friend Rome was now disengaged from its long war with Carthage and was as annoyed at Philip as was Athens.

Athens was thus fortunate in its timing in appealing to Rome. King Attalos came across from Pergamon to give his support, and Roman legates arrived to investigate and to collect allies among the Greeks and in search of convincing excuses to declare war on Philip.[45] This was the effective end of the pretence of Athenian neutrality, though it was disguised by Roman forbearance for the next half-century or so, just as earlier it had existed only because of Ptolemaic protection. Once within Rome's system, however, there was no way out: one did not resign from the Roman Empire, no matter how distant and polite Rome's control. The city's neutrality was still imagined to continue for a few decades, and Rome respected the city's autonomy, but only because the city was weak, quiescent, and no threat.

The idea of neutrality for a small city was no longer, if it ever had been, a tenable proposition, not even as a pretence. The only interpretation of Athenian policy as 'neutrality' which makes any sense is in the local Greek conflicts between the wars of the 220s and the attack by Philip V in 200, when Athens was not involved in the fighting. In terms of the wider Mediterranean political world it was a city under Ptolemaic protection until about 205. It was the collapse of Ptolemaic power from 205 which cast it adrift, just as the Macedonian collapse in 229/228 had 'freed' it. When Roman protection arrived in 200, Athens could breathe again. Attika remained at peace because of these circumstances, not just because it was a successful diplomat in practising neutrality – it was protected by a great power.

## Aratos and the Spartan revolution

To return to Aratos and the wars of the 220s, which Athens largely escaped, it was in part the removal of its Macedonian garrisons which began the diplomatic changes in Greece and the Aegean which paradoxically led to the revival of Macedonian power. In the Peloponnesos the Achaian League pursued Aratos' policies for another year or so. The death of Demetrios II acted on the tyrant Aristomachos II of Argos as the living king had earlier on Lydiadas of Megalopolis. (Aristippos II had been killed in an ambush conducted by Aratos about 235.[46]) Achaian pressure and Aratos' diplomacy persuaded Aristomachos to follow the part of Lydiadas, resign his tyranny, and bring his city into the league. This was, as with the accessions of Corinth and Megalopolis, followed by other cities joining the league as well – Hermione, Phlius, and Aigina.[47] However, at about this time the four Arkadian cities which had joined and then left the league several years before now deserted Aitolia in turn and were taken over, probably quite willingly, by Sparta. Aratos attempted one of his clandestine attacks in response, but failed. A move by Sparta into another part of Arkadia, however, brought the Achaians to declare war.[48]

This was not the sort of action Aratos favoured; it seems to have been a decision taken when the former tyrant Aristomachos was Achaian *strategos*. Aratos much favoured undeclared warfare, raids and intrigues and *coups d'etat*, presumably because such a policy could be turned on and off at will and could be integrated more easily with his diplomacy, or could often be hidden or disowned if he failed; the continuing military weakness of the Achaian League must also have been an influence. Sure enough, the result of this new war was a couple of battles in which the Achaians were defeated; in one of them Lydiadas was killed, so Aratos was rid of one of his internal rivals.[49] Then the Spartan King Kleomenes III carried through the internal revolution which his brother-in-law Agis had failed to complete fifteen years before; suddenly Sparta emerged as a locally potent military power.[50] This was not something Aratos was equipped – mentally, militarily, or diplomatically – to cope with.

Nevertheless it was diplomacy he used to get his league out of the trap it had blundered into by following his policies. Kleomenes' revolution was very attractive to many of the poor in the Peloponnesos, where the economic and social distance between the few rich and the many poor had widened in the past century. Aratos had seen Sparta win victories even before the revolution had enhanced its military power, and he clearly understood that the increase in strength the revolution brought to Kleomenes meant that the Achaian forces, never numerous and never particularly valiant, were liable to defeat, and indeed that the loose-knit league itself was threatened with disintegration.

There was a proposal to make Kleomenes *hegemon* of the league,[51] no doubt intending that it would be an honorary position as when Ptolemy held it and perhaps hoping that he would come under Aratos' influence, as Lydiadas and Aristomachos had. This has the air of a suggestion by Aratos, but Kleomenes was unlikely to take up the presidency, or even to listen very closely to Aratos, who was hostile to the social implications of Kleomenes' revolution. Aratos looked for external support. Of the available powers, Athens was aligned with Ptolemy III, but Ptolemy was, and always had been, quite unwilling to be involved in Greek affairs on land; Aitolia was unavailable after the desertion of the four cities and unwilling to become involved in the Peloponnesos; and there was Macedon and Antigonos III. Kleomenes began winning battles, and characteristically Ptolemy III switched his financial, and so his diplomatic, support from Achaia to Sparta. Not only was his old sponsor and supporter unwilling to help, but Aratos found that Ptolemy was supporting the enemy.

While these events were playing out in the Peloponnesos, Antigonos III had secured control of Macedon in the face of invasions from the north and a possible Roman threat from the west (see Chapter 7). But, as ever, Macedon's main enemy was Ptolemaic Egypt. The expulsion of his forces from Athens had been followed by the reception of Ptolemaic protection for the city; Antigonos had replied with a naval expedition to Karia, where he campaigned for a time.[52] This is always regarded as a curious move, difficult to account for, but it was surely provoked by Ptolemy's success at Athens, and one of the reasons for Ptolemy's new support for Sparta was as a tit-for-tat for Antigonos' interventions in the traditional Ptolemaic area of Karia. The two powers were clearly shadow-boxing but also possibly heading for war.

For Aratos this switching of Macedonian and Egyptian interests provided an opportunity to counter Kleomenes – not to mention the fact that he was without any possible help elsewhere. In order to keep Kleomenes out, Aratos turned to Macedon. This required some diplomatic finesse, to put it mildly. First he sent two Megalopolitans with whom he had a family relationship to sound out Antigonos III on giving help against the Spartans. There were to be two layers to the help he needed: first, a public agreement, embodied in a letter, to send some limited help; second, a secret agreement to supply much greater help, including a declaration of war if Sparta continued to be successful.[53]

By 225, however, Kleomenes was invading and conquering cities of the league. The Achaian army was trounced. Kleomenes besieged Acrocorinth and then blockaded Aratos himself inside Sikyon. By this time Aratos had sent his son (also Aratos) to Macedon to activate the second part of the agreement with Antigonos. When he returned with the terms, the elder Aratos escaped from Sikyon – clearly with little trouble, so perhaps he had remained there to emphasise his suffering in the cause – and presented them to the assembly. Antigonos wanted the league to send hostages to ensure that it remained on-side, and he wanted to place a garrison of Macedonian troops in Acrocorinth. With half the league in Kleomenes' hands and no Achaian army in existence capable of relieving the sieges, the assembly had no choice but to agree.[54] One's suspicions must be strong that Aratos waited until the Achaians were desperate before producing the Macedonian solution. Certainly Antigonos' timing was precise.

## Antigonos III Doson

Aratos might be a cunning intriguer and the man who preferred clandestine plotting and diplomacy to open warfare, but his methods were hardly popular. He had now met his match in this, even his master, in Antigonos Doson. This man was a cadet member of the Antigonid royal house, the nearest male relative of King

Philip V, who had succeeded his father as king in 229 at the age of eight. A Macedonian Assembly made Antigonos Philip's guardian with the title, or position, of *strategos*. In true traditional style he married Philip's mother, Chryseis, and an early victory persuaded the Macedonians, willingly enough, to make him king. He faithfully protected and reared Philip, and eventually opportunely died just as Philip was about to reach adulthood.

Antigonos' rapid advance in power at home is a testament to his diplomatic sense and his political savvy. His political skill is apparent in his command of the trust of the generality of the Macedonians, and this ensured his command of his kingdom, with no serious internal opposition to hold him back. When he was approached by the two Megalopolitans, Nikophanes and Kerkidas, sent by Aratos to negotiate the alliance against Kleomenes III, he could seize the opportunity they inadvertently offered.[55] This was one of the moments when a king was presented with a clear set of alternative policies when any choice he made would lead to a significantly expanded power for his kingdom.

Aratos had been an almost consistent enemy of Macedon for thirty years – 'almost' because his preference for diplomacy was also an abiding diplomatic flexibility. But if there was one man and one state which were perceived as inveterate Macedonian enemies, it was Aratos and the Achaian League, and Aratos' participation in the removal of the Macedonian force from Corinth and then from Attika can only have confirmed this impression. So when the envoys arrived from the league asking for help, Antigonos could have been expected to reject them and then watch with undisguised pleasure as the league was destroyed by the Spartans; all that was required in such a case was that he do nothing, though this would leave him without any voice in the subsequent settlement of affairs in Greece. Alternatively, he could favour the current Achaian enemy, King Kleomenes, whose internal revolution had released the military energies which were in the process of destroying the league. This might give him some control over Kleomenes' actions, though this was doubtful – revolutionaries and Spartan kings rarely acceded to outside pressures, and Kleomenes was both. Or, third, Antigonos could accept Aratos' offer of an alliance and rescue the Achaian League. That is, Antigonos had the luxury of an almost free choice of policy.

It is a mark of the cunning of the diplomacy of Aratos that his envoys did not insist that Antigonos reach an immediate decision. Antigonos was given time to make his choice, Aratos apparently being certain that in the end he would assist the league. In particular Aratos asked for only a small measure of help at first; having given it, of course, Antigonos had thereby aligned himself against Kleomenes, who was thus identified as the aggressor, and the league could then demand more help, which did in fact in the end arrive, if with strings.

It turned out that Aratos was dealing with a diplomat as cunning as he was, and Antigonos had plenty of time. It took two years to move from the preliminary help to a full Macedonian expeditionary force marching into the Peloponnesos. It was in Antigonos' interest to wait until whoever he was going to help was in such straits that he could make his own terms. It was always possible for him to switch back to neutrality or even into assisting Sparta if the Achaians should show some unexpected martial ability and start winning – Ptolemy III had done just that. Antigonos placed himself in a position where he would only need to arrive in the Peloponnesos with his Macedonian army to win. Hence the two-year delay while the two antagonists fought and mutually weakened each other.

Antigonos must also have appreciated that a war in the Peloponnesos could be waged without seriously tangling with Ptolemy, who was subsidising Kleomenes but would not intervene physically. This did mean that Antigonos had to avoid Athens, which he must have wished to dominate once more, but to attempt to do so might just tip Ptolemy over into overt hostility. And yet it followed that the solution to a Greek political problem which did not involve Ptolemy would be an effective reduction in Ptolemaic power and prestige. Both winners and losers in Greece would be beholden to Antigonos.

Ptolemy III showed uncharacteristic clumsiness in dealing with the problem. (He died in 222, so perhaps he was ill, but he largely relied on a very able minister, Sosibios, so perhaps the apparent clumsiness is more a sign of a diplomatic bluff, which was then called). Athens had already aligned itself with Ptolemy by 227/226, and as the crisis in the Peloponnesos developed, the city very publicly emphasised again and again this alignment by means of its succession of honours directed at Ptolemy, which he reciprocated. It was all a masterpiece of diplomatic emphasis and exchange which left no one in any doubt that the city was under Ptolemy's protection. By contrast the Spartan subsidies were cheap and clearly aimed at keeping Kleomenes fighting – and Kleomenes scarcely needed Ptolemaic protection.

This was a successful policy by Ptolemy, and Athens was ignored in Antigonos' plans. Antigonos' actions effectively trumped both the wiles of Aratos and the Ptolemy-Athens alignment. He had plenty of time to make thorough diplomatic preparations. He gathered his Greek allies – that is, almost everyone but Athens and the Aitolians – into a new super-league, imitating that which had been formed by Philip II after his victory in 338 and which had been briefly revived by Demetrios I, Antigonos' grandfather, eighty years before. This put Antigonos in full control of the war, of the peace, and of Greece itself in large measure. This 'Symmachy', as it is termed, was not really something intended to be permanent, as Philip II's League of Corinth had been. It was seen to be all too obvious an instrument of Macedonian power after Antigonos' death; it was essentially a short-term wartime alliance which put Antigonos in the legal position of commander-in-chief of all the allied forces.

Ptolemy agreed to continue subsidising Kleomenes, who sent his mother and son to Alexandria, supposedly as hostages;[56] presumably Ptolemy hoped this would give him some control over Kleomenes' actions. The whole transaction implies that the two kings were in a sort of working alliance, and no doubt this was what Kleomenes hoped would develop. Antigonos tried by a diplomatic approach to persuade Ptolemy not to pay the money, but this failed.[57] A couple of battles in which Kleomenes was beaten were more persuasive. After only a year Ptolemy saw who was losing and cancelled the subsidy; the news reached Kleomenes as Antigonos' army approached Sparta's borders, though the decision had clearly been reached in Alexandria some time earlier.[58] Kleomenes was on his own again and went down to total defeat in battle at Sellasia. Ptolemy honoured his semi-alliance to the extent that he gave Kleomenes political asylum at Alexandria after his defeat.[59] (This was a standard Ptolemaic ploy: the Athenian politicians Demetrios of Phaleron and Khremonides had both been given employment by Ptolemy II when they were driven from Athens.)

Kleomenes had also been desperately trying to get the Achaians into negotiations in the hope of achieving a peace and so escaping from the war before Antigonos could attack him. During 224, therefore, a complex set of negotiations – Kleomenes with Aratos and Ptolemy, Ptolemy in contact with Antigonos as well as Kleomenes, the Achaians awaiting Antigonos' arrival yet talking with Kleomenes – was going on. The arrival of Antigonos at Aigina late in 224 was followed by the abandonment of Kleomenes by Ptolemy and, finally, by the organisation of Antigonos' allies into the Hellenic Symmachy. At that point the war was over except for the final battle. It had been diplomacy which had all along been decisive. The battle of Sellasia was only the public result.

The Achaians had probably been relieved to discover that Antigonos' terms for helping them were the surrender of Acrocorinth and the delivery of hostages to Macedon; no doubt the leniency of these terms was deliberate, for Antigonos would not wish to drive the Achaians to desperation. The Achaians agreed with relief, but as the war went on they found that other terms were demanded (just as Aratos' original suggested terms were designed to bring Antigonos' help by first a minor assistance, and then to a full military alliance). Megara, separated from the rest of the league by Kleomenes' control of Corinth, was taken over by Antigonos in the course of the fighting.

The victory of the Macedonians came in two stages, which were separated by further negotiations. First was the breaching of the Spartan fortified line at the Isthmus, the seizure of control of Acrocorinth by Antigonos, and then the capture of Argos, which had rebelled against Kleomenes. These events were followed by negotiations between Antigonos and the Achaian League, which fully accepted that Antigonos should be commander-in-chief of the forces operating against Kleomenes. Antigonos then embarked on the difficult campaign southwards and eventually defeated Kleomenes, who fled to Egypt and asylum. But even after Kleomenes had left, Sparta remained a continuing problem, a matter which suited Antigonos perfectly, since it would remain a constant thorn in the Achaian side in the Peloponnesos but not in his. The Ptolemaic alliance with Athens continued, so much of Greece was effectively divided between the adherents of Macedon and Egypt. The exception was the Aitolian League, isolated and surrounded by the allies of Macedon.

Aratos' diplomatic methods had included such 'undiplomatic' ploys as assassination, raids on foreign states in peacetime, the promotion of subversion, and clandestine attacks, and in diplomacy of this type he was clearly a master. His methods were an interesting variation on the usual Hellenistic diplomatic style, but they were based essentially on the weakness of the Achaian state as well as the character of Aratos himself, and so they could lead nowhere other than to degrade normal diplomatic practice. Similarly the apparent condition of neutrality into which Athens had slid was no more than a cowering under Ptolemy's shadow. The clear victor in the Greco-Aegean conflicts had been Antigonos III Doson and Macedon; diplomacy always succeeded best when it was based on real power.

## Notes

1 *IG* XII 7.506 (= Burstein 92 = Austin 256); Gary Reger, 'The Political History of the Kyklades, 260–220 BC', *Historia* 43, 1994, 32–69.
2 Detailed by Bagnall, *Administration*.
3 Holbl, *Ptolemaic Empire*.
4 Ibid.
5 Christian Habicht, *Athens from Alexander to Antony*, Cambridge MA 1997, 127.
6 Paul Cartledge and Antony Spawforth, *Hellenistic and Roman Sparta*, London 1989, 36–37.
7 Schmitt, *Staatsverträge* 3. 476; Burstein 56; Austin 61.
8 Habicht, *Athens*, 143–144.
9 J.D. Grainger, *The Syrian Wars*, Leiden 2010, 119–122.
10 Bagnall, *Administration*, 159–162.
11 L. Basch, 'The *Isis* of Ptolemy II Philadelphus', *The Mariner's Mirror* 71, 1985; there is disagreement over the size of the ship, either a quinquereme or a trireme; there is no disagreement that it was a visit by a Ptolemaic warship to a distant kingdom.
12 *IG* XI.4.1038.
13 *IG* IX.12.56.
14 Polybios 2.43.2.
15 Plutarch, *Aratos* 9.3–4.
16 J.A.O. Larsen, *Greek Federal States*, Oxford, 1968, 227–229.
17 Plutarch, *Aratos* 11.2.
18 Ibid., 12.1–2, 13.4.
19 Livy, *Per.* 14.
20 Plutarch, *Aratos* 16.1.
21 Ibid., 15.1–3, where Antigonos is quoted as praising Aratos; Plutarch interprets this as an attempt to sow doubts among Aratos' supporters, but it may be a reflection of Antigonos' policy of the moment.
22 *IG* II(2) 774 + *SEG* 39, 131.
23 *IG* II(2), 774.
24 Plutarch, *Aratos* 17.2–5.
25 W.W. Tarn, *Antigonos Gonatas*, Oxford 1913.
26 Plutarch, *Aratos* 18.2–24.1.
27 Ibid., 24.3.
28 Ibid.
29 Habicht, *Athens*, 163; L. Migotte, *Les souscriptions publiques dans les cites grecques*, Quebec 1992, 28–34.
30 Plutarch, *Aratos* 23.2.
31 Ibid., 25.2–4.
32 Ibid., 24.4.
33 Ibid., 30; Pausanias 8.10.6 and 27.12.
34 Plutarch, *Aratos* 31.2–32.3.
35 Ibid., 33.1.
36 Ibid., 33.2–4.
37 Ibid., 30.
38 Ibid., 34.5–6; Pausanias 2.18.6; Habicht, *Athens*, 173–175.
39 Polybios 5.106.6–8, in scathing terms.

40 Ibid., 5.106.7.
41 *ISE* 28 and *IG* II(2) 828.
42 Pausanias 1.5.5 and 10.10.2; Stephanos of Byzantion, 'Berenikidai'; see also Holbl, *Ptolemaic Empire* 52, and Habicht, *Athens*, 182.
43 Polybios 3.2.8 and 16.2.9; Livy 31.31.4; Appian, *Macedonian Wars* 4.1.
44 Habicht, *Athens*, 196.
45 Polybios 16.2.7.
46 Plutarch, *Aratos* 27–29.5.
47 Ibid., 35.1–3.
48 Polybios 2.46.2–3; Plutarch, *Kleomenes* 5.1.
49 Plutarch, *Aratos* 36.4–37.5, and *Kleomenes* 6.3.5; Polybios 2.51.3.
50 Cartledge and Spawforth, *Hellenistic Sparta*, 50–53.
51 Plutarch, *Kleomenes* 15.
52 Polybios 20.5.7–10; Trogus, *Prologue* 25.
53 Polybios 2.48.4–49.10.
54 Polybios 2.51.4–52.4; Plutarch, *Aratos* 41.
55 Polybios 2.47–51; Plutarch, *Aratos* 38.11–12.
56 Plutarch, *Kleomenes* 22.4–10.
57 Ibid.
58 Polybios 2.63.1.
59 Plutarch, *Kleomenes* 32.

# 6 The diplomacy of Antiochos III – I

## The Greek world

One of the few Hellenistic kings of whom it is possible to write a consecutive history is Antiochos III, and he is therefore a necessary study in terms of diplomacy, all the more so in that, since he reigned for thirty-six years, one can discern an individual method in his work, though the man himself does not seem to have been in any way extraordinary. He was generally competent as a war commander – that is, he won some battles, but also lost others; his ability as an administrator seems similarly competent, though he merely ensured that the Seleukid government machine, such as it was, ran generally smoothly. He was ambitious, with the general aim of 'restoring' the boundaries of his kingdom as set by the founder Seleukos I, but he was fully capable of both cutting his losses in defeat and in realising the limits of his power in success, even if he misjudged Rome. His prominence in this study is due largely to his long reign, longer than any other member of his family, and to the fact that his exploits were chronicled by Polybios, a younger contemporary. It follows therefore that his very ordinariness – as a king, to be sure – will show Hellenistic diplomatic practices under 'normal' conditions at a time when those practices had solidified into a system.

There are four crucial episodes in his career as king which display him in action as a diplomat: the Fourth Syrian War (221–217), his expedition to the east (211–206), the Fifth Syrian War (202–195), which included the preliminary partition agreement with Philip V, and the long-drawn-out negotiations with Rome which in the end culminated in his war with that city and the negotiations for peace (200–188). Within these episodes there are some subsidiary diplomatic sequences which are the most revealing of Hellenistic practices. The first three of these are considered in this chapter; the Roman episode is discussed in Chapter 10.

## The Fourth Syrian War

The Fourth Syrian War was triggered by the death of Ptolemy III at the end of 222.[1] The previous peace between Seleukid and Ptolemaic kings had expired with the death of Seleukos II in 226. His successor Seleukos III had been too busy and too short lived to begin a new Ptolemaic war, but Antiochos III was entirely free of any obligations to Ptolemy and had reasonably good grounds for commencing a new war, for Ptolemy III had been supporting Seleukid enemies in Asia Minor, the campaigns by Attalos I of Pergamon and later the rebellion of Akhaios. Antiochos was also persuaded by his minister Hermeias that it was the proper work of a king to fight other kings;[2] that the successor to Ptolemy III was a child was no doubt an added inducement.

There were, it seems, no preliminary diplomatic moves before launching an attack, though Hermeias did produce a letter which suggested that Ptolemy (III or IV) was in contact with the rebel governor of Asia, Akhaios. This is condemned as a forgery by Polybios,[3] but the context makes it by no means unlikely, and it is certain that similar intrigues took place later. The best way for the Ptolemaic government to prevent a Seleukid attack on Syria – which the death of Ptolemy III must have rendered likely, as did the accession of Antiochos III – would be to distract Antiochos by a rebellion within his kingdom. In fact Akhaios did not come out into open rebellion until later, so any Ptolemaic intrigues had been unsuccessful, but the mere fact that contacts between Ptolemy and Akhaios took place would inevitably engender suspicion, particularly in Hermeias' mind.

There was, however, a rebellion in 222 in Media by the viceroy of the eastern satrapies, Molon, and a suspicion of Ptolemaic involvement in promoting dissension was natural in the paranoid circumstances. The king's council in session in Antioch assumed that the best way to eliminate the threats would be to attack the source of them all, the Ptolemaic kingdom. The death of Ptolemy III and the succession of an inexperienced king would inevitably create confusion in the Ptolemaic court. In fact it was confusion in the Seleukid kingdom which followed.

So the Fourth Syrian War began with the sudden invasion of Ptolemaic Phoenicia by the Seleukid royal army.[4] This was defeated by a solid Ptolemaic defence in the Bekaa Valley led by the Ptolemaic mercenary commander Theodotos the Aitolian. Then Hermeias and Antiochos turned to deal with Molon, only to find that Akhaios in Asia Minor finally came out in rebellion as well, evidently concerned that Antiochos would not last long. But Akhaios' troops refused to march to invade Syria, a destination Akhaios had kept secret until the march was well on its way, so Antiochos was able to defeat Molon, and then mount a *coup* to remove the overbearing and threatening Hermeias. It then became possible to concentrate once again on the Ptolemaic war, which had remained in suspense while Molon was removed.

There is no evidence of any diplomatic processes involved in any of these events by the Seleukid government directed by Hermeias. There was no declaration of war, no negotiations with either Molon or Akhaios or with the Ptolemaic regency government. The one development which has evidence of diplomacy in these years was the negotiation conducted, probably by Antiochos' naval commander Diognetos, for a wife for his king.[5] The chosen girl was Laodike, daughter of Mithradates II, king of Pontos (another of Antiochos' cousins). The marriage was vital to the dynasty; since Antiochos was the only living male member of the family by direct descent, his marriage and the production of an heir was clearly of crucial importance.[6] The rebellions of Molon and of Akhaios were probably due to the realisation that if Antiochos could be killed, the kingship was vacant; both men took the royal title after their rebellions began, presumably having determined that they had what seemed to be sufficient support.[7] Akhaios did probably have a family link to the dynasty, but his soldiers, recruited from Greek and Macedonian settlers in Asia Minor, refused to fight 'the king' – meaning Antiochos – though their real reason was presumably an unwillingness to be marched far from home to fight a much bigger army. Had he waited until Antiochos was dead, they would perhaps have been less unwilling.

The lack of the use of diplomacy by Hermeias and Antiochos in these early crises was presumably due to Hermeias' preference. He dominated both the king and his council, and his priority may well have been to control Antiochos rather than to win the wars. With his removal (by a court intrigue and assassination) the Ptolemaic war was resumed, in 219. This time the diplomatic and military campaigns alike were marked by a much greater display of subtlety and diplomacy, and this change is probably due to Antiochos' accession to power in place of Hermeias and to his own preferences to use diplomacy as well as, or in place of, warfare. This was a trait he exhibited all through his life.

The city of Seleukeia-in-Pieria, held since 241 by Ptolemy III, was now besieged. An intrigue fairly quickly persuaded the junior Ptolemaic officers to overthrow their commander and to surrender the city.[8] Then, before a new attack into the Bekaa Valley, another preliminary intrigue was mounted, targeted at persuading the Ptolemaic commander, the Aitolian Theodotos, to defect. He had already beaten Antiochos in the earlier invasion but was now persuaded to change sides.[9] The Seleukid army therefore got through the main Ptolemaic defences. In the next year a series of similar intrigues brought most of Palestine into Antiochos' control,[10] and by early 217 Antiochos had assembled a great army at Gaza in preparation for an invasion of Egypt.

It must be emphasised that the use of such terms as 'intrigue' and 'negotiate' are synonyms for 'diplomacy' and that persuading officers to subvert either their commander (as at Seleukeia) or their government (as in the Bekaa Valley) or to surrender their garrisons (as in Palestine) are all diplomatic acts. In the same way, preparations for a future war, as in the preliminary alliance with Lyttos in Crete or the Ptolemaic contacts with Akhaios and (possibly) Molon, are all part of the diplomatic background to the much better-known military events. This is borne out by the various negotiations, intrigues, and contacts in 218 and 217.

Antiochos had shown in his campaigns that he was very ready to win points by diplomacy, even more so perhaps than by violence. This was a characteristic which was personal to him and was perhaps a legacy of the lack of success of his father and brother in their wars, where diplomacy seems to have been at a discount. But in the first stages of the Fourth Syrian War, he met his match in diplomatic intrigue. The Ptolemaic government was in the hands of two men, Sosibios and Agathokles, who had established a firm control over the regency for Ptolemy IV, largely by having any possible competitors killed off.[11] They proposed a truce for the winter of 218/217, which was the normal military practice – which Antiochos accepted.[12] Both sides required time for further military recruitment, but Sosibios also became very busy diplomatically. He contacted Akhaios, urging him to join in the fight, though since Akhaios' army would not march to Syria, this was impossible, as

## 106   *Diplomacy in action – the East*

Antiochos well knew. Ptolemaic envoys went to Greece to recruit mercenaries.[13] Four Greek states, Rhodes, Byzantion, Kyzikos, and Aitolia, were persuaded to send mediators to try to arrange a peace.[14] Since all four of these states were in fact friends or allies of Ptolemaic Egypt, they would be regarded as partial and so were unlikely to have any success, but it was good public relations.

The process of negotiation was long and slow, made deliberately so by Sosibios, who required time to rebuild and organise the Ptolemaic forces. Envoys passed to and fro between Memphis and Antioch and Greece. These men are unnamed, and their precise purposes are never stated, but the eventual result was an agreement to conduct peace negotiations at Seleukeia-in-Pieria.[15]

The choice of venue for the negotiations, Seleukeia-in-Pieria, was Antiochos'. Technically Seleukeia might be reckoned a Ptolemaic possession in temporary Seleukid occupation, but it had been captured by Antiochos, and he was clearly not going to give it up. The obvious place for these negotiations was Antioch, only a few miles away, the site of the royal palace and the Seleukid government centre. Making the Ptolemaic delegation meet at Seleukeia was therefore Antiochos' method of indicating that possession of the city was not for negotiation.

With the Greek audience of (Ptolemaic-selected) 'mediators' in the captured city, and with his army in occupation of a large parts of the Ptolemaic Syrian province, Antiochos used the meeting to expound his claim to Koile Syria, detailing the origin of the problem eighty years before. The Ptolemaic delegates replied by basing their own claim to its recovery on continuous possession and the repeated failure of the Seleukid kings to make that claim good. The real sticking point in the negotiations, however, was the request of the Ptolemaic delegates that Akhaios be included in the peace treaty, which Antiochos adamantly refused even to consider. The delegates must have known this, so it was a deliberate inclusion designed to prevent any agreement.[16] In this it was successful.

The battle which the two sides then contrived in the summer at Raphia was a Ptolemaic victory. As Antiochos retreated he first requested a truce to bury his dead troops – so admitting defeat – then sent plenipotentiaries to negotiate a longer truce. Finally he retreated all the way to Antioch. Ptolemy was able to recover control of Palestine and Phoenicia, the recaptured cities hastening to present their tribute and congratulations after having surrendered, more or less willingly, to Antiochos a year earlier. Antiochos' envoys, his nephew Antipater and his general Theodotos Hemiolios, had to endure a tongue-lashing from Ptolemy when they met but were then granted a truce for a year.[17]

Sosibios went with them to meet Antiochos on their journey to negotiate a definitive peace. The meeting this time took place at Antioch. The terms are not listed, only the conclusion of peace being mentioned,[18] but they can be inferred from later events. Antiochos is said to have been under pressure to agree because of his defeat, the damage his army had suffered, and the danger that Akhaios would attack,[19] but these are probably only assumptions by historians. He clearly held out during the negotiations for keeping the city of Seleukeia, which he is known to have held later, and it is evident that Sosibios did not repeat the demand that Akhaios be part of the treaty. In other words, Sosibios was by not confident of being able to carry the war into north Syria if Antiochos failed to agree, nor was he sure that if the war continued the Ptolemaic army might again be victorious; his terms therefore were designed to be acceptable; it also seems that Ptolemy IV was complacently satisfied with his victory and unwilling to go on fighting. As a gesture, he appointed Andromachos, Akhaios' father, as the governor of the reconquered Koile Syria province. Polybius remarks that the Egyptians were surprised at Ptolemy's success 'in view of his character in general'.[20] He reverted to his habitual lethargy; by the peace he was protected from any attack from Syria, so he could afford his laziness.

The diplomatic processes as revealed by this war are reasonably clear and straightforward. Envoys were able to reach Antiochos in the midst of the war to negotiate a truce, and Antiochos was able to send his own envoys after the battle, even as Ptolemy's forces were advancing into Palestine; both groups clearly made their journeys without impediment, no doubt under the sacrosanctity accorded to heralds. The negotiations in Seleukeia in the winter of 218/217 were evidently never going to succeed, since both sides still thought they could win the war; both sides used them to set forth their justifications for the fighting, presumably with several audiences in mind: the Greek mediators and therefore the rest of the Greek world, also perhaps their own subjects. Polybios' knowledge of the details of these private discussions suggests that a summary was published; with the emphasis on Antiochos' lecture, it may well have been produced by his chancery. The Greek city mediators being Ptolemaic friends or allies, Antiochos' lecture on his 'rights' indicates that this was fully understood. The terms demanded by each side in view of the balanced military situation – complete surrender of Koile Syria demanded by Antiochos, evacuation of his conquests required by Ptolemy, and the inclusion of Akhaios in the treaty, so making him independent – were clearly designed to make agreement impossible. The Seleukeia conference was thus mainly for show to indicate that both sides were keen to make peace while in reality aiming to justify their rival claims and their continuing conduct of warfare.

The real negotiations, after Antiochos' defeat at Raphia, were shown to be serious by the status of the envoys each side sent. None of those at Seleukeia at the first meeting are named by Polybios, either because he did not know who they were or, more likely, because of their generally low status, which would again imply an expectation of failure. After the battle Antiochos' envoys were his own 'nephew' Antipater[21] and one of his most prominent generals, Theodotos Hemiolios; Ptolemy's envoy was Sosibios, his most senior minister; their status and the meeting each group of envoys had with the enemy king guaranteed that this time the negotiations were intended to succeed.

## The suppression of Akhaios

The real victim of the Fourth Syrian war, apart from the soldiers who were killed or maimed in the fighting, was Akhaios. By failing to get him included in the treaty, Ptolemy had effectively abandoned him, and sure enough, next year (216) Antiochos began a campaign to suppress his rebellion. This was a slow process, but by 214 or 213, Akhaios' part of Asia Minor had been recovered except for the citadel of Akhaios' main city, Sardis. The advance of Antiochos' forces had been accompanied by diplomatic contacts he made with the Attalid King Attalos I of Pergamon. Attalos had been a momentary victor intervening in the complex Seleukid dynastic war in the previous decade and had been driven out of his conquests by Akhaios when the latter was still a loyal Seleukid governor.[22] Since both Attalos and Antiochos were enemies of Akhaios, it was clearly sensible of Antiochos to contact Attalos and secure his alliance. So Akhaios was under threat from the Attalid power to his north just as Antiochos' forces were advancing from the east.

Antiochos had therefore made two treaties in 217. The first, with Ptolemy IV, as a result of his defeat, was a guarantee of peace between them until one of them died. Both were in their early twenties, so both could assume that the peace they had reached would last for a fairly long time. (It actually expired in 205 or 204, with Ptolemy's death.) Antiochos' treaty with Attalos is not detailed anywhere, except for its existence,[23] but it must have at least implied a secure condition of peace until one party died.[24] (This treaty might also be reckoned the Seleukid recognition of Attalid independence.)

Akhaios' exposure to attack by Antiochos and Attalos was no doubt quite clear to him from the beginning. His only hope of survival, apart from a most unlikely military victory, was in enlisting Ptolemaic help – but Ptolemy could hardly break his treaty with Antiochos. The help he did provide had therefore to be clandestine, otherwise Ptolemy would expose himself to accusations of bad faith and treaty violation. The early contacts of Akhaios with Ptolemy IV's ministers are not known, nor are those with his predecessor Ptolemy III (though some sort of Ptolemaic military assistance appears to have been provided before Ptolemy III died).[25] The attempt to include Akhaios in the terms of the peace treaty negotiations at Seleukeia-in-Pieria suggests that such contacts had continued until then. Indeed Akhaios' father Andromachos is known to have gone to Egypt at one stage, during the earlier war in the 220s, and had been appointed governor of Koile Syria in 217.[26] Encouraging rebellion is a difficult matter for any king, however, and Akhaios was apparently unable to secure a firm recognition of his independence, which, like the Seleukid recognition of the kingship and therefore independence of Magas in Cyrenaica in the 270s, would be regarded by Antiochos as a *casus belli*. Since Akhaios had been excluded from the peace after Raphia, despite Ptolemaic requests to include him, his status as a rebel had in effect been accepted by Ptolemy. This did not mean, however, that Ptolemy was willing to let Akhaios go down to defeat without making some attempt to help him. After all, taking a leaf out of Antiochos' diplomatic book, Akhaios under Ptolemy's protection would be a useful tool with which to threaten Antiochos, just as Antiochos had intrigued his way into Seleukeia.

The war eventually centred on the siege of the acropolis of Sardis, which began probably in 214, after the conquest of the rest of Akhaios' (former) territories. The siege was long and slow, and there was plenty of time for a plot to be organised from Egypt. Polybios describes in some detail the attempt which was made by

Ptolemaic agents to extract Akhaios from the besieged acropolis.[27] It was not possible to do this openly, since it would have broken the terms of the recent peace treaty for Ptolemy to be seen to be directly involved, so agents at some remove had to be employed. These turned out to be Cretan mercenaries, who were efficient only in betraying each other, their employers, and Akhaios himself, fully justifying Polybios' scornful comments about them. Akhaios fell into Antiochos' hands and was executed. The Ptolemaic involvement was quite clear to Polybios half a century later, and it was probably clear to Antiochos at the time, but the use of the Cretan mercenaries made Ptolemy's involvement deniable. Antiochos was apparently satisfied that the plot had failed and was content to abide by the peace terms with Ptolemy. By accepting that the treaty still stood, he was able to set about other adventures, without any threat of Ptolemaic interference.

## The eastern expedition

Antiochos' basic campaigning method had now developed, and became the normal pattern of his work for the rest of his reign. Having identified his enemy, he contacted an ally: Theodotos in Palestine to rebel against Ptolemy IV's government; Attalos I to take Akhaios in the rear. This necessarily required the services of competent and perhaps secret envoys; it is unfortunate that the names of none of these men have survived, but the work was clearly at times dangerous and appears to have been competently done (contrasting with Sosibios' use of Cretans). The earliest case was the intrigue which undermined the governor of Seleukeia-in-Pieria; even before that, the campaign against Molon had been helped by the continued loyalty of Zeuxis, a local commander in Babylonia. We can perhaps see the gradual elaboration of the method in these cases, and Antiochos used it consistently over the next decades.

The new adventure which Antiochos III set himself was the recovery of territories which had been lost by his royal predecessors over the previous generation. He had, of course, already done this by the conquest of Seleukeia and, in Asia Minor, by suppressing Akhaios. This restoration policy – which included the conquest, or 'recovery', of Koile Syria from Ptolemy – may be seen as the life-task he had set himself. What he did and what he accomplished provides a revealing view of the methods of diplomacy and of the sanctity of treaties in his world.

The eastern lands he wished to reclaim were those between the Caspian Sea and the Khyber Pass. In the aftermath of the suppression of Molon's revolt he had re-established his supremacy over the kingdom of Media Atropatene in Iran.[28] In terms of the former provinces of his family's kingdom, in his new expedition he was seeking to re-establish control over Armenia (which he achieved in 212), the eastern half of Hyrkania, the satrapies of Parthia, Baktria and Sogdiana, Areia, Arachosia, and 'India', and, perhaps, Karmania. In other words, during the dynastic civil wars from which his kingdom had just emerged, a good half of the former kingdom had been lost.

On a bare telling it can seem that the expedition was a failure. Antiochos eventually became entangled in a two-year siege of a single city, Baktra, which he failed

110  *Diplomacy in action – the East*

to capture, and the quantity of territory he recovered for his own direct rule seems to have been relatively small; meanwhile all the kings he encountered survived, as did their kingdoms. Despite this apparent relative failure, when Antiochos returned to the western part of his kingdom, he was called *megas*, 'Great'.[29] It follows that both he and his contemporaries clearly thought of the expedition as having been successful. The assumption of failure stems from a misunderstanding of Antiochos' aims. Moderns assume that his aim was outright conquest and the restoration of direct Seleukid rule,[30] but if we reduce the expectation to closer to what he actually achieved, a better estimate of his achievement may be made. This alteration in viewpoint has a clear effect on the perception of his diplomacy.

Antiochos distinguished between rebels and ruling kings. Rebels (Molon, Akhaios) were executed under conditions of maximum humiliation; ruling kings had his overlordship imposed on them. So Molon was executed; his (presumed) supporter Artabarzanes of Atropatene, who submitted when summoned, was confirmed as king. In Armenia, King Xerxes was defeated but was then confirmed as king, had his treasury confiscated, and was then married to Antiochos' sister. Antiochos supposedly rejected a suggestion from a member of his court that he seize the young man when he came to negotiate, possibly an apocryphal story intended to imply the king's honourable conduct. The total effect was to make Xerxes a subordinate ruler within Antiochos' kingdom. There are clear problems with the details of the story, but the point here is that Xerxes, like Artabarzanes, survived (though Antiochis later killed her husband and returned to her brother, a separate matter[31]).

So when Antiochos began his march to his eastern lands in 210, his intentions and his methods had been made reasonably clear by his previous actions. If the ruler was a rebel, he would be removed and probably killed, as were Molon and Akhaios. If he was an independent king whose kingdom had existed for several decades already – like Armenia and Atropatene – he would be reduced to vassalage and expected to agree to a lasting peace treaty and pay tribute. Therefore his intention was less to conquer than to renegotiate his empire, with the army as his necessary backup.

Needless to say, threatened kings fought, as had Xerxes. First the Parthian king, then the Baktrian king, whose royal city Baktra was besieged for 'two years', were reduced to vassalage, defeated and then admitted to negotiations. It is said that the Indian King Sophagasenos, whose kingdom was probably in the Parapamisadai, was already allied with Antiochos when he arrived, and so he was similarly subjected. In each case the king was left in place, having made a treaty with Antiochos. Arachosia, Areia, and Drangiana were brought back under his authority, and he returned through Karmania, Gedrosia, and Persis, another kingdom on which he imposed his suzerainty. The major work was thus diplomatic. Fighting had taken place in Parthia and Baktria, but both conflicts had ended in negotiated treaties; the other regions, from the Paropamisadai to Persis, had succumbed without fighting.

Certain diplomatic procedures and practices emerged in these conflicts during Antiochos' first decade and a half. Imposition of tribute and royal marriages were used to signal the subordination of minor kings such as Xerxes. Treaties were used to bind kings to peace if they were not under Antiochos' direct authority, such as Attalos and Ptolemy. Tribute was imposed in other cases, either by itself, as with Atropatene, or in combination with another scheme, as with Xerxes (who was 'forgiven' his arrears of tribute but had to pay it in future and had his treasure confiscated). There was evidently no standard method for dealing with a king, but there was a range of possibilities to be selected from which a method would be chosen to fit a particular case; in every case, however, subordination was implied – except with Egypt.

Antiochos was usually personally involved in the negotiations. It is possible he did not take part in the conference at Seleukeia in the winter of 218/217, except to deliver his lecture, but after the battle of Raphia the peace negotiations took place at Antioch, and that means in the royal palace there. In his eastern expedition he negotiated directly with Xerxes of Armenia and with the envoy of Euthydemos of Baktria. In this, therefore, as in his diplomatic tactics, Antiochos was fully in control. He did not insist on 'summit meetings' and never actually met either Ptolemy IV or Euthydemos. The ratification process in the treaties involved an exchange of oaths made by the kings. These were thus performed before envoys acting for the kings, so Antiochos would not need to ratify anything negotiated with his enemy's envoys until the enemy king had sworn.

It may also be noted that in the east there are clear signs that Antiochos used his normal method of allying with a power to the rear of his enemy before launching his attack. It is possible that in his Parthian campaign he had an alliance with the Baktrian King Euthydemos, who was Parthia's eastern neighbour, though this is not certain;[32] Euthydemos was next on Antiochos' list, so it is perhaps unlikely. When he attacked Euthydemos, he had an alliance with Sophagasenos, situated to the south of Baktria. This might be the reason that the war was reduced to a siege of Baktra city; it also implies that most of Baktria had been conquered.

In the end negotiations took place, though in fact it is likely that the talks had been more or less continuous from the beginning of the siege, and the siege itself was part of the negotiating process. Euthydemos eventually persuaded Antiochos that he could call in allies from the north, nomad warriors who had gained control of Sogdiana – thus neutralising Antiochos' alliance with Sophagasenos. This would cause much difficulty for Antiochos, though it was, of course, a desperate measure on Euthydemos' part, which would cause much destruction in Baktria itself. Yet this was the sort of threat to which no king with Antiochos' aims could give way, so there must have been rather more to their discussions than a mere threat by one side. The two-year siege would very likely soon end in the capture of the city – hence the desperate threat by Euthydemos – and it had always been likely that the conflict would be ended by a negotiated treaty.

The negotiations succeeded in reaching a compromise, though the way that this episode is presented by Polybios makes it seem as though Euthydemos' threat to call in the nomads forced Antiochos to negotiate. It surely had an effect, but in actual fact the terms which were agreed show quite clearly that it was Euthydemos who gave in. The terms included Euthydemos' surrender of his war elephants, payment of a substantial treasure, and his acceptance of Antiochos' confirmation of his royal status. This is indicated by an offer by Antiochos to give his daughter in marriage to Euthydemos' son Demetrios. Antiochos only made such offers to other kings, such as Xerxes, and later to Ptolemy V. Euthydemos obviously accepted Antiochos' overlordship, as had Tiridates of Parthia.[33]

The marriage never did take place, so far as we can see. It may be that the daughter Antiochos had in mind was too young. His earliest child was not born before 220 or 219, and seems to have been a son. Therefore any daughter had a maximum age of 12 or 13 years at the time the siege ended, in 206, and probably less, several years too young for a marriage at this time. Whether the offer of a daughter was accepted is also in question. (We must be careful to avoid assuming that an offer of such a union automatically meant its acceptance and its eventuation.) But the offer was clearly intended as a public mark of Euthydemos' defeat, so it will not have been welcome to him, nor perhaps to Demetrios. If it was made, the offer was thus clearly later rejected, or more likely evaded, or perhaps the matter was simply allowed to drop. We may take it therefore that this failure of the marriage to take place, whether the offer was made or was made and rejected, or later refused, or forgotten, is a clear sign that for Euthydemos his subordination to Antiochos was most uncomfortable. Nevertheless Euthydemos had accepted the treaty and had agreed to his new status as a subordinate king.[34]

Antiochos went on to campaign beyond Baktria against Sophagasenos, whose kingdom appears to have been on the borders of India, probably in the Paropamisadai. He was certainly regarded as an Indian king, and his name appears to have been Indian (interpreted as originally 'Subhagasena'). The region he ruled had been part of the great Mauryan Empire until that began to break up from about 230 BC.[35] What fighting there was against him, if any, is not known, but Sophagasenos made a treaty with Antiochos on the same lines as that with the other kings Antiochos had dealt with recently. This may have been the original alliance which was renewed when Antiochos arrived. Sophagasenos accepted Antiochos' overlordship and surrendered to him a stable of war elephants, and presumably some treasure as well, and Antiochos left a man behind to collect the tribute and convoy the animals to the west. The movement of these two elephant herds to the west will have demonstrated very clearly of the extent of Antiochos' success. No doubt Androsthenes of Kyzikos, given the task, took a less onerous route to the west than Antiochos and the rest of the army. Such a herd would need access to considerable supplies of fodder.[36]

Polybios comments that the treaty with Sophagasenos was a 'renewal' of one made earlier.[37] This would seem to be another example of Antiochos' preliminary diplomatic preparations, by which he contacted a ruler or a potential traitor in the rear of his immediate enemy whose threat of participating in the war would divide the enemy's attention and perhaps his forces – Attalos against Akhaios, Theodotos against Ptolemy. Of course, the preliminary treaty also rendered the new ally into another subordinate, and the later treaty confirmed this.[38]

From Sophagasenos' kingdom Antiochos returned to the west by a more southerly route. He is said to have crossed the 'Caucasus' Mountains – the Hindu Kush – into 'India', which was the kingdom of Sophagasenos. He went on into Arachosia, then on to Karmania, wintering there (winter of 208/207), as had Alexander.[39] Arachosia, like the Paropamisadai, had been surrendered to the Mauryan Empire a century before by Seleukos I and had been part of Asoka's empire until about two decades before. Antiochos had thus 'recovered' territories his family had hardly ever ruled. He was in Persis in 206, where his presence is recorded in an inscription.[40] In all these regions he had, by his very presence and transit, enforced his authority. Persis was another region with a tendency towards independence and where at least one local ruler had minted his own coins – a mark of sovereignty – in the recent past; Antiochos' presence will have been salutary.

After all this, when he returned to the west, therefore, Antiochos was quite right to proclaim, by adopting the epithet *Megas*, that he had achieved a major victory in the east. He had recovered some territory, but this was perhaps the least important part of his achievement. He had collected a considerable treasure, which would be very useful in later wars, as would his new stable of trained war elephants. He had secured his authority in a series of distant and perhaps until then semi-independent regions. But above all he had established his clear superiority over a whole series of kings. In particular the three kings in the east, of Parthia, in Baktria, and Sophagasenos, and perhaps in Persis, were now all bound to him by international treaties.

There is no indication that Antiochos was able to call on any of these kings for any assistance in his later wars, though he certainly recruited soldiers from amongst the nomads of the lands close to Baktria and the Parthian kingdom. The main results of his campaign were less military than diplomatic and political. By binding the three kings to him by oath-sworn treaties, he had constructed a diplomatic network which compelled them to keep the peace with him, and so between themselves. It seems clear that the principal gainer from all this, apart from Antiochos, was Sophagasenos. After Euthydemos' death, sometime about 190 or a little before, his son Demetrios, now king, conducted an invasion of 'India',[41] presumably meaning Sophagasenos' kingdom, which was regarded by Polybios as in 'India' and was Baktria's immediate neighbour to the south. It was probably this development and Euthydemos' death which partially dismantled the diplomatic network he had set up in the east, which provoked Antiochos' new eastern expedition, which he began in 187 and in which he was killed.

Antiochos' diplomatic gain, apart from the tremendous prestige of an eastern campaign and victory, was the assurance that he could ignore the east in future so long as his diplomatic partners lived, just as he was earlier confident that Ptolemy IV would leave him at peace after the 217 treaty. Having concluded solemn treaties with these kings, he was assured that peace would prevail in the east for the foreseeable future. This was the same attitude as he had displayed when he set off to the east, even though he had left Ptolemaic Egypt, the inveterate enemy of the Seleukid kingdom, with something of a grievance in his rear. It follows, since Antiochos was quite clearly a king who was as adept at intrigue as anyone in his time and could expect to be intrigued against, that he knew that once a treaty had been concluded, it remained in force.

## The Ptolemaic partition agreement

Antiochos III's return from his eastern expedition coincided with the death of Ptolemy IV in 205. This was concealed by his ministers (Sosibios and Agathokles) for several months, in part because the leading ministers wished to retain power in their own hands and feared competition from other courtiers and from Ptolemy's widow. The late king's successor was a child (Ptolemy V) whose regent was probably intended to be that mother, Arsinoe. To prevent this, the two leading ministers had Arsinoe murdered and only then announced the succession, with themselves as regents.[42]

Of course, the death of Ptolemy IV opened the way for Antiochos III to begin a new Syrian War, and it was the knowledge of this imminent possibility or threat which was another major factor in the regents' calculations. There was also the major problem that the great rebellion in southern Egypt continued. Its leader had been able to seize control of Thebes and there have himself proclaimed Pharaoh. This was partly blamed on the success of Ptolemy IV at the Battle of Raphia, where it had only been by recruiting a large force of native Egyptians and training them in the techniques of Macedonian warfare that the battle had been won. The troops were discharged afterwards, but some of them at least seem to have joined the rebellion in the south. So the Ptolemaic forces were not only faced by a well-trained and well-motivated enemy, but it was no longer possible to recruit native Egyptians, for they might well take their weapons and desert. The rebellion spread intermittently to the rest of Egypt in the next years. It was clearly a powerful distraction for the politicians in Alexandria, and they reacted sensibly by aiming to avoid further wars.[43]

The regency government in Alexandria tried to prevent war with Antiochos by diplomatic means. High-ranking envoys were sent to the three other Great Powers in the Mediterranean world – Antiochos III, Philip V of Macedon, and Rome – but the men were all political enemies of the regent, Agathokles (Sosibios died soon after Arsinoe),[44] and the suspicion must be that Agathokles was as much concerned to remove these envoys from Alexandria as for their diplomacy to succeed. How far this internal political rivalry affected the conduct of the envoys is not clear, but it was surely in the interests of all factions at the court to avoid a new Syrian war, if possible, something which Agathokles no doubt counted on.

The absent envoys must have known that Agathokles' position in Alexandria was unstable – and in fact he and his family were overthrown and murdered about the end of 203.[45] This cannot have helped the envoys' positions as diplomats, and their authority in their missions clearly fluctuated with the instability in Alexandria. This can only have encouraged the enemies of Ptolemy and discouraged any friends.

The envoy sent to Antiochos III was Pelops son of Pelops, who had been the Ptolemaic governor in Cyprus for over a decade.[46] His appointment as envoy may well have been a ploy to remove him from Cyprus, where he commanded considerable naval and military forces and where his long tenure of office will have allowed him to develop good local support, both in the armed forces and among the civilians. He reached Antiochos in Asia Minor, where the king was busy gathering into his system those cities which were of uncertain allegiance. This certainly included some which were claimed by Ptolemy – the matter was somewhat uncertain, the cities in question being on the borderlands of the two empires. If either side required an excuse for war, these places provided them ready made. Pelops protested at Antiochos' actions, but he could do little more than that to prevent the encroachments. The only way to stop Antiochos was to invoke a credible threat of force, and it was clear that Pelops had no authority to issue any such threat. Nor had he any forces at his command with which he could protect the disputed cities – indeed his brief was to prevent a war, not instigate one, so Antiochos in effect had a free hand.[47]

Pelops reminded Antiochos of the terms of the peace treaty which had ended the previous (Fourth) Syrian War in 217, notably stressing the new state of friendship (*philia*) which the treaty had created.[48] What he perhaps did not point out, but which Antiochos surely did, was that this *philia* was between the two kings in particular, that is, himself and Ptolemy IV, and with one of them dead that condition had obviously ceased to exist. Antiochos' reaction to Pelops' reminder is not recorded, but as an experienced diplomat it is likely that all he would do was issue some bland non-committal statement, thereby reserving his position; this would imply that he might well launch a new war. The very fact that Pelops was making such an argument, of course, meant that he feared such a war, and this can only have encouraged Antiochos.

The envoy to King Philip V of Macedon was Ptolemy son of Sosibios. With Sosibios' death Agathokles took his place as senior minister and regent, but he rightly feared his sons, one of whom was responsible in the end, with others, for his overthrow and death. Sending Ptolemy, who was probably Sosibios' eldest son, to Macedon was therefore Agathokles' way of removing another enemy from the immediate Alexandrian political scene. There was also another motive. There had already been discussions between the Ptolemaic and Antigonid courts for a marriage treaty by which the child Ptolemy V would eventually marry a daughter of Philip. These discussions had been begun before Ptolemy IV's death and had presumably been conducted by Sosibios, quite possibly by sending that same son Ptolemy as his envoy to Macedon. Agathokles hoped to advance these negotiations.[49] If they succeeded, Philip might be brought over to the Ptolemaic side. It would not necessarily create a firm alliance between the two states, but it would probably neutralise Philip in any Ptolemaic conflict with Antiochos and might even persuade him to mount a threat to Antiochos' territories in Asia Minor. Even if Philip stayed neutral, this would eliminate the Aegean area as a theatre of warfare.

The third envoy was Ptolemy son of Agesarchos, originally from Megalopolis in Arcadia,[50] who was to go to Rome, ostensibly to announce the death of Ptolemy IV and the accession of his son – a normal diplomatic task in the circumstances. There was no point in asking help from Rome, which was still fighting Carthage in Hannibal's War, so Ptolemy was in no hurry to get to the city. He was instructed to delay in Greece on his way, possibly in hopes that the Romano-Carthaginian War might end quickly and that Rome could then be persuaded to help. Ptolemy came from a major city of the Achaian League, so he was to contact his 'friends and relatives' in the Peloponnese, presumably to enlist them as friends of King Ptolemy.[51]

In addition to these three men sent on specifically diplomatic missions, Skopas, an Aitolian, was sent to his homeland to enlist a mercenary army for service in Egypt. Skopas was an experienced Aitolian politician, and he had no difficulty in raising a major force. The recent restoration of peace in Greece and Macedon by the treaties of 206 and 205 had no doubt left considerable numbers of soldiers unemployed. Ptolemaic gold would mop them up, providing welcome reinforcements for the Ptolemaic army, and also to the relief of their homelands.[52]

Agathokles, therefore (or perhaps it was Sosibios before he died), was conducting an intelligent diplomatic campaign. He was investigating what Antiochos intended, angling for an alliance with, or the neutrality of, Philip, and recruiting troops and friends in Greece. By harking back to the peace with Antiochos and emphasising the youth of the new king, he was evidently hoping for public sympathy, and Polybios for one fell for this line.[53] The recruiting drive in Greece implies that peace with Antiochos was not expected to continue, and it was obviously necessary to be prepared. Polybios also suggests that Agathokles could not depend on the mercenaries already in Ptolemaic service and that the new recruits could be assumed to be more biddable.[54] If war did break out, the mercenaries would be useful, and Ptolemy could have a set of international friends who might help, or at least stay neutral. If war did not happen in Syria or Greece, the soldiers could be used against the Egyptian rebels in the south.

It is surely curious that this Ptolemaic diplomatic and military preparation is so widely ignored by those who discuss these matters. Attention is generally fixed on the subsequent agreement between Philip V and Antiochos III to partition the Ptolemaic possessions, but the earlier Ptolemaic diplomacy is often omitted. For example, Eckstein devotes two long chapters to the partition treaty but never notes the preliminary Ptolemaic activity.[55] Of course, for those studying these events, the puzzle of the partition agreement is absorbing, and conclusions concerning it have ranged from dismissing it as never having existed to Polybios' strange outrage that it amounted to the theft of a child's heritage.

The fascination of the hunt for the agreement has clearly blinded too many researchers to the actual events of the time. The preparatory activity was all Ptolemaic, and to ignore this is to distort the situation. The Ptolemaic governments – of Sosibios, of Agathokles, of Tlepolemos – were quite certain that they were facing, or about to face, a war. Their diplomacy was designed to enlist Philip, and perhaps Rome, on the Ptolemaic side, while portraying Antiochos, whom they obviously did not expect to be deterred, as the thief Polybios portrayed. This diplomatic campaign was no less cynical than the widely condemned partition agreement.

It is, of course, nonsense to discuss the crises which were developing in terms of stealing a child's inheritance, and if Polybios truly believed that was happening, he was being ludicrously naive. (In fact, one cannot accept that he did so believe, and his motive was perhaps to be able to portray Philip and Antiochos in black terms so as to allow others – Rome especially – to be portrayed as less cynical. Probably it was the Roman deviousness in attacking Philip in 200 which was in his mind.)

The agreement between Philip and Antiochos was a sensible move in response to Ptolemaic diplomacy in the crisis.

It needs to be recalled that the Ptolemaic Empire's reach extended to close to Antiochos' Syrian cities, all along the Asia Minor coast from Kilikia to the Propontis and the coast of Thrace, and close to Philip's kingdom, through much of the Aegean Sea and its islands; Ptolemy was the protector of Athens, had given refuge to the revolutionary King Kleomenes of Sparta, and had subsidised the lively, awkward, and unprincipled Aratos of Sikyon and the Achaian League. Both Antiochos and Philip had suffered at Ptolemaic hands in the recent past, and they could not know just how hollowed out the king's power had become. There was certainly confusion in Alexandria, and there was a rebellion in Upper Egypt, but neither of these marked a serious or obvious reduction in Ptolemaic power. When the war came, it took Antiochos seven years to complete his conquests, and Philip found even conquering the Ptolemaic cities on the Asian coast beyond him. Ptolemaic Egypt might seem a hollow shell to those using hindsight, but it cannot have seemed so to the two kings at the time. They had to assume they faced a difficult task – and their difficulties in the event showed that this was a correct estimate. In the circumstances an agreement between them made good sense.

It is not known who initiated the discussions which led to the partition agreement, but they evidently took place while Antiochos was in Asia Minor. The two kings had been in contact with each other on the subject of Egypt earlier and had sent a joint suggestion that they might assist in Egyptian government in its internal troubles. This was a clever diplomatic move; if it was rejected, as was most likely, the kings could act affronted and could claim they were sympathetic to the plight of the Ptolemaic government; if it was accepted, they would gain some control over the government and possibly over the kingdom, or could demand a price for their help. The offer was, of course, rejected.[56]

Philip was more likely to make serious gains by war than he could ever acquire by any dowry agreement. The details of the proposed division of Ptolemaic territories are not clear,[57] but Koile Syria was clearly going to be Antiochos' share, as were the several Ptolemaic towns and cities on the southern and western coasts of Asia Minor, where he had been operating when Pelops met him. Philip's share was probably to be the Ptolemaic posts in and around the Aegean area, but it may also have included Cyrenaica, which his great-uncle Demetrios the Fair had briefly ruled half a century before.[58]

The intentions of the kings towards Egypt itself are not known, though at one point in his campaign it may be that Philip intended to sail there to seize control.[59] If so, it is highly unlikely that he would have succeeded and that any conquests in the Aegean would be lost while he was away. Antiochos showed no intention at any time of invading Egypt, and he had a much better opportunity of doing so after his conquest of Palestine.

One might have expected Antiochos also to contact the Egyptian rebels, but there is no sign that he did so. Probably he did not need to, since they were doing well enough at destroying Ptolemaic strength without his help; without his encouragement they were acting as a threat to the rear of his enemy, which was his standard operating method. The probability that Egypt itself was excluded from the partition agreement of Antiochos and Philip rather suggests that there was no intention to eliminate the Ptolemaic dynastic kingdom altogether. Of course, neither king could wish Egypt to fall to his rival, for power reasons. The obvious man to claim it would be Antiochos, but if he wanted Philip's agreement to a partition, he would need to be moderate in his own demands – though either might be able to get Egypt in a later war. It is noticeable that Antiochos did not overstep the (presumed) division when he made peace, even though Philip had by then been reduced to impotence by Rome.

This agreement has been described as a 'diplomatic revolution', but it was nothing of the sort, except in revealing a new yearning of minor Aegean powers for Roman protection, brought on largely by Philip's brutality.[60] Both Antiochos and Philip had been long-standing enemies of the Ptolemaic kingdom, the one over the question of Syria, the other in the Aegean, an enmity going back several generations. Not only that, but the two dynasties had long been associated, in particular in three intermarriages, in 299, in 277, and in about 240. They had repeatedly cooperated informally in wars, especially when one of them was fighting the Ptolemies. This partition agreement was thus little more than the reformulation in writing, for a specific purpose, of a relationship which had existed for eight decades – if indeed the agreement was ever reduced to writing. It was, given the exigencies of the situation, more likely to have been an informal understanding.

A 'diplomatic revolution' would mean a sudden change in alliances in which former allies became enemies and vice versa, and it would need to apply to the great powers, not merely the second- and third-level states such as Rhodes and Athens.[61] This is not what happened in the eastern Mediterranean in 203 BC. The agreement was how to partition the overseas possessions of the Ptolemaic dynasty, no more. The war which then broke out was actually inevitable, given the political practices of the kings and the internal collapse of the Ptolemaic state.

The agreement has gained notoriety because it was secret, or at least not announced – there was, of course, no reason it should be publicised, and many why it should be kept quiet. It was detected by the Rhodians, and because the Rhodians felt threatened by it – as friends and allies of Ptolemy, they were right to feel so – they publicised it. But they reacted by exaggerating the agreement's threat and by implying that it made the two kings into active allies and that this alliance was a threat, not just to Rhodes, but to Rome. The Rhodians now looked to Rome as their (at least potential) protector, since Ptolemy was no longer capable.[62]

This had not been the intention of the kings, who were probably – the details, or course, are not known – more concerned not to collide with each other. If they both snatched at Ptolemaic provinces, Ptolemaic ability to resist would be distracted. It must be noted that when, in 197, Antiochos had the opportunity to seize Rhodes, he did not bother, and next year, in his dispute with Rome at the Lysimacheia conference, he nominated Rhodes as the possible arbitrator. From the point of view of Antiochos, of course, the partition agreement was another example of his diplomatic preparations to attack the Ptolemaic power, just as he had suborned Ptolemaic officers in the previous war. Philip was never that subtle, and he carefully waited for Antiochos to start the war in Syria before making his own moves in the Aegean area. And, for once, we have an indication of the extent of diplomatic preparations for a major war, just as we can discuss Roman preparations for wars in Sicily, with Carthage, and with Philip.

## Notes

1 Polybios 5.41.3.
2 Polybios 5.45.6; E. Will, 'Les premiers annees du regne d'Antiochos III (223–219 av. J-C)', *Revue des etudes grecques* 75, 1962, 72–129.
3 Polybios 5.42.7; now often accepted as genuine; as examples, Will, *Histoire Politique* 2.25–26; H.H. Schmitt, *Untersuchungen zur Geschichte Antiochos des Grossen und seiner Zeit*, Wiesbaden 1964, 161–164; and E.R. Bevan, *The House of Seleucus*, London 1902, 1.302 have varied opinions.
4 This war thus began in 221; it is frequently stated to have begun only in 219 (e.g. Austin 182). The lethargy of the Ptolemaic regency government is clear in its failure to exploit its defensive victory in the Bekaa Valley in 221.
5 Polybios 5.43.1–4; Diognetos escorted the bride to Syria; it seems reasonable to assume he was the negotiator.
6 It was only a century since the death of Alexander the Great without adult heirs; the chaos following his death was quite likely in everyone's mind.
7 Polybios 4.48, claims that Akhaios had been urged to take the royal title after defeating Attalos I.
8 Ibid., 5.60.1–61.1.
9 Ibid., 5.61.3–5.
10 Polybios' account (5.70–71) indicates very little fighting; the places Antiochos took must therefore have fallen to him by negotiation.
11 Holbl, *Ptolemaic Empire*, 127–128.
12 Polybios 5.66.2.
13 Polybios 5.63.7–65.11.
14 Polybios 5.63.5; Ager, *Interstate Arbitrations*, 53.
15 Envoys are mentioned at Polybios 5.63.6, 66.8, 67.1.
16 Polybios 5.67.3–68.1; the attempt to include Akhaios is, of course, a clear indication of Ptolemaic relations with the rebel.
17 Polybios 5.87.1–6.
18 Polybios 5.87.6.
19 He apparently feared one before the conference (Polybios 5.66.3).
20 Polybios 5.87.1–7; for the treaty see Will, *Histoire Politique* 2.38, 39–40; Holbl, *Ptolemaic Empire*, 131–132.
21 Polybios certainly used the Greek for 'nephew', but given Antiochos' age this is unlikely to be Antipater's actual relationship with him; perhaps 'cousin' might be a better translation.
22 Polybius 4.48.11.
23 Polybios 5.107.4.
24 This was presumably the basis of Attalos' complaint in 198 of encroachments on his territory by Seleukid forces. He complained to Rome on this; but he presumably also complained to Antiochos, and since the encroachments ceased, no doubt that complaint was successful (Livy 32.8.9–16).
25 P. Haun 6; W. Huss, 'Eine ptolemäische Expedition nach Kleinasien', *Ancient Society* 8, 1977, 187–193.
26 Polybios 4.41–6.
27 Polybios 7.55.1–18.10.
28 Polybios 5.55.1–10.

29 *OGIS* 230, which may be a personal compliment by the author; Ma, *Antiochos III*, 272–276, provides a list of references.
30 In the first version of *CAH* VII, the eastern expedition is ignored; in the new edition (VII, part I) it merits a single paragraph; Musti there insists that it 'did not result in a renewed subjugation' of Parthia and Baktria; Polybios was more positive (11.34.14–16); Will, *Histoire Politique* 2.68–69, summarises the varied modern reactions.
31 John of Antioch 4.557.
32 The final result of the Parthian war is not certain, but Justin 41.5.7 considers the end was a negotiated 'alliance' – that is, Antiochos compelled the Parthian king to submit; Malcolm A.R. Colledge, *The Parthians*, London 1977, 28, concluded that 'the kingdom of Parthia had been reduced in size . . . but it had survived'.
33 Polybios 10.49.1–15 (the campaign), and 11.39.1–10 (peace). Paul J. Kosmin, *The Land of the Elephant King*, Cambridge, MA 2014, 121, interprets the agreement to understand that 'Antiochos acknowledged the sovereign independence of . . . Baktria'.
34 No ancient source goes further than the suggestion of a betrothal; this had been enough for some moderns to assume that the actual marriage took place; W.W. Tarn, *The Greeks in Baktria and India*, 2nd ed., Cambridge 1966, 82, did not accept it, for example, most unusually for him; Will, *Histoire Politique* 2.61, notes that 'hypotheses flourish'.
35 A.K. Narain, *The Indo-Greeks*, Cambridge 1957, 21.
36 Polybios 31.39.11–12.
37 Polybios 11.34.11–12.
38 None of these treaties made by Antiochos between 217 and 206 are listed in Schmitt, *Staatsverträge*.
39 Polybios 11.35.13.
40 Austin 190.
41 Strabo 11.11.1; Klaus Karttunen, *India and the Hellenistic World*, Helsinki 1997, 273–274, and references there: Narain in *CAH* (2) 1989, VIII, chart on 421, suggested that Demetrios' conquests were small.
42 Polybios 15.25.1–5; Justin 30.2.6; Holbl, *Ptolemaic Empire* 134.
43 W. Peremans, 'Les Revolutions Egyptiennes sous les Lagides', in H. Maehler and V.M. Strocka (eds.), *Das Ptolemäische Ägypten*, Mainz 1978, 39–50; A.-E. Veisse, *Les 'revoltes egyptiennes': recherches sous les troubles interieures en Egypte du Regne de Ptolemee III a la conquete romaine*, Paris 2004.
44 Polybios 15.25.13–15.
45 Polybios 15.25.20–23; Holbl, *Ptolemaic Empire*, 135–136.
46 Polybios 15.25.13; *Prosopographia Ptolemaica* 6.1.15064; Bagnall, *Administration*, 252–253.
47 Ma, *Antiochos III*, 63–73 for the cities Antiochos was collecting at the time.
48 Polybios 15.25.13
49 Ibid.; M. Holleaux, *Rome, la Grece et les monarchies Hellenistique au IIIe siecle avant J-C*, Paris 1935, 78–79.
50 *Prospographia Ptolemaica* 6.1.15068 and 16944.
51 Polybios 15.25.14.
52 Polybios 15.25.16.
53 Polybios 3.2.8, 15.20, and other places.
54 Polybios 15.25.11.
55 A. Eckstein, *Rome Enters the Greek East*, Oxford 2008, part II.
56 Polybios 15.20.1.
57 Polybios may have given details in part of his account which is missing. The various items of evidence are collected by Schmitt, *Staatsverträge*, III, 547, and see Austin 192. The existence of the agreement has been demonstrated by an inscription from Bargylia which records transfers of conquests between the kings: H.-U. Wiemer, 'Karien am Vorabend des 2 makedonischen Krieges: Bemerkungen zu einer neuen Inschrift aus Bargylia', *Epigraphica Anatolica* 33, 2001, 1–14.

58 Polybios 25.20.2; Livy 31.14.5; Appian, *Macedonian Wars* 4.1; Justin 30.2.6; Austin 192; the agreement is much discussed, notably by R.M. Errington in Athenaeum 49, 1971, who was very sceptical; see also Erich S. Gruen, *The Hellenistic Kingdoms and the Coming of Rome*, California 1984, 387–390 and Ma, *Antiochos III*, 74–82.
59 This is Eckstein's argument, *Rome Enters*, but it is based on very flimsy evidence.
60 Eckstein, *Rome Enters*, ch. 5.
61 It is a term applied to the apparently sudden alteration in political and diplomatic alignments in Europe in 1756, a change which introduced the Seven Years' War.
62 Livy 31.2.1: Appian, Macedonian Wars 4; H.R. Rawlings, 'Antiochos the Great and Rhodes', *American Journal of Ancient History* 1, 1976, 2–28.

# Part III
# Diplomacy in the West

# 7 Ionian Sea diplomacy

The Ionian Sea, between Greece and Italy and Sicily, is not usually taken as a specific region for study, but during the late fourth and third centuries it was a veritable cockpit of conflict and diplomacy. It had been a political unit earlier, under the Syracusan monarchy of Dionysios I and II, but the complexity of the political, strategic, and diplomatic situation there between 342 and 212 was new. These conflicts have usually been detailed in separate and discontinuous sections – Romans and Carthaginians, the adventures of Pyrrhos, the time of Agathokles – but taking up a viewpoint, metaphorically speaking, somewhere in the sea from which the events in western Greece, southern Italy, and Sicily can be followed makes it clear that they were interrelated.

The events fall into two parts, of which the second is the long conflict of Rome and Carthage (264–201), which will be dealt with in Chapters 7 and 8; here the events between 316 and 264 are considered, without assuming that they are a mere preliminary to that First Romano-Carthaginian War. They deserve consideration in their own right.

## Agathokles

Agathokles seized power in Syracuse in 316 and campaigned to extend his authority over Sicily, at first without much success. In 310 he invaded Africa to attack Carthage in its home territory. In his Carthaginian war, diplomacy was almost as prominent on both sides as the actual fighting. Envoys were exchanged during the siege of Syracuse; Agathokles sent a special envoy, Orphon, to persuade Ophellas in Cyrenaica to bring his forces to assist in the war; many of the African towns outside Carthage negotiated their own surrenders; the Carthaginians sent envoys to Agathokles' troops when they mutinied.

The expedition of Ophellas is one of the most revealing in diplomatic terms. Agathokles was unable to prevail in Africa, not least because Carthage repeatedly put new armies in the field after being defeated. If that continued, in the end Agathokles' forces would be worn down even if they won every battle. The proposition put to Ophellas by Orphon was that he should take an army from Kyrene to Africa and that he would be installed as king of 'Libya' after the victory; Agathokles would be content with Sicily. To this Ophellas, a former soldier of Alexander's who had been installed as governor of Cyrenaica by Ptolemy I, agreed.[1] He set about recruiting extra forces, principally in Athens, for he was married to a prominent Athenian, Eurydike daughter of Miltiades (later one of Demetrios I's wives), and he also angled for an alliance with that city.[2] This was all apparently fairly public knowledge, and Carthage sent envoys to seek Athenian friendship, presumably aiming to deter the recruitment of more Athenian troops by its enemies.[3] Ophellas collected a considerable force: ten thousand is the (suspiciously round) figure mentioned – they were surely not all Athenian – but they came with an equal number of dependents.

After a two-month march from Cyrenaica, the survivors were met in southern Tunisia by Agathokles. The two leaders soon quarrelled, and Ophellas was killed.[4] The sources are contradictory on what caused the dispute, but it probably originated in an argument over the terms of the treaty negotiated by Orphon. The prospect of a kingdom for Ophellas was one which no doubt made him assume that he would command the joint forces of both men, and perhaps his experience as one of Alexander's commanders made him arrogant. Agathokles' arrogance no doubt matched his, and he was certainly not going to cede command over his own Sicilian troops. In the sequel Ophellas' force enlisted with Agathokles without further argument. Their dependents were shipped off to Syracuse, though the ships were wrecked on the way and most of them died.[5] The whole episode is often interpreted as an example of Agathokles' cynicism and contrivance; it looks more like a series of misunderstandings and accidents. There are, of course, plenty of problems with the story, such as the anachronistic promise of the position of 'king' to Ophellas – this was in 309, well before the assumption of royal titles became common.[6] Essentially, however, we can see that it was an episode of diplomacy involving the two leaders and Carthage, plus Athens. Until the knife struck down Ophellas, there was no violence, and it was very largely a failure of diplomacy – the dispute between the two men – which spoiled the plan.

In Sicily a league of cities was formed centred on Akragas, with the aim of driving out both the Syracusans and the Carthaginians from their lands. Agathokles divided his army to combat this new threat and took part of it back to Sicily. He ended up under blockade in Syracuse, while his son, who had been left with half the army in Africa, was defeated by the Carthaginians and then blockaded in Tunis.[7] It is an object lesson in not dividing one's forces.

Agathokles turned to diplomacy again and sought another ally. In Italy, Rome had recently defeated a coalition of Etruscan cities, dealing with each one separately, dividing the enemy coalition, and ending the war in 308, with a series of treaties with the several enemy cities intended to last for thirty years.[8] In addition a new treaty was made between Rome and Tarquinii, a renewal of a forty-year peace treaty to last for another forty years.[9] The terms of these agreements were fairly simple – merely to refrain from mutual hostilities. This left both sides free to conclude agreements with other cities, and Agathokles did so with some of the Etruscans, probably principally with Tarquinii, the only major Etruscan seaport; the agreement was for a fleet of Etruscan ships to assist Agathokles at Syracuse.[10]

Carthage's diplomatic antennae had been alert to Agathokles' alliance with Ophellas, as its contact with Athens showed, and a Carthaginian embassy was now quickly sent to Rome. At least that is what may be presumed, but the existence of any treaty which resulted has been much disputed. If the international context is considered, and the contacts of Agathokles with the Etruscans is taken into account, then contact between Carthage and Rome seems very likely on the basis that both seemed to be threatened. Rome may well have feared the intervention of Agathokles in the events in Italy and may have been concerned to ensure that he was kept fully occupied in his Carthaginian war.[11] Diplomatic contact between Rome and Carthage fits well with the general situation, in that Agathokles was clearly interfering in both cities' areas, and such contacts were repeated in later wars; the treaty of 306 is thus likely to be genuine, though it was not a full alliance.

The Etruscan intervention turned out to be decisive for Agathokles' war. A squadron of Etruscan ships helped to break the blockade of Syracuse by the Carthaginian fleet, and Agathokles' army was then able to defeat his enemies. The Carthaginians recovered, and Agathokles was once again blockaded.[12] He was facing three enemies: the Carthaginians, the exiled Syracusans whom he had displaced, usually described as 'the oligarchs', and the commander of their army, the Syracusan Deinokrates, who had the overall command. Agathokles tried again in Africa but was defeated by the Carthaginians, and negotiations for peace followed. When it became clear that Agathokles himself would have to be surrendered to Carthage as the price of a peace treaty which was being negotiated between the army and Carthage, he deserted – or perhaps he would have said he had already been abandoned by the army; once he had gone, the army quickly made peace.[13]

It is obvious that Agathokles had decided to reduce his ambitions. In Syracuse he skilfully picked off his enemies one at a time. He proposed peace to Deinokrates on terms he knew would not be accepted, then let the oligarchs know that they had thereby been denied the chance to return to the city. He contacted Carthage and swiftly made peace on terms which surrendered the western end of Sicily to Carthaginian control. This included some of the territory which was occupied by the exiled oligarchs. Since they and Deinokrates now distrusted one another, it seems that Agathokles was able to persuade some of the oligarchs that they could return. In a final battle Deinokrates lost control of part of his army, which changed sides, presumably by pre-arrangement with Agathokles. Possibly Deinokrates was also suborned, for he was welcomed back by Agathokles and joined him in securing Syracusan control over the non-Carthaginian part of the island. It is possible that the city of Akragas was left independent, no doubt by treaty.[14]

This three-sided war – oligarchs, Syracuse, Carthage – was thus brought to an end by a series of negotiated agreements and treaties, with Carthage, with some of the oligarchs, probably with Deinokrates, with the non-Syracusan cities. Agathokles' African army had made its peace with Carthage and accepted lands in western Sicily as their new homes. The complexity of the overall settlement is a testimony to the difficult political situation in Sicily; it was only after an exhausting war, in which it became clear that no one was likely to win, that the several sides could be brought to a condition where negotiations could hope to succeed.

During the conflict it may be noted also that Cyrenaica, Athens, Rome, and the Etruscans had been drawn in one way and another. The masterly way in which Agathokles divided his enemies at the end and dealt with them singly has to be admired; he was clearly a much better diplomat than he was a general.

## Taras

Agathokles' full control of Syracuse and the eastern two-thirds of Sicily widened his horizons to include the situation in south Italy and western Greece. He was hardly ignorant of the region – during his pre-tyrant career he had been a soldier there, and since then there had been developments which came to involve him. The central power was Taras, a Greek city (Tarentum to the Romans) which at intervals aimed to establish its control over southern Italy. In this it was a sort of Italian Syracuse, and most of its enemies were the other Greek cities (as also was the case for Syracuse); it also aimed to control the hinterland, the areas now called Apulia, Basilicata, and Calabria. It had developed the practice of inviting a commander from old Greece to lead its armies, reinforced by mercenaries recruited elsewhere. That is, its democracy probably did not trust a Tarentine in command of its forces, fearing he might establish a tyranny; at the same time the city's population was apparently not large enough to field a sufficient army to undertake the task of conquest.

These campaigns were, of course, as much diplomatic as military/naval events, perhaps even more so. On the first occasion, in 342, envoys from Taras went to Sparta (Taras' mother city) to ask for help. The Tarentines on this occasion seem to have been under some pressure from their inland neighbours, and the subsequent fighting came very close to the city, whose *chora* was a thin strip of land along the coast stretching for a hundred kilometres, but never more than twenty kilometres wide. The Spartans replied by sending a mercenary force under the command of one of the Spartan kings, Archidamos. He fought the Lucanians, inhabitants of the present-day Basilicata, intermittently for several years before being killed in a fight at Mandonion, only a few miles from Taras. The Lucanians then destroyed his remaining mercenaries.[15]

The Tarentines had induced Spartan help by offering to pay for the mercenary army, and it was in hopes of getting loot and wealth for his home city that Archidamos came to Italy. The Tarentines' lack of trust in one of their own citizens to command the army, of course, also demonstrated deep suspicion of any commander with troops at his call, a suspicion not unnaturally returned. It was evidently assumed that a Greek king would be more interested in eventually returning home then in seizing power in Taras, but this was a repeated miscalculation. At least Archidamos, though he eventually failed, conformed to Tarentine expectations.

Five years after Archidamos' death, in 333, the Tarentines contracted King Alexander of Epeiros to command an attack on the Bruttii, in the long 'toe' of Italy. This was a different war from the earlier, for this time it was Taras which was the aggressor. The details of the negotiations are not known, but Alexander seems to have been easy to persuade, hoping to emulate the conquest career of his nephew/

brother-in-law Alexander of Macedon. The two kings set off in opposite directions in the same year.

The Epeirote Alexander was an accomplished strategist and diplomat. Ignoring the Bruttians in the west, he first attended to Apulia, Taras' neighbour to the north, and the Messapians in the 'heel', its immediate neighbour to the east. This was a brief conflict and was ended by negotiations by which he and an Apulian king became allies. The subsequent fighting involved the recapture of Herakleia, a Tarentine outpost on the 'instep' of Italy which had been taken by the Lucanians, and further campaigns into the territories of the Lucanians and the Bruttii. He also clashed with some Samnites 'while marching from Paestum'. As a result he came into contact with Rome and concluded a treaty of peace with that city.[16] Exactly what this means is not clear, for he was not at war with Rome; probably it was merely a friendly contact, since both were hostile to the Samnites.

Alexander had thus constructed a kingdom for himself in Italy composed of alliances and subjects spread from Paestum (presumably) to Apulia. He had shifted the headquarters of the Italian league from Herakleia, where it was under Tarentine influence, to Thourioi, and he dominated or controlled almost all of the Greek cities along the southern coast and had temporarily crushed the Bruttii and the Lucanians. But his ambitions alienated his employer, Taras. It may be that Taras now reneged on the original agreement, whatever it consisted of, but Alexander was then killed in battle with the Lucanians.[17] His kingdom broke up, but for Taras the result seems to have been reasonably satisfactory, for the city did not search out a new commander for nearly thirty years.

For a brief period, no more than two years, Alexander controlled a kingdom which included the southern part of Italy and his homeland of Epeiros, an Ionian Sea empire, stretching from the toe of Italy to the border with Macedon. Had it endured it could have been a formidable competitor with both Rome and Agathokles.

Both Archidamos and Alexander had been hired as commanders with a mercenary army, but their most effective work had been diplomatic. Archidamos seems to have done relatively little fighting. Alexander did more, but then he ranged over a larger area. His masterstroke, had he lived, might have been his treaty with Rome, described as a 'peace' treaty, Livy's term, for Livy generally assumed that a treaty followed a war, though it was more a treaty of partition in which the two powers recognised separate spheres of power in Italy. It is evident that the main result of Alexander's career was to mould much of the south into a Tarentine state. With his death it ceased to be a kingdom but remained a city empire.

The practice of hiring a Greek army and commander was taken up by the league of Sicilian cities which opposed Agathokles. They also, in 314, went to Sparta for a commander. The object in this case was less to find a proven military commander than one who was neutral in respect to the various Sicilian cities and other exile groups in the island. This meant avoiding a Greek commander from any of the smaller Sicilian cities – a similar response to the Tarentines. They chose Akrotatos, son of King Kleomenes II, who was unpopular at home and glad to get away. He started out with 'a few ships', which means a fairly small armed force. On the way he intervened at Apollonia on the Adriatic coast, which was at war with King Glaukias of the Illyrians, and persuaded the two sides to make peace. There is no sign of any fighting by the Spartans. 'A few ships' would hardly carry enough soldiers to make a serious difference in such a war. Akrotatos was operating as a mediator, and, though his visit is said to have been accidental, it is quite possible he was invited to intervene.[18] He called at Taras, where, since he was going to fight Agathokles, he was provided with twenty ships, but went off before they were ready (they arrived later).[19] The sequence of visits – Apollonia, Taras, Sicily – looks very like a series of diplomatic contacts being made before reaching his destination at Akragas.

Akrotatos is said to have slipped into lethargy and vice when he got to Akragas, one of the ancient examples of Spartans going to pieces when away from their home city; but another interpretation is possible, more a matter of frustration at the internal wrangling amongst the allies and a consequent inability to achieve anything. This may well be the explanation for a quarrel in which he is said to have murdered one of the leading Syracusan exiles. He was eventually deposed from his command and driven out.[20] The alliance between the cities and exiles then swiftly collapsed, which suggests that it was only Akrotatos who had held it together. His intervention in Sicily, as it had been at Apollonia, was mainly diplomatic; at no point is he recorded as doing any fighting. This is an unusual conclusion to come to for a Spartan prince, but the evidence is clear.

Taras had no apparent need of help at that point, since it was able to supply him with twenty ships, which probably carried a force of troops as well as sailors. The reason for the city's calm was probably that Agathokles' wars in Sicily and Africa had drained off large numbers of soldiers from the mercenary sources in Italy, including Bruttians and Lucanians, while in central Italy the Roman wars preoccupied Taras' neighbours enough for them to leave the city alone. Taras did attempt to exert its power until about 320, when a set of envoys proposed to insist on peace between Rome and the Samnites. Its envoys suggested that a peace be agreed and that if one side did not agree, the city would join the other – classic arbitration technique.[21] The Tarentines obviously felt they had some authority as far as Campania, and they gambled that Rome would accept this. The diplomatic approach failed in the face of Roman intransigence and their determination to avenge their defeat at the Caudine Forks.

A better date than c. 320 for the meeting might be after the revival of the Roman-Samnite fighting in 316 and therefore after the passage of the diplomatic Akrotatos across the Tarentine horizon. The success of his arbitration at Apollonia may have inspired the Tarentines to attempt the same feat. The sources are difficult and have clearly been over-interpreted in an attempt to justify Roman intransigence. It may be seen as an honest attempt to calm matters in central Italy, just as they had been calm in the south for two decades. It failed.

The victory of Agathokles and his proclamation as king (306–304) in Syracuse and eastern Sicily brought Taras to a recognition that help was now needed once more. The Lucanians, trapped between Agathokles, Rome, and Taras, struggled to maintain their independence. Rome had reached into northern Apulia with its colonial foundation at Venusia, which no doubt was felt to be an intrusion into

Taras' area or at least seemed to be a threat, though it was a manoeuvre in Rome's Samnite war.

Envoys were sent to Sparta once more, where they recruited another discontented Spartan prince, Akrotatos' brother Kleonymos. He had been passed over for king and resented it, so the Spartans were, as with Akrotatos, pleased to see him go. He recruited mercenaries at Cape Tainaron, the great mercenary market in Spartan territory, no doubt with Spartan permission, though the money was once again Tarentine; ships of Taras carried the men to the city, where more mercenaries (recruited by the city) and a large force of local troops joined him. The army consisted of one-third mercenaries and two-thirds Tarentines, said to be a total of 30,000 men.[22] That is, Kleonymos was being hired, like the rest, for his name and his military and diplomatic skills, but the intentions, the ships, the finance, and most of the forces were Tarentine.

Kleonymos' arrival, name, and army succeeded in attracting a set of allies, a process clearly achieved by diplomacy. From the wording of Diodoros' account it seems that the recruiting of the Tarentine forces was simultaneous with the diplomatic contacts. The Messapii of the heel of Italy, old enemies of Taras, and 'most' of the Greek cities were brought into the alliance. The exception among the cities was Metapontum, another old Tarentine enemy and its immediate neighbour. Kleonymos allowed it to be sacked by the Lucanians, then drove the attackers out. He fined the Metapontines heavily enough to drive the city into poverty, then made allies of the city and the Lucanians.[23] He had thus achieved the revival of much of the kingdom of Alexander thirty years before, though the relative ease of the achievement rather suggests that much of the region had remained in Tarentine control all along.

It may be at this point that Rome and Taras made a treaty, one item in which was that Roman ships should not sail past the Lacinian Cape, across the Bay of Taranto from the city.[24] This left the main part of the Ionian Sea to Taras, with Roman influence restricted to Bruttium. Kleonymos used his sea power to take the island city of Kerkyra, and is said to have mused aloud about taking on Agathokles in Sicily.[25] Note that in all this he had done very little fighting. The existence of his large force had brought in the allies; at Metapontum he had occupied and freed the city after the Lucanians took it; the only other violence he had undertaken was at Kerkyra, which he now garrisoned with a substantial force. At this point he controlled all the Ionian Sea coasts from the Lacinian Cape to the southern tip of Kerkyra and the Italian Adriatic coast for 150 kilometres. He conducted a raid north into the Adriatic, into the land of the Veneti, and was defeated. Presumably this expedition did more than simply face disaster at the northern end of the sea, as our source implies; it looks more like a reconnaissance for future expeditions. Geographically it also seems as though Kleonymos was looking to box in the Romans; with control of southern Italy and Venetia (and possibly an alliance with the Cisalpine Gauls) Roman expansion could be blocked; this sounds very like Tarentine policy, fearful of the approach of Roman power into Apulia and Bruttium. Kleonymos is said to have fought in the land of the Sallentini on his return, his enemy said to be Romans;[26] Rome could well have intrigued to persuade the people of the heel of Italy to make trouble for Kleonymos, just as he was apparently aiming to make trouble for Rome in Venetia.

At that point Kleonymos disappears from the story with the loss of Diodoros' text. He had reached a position where he had control of much of southern Italy, and by taking over at Kerkyra he had established a dominating position by sea. The comment that he was thinking of attacking Agathokles may only have been an assumption from the political situation he had achieved, or from what Pyrrhos attempted later – and he was, of course, the brother of Akrotatos. But he had one clear advantage over Pyrrhos: Taras had a treaty with Rome, which in effect recognised Taras' (and his) local supremacy in southern Italy. It seems clear that the combined military might and naval strength of Kerkyra, Taras, and Apulia was sufficient to deter Rome, which had already reached into northern Apulia at Venusia but for the time being came no further.

Kleonymos left Italy before 300, for in that year Agathokles took control at Kerkyra, in competition with Kassander of Macedon; clearly Kleonymos' absence from the event indicates that he was no longer in the region. It is just possible that his personal policy was really not to construct a kingdom for himself, but that, like his brother Akrotatos, he depended on local support, which faded with his success. Perhaps he felt he had done the work he had been hired for by beating back the Lucanians, so he left, job done. (This does seem unlikely behaviour for a Spartan; but note his brother's response at Apollonia and Akragas earlier; it could be that both men were simply following strictly the terms of their contracts.)

## Agathokles' kingdom

The way was thus open for Agathokles. He pre-empted Kassander's attempt to seize Kerkyra but was careful to allow the Macedonian forces to withdraw after being beaten.[27] He gained control of the Lipari Islands[28] and attempted a campaign into Bruttium, which failed.[29] An appeal for help from Taras is reported,[30] but it is difficult to see why the city should bother; Taras was not under any pressure at the time, and Agathokles' actions will have preoccupied any other local powers in the region. Diplomatically he was drawn into the wide network of semi-formal alliances constructed by Ptolemy I. He was presented with Ptolemy's daughter Theoxene as his third wife and arranged a marriage of his own daughter Lanassa, by an earlier wife, with Ptolemy's client Pyrrhos when Pyrrhos became joint king in Epeiros; Kerkyra was her dowry.[31] Supposedly, on the way to the marriage ceremony, Agathokles seized the city of Kroton.[32] This was close to the Lacinian Promontory, which Taras had marked out in its Roman treaty as its western boundary.

He also circled round into the Adriatic, making alliances with two groups in northern Apulia, the Peucetii and the 'Iapygii',[33] both located north of Taras and allied with that city. Agathokles was following the trail blazed by the Spartans – Akrotatos had been active at Apollonia on the east Adriatic coast, Kleonymos among the Veneti, in Apulia, and at Kerkyra, and now Agathokles was active in Apulia and Kerkyra. An alliance with Pyrrhos was part of this pattern, and when Lanassa was married to Pyrrhos, a little after the capture of Kroton, Kerkyra was her dowry. Looking at the geography, it seems obvious that Agathokles' main concern was to restrict Roman expansion southwards, and in this he and Taras were at one. His activities may also have been aimed at encircling Taras; the 'appeal' sent to him by Taras could have been an agreement and an alliance. Certainly the Tarentines do not seem to have objected to his actions in their neighbourhood as they did later to those of Rome.

The expansion of Agathokles' power, be it noted yet again, was only partly by means of military expeditions. His defeat in Bruttium was offset by the successful captures of Kerkyra and Kroton. But it was his diplomacy which brought him into the Adriatic and to his Epeirote alliance. His relations with Taras are not recorded (other than the supposed appeal), but it is evident from these other diplomatic contacts that he was being very careful to avoid treading on Tarentine toes. He and Taras were both at enmity with the Bruttians, as well as suspicious of Rome. He made a second attempt on the Bruttians, who waited until he had gathered a large army in preparation for a campaign against them, then attempted to make peace, even suggesting an alliance. They were following the same diplomatic tactics as those which had been used by the Lucanians and others in the face of earlier attacks. Agathokles required a victory, however, and succeeded in taking control of Hipponion, on the north coast of the Italian toe, to complement Rhegion at the tip and Kroton on the southern side.[34] It is evident he had no intention of campaigning to conquer the whole region.

The Bruttians, the Lucanians, and the tribes contacted by Agathokles on the east coast formed a band of territory across southern Italy separating the now-Roman central Italy from the lands of Agathokles and Taras in the south. The alliance of these last was apparently sufficient to block any further southern moves by Rome, except the plantation of the new colony of Venusia in 291. Agathokles' daughter fled from Pyrrhos and gave herself and her island-dowry to Demetrios of Macedon, at which Agathokles contacted Demetrios and formed an alliance with him – as distant a connection as that which he had with Ptolemy. Demetrios was visited by Agathokles' grandson (also Agathokles), who was accompanied on his return to Sicily by Demetrios' friend Oxythemis; Diodoros' interpretation of this is that Oxythemis was actually sent as a spy,[35] a plausible interpretation.

Agathokles sent Theoxene and her two children back to her father,[36] which might indicate a severing of the friendship with Ptolemy in favour of one with Demetrios, or it might be in preparation for a decision on naming Agathokles' successor. He had in fact chosen his grandson Agathokles to succeed him, but this stimulated his surviving son Archagathos to murder the younger Agathokles; he was himself then killed by Meno, a Segestan exile. In the midst of all this killing the elder Agathokles himself died.[37] The kingdom soon collapsed, and so, inevitably, did the complex of alliances Agathokles had constructed in southern Italy, largely by means of his diplomacy.

## The arrival of Rome

The way was thereby opened for a renewal of the competition to control southern Italy. The Syracusan kingdom descended almost at once into civil war, and the Carthaginians soon intervened. The Italian territories and allies of Agathokles felt themselves again in danger. In south Italy the one city which escaped control by either Taras or Agathokles was Thourioi. It was probably reckoned to be within Taras' region, but the two cities were never friendly. In 285 Thourioi, menaced by

134  *Diplomacy in the West*

Lucanian enmity, turned to the one Italian power which seemed capable of providing assistance, Rome.[38]

Rome was turned to because by this time Sicily was no longer in a position to assist. Agathokles' kingdom had broken down into its constituent cities, most of them controlled by individualistic and unstable tyrants; Syracuse itself was locked into a multi-sided civil war. A group of Agathokles' mercenaries seized control of Messene, and from there raided throughout the island. They called themselves the Mamertines, from Mamers, the name of the war god used in Campania, whence many of the men had originated. The Carthaginians intervened, perhaps as much to ensure that their Sicilian territories remained under control and were defended against Mamertine attacks as to extend them.[39]

The request to Rome from Thourioi was for a commander and an armed force to assist the city in protecting itself. That is, Thourioi was doing exactly the same as Taras in its requests to Sparta and Epeiros over the previous half-century. The Romans sent a detachment commanded by a tribune, who was honoured with a golden crown by the city in the best Hellenistic style. Three years later another appeal produced a larger army and the consul C. Fabricius Luscinus; he drove the city's enemies away, and a Roman garrison remained in the city under the command of a military tribune called C. Aelius.[40]

The Romans' arrival seems to have successfully relieved the city of the Lucanian pressure. This involved Rome in a conflict with the Lucanians, but the arrival of the Roman garrison also annoyed Taras, though there was no direct reaction until a Roman naval squadron sailed west along the southern coast as far as Taras itself.[41] This was in direct violation of the Rome-Taras treaty, in which Rome had agreed not to send any ships past the Lacinian Promontory. The purpose of the naval cruise is not known, but quite possibly it was a diplomatic mission. The local political situation had changed since the Lacinian treaty had been negotiated, and the extension of Roman power over Thourioi had further changed matters, while the new Roman colony at Venusia, together with the accession of several places in northern Apulia to the Roman alliance, had brought Roman power closer to Taras in another region. The treaty was thus now somewhat out of date, and it would be reasonable for Rome to wish to revise the treaty, in part to allow naval access to Thourioi; it is therefore possible that the purpose of the voyage of the ten ships to Taras was to renegotiate the treaty.

If it was a diplomatic mission, the Tarentines did not realise it. When the Roman ships appeared they were attacked by Tarentine vessels, and, of the ten ships in the squadron, four were sunk and one was captured. The Tarentines were obviously in greater naval strength than the Romans; the latter must have known this before they set out, so the ten-ship squadron cannot have been intended as a threat. (Appian calls it a voyage of inspection and refers to the crew as 'sight-seers'; the first suggestion is quite possible, the second ludicrous; he betrays later Roman excuses here.) The Tarentines were roused to action by a demagogic politician, Philocharis, who claimed the ships' visit was in breach of the old treaty; the reaction of the Tarentines does strongly suggest that they were already apprehensive at the wider Roman approaches. Having clashed at sea in defence of the treaty, the Tarentines mustered an army and took Thourioi, expelled the oligarchic rulers, dismissed the Roman garrison under a flag of truce, and established a democratic, and therefore friendly, government.[42]

Rome's reaction was to try diplomacy first. The fact that the Tarentines had released the Roman soldiers taken at Thourioi suggested that elements in the city wanted to avoid a conflict. The attack on the ships had been brought about by the demagogue Philocharis, but it was known that the wealthy classes were less anti-Roman. Taras was a major city, powerful and rich, which only twenty years before had put an army of 30,000 troops into the field and had access to the mercenary market in Greece and to the services of Greek commanders. The Romans knew that it was a city to be wary of. The actions at Thourioi implied no more than a minor escalation of a putative conflict and could be justified, just as could the Roman naval arrival.

The Romans sent envoys to Taras, the chief of whom was 'Postumius' (probably L. Postumius Megellus, thrice consul, and the captor of Venusia twenty years before). In a notorious scene he attempted to present Rome's demands in the Tarentine Assembly, only to be laughed at and insulted – or so later Romans claimed.[43] Yet the terms he presented were undoubtedly understood by the Tarentines and were reasonable, given that Roman allies and forces had been defeated – release the prisoners (presumably Thourians, or perhaps Roman sailors, since the Roman soldiers had already been released), restore the expelled Thourians and their looted property, and hand over to the Romans 'the authors of these crimes'. The rejection of these terms and the insult to their envoy meant that the Romans had no option but to resort to force. The Tarentines had in effect refused to negotiate, even though the terms which Postumius presented were clearly open for discussion. The consul L. Aemilius Barbula was sent with his army to enforce Roman terms.[44]

There was a lapse of time of several months between the insult to Postumius and the arrival of Aemilius outside Taras. In that time that Tarentines instituted their own diplomatic process, requesting the services of the Epeirote King Pyrrhos, by now a famous commander. This approach was apparently known to the Romans, and it was one of the reasons for Aemilius' advance towards Taras, complete with army, when he had in fact been sent at first against the Samnites – a priority which seriously reduces the importance of what had happened at Taras. When Aemilius arrived at the city, the same terms Postumius had suggested were presented to Taras but were again rejected, in particular because of the final clause: they could not surrender the political leaders who had brought Taras to this crisis.[45] Whether there were any negotiations is not clear. The other demands could possibly have been accepted, but no city would give up its political leaders and still believe itself to be free and independent. If Rome seriously wanted to avoid a fight, this was the clause which had to be abandoned in any negotiation. It seems neither delegation would, or perhaps could, deal with the issue.

The whole sequence, from the visit of the ships to Aemilius at Taras, is an example of two sides stumbling unwillingly into war, both of them making serious miscalculations about the other – shades of the messy diplomacy leading to Demetrios' siege of Rhodes. It would seem that both sides had carelessly failed to inform

136  *Diplomacy in the West*

each other what was happening: Rome had failed to tell Taras in advance about the ten ships; the Tarentine naval response to the appearance of the Roman squadron was clearly disproportionate. Whether or not the 'old treaty' still applied, it must have been obvious at Taras that the small number of ships involved was not an attack on the city; an inquiry rather than a battle would have been the most appropriate response. Had the Romans sent only a single ship, this would have been a more intelligent approach. At the same time, and given the geographical position of Thourioi, a warning to Taras of Rome's intention to rescue that city would have been sensible (unless, of course, that was the mission of the squadron). Finally, both sides having adopted non-negotiable positions, they found themselves at war. The Tarentines reverted to their previous pattern, inviting another king of Epeiros to come to help them. And so Rome for the first time had to face the full strength of a Hellenistic army commanded by a professional warrior.

## Pyrrhos

Pyrrhos was a well-experienced soldier famed for some impulsiveness, but he was also a canny diplomat. He had had to struggle to achieve his kingship, and in doing so he had learned diplomacy as well as intrigue and war. Installed as king of the Molossi in 306 as a teenager, he was expelled in 302. He moved about as a commander for hire, learning his military trade, and was a hostage with Ptolemy I for five years. In this time he struck up a very useful friendship with Ptolemy, who gave him his stepdaughter Antigone in marriage. With Ptolemy's considerable assistance, military and financial, he was able to return to his Epeirote kingship in 297.[46]

His throne was by no means stable. He was the head of a complex federal state composed of the voluntary association of three tribes. He was subject to distinct limitations on his royal powers, though he had control of foreign affairs, and of course he had command of the army. He used these powers adroitly to expand his authority at home. He had been an enemy of Kassandros of Macedon, but he assisted Kassandros' son Alexander V to gain the Macedonian throne. As his fee he took two of the border provinces, located between Epeiros and Macedon, and the non-Macedonian region of Amphilochia and the city of Ambrakia to the south.[47] These were his personal lands, not a part of the Molossian or the Epeirote state, so he was now largely independent of the constitutional restraints on his kingship. In 294 he married Lanassa, the daughter of the Sicilian King Agathokles, and received Kerkyra as her dowry.[48] So within three years of achieving a royal title he had built himself a considerable personal kingdom, and he had done it very largely by diplomatic means – first by convincing the Molossians, and so the Confederacy, to accept him, then by his agreement with King Alexander V, and then by marriage to Lanassa.

At this point his capacity for peaceful expansion came to an end. There were no more areas he could claim. He took two more wives, the daughters of the kings of the Paiones and the Illyrians, who were the inland neighbours of Epeiros. He married them more or less simultaneously and for good diplomatic reasons, for these marriages were prizes of victories which acted to protect his northern frontier. Lanassa now left him, for this sort of harem-diplomacy was going out of fashion, and one-wife-at-a-time was becoming the normal royal posture. She took Kerkyra with her and married Demetrios Poliorketes, who had just made himself king in Macedon.[49] Since Pyrrhos' ambitions were now directed towards Macedon, Demetrios became his enemy, and Lanassa presumably knew this full well. So Pyrrhos' diplomacy had finally failed. The two men conducted a desultory war against each other for the next few years, neither able to win, though Pyrrhos certainly impressed the Macedonians with his personal warlike prowess. Demetrios finally annoyed the Macedonians so much that they left him, just as Lanassa had left Pyrrhos. In the aftermath Pyrrhos managed to seize control of part of Macedon in concert with Lysimachos, who was advancing from Asia. But Lysimachos was too powerful and too cunning; Pyrrhos soon had to withdraw into his own kingdom.[50] There must have been negotiations over this, but we know nothing of them.

This was the king who was supposedly restless and impulsive but who had just developed Epeiros into a considerable power largely by diplomatic means. His later ambitions had been directed to securing Macedon, but the competitors – Kassandros, Demetrios, Lysimachos – were too powerful. He made a treaty with Demetrios' son Antigonos Gonatas against their mutual enemy Lysimachos, but the combination could make no headway. Such was the situation in 281 when, in rapid succession, Lysimachos was defeated and killed in Asia Minor by Seleukos, who was then murdered; and Pyrrhos received the invitation from Taras to come to that city's assistance against Rome.

The invitation arrived in 281, but it was not for another year that he went to Italy, with a large army. Between receiving Taras' request for assistance and his arrival in Italy he had indulged in extensive diplomacy. He persuaded three of his competitors in the Aegean area to provide him with assistance: Antigonos Gonatas gave him some ships, Antiochos I, Seleukos' successor, provided some soldiers, and Ptolemy Keraunos, now king in Macedon, the murderer of Seleukos, handed over a squadron of elephants which he had captured (presumably from Seleukos).[51] The purpose of these loans and gifts has been presumed to be a means to get rid of Pyrrhos from Greece, since he was a disruptive presence, but it may also be a gesture of Panhellenic feeling – the Greeks in Sicily were being threatened by Carthage again, and those in Italy by Rome.

Pyrrhos brought to Italy a force of 20,000 hoplites, 2,000 archers, 500 slingers, 3,000 cavalry, and 20 elephants, recruited from his homeland and from the many available mercenaries,[52] though most of them were men of his own kingdom. He sent an advance force of 3,000 men on ahead commanded by Kineas of Thessaly, a diplomat, and the general Milo. They arrived to discover that the Tarentines had not been negotiating with Pyrrhos alone.

The consul Aemilius had been campaigning in Taras' territory, presumably hoping to provoke the city either to fight or to negotiate. In the city a politician called Agis had been elected general and had attempted to open negotiations, which suggests that Taras was less than enthusiastic about a new war. The terms of the alliance between Taras and Pyrrhos were that his troops would occupy Taras' acropolis, that he would exercise command of both his own and the city's forces, that Taras would supply the city's troops and pay for them and would provide ships to transport Pyrrhos' army to Italy. This arrangement was one which the Tarentines no doubt allowed Rome to hear about; when Agis achieved power he began his negotiations with Aemilius. Agis and his followers, who may well have been a majority in the city by now, were using the possibility of Pyrrhos' arrival to deter the Romans and bring them into talks. This is all good devious diplomatic practice, of course.

Therefore, when Kineas and Milo landed, their first task was to displace Agis, which was accomplished when Milo took control of the acropolis in accordance with the treaty with Pyrrhos. Several members of the Tarentine diplomatic delegation with Pyrrhos had stayed on in Epeiros, possibly as hostages, though it may also be that Pyrrhos held them back because they were Agis' supporters. Pyrrhos' people had in effect carried through a *coup* at Taras, and this immediately halted the negotiations with Aemilius,[53] who withdrew his forces, under attack, to winter at Venusia. Evidently his mission really had been to negotiate; the Tarentines, putting their faith in Pyrrhos, had resisted his violent blandishments while keeping him in play with talks, perhaps simply by allowing Agis to go on with his own aim of reaching a settlement – the motives of all these men and groups are obscure, but clearly they clashed. When Pyrrhos and his army arrived, he was quickly able to gain a secure base in the city; he had a large army – his own could be doubled from the levy of Taras and its Italian allies – and he could campaign effectively and negotiate from a position of strength.

Pyrrhos' campaign in Italy was a careful mixture of war and diplomacy, much like that which Aemilius had evidently been attempting. He negotiated with the consul P. Valerius Laevinus before the first battle at the River Siris near Herakleia.[54] He had already secured promises of help and recruits from the Lucanians. After his victory at Herakleia he received concrete support from them, the Bruttians, some of the Samnites, and other Greek cities, including Kroton. That is, he had achieved much the same position as his cousin Alexander the Molossian fifty years earlier (and perhaps that of Kleonymos of Sparta as well): a series of alliances which reached to the Roman borders at southern Campania and south of Venusia. He took over Lokroi, but Rhegion was held firmly by its Roman garrison.[55] He marched north towards Rome, probably hoping to extend his alliance system into Etruria so as to isolate Rome, but the Greek cities in Campania were held by the Romans, and when he went beyond Campania to the north he was in danger of being trapped in hilly country between two consular armies, one coming south from Etruria, the other in Campania. Nevertheless, he could be well satisfied, and, leaving garrisons, he retired to Taras for the winter of 280/279.[56]

The two sides exchanged embassies during the winter. The Romans, led once more by C. Fabricius Luscinus, arrived at Taras to negotiate the recovery of Roman prisoners. Pyrrhos released them without ransom, and Kineas accompanied them back to Rome. It was therefore made clear that Pyrrhos was seriously interested in negotiating a peace. Kineas presented the king's terms to the Senate. If they are reported correctly, they were sufficiently realistic to form a basis for an agreement.

The cities in south Italy were to be free and autonomous, the lands conquered by Rome from the Samnites, Lucanians, and Bruttii were to be freed, and Rome and Pyrrhos were to be allied.

It is customary to make these demands even more extreme by suggesting that some of Rome's colonies in the south and the Greek cities of Campania were also included and to suggest that the Romans were to be reduced to little more than 'Latium alone'.[57] But the terms as recorded make sense without too much interpretation, exaggeration, or invention. The Greek cities of the south and the three peoples mentioned were all Pyrrhos' allies; they were to be free and autonomous, a condition fully in accord with normal Hellenistic practice. The 'alliance' suggested was to be between the king and Rome, both of whom were leading elements in rival alliances-cum-confederations. That is, Rome would retain its central Italian and Campanian allies and subjects (and those north of Rome), and the two principals' alliance would guarantee the peace. In Hellenistic terms – and Kineas was acting as a Hellenistic diplomat, as his supposed attempt to give presents to the senior men in Rome shows – the alliance was to be the sort of lifetime peace now normal amongst the kings in the east. Pyrrhos was pledging himself to peace with Rome for the rest of his life.

There were clearly details which were to be negotiated – the Roman colonies in Apulia at Venusia and Luceria are examples, as was the Roman position in Samnium, which the city was unlikely to give up easily, also the garrison in Rhegion – but if the terms as stated by Plutarch are taken to be those announced by Kineas, they were probably a first statement, a negotiating position, and as such they were not unreasonable, given the military and political situation at that moment. The Roman Senate, however, supposedly inflamed by a stirring speech by Ap. Claudius Caecus, rejected the terms. Fabricius was sent back to Pyrrhos to deal with the issue of the prisoners, who had been released only on parole, and this was clearly an opportunity for further negotiations. Pyrrhos generously gave up any claim on the prisoners, but it seems that Fabricius had no leeway in further negotiations. The drawback, of course, was the public nature of the Roman terms. Having been discussed openly in the Senate and agreed there it was very difficult to modify them, especially after Caecus' outburst, though this is not necessary as an explanation for the Roman mulishness. So, once again, the Romans were being intransigent. A new battle in the spring was another victory for Pyrrhos. It is said that he was bothered by the casualties he had suffered, but the Roman forces suffered even more. This story of his fearing to fight on is probably a Roman attempt to explain his next move.

An appeal for help came to Pyrrhos from Syracuse. The city's forces had been defeated by Carthage, and other appeals came from Akragas and Leontinoi.[58] These were the main Greek powers in Sicily, and the implication was that Pyrrhos was being invited to take up a similar position as that which had been held by his ex-father-in-law Agathokles. Kineas was sent to negotiate the terms of his intervention, and Pyrrhos made arrangements for his absence from Italy. In addition to these demands, he was also being asked to go back home to Epeiros, where Greece and Macedonia were under threat from raids by the Galatians.[59] He appears to have calculated that a quick war in Sicily would bring him such an increase in strength as would persuade the Romans to make peace, then he could return to Greece. (Most sources suggest that he may have planned to invade Africa; the quantity and difficulty of the problems already facing him makes such a plan, even as an idea, highly unlikely.)

Kineas' negotiations in Sicily were successful, and Pyrrhos was able to occupy the appellant cities and drive the Carthaginians back to their basic position in the western end of the island, apparently having had to fight seriously only at Panormos and Eryx, within the Carthaginian area.[60] Carthage took diplomatic countermeasures. A fleet had sailed to Ostia the year before, and its commander Mago had offered to help the Romans in their war against Pyrrhos and Taras. The object of the Carthaginians was obviously to keep Pyrrhos active and busy in Italy, and so this was a sensible Carthaginian move; it also implies that Sicilian requests for his help were already being discussed in the island a year before they reached him. Rome, equally sensibly, refused the offer, presumably hoping that Pyrrhos really would go elsewhere, most likely to fight Carthage.[61] If the senators had not yet thought he might go there, the Carthaginian approach surely suggested it to them. This was also no doubt one of the factors which persuaded the Senate to reject Pyrrhos' peace terms – it seems unlikely that a single speech by a blind old senator would have been sufficient, no matter how eloquent and vehement.

When it was clear that he really was going to Sicily, once Kineas' negotiations had been successful, Carthage tried again with Rome. This time an alliance was agreed by which Rome and Carthage would fight their separate wars, but Carthage would assist Rome with ships when necessary.[62] Therefore, when Pyrrhos went to Sicily the forces left in Italy were subject to Roman attacks, but these were never serious, and his commanders seem to have held on to most of the territory Pyrrhos had already secured.

The war in Sicily lasted longer than Pyrrhos perhaps expected, as wars tend to, but by 277 he had driven the Carthaginians back to their last stronghold, Lilybaion. They offered peace, a large indemnity, and a maritime alliance. Pyrrhos, perhaps persuaded by his Sicilian Greek allies, held out for the total evacuation of Sicily.[63] At this point he was in command of Epeiros, the Greek cities of southern Italy, and all Sicily except for Messene (the Mamertines) and Lilybaion (the Carthaginians). He also may have held Kerkyra. For the first time, the whole area of the Ionian Sea was under one political regime, from the watershed of the Pindos Mountains to the western end of Sicily and north as far as the borders of Campania. This polity could be interpreted, had it held together, as the culmination of the various efforts made over the past century and a half by kings and commanders, from Syracuse, from Sparta, and from Epeiros, to create such a state, efforts which had intensified since the time of King Alexander, Pyrrhos' great-uncle. It may be noted also that such a prospect had brought Rome and Carthage together twice, in the face of Agathokles' power and that of Pyrrhos.

Almost at once, however, this potential empire began to crumble. The Sicilian cities began to decline to contribute, and the only way to hold the new kingdom together would be by crushing the freedom enjoyed by the Greek cities. Pyrrhos was at war against both Rome and Carthage, and his home kingdom was under threat from the Galatian invasions. He needed to be able to direct the total resources of all the areas, but the requirement to go on fighting was so large that the Greek cities had no wish to be part of an empire. The advance of the Romans against his Italian lands called him back.[64]

Neither Rome nor Carthage showed any more willingness to negotiate; they could now afford to wait, since it was clear that his support in Italy and Sicily was collapsing. He was still able to campaign as far as the borders of Samnium and fight a drawn battle against a Roman army, but to get more troops he needed to go to Greece. He had proclaimed his son Alexander (Lanassa's child, and therefore Agathokles' grandson) as his heir to the kingdom of Sicily, and he left another son, Helenos, in charge in the acropolis of Taras when he left. There seems no doubt he hoped to return. During his absence in Sicily, Rome had not made much progress; the Carthaginians did recover their lost lands and took control of parts of central Sicily. The east of the island, including Syracuse, remained independent, as did most of southern Italy. Had he returned to the west fairly soon, therefore, there was a substantial geographical base left for him upon which to construct and maintain an Ionian Sea kingdom, but he died in 272. Rome was then able to persuade Taras to join its alliance as a free and autonomous city, an agreement reached by negotiation.[65]

The reason for the detail of this chapter is to emphasise, as elsewhere in this study, that most of the history of the region can be best explained in terms of diplomacy rather than warfare. The ancient sources are besotted with the battles of Agathokles and Pyrrhos, not to mention the Romans, but for every day of battle there were days, even weeks, of negotiation. Pyrrhos is said to have noted that he gained control of more cities through Kineas' negotiations than he did by fighting. He constructed his kingdom in southern Italy by negotiation, just as he had in Epeiros. His extended kingdom, of course, collapsed as quickly as had that of Agathokles, but so had Roman dominion in the south under his pressure; it was rebuilt by conquest, until a new opportunity came to escape Roman rule with the arrival of Hannibal.

## Notes

1 Diodoros 20.40.1–3.
2 Diodoros 20.40.1–2; Justin 22.7.4; Schmitt, *Staatsverträge* 432; Tillyard, *Agathocles* 144–152.
3 *IG* II(2) 418.
4 Diodoros 20.42.3–4; Justin 22.7.5; Polyainos 5.3.4.
5 Justin 22.6–7.
6 The Loeb translator of Diodoros renders the offer as 'dominion over Libya', and the Greek is not more than lordship; but the sense is clear.
7 H.J.W. Tillyard, *Agathocles*, Cambridge 1908, 157–162.
8 Livy 9.41.5–7.
9 Livy 9.37.12 and 41.2; Schmitt, *Staatsverträge* 435.
10 This follows from the later appearance of Etruscan ships as his allies – see note 12.

## 142   Diplomacy in the West

11  Livy, 9.43.26; Schmitt, *Staatsverträge* 438; Will, *Histoire Politique* I, remarks that 'knowledge of the treaty seems necessary to comprehend the events of the time of Pyrrhos' – still more is it necessary to comprehend the time of Agathokles.
12  Diodoros 20.61.6–8; Schmitt, *Staatsverträge* 436.
13  Diodoros 20.68.1–69.13; Justin 8.2–14.
14  Diodoros 20.77.3–79.4–5 and 89.1–90.2.
15  Diodoros 16.62.4.
16  Livy 8.3.5 and 17.6.
17  Livy 8.24.1–7.
18  Ager, *Interstate Arbitrations* 9.
19  Diodoros 19.70.4–8.
20  Diodoros 19.71.1–5.
21  Livy 9.14.1–4; Ager, *Interstate Arbitrations* 8.
22  Diodoros 20.104.1–2.
23  Diodoros 20.104.2–3.
24  Appian, *Samnite Wars* 7.1; Schmitt, *Staatsverträge* 444.
25  Diodoros 20.104.4.
26  Diodoros 21.3; Justin 23.1.6–9.
27  Diodoros 21.2.
28  Diodoros 20.10.1.
29  Diodoros 21.3.1–2.
30  Justin 23.1.17.
31  Theoxene: Justin 23.2.6; Lanassa: Diodoros 21.4, Plutarch, *Pyrrhos* 9.3.
32  Diodoros 21.4.
33  Ibid.
34  Justin 23.2.3; Diodoros 21.8; Strabo 6.1.5.
35  Diodoros 21.15.
36  Justin 23.2.
37  Diodoros 21.16.
38  Livy, *Per.* 11.
39  Summarised by Franke, *CAH*, VII.2, 471–474.
40  Pliny, *NH* (see 'Abbreviations' section for full information) 36.12.
41  Livy, *Per.* 12; Appian, *Samnite Wars* 7; Cassius Dio, frag 39.4.
42  Appian, *Samnite Wars* 7; on all this see Kathleen Lomas, *Rome and the Western Greeks: Conquest and Acculturation in Southern Italy*, London 1993.
43  Appian, *Samnite Wars* 7.
44  Ibid. 7.3.
45  Ibid.
46  Plutarch, *Pyrrhos* 1–5.
47  Ibid. 6.
48  Ibid. 9; cf. P.R. Franke, 'Pyrrhus', *CAH* VII.2. 459–462, for Pyrrhos' escape from the restrictions of Epeirote kingship.
49  Plutarch, *Pyrrhos* 10.5.
50  Ibid. 11–12.
51  Ibid. 13–15; Pausanias 1.12; Justin 18.1–2.
52  Plutarch, *Pyrrhos* 15.1.
53  Zonaras 8.2.
54  Plutarch, *Pyrrhos* 16.3–4; Dionysios 19.9.2–4; Zonaras 8.3.4; Ager, *Interstate Arbitrations* 27; Schmitt, *Staatsverträge* 467.
55  Plutarch, *Pyrrhos* 17.5; Justin 18.1.8; Cassius Dio 9.7.
56  Zonaras 8.4.
57  Plutarch, *Pyrrhos* 18.2–3; Franke, *CAH* VII.2, 470–471.
58  Plutarch, *Pyrrhos* 22.1; Zonaras 8.5; Diodoros 22.8.1.

59 Plutarch, *Pyrrhos* 22.1–3; Diodoros 22.8.3.
60 Plutarch, *Pyrrhos* 22.6; Diodoros 22.10.
61 Justin 22.1–3.
62 Polybios 3.25.1; Livy, *Per.* 13; Schmitt, *Staatsverträge* 466.
63 Plutarch, *Pyrrhos* 23.2.
64 Polybios 3.25.1; Livy, *Per.* 13.
65 Livy, *Per.* 15; Zonaras 8.6.13; Schmitt, *Staatsverträge* 475.

# 8 The diplomacy of Rome and Carthage – I

The relations of Rome and Carthage went through a long series of stages. Their early relations, from the sixth to the fourth centuries BC, were apparently mainly commercial, as indicated by the treaties made between them. The wars they fought from 264 BC onwards were centred on control of Sicily and were largely a development of the preceding series of crises discussed in the last chapter. The first stage in their relationship which was overtly political is their joint opposition to King Pyrrhos in south Italy and Sicily.

## The war against Pyrrhos

The first politically significant treaty between Rome and Carthage was that concluded in 279/278 which made them allies of a sort against King Pyrrhos (see also Chapter 7).[1] In their earlier treaties, all apparently essentially commercial in nature,[2] it was Carthage which had taken the initiative, responding to the successive stages in the Roman conquests in Italy with the intention in the end of blocking any Italian commercial expansion into the western Mediterranean.

Those early treaties, by their existence and their terms, demonstrate that developments in both cities were well understood. Rome, for instance, was fully aware of events in Sicily and knew of those in the east sufficiently well that a Roman embassy went to Babylon to greet Alexander the Great on his return from India in 324,[3] and no doubt to investigate his further plans; similarly, Carthage had been concerned at Alexander's brutal destruction of Tyre and had envoys in that city when it was destroyed.[4] The repeated campaigns of Greek warrior rulers and adventurers in southern Italy between 342 and 272 were obviously of concern to Rome, particularly in the apparently expansionist plans of Kleonymos and Agathokles, and the contacts Agathokles had with the Etruscan cities will have been noted in Rome, but it was Pyrrhos who posed the first serious threat to the city, and he threatened Carthage's position as well.

The only one of the early treaties about which we have any precise information is that concluded in 279/278 (considered in the previous chapter). The agreement envisaged some cooperation, but the two cities actually cooperated in very few actions – Carthaginian ships transported a small Roman force to attack Rhegion, though this action was unsuccessful.[5] Carthage was left to fight Pyrrhos alone in Sicily and, at a moment of desperation, proposed a peace which, had it been accepted, would have left Rome fighting alone once again.[6]

Rome similarly ignored Carthage while conquering southern Italy, but in 272, as Rome finally closed in on Taras, a Carthaginian fleet approached the city from the seaward side. This is claimed, by Livy almost three centuries later, to be an intervention by Carthage in Rome's territory and Rome's internal affairs,[7] but at the time Taras was held by troops of Pyrrhos under his general, Milo, and Rome and Carthage were allies and were both at war with the king. Milo commanded a considerable force, which Rome had not attempted to tackle in the three years since Pyrrhos sailed to Greece. Disregarding the later Roman interpretation, it is worth considering the wider context of this Carthaginian intervention.

Pyrrhos was killed in fighting in Argos late in 272.[8] By then he had been in Greece for several years and had shown few signs of being able to return to Italy, though by leaving Milo and his garrison in Taras he indicated clearly enough that he hoped to do so. By the time he was killed Rome had at last attacked Taras, and Carthage's squadron joined in. Livy's claim that Carthage was interfering in the Roman area ignored the treaty they had agreed in 279/278; Carthage was clearly free to fight by sea and to bring assistance to Rome by sea and was obviously as anxious to eliminate Milo's army before Pyrrhos came back as was Rome. So another possible interpretation of these events, not one which requires Roman-Carthaginian hostility, is that they were cooperating in the attack on Taras in order to remove Pyrrhos' last active post in the west before the king could return. The Romans had already laid siege to the city when the fleet arrived, and Carthage's assistance was hardly necessary, except to complete the blockade; but the Roman account pays no attention to any Carthaginian actions.

What is significant, of course, apart from the distortion of motives and timing in the (Roman) record of Carthaginian activity, is that the Roman historical tradition found it necessary to claim that Carthage was acting against the treaty's provisions by moving against Taras. Quite evidently it was not, but the Roman tradition, always self-justificatory in its most guilty moments, had to try to put Carthage in the wrong in an interpretation which anticipated later hostility.

Of course, neither city trusted the other; this was in the nature of the geopolitical situation. Carthage had tried to make peace with Pyrrhos, and Rome had certainly delayed attacking his forces in south Italy, while the king was in Sicily, so when both parties turned up at Taras, undoubtedly they were mutually suspicious. Both cities always put their own actions and intentions well ahead of any treaty obligations and were prepared to ignore the treaty if they felt it necessary. Their alliance, being directed against Pyrrhos, was never more than a temporary arrangement and expired with Pyrrhos. Mutual suspicion continued but was hardly a critical factor in events.

## The Mamertine crisis

The first Romano-Carthaginian War originated in a dispute centring on the brigands who had seized control of the Sicilian city of Messene amid the general collapse of Agathokles' brief kingdom. The historical sources for the outbreak of the war are a complex tangle of sometimes contradictory elements[9] in which it is

146   *Diplomacy in the West*

difficult to discover what actually happened, but it seems that diplomatic misunderstandings were at the root of events.

The sources which have to be used are overwhelmingly concerned to explain why Rome went to war with Carthage. This is a reasonable retrospective viewpoint, but it avoids any discussion of the situation inside Messene and of most of the policies of both Carthage and Hiero, the original participants, whose policies led to the Roman intervention. Above all, it removes from the story virtually all record of diplomatic activity and any discussion of the possible alternatives to what happened.

It must therefore first be insisted that none of what happened was inevitable. Rome was not predestined to fight Carthage. It was quite possible that Rome could visit its aggressiveness on other victims – Cisalpine Gaul would be a prime target. But the Roman decision for war was, in effect if not explicitly, made before its army reached Messene and is signalled above all by the size of the army which was sent south. This was a sure sign to all in Sicily that a magnified Mamertine expedition had arrived and that Rome's terms would be those which everyone else must accept. Until then the main activity in dealing with the Mamertines' potential for causing trouble had been diplomatic. The arrival of the Roman consular army significantly increased the stakes and made war much more likely. The initial activity was a mixture of diplomacy and occasional fighting, with diplomacy the crucial element. It is worth examining the crisis as a failure of diplomacy rather than, as is often done, as a clash of ambitions, and still less as an inevitable conflict. The diplomacy tends to disprove both of these contentions.

The centre of the problem was the position of the Mamertines, a group of Agathokles' former mercenaries who had seized control of the city of Messene, had expelled or killed the citizens who resisted, then had appropriated their wives and their property.[10] They had then spent their energies in raids over the nearby countryside[11] and succeeded in maintaining control over the north-eastern corner of Sicily for over two decades.

Their origin as mercenaries and their aggressiveness were sufficient to damn the Mamertines in the sources as brigands, but they were not the only group to act in such a way, and they do not seem to have been treated by any of their Sicilian contacts in any way other than as the people of the city. As a community, they appear to have been a functioning democracy in which decisions were taken in public assemblies. Only one man of the city is ever named in any of the existing sources, not even the commanders of the raids; it thus seems that, amid the civil wars and tyrannies of Sicily, the Mamertines may well have been the only democratic state which would have been recognised as such by, say, the Athenians two centuries earlier. That they were aggressive was a characteristic which they shared with most Greek cities, starting with their neighbour Syracuse (and Aratos of Sikyon in old Greece a little later – see Chapter 5). They were originally from central Italy, mainly it seems from Campania, and the ethnic name applied to them commemorated the god of war of the Oscan people, Mamers (who was Ares of the Greeks and Mars to Romans), who was portrayed on their coins. Their origin connected them in an indefinite way back to Italy and thus to Rome, which had incorporated their claimed homeland into its system since 326; the Campanians in the band will have been familiar with the conditions at 'home'.

The second element in the crisis was the city of Syracuse. Agathokles' kingdom had been partly revived by Hiero, originally elected as Syracusan general, who secured his promotion to king by the usual method, using his command to seize full power.[12] He assisted the Romans in their campaign to recapture the city of Rhegion from a group of mutinous soldiers in 270, but this was not a sign of an alliance for more than this single operation; Rome and Hiero were not allies.

Carthage recovered its position in western Sicily after Pyrrhos' withdrawal and was as unhappy about the conduct of the Mamertines as anyone else. A Carthaginian squadron was stationed in the Lipari Islands, presumably to suppress any Mamertine seaborne piratical activity.[13] The real danger to Carthage, of course, was that successes by the Mamertines might encourage those Greek cities in its part of the island to opt for Mamertine support rather than Carthaginian. This in turn would undermine the positions of the local Carthage-supported tyrants; hence the importance of the democratic ethos of the Mamertines.

The main states of Sicily after Pyrrhos' withdrawal were thus Carthage, the Mamertines, and, growing in strength, Syracuse. The other cities had freed themselves from Syracusan rule when Agathokles died and from Pyrrhos' regime when he left: Akragas was the most important, and there were numerous others; however, the crisis which led to the new war involved only Messene, Syracuse, and Carthage, and eventually Rome, with Messene as the storm centre.

Hiero, emerging as a Syracusan tyrant, and the democratically inclined Mamertines, both aggressive, fell into war with each other about 270; the Mamertines were at enmity with Syracuse no matter who ruled there. Hiero had established friendly relations with Rome over the problem of the mutineers in Rhegion, while the Mamertines had felt friendly towards their fellow ex-mercenaries across the strait. Rome showed no interest in following up the contact with Hiero although it was clearly fully aware of the situation, but it was not involved after solving the Rhegion problem.

Hiero, having assisted in the destruction of the Rhegion pirate nest, turned to deal with the Mamertines. He won a decisive victory at the Longanos River in 270,[14] and the Mamertines as a result lost control of some of their territory. Hiero now had himself proclaimed king. He spent some years consolidating his power at home, then moved to besiege Messene city in 265. The precise purpose of the siege is unknown – Hiero may have been aiming to destroy the Mamertines or just bring them to some sort of subordinate terms – but it was crucial in complicating the whole situation. The Carthaginian commander of the squadron based at Lipara Island intervened. His task had presumably been to block any maritime enterprise out of Messene, but now he saw an opportunity to extend Carthaginian power. He contacted Hiero, who accepted his offer to intervene, then contacted the Mamertines and offered his protection – that is, against Hiero. Badly damaged by their battle losses, they accepted a Carthaginian force to occupy their acropolis.[15] This was clever diplomacy by the Carthaginian commander but not a procedure likely to establish trust between him and Hiero or between Syracuse and Carthage.

148   *Diplomacy in the West*

These two cities were mutually and traditionally hostile. It was clearly Hiero's ambition to eliminate the Mamertine problem, but this was not necessarily in Carthage's interests. Establishing a Carthaginian-Mamertine alliance was a useful extension of Carthage's reach, and since the garrison remained in the acropolis of Messene after its installation, the commander's initiative evidently met with approval at Carthage. It was also presumably acceptable in the short term to Hiero and the Syracusans, who were relieved of the raids they had suffered. Until this point, be it noted, there had been just two military actions: Hiero's victory at Longanos and the later siege of the city. Every other move had been by way of diplomacy.

Hiero's forces had done the fighting, but the Carthaginians had reaped a good part of the benefit, and the assumption must have been that Messene was going to become part of the Carthaginian section of Sicily on a permanent basis, while Hiero had taken control of part of the Mamertine lands after his victory. So both had gained at Mamertine expense, and the suppression of Mamertine raids was a gain for both. Further, Hiero had parlayed his victory into a kingship, and Carthage had gained a useful base in Messene with its comfortable harbour and strategic position.

The Mamertines had now ceased to be an immediate threat to their neighbours, but Carthaginian protection cannot have been comfortable. Tensions developed among the citizenry over how to get rid of the garrison. One group wanted to arrange a more formal agreement with Carthage, by which the city's autonomy would be guaranteed in exchange for an alliance and perhaps the garrison's removal. The second group, rather belatedly remembering their Italian origins, wanted to submit to Rome and so get rid of the Carthaginians, presumably peacefully. Both groups appealed for help when Hiero came again to attack, acting in response, presumably, to these moves within the city.[16]

If either party in the city was assuming that there would be a peaceable evacuation of the Carthaginian garrison, this was very naïve of them. Carthage may have been bounced into the situation by its local commander acting on his own initiative, but the Senate in Carthage was obviously quite happy for the force to remain. No doubt friction developed between citizens and garrison, and this would be one of the reasons for the pro-Carthage party to look to the garrison's removal. The motivation for the pro-Roman party is less obvious. Since the original group of mercenaries had been men recruited by Agathokles (who died in 289), by the time the Carthaginians took over the acropolis in 265 most of them were probably dead; perhaps three decades had passed since any of the original group still alive had lived in Campania, and despite their apparent devotion to Mamers it is not by any means certain that they were all from Campania, and one may surely discount any nostalgia influencing Mamertine policy. But the only alternative to Carthage or Syracuse was Rome, which was established just across the strait, in Rhegion.

Rome was divided over its response. Polybios details the pros and cons: dislike of the Mamertines; fear that Carthage looked to be taking over all Sicily, which would block any Roman expansionary interests; within living memory Carthaginian fleets had appeared off Ostia and off Taras, and a squadron was based at Lipara and now perhaps at Messene; Carthage's naval reach was long. There is no indication that Italian solidarity played any part in the Roman decision, any more than the Mamertines were pro-Roman or pro-Italian. In the end the decision rested on Roman ambition, that in order to continue expanding Rome must move into Sicily. These Roman reasons are not necessarily the only ones considered; Polybios, after all, was writing a century later, when Rome had become the Mediterranean superpower; in 264 it was just the city which had established itself, precariously, as lord of Italy; Polybios' reasons were coloured by hindsight. Above all, the prospect of a Carthaginian war is not likely to have been a Roman consideration.

The experience of the Romans at Rhegion was, however, relevant. There, Carthaginian assistance had been ineffective, but Hiero had helped the Romans succeed. In both cases that part of Italy was shown to be more accessible to Sicilians than to Romans. Roman control of Messene – which was the issue in the beginning – would push these potential interferers away from Italy and secure Roman control of the strait, an important strategic objective. The line of communication between Rome and Taras, and Rome and the eastern Mediterranean, lay through the strait; also, the issue of Messene and the Mamertines was a continuing aspect of the problem of the Ionian Sea kingdom.

Rome's choice was to intervene, and the prospect of a conflict with Carthage was not ignored.[17] Polybios portrays the decision as driven by the people after the Senate had decided that the Mamertine request should be denied. Polybios' account is perhaps contaminated by later Roman justifications, but once the decision was taken, it was followed through, and the appointed commander, the consul Ap. Claudius Caudex, was given wide war-making, that is, diplomatic, powers.[18]

The two Messenian/Mamertine parties had therefore set up a confrontation between Rome and Carthage, though none of the parties involved had seen it coming or had intended it. The Carthaginians at Carthage may not have understood what was happening, though surely the commander of the occupying garrison kept in touch with the local politicians, and the pro-Carthage party could tell him what their opponents planned. The Romans – the Senate, the consuls, and the assembly – understood that they were entering a dispute with Carthage if they accepted the Mamertine invitation, though a wider war was not envisaged. The motivation clearly varied with each interest group and probably among individuals as well. The issue, however, was not the launching of a great war but the situation in Messene.

The precise events which followed at the Strait of Messina are no clearer than these earlier events, but at some point the Carthaginians were induced, or forced, to leave Messene's acropolis by the Mamertines.[19] The pro-Carthaginian group could argue that the Carthaginian garrison was attracting the enmity of both Hiero and Rome; the pro-Roman group was in favour of any move which would remove the Carthaginians; they could together work to persuade the commander of the garrison to leave. If he had originally put his force into the acropolis by invitation, he may well have had no choice in honour but to leave when asked to do so by the Messenian Assembly.

150  *Diplomacy in the West*

We have to assume that the Mamertines knew what they were doing, that their decisions were arrived at by open discussion in a civic assembly, and that they were not merely victims of great power manoeuvres. This was neither a tyranny nor a secretive monarchy, even if the citizenry was composed largely of former mercenaries. The Carthaginians had been invited in to pre-empt the Syracusan conquest, a move which had succeeded; they were now being invited out by a similar process of a popular decision by the assembly. It was also a decision of the assembly which opened the way for the installation of a Roman force to replace the Carthaginians. It is reasonable to assume that in this case the Mamertines also knew what they were doing. A Roman garrison, like the Carthaginian, would be a protection against Hiero; it might well lead to the incorporation of the city into the Roman Commonwealth, but this was a more comfortable prospect for the ex-Campanians than being a Carthaginian ally. Carthage's protection had been valuable, but, having received it, the Mamertines were still vulnerable, both to Hiero as an enemy and to Carthage as an ally. The removal of the Carthaginian garrison was achieved by the citizens, and the installation of a Roman garrison was inherent in the original request by the Mamertines for Roman help. The prospect was not unpleasing to various Romans: the consul would have an active command, and for the ordinary soldiers, as Polybios puts it, there was the prospect of plunder.[20]

Polybios' account makes it clear that the Romans fully understood that to move into Messene would probably involve them in a war in Sicily against both Hiero and perhaps Carthage; the prospect of plunder[21] was hardly to be expected by merely occupying the citadel of Messene. A war was certainly therefore envisaged. Neither of the prospective opponents was a negligible power, and they would surely become allies once Rome intruded on their patch; they were already in part allied over the issue of Messene.

It is somewhat of a surprise, however, that the only diplomatic move was a new joint Carthaginian-Syracusan action against Messene.[22] Neither Hiero nor Carthage appears to have attempted to persuade Rome to stay away, even though both had made friendly diplomatic and military contact with the city in the recent past. This omission was not the result of a speedy Roman arrival, since the decision at Rome took some time to be arrived at, and both Hiero and Carthage clearly had good sources of information about events there – just as it is clear that Rome knew of affairs in Sicily. The Roman army took some time to march to Rhegion, and ships had to be collected there for the crossing: Rome's decisions and moves were as open and public as were those of the Mamertines. By the time the Roman army arrived, forces from both Syracuse and Carthage were menacing Messene, hoping to seize the city before the Romans crossed the strait.

With the Roman army at Rhegion, there were four elements involved in deciding what was to happen next. The weakest was Messene itself; the most powerful was the Roman army, with the consul; Messene was under siege by (third) a Carthaginian force and (fourth) the Syracusan army under Hiero. The consul Caudex's task was to occupy Messene; neither Carthage nor Hiero liked the idea, partly because both hoped to occupy the city themselves and partly because they hoped to exclude Rome from the island. In diplomatic terms Hiero and Carthage were operating as allies, though we do not know if they had a formal agreement; the Mamertines clearly took the Roman side, if only to free themselves from the siege.

For Caudex the precise situation at Messene had changed between the time he received his powers from the Senate and the time he arrived at Rhegion. When he set out he knew that both Syracuse and Carthage were involved in the city and had been, either competing or cooperating, for some years; but an active siege was new. The Roman garrison at Rhegion was only a mile or so away; the commander there could inform Caudex of the situation in detail as soon as he arrived.[23]

Having arrived at Rhegion, Caudex had to get some of his troops into Messene if he was to execute his task. This was not acceptable to Carthage or to Hiero, and the transfer of Roman forces into Sicily was hindered by Carthaginian ships, though neither Hiero nor Carthage was willing to initiate hostilities. The Romans therefore had the initiative and had been invited by Messene. Caudex evaded interception and put a force into the city, by which time the Carthaginians had left. There is an elaborate story in Diodoros and others which seems to be designed to cast the blame for the start of the fighting on Carthage, but Polybios is clear that the Carthaginian garrison had left the city before the Roman forces arrived.[24] The ineffective Carthaginian opposition came from the ships based at the Lipari Islands, commanded by the (never named) man who had originally installed the Carthaginian forces in the Messenen citadel. He may well have been again acting once more on his own initiative – it is said that the Carthaginians soon executed him. The assumption has been that he was executed for failing to hold on to Messene; his several personal initiatives may well have been his real fault in Carthaginian eyes.

It was the size of the Roman army which was the key to the situation. Rome's military presence in Messene was clearly by invitation (just as that of Carthage had been, and as was its withdrawal). This was the major diplomatic card in Caudex's hand. On the other hand, the arrival of a Roman consul with a full consular army was hardly what the Mamertines had expected. What they had presumably hoped for was a token force whose presence would deter Carthaginian or Syracusan attack. Twenty thousand soldiers was not just a protective garrison; it was an aggressive force designed if necessary to campaign over large areas of Sicily. It is therefore not just the prospect of Roman involvement but the sheer size of the obviously aggressive Roman army to which both Carthage and Hiero reacted. The Mamertines in Messene had been bad enough, but to have the city which controlled all Italy also in control of Messene with twenty thousand men was a much more unpleasant prospect for everyone.

Here was a new chance for diplomacy, though the size of the Roman force made it of doubtful utility. The forces of Hiero and Carthage seem to have taken up defensive blockading positions, and so without overt hostilities, possibly in the hope of persuading Caudex to negotiate. It is likely enough that they would have been willing to accept a controlling Roman garrison in Messene's citadel, just as Hiero had accepted a Carthaginian one, if it had been reasonably small and so not a threat. The original aim of both Hiero and Carthage, after all, had been to stop the Mamertine raids; a small Roman force in Messene would probably do this. The consul, however, with a large force at his disposal, could ignore diplomacy in favour of a short sharp war. As protector of Messene he could argue that the removal of the blockading forces was necessary.

Throughout the Mamertine crisis diplomacy and fighting had gone together. Hiero's diplomatic tactics in 270 assisted Rome against the rebels in Rhegion and so isolated the Mamertines, so denying them the potential support for the Rhegion rebels. Hiero was then able to defeat them in the field at the Longanos River. This clever mix of diplomatic and military manoeuvring gained him substantial advantages – a crown at home, control of more territory at Mamertine expense, and the end of further raids. The price was the acceptance of the Carthaginian force in the Messene citadel and a tacit alliance with Carthage.

The Mamertines had proved to be active diplomats as well. They made friends with the Rhegion rebels, which could have provided them with a powerful strategic and economic position astride the strait. This must have seemed a good idea at the time, though they had perhaps failed to appreciate that more powerful states would object. They were isolated diplomatically after Hiero's victory the next year but quickly recovered by accepting a Carthaginian force in their acropolis. That the garrison stayed in Messene for some time means that its presence was generally acceptable to all parties, Mamertines, Hiero, Carthage, and presumably Rome, whose forces were now firmly ensconced in a similar garrison in Rhegion just across the water. This was nimble diplomacy by a minor state surrounded by bigger beasts.

The next Mamertine initiative was to cajole the Carthaginian garrison to leave and to invite the direct participation of Rome in their affairs. The basic Mamertine policy was to gain protection against Hiero, whom they knew would destroy them; the greater powers were not interested in doing so. The arrival of the large Roman consular army and its admission into their city effectively ended Mamertine participation in events, for nothing could now be done without Roman permission. Probably the Mamertines reckoned that they had come out of the whole crisis more or less as winners; the Roman occupation of their city was in effect its incorporation into the Roman state, thereby providing full protection against its enemies while not interfering with internal matters.[25] It is even possible that some of the Mamertines knew that they could go back to raiding if they joined with the Roman army, since that turned out to be the main Roman military activity for the next few years – and this was implicit in the expectations of plunder among the Roman rank-and-file.

## Caudex at Messene

When consul Caudex, from his position within the circuit of Messene's walls, examined his situation, he found he was faced by two enemy forces – note that they are enemies of Messene but not (yet) of Rome. The removal of the Carthaginians from the acropolis had been followed by Carthaginian annoyance, expressed by the military and naval blockade and the execution of the commander who evacuated the place; the city was also under attack by Hiero. This had been the situation before Caudex got his forces into the city, and it continued, but no fighting had

## The diplomacy of Rome and Carthage – I 153

yet taken place between the Romans and the blockaders. Caudex's next task was therefore to rescue Messene from its enemies. Whether Rome came to be at war with those blockading states depended on his next move.

Caudex began negotiations; no source gives any indication of his terms, but they can be conjectured without difficulty: the allies should withdraw their forces and evacuate all the lands claimed by the Mamertines. In exchange Caudex must at the least have promised no resumption of the old raiding policy. For Hiero this would mean surrendering the territory he had won by the Longanos victory five years before, entailing a serious loss of prestige at home, which might be fatal. However, by (presumably) refusing these Roman terms, Hiero laid himself open to attack. Caudex obliged.

The Carthaginian forces did not assist their associate. Perhaps they did not have a large enough military force available; perhaps the two armies were camped separately, so they did not realise Hiero was being attacked; more probably, perhaps Caudex was still negotiating with them. He certainly fought them one at a time. After a hard fight, the Romans inflicted a marginal defeat on the Syracusan army. After that, without Carthaginian support Hiero could scarcely continue; he abandoned his camp and took his army home. The day after, Caudex attacked the Carthaginian forces, which would seem to have been weaker than the Syracusans', and drove them back.[26]

The war was now truly begun, though it was still only a local quarrel in northeastern Sicily. Caudex faced two armies, neither of which had been seriously damaged, that were still near Messene. He may have made a tentative move against Syracuse itself, but the nearby presence of the Carthaginian forces will have restrained him; on the whole it seems unlikely that he was able to move very far from his base. His achievement was thus limited to holding Messene; the enemies were still in the field.

These events took place in a very restricted geographical area and in a relatively short period of time. Only Hiero was fully in control of both his forces and his state. Both Caudex and the Carthaginian commander(s) were subject to restrictive orders from their home governments, and their actions must be interpreted in that knowledge. Caudex had powers of waging war, but he was also more than willing to use diplomacy. The Carthaginian commander was in a much weaker position than the others: he would be criticised, at least, if he brought on a major war. His decision was to withdraw from the city and not to assist Hiero; his force was probably a weak one, for it was defeated by the Romans very easily – or perhaps he simply withdrew when an attack seemed inevitable. Roman and Carthaginian forces, naval and military, had so far only skirmished with each other, but Rome and Syracuse were clearly at war.

The Roman decision to send a full consular army had given Caudex a formidable power to back up his diplomatic moves. It is worth emphasising that for most of the time he was very willing to negotiate – but having a large army at his back meant he was not willing to accept that 'negotiating' was a process in which he should make concessions to secure an agreement. The only offer he could make which Hiero and Carthage might accept was to remove most of his army from

Sicily; a Roman garrison in the acropolis of Messene would be acceptable, but no more. Caudex's demands would be for Syracusan and Carthaginian forces (military and naval) to be removed from the vicinity of Messene. There was clearly the basis for agreement in these positions, but it is equally clear that Caudex's demands – returning the conquered territory, for instance, and perhaps other demands – were too much for Hiero.

Caudex was also under pressure of time. His command would expire in the autumn, and several months had elapsed between taking up the command at Rome and reaching Rhegion. When he reached Messene, his time for action was fairly brief. His attacks on both Syracusan and Carthaginian forces may well have been an attempt to force them to agree to treaties before he had to return to Rome. He failed in this, but his successors continued his policy, with as little success. He had done his best to avoid all-out war and had set up a situation in which it would still be possible to avoid it, if his successors' diplomatic skills were good enough. But it turned out that the decision was not in their hands.

## The Sicilian War

Caudex's report of his actions was made to the Senate in the autumn, which then had the winter to consider its options. The decision was that Rome would increase the stakes, sending both consuls, each with a full consular army – double the force Caudex had – to make war on their two enemies; the two consuls were clearly intended to attend to the two enemies separately, but they also sensibly worked together.[27] The active part of the campaign was led by M. Valerius Maximus, who invaded Syracusan territory. One town, Hadranon, was captured and sacked by Maximus; a second, Kenturipa, was besieged; both of these are on the Syracusan side of Mount Aetna but not really very close to the city.[28] The other consul, M'. Otacilius Crassus, has none of his exploits recorded, and we do not know what he was doing. The Carthaginians are said to have distributed their forces to hold various (unnamed) towns, so the most plausible assumption is that he was controlling the garrison in Messene and confronting whatever Carthaginian forces were still nearby, so allowing Maximus to polish off the Syracusan war first. There was still no Carthaginian war.

Diplomacy soon reaped much greater dividends than warfare. While Kenturipa was still under siege by Maximus' army, envoys began arriving from other cities in the island to see the consuls.[29] At least that is how the event is portrayed, but one wonders. For most Sicilian cities and their citizens – and their tyrants – the perception of Roman motivation and purposes and intentions can only have ranged from ignorance to fear. That the Roman army was assisting the Mamertines was something which could only strike fear into Sicilian hearts. A knowledge of Roman methods of warfare, based on stories of the conquest of central and southern Italy, was probably fairly widespread, for it had been the victor in a long series of brutal wars during the previous eighty years, and the fight against Pyrrhos was surely well known. The size of the Roman armies – at first twenty thousand men, then double that – was threatening and intimidating, indicating clearly that the Romans were going to stay and that all Sicily was their field of action.

The various Sicilian cities not involved so far might have felt they now faced a series of super-Mamertine raids by Roman forces. No doubt Carthage had had the tacit support of the other cities in garrisoning and so controlling the Mamertines, though only Syracuse appears to have provided actual support. Now the Roman army had taken the side of Mamertine Messene in the conflict and was fighting Syracuse. It was a large, violent, and threatening force – no doubt the expectation of loot was known – yet Rome was not a piratical state composed of semi-retired mercenaries. It was an organised and victorious city, and the ways to deal with a threat by such a city were to form an alliance to fight it, or to submit to it, or to ally with it. This last was clearly preferable – it was what Messene had done – and this was what the Sicilian cities now did.

Later Roman historians knew full well that by the end of the war all Sicily had become either Roman or Syracusan, so they assumed that the Sicilians were submitting to Rome. But in 263 the Sicilians could only assume that what the Roman army intended was a fight against Syracuse and possibly raids on the Mamertine pattern. There was therefore scope for diplomacy. Apart from Syracuse, the cities were generally weak, and their way to survival was to join the most powerful force around, which for the moment seemed to be Rome's; the cities would thereby neatly prevent any Roman raids. The Sicilian response was therefore the same as that of their Mamertine enemies, to shelter under the wing of the temporary winner.

During 263, therefore, most of the cities of Greek Sicily formed alliances with Rome.[30] Syracuse dominated the east of the island, and Carthage held her traditional section in the west and north. The centre of the island, some of the south, and Messene in the north-east were now allies of Rome. Hiero took the point and followed his fellow Greeks into contacting the consuls and making an alliance with Rome, though in his case the process was a treaty of peace. In what became a later avaricious Roman pattern he was sentenced to a fine of a hundred talents to be paid in instalments over fifteen years.[31] This was a minor inconvenience to such a rich city, and, in exchange, for that period Hiero would be under the protection of a powerful city. The contract was between Rome and Hiero as king, and therefore he had also gained a powerful protector for his position in Syracuse as king. It may have seemed a bargain made in heaven.[32]

At this point it would seem reasonable for the Carthaginians to make their own alliances with Sicilian cities or to contact the consuls and make peace. Their involvement in Messene had been aimed at suppressing the piratical mercenaries, an action probably precipitated by the unauthorised actions of the local commander in the Lipari Islands, now executed. Carthage had not been seriously damaged by the Roman success; indeed, as with the Greek cities, the Roman control of Messene could be welcomed, as an action by an old ally, a civilised city, and one which would preserve the freedom of navigation through the strait for all and suppress the Mamertine raids. The skirmishes between their forces clearly called for a treaty to resolve their differences.

No Carthaginian diplomatic initiative resulted, even though the situation clearly called for one. The reason was that Carthage was suffering from a problem of its own. The movement of the Greek cities of central Sicily to join the Roman side spilled over into the Carthaginian province. Segesta, Halikyai, and perhaps Makella, all cities under Carthaginian suzerainty, 'turned to the Romans', as did three smaller places; Tyndaris was just prevented from doing so when the Carthaginians imprisoned the most prominent citizens.[33] This was the real spark for the Romano-Carthaginian war; the clear threat of the collapse of its Sicilian dominion propelled Carthage into fighting Rome.

A Carthaginian force was approaching Syracuse to assist in its defence when the Roman-Syracusan peace treaty was agreed, so Carthage was quite serious and may well have contacted Hiero already by that point, but he chose the Roman side, as had so many other Sicilian rulers. The Carthaginian commander pulled back when he heard the news. When the Roman forces moved westwards they clashed with those of Carthage, by then not unexpectedly. Carthage replied with naval and military forces. And so the war, which had been confined to the north-east corner of the island, with minimal Carthaginian involvement, developed into the major conflict which was to last for more than twenty years. There is no sign that the Romans had instigated the attempted defections from the Carthaginian province, though it would not be surprising if they had; without them there would be no Carthaginian war and therefore no glory for the consuls and no loot for the soldiers. On the other hand, Carthage had done little or nothing to avoid the conflict; the war came because both cities willed it; it could have been avoided fairly easily by the use of some intelligent diplomacy; neither was prepared to make the attempt.

Thus it was only in 262, when the Roman armies began to fight Carthaginian forces, that the Romano-Carthaginian war began. The Roman takeover of Messene, the defeat of Syracuse, and the alliances with the Greek cities are best seen as extensions of the Roman actions in southern Italy, where a whole series of Greek cities, from Naples to Taras, had come under Roman control over the past sixty years or so. Until 262 it was not a Carthaginian war at all; it was a war between Rome and the Greek cities, most of which gave themselves up without fighting. In that war the main action had been diplomatic. There had been some fighting between the Roman army based at Messene and the Syracusan forces, but this soon ended in a compromise peace which left Hiero as king in Syracuse under Roman protection, just as, without fighting, many of the Greek cities of the island had come under Roman protection, as they might see it, as a way of avoiding Romano-Mamertine raids. The movement towards Rome in the Carthaginian part of the island threatened Carthage's position; to this Carthage had to react.

The war having changed, therefore, from one of Rome against a number of weak Greek cities to one of Rome against the more powerful Carthage, both of the principals being cities at a good distance from the fighting, there was much less scope for diplomacy. Neither Rome nor Carthage showed much interest in anything but military victory until, during the last decade or so of the fighting, Carthage tended to ignore events in Sicily. Only the invasion of Africa by the Roman forces under M. Atilius Regulus in 255 produced a moment of diplomacy. When he was initially successful, Regulus, the commander of the Roman forces in Africa, suggested negotiations to the Carthaginians. He then presented them with such harsh terms that the Carthaginians not only rejected them but began a serious process of military recruitment, with the result that Regulus was defeated and had to surrender.[34]

In its last years the war centred on interminable sieges of Lilybaion and Drepana. Carthage was pleased to let the Roman forces suffer hunger, exposure, and disease, while Hamilcar Barka used a small force to harry the Roman rear areas from a series of strongholds. In the end, such defensive tactics inevitably produced defeat. A Carthaginian relief fleet was beaten at the Aegates Islands, whereupon Hamilcar Barka was given full powers to treat for peace. He negotiated with Q. Lutatius Catulus, who, like Hamilcar, was concerned that his home city was close to exhaustion.

The story of the negotiation is as contaminated by Roman myth-making, exaggeration, and invention as other elements in the history of this war, but it is reasonably clear that both sides were under serious home pressure to conclude an agreement, though neither was prepared merely to submit to the other's demands. It was clear that Carthage had been defeated, in that it had lost control of almost all Sicily and had seen its fleet beaten, but its government had hardly been much concerned about the war for several years before the end. Hamilcar eventually accepted that the ancient Carthaginian foothold in western Sicily would have to be abandoned, a decision probably made on instructions from home; this had been Carthage's original reason for fighting, and once that was accepted the rest of the terms were straightforward: exchange of prisoners, surrendering Roman deserters (if Hamilcar still held any – there had been plenty of time for them to get away), and the payment of an indemnity.[35]

At this point a new Roman diplomatic tactic emerged to complicate matters. Catulus agreed to the terms, but they had then to be ratified by the Senate in Rome. Hamilcar had also been given powers to conclude a treaty, and his terms were probably ratified in the Carthaginian Senate without delay. (We can be sure that, if the Carthaginians had objected to the terms, they would have subsequently been accused of bad faith.) The Roman Senate, in the full knowledge that the enemy had relaxed his guard and was unwilling to resume the fighting, appointed ten commissioners to investigate the terms, with authority to impose new ones. This became a standard Roman ploy to screw even more out of an enemy than the initial negotiation had obtained. In this case the chief of the commissioners was Catulus' brother Q. Lutatius Cerco, who persuaded the Carthaginians to make minor concessions, just sufficient to pacify those senators who still wanted to go on fighting. The indemnity was increased and a clause added that Carthage should evacuate the islands between Sicily and Italy. In the context of 241, this meant the Lipari Islands, which had been an annoying Carthaginian naval base all through the war. The new agreement was finally ratified at Rome, and Hamilcar evacuated all the Sicilian bases.[36]

The diplomatic history of the war shows a whole list of missed opportunities on both sides, especially at the beginning. It would have been possible in 263–262, in the afterglow of the treaty with Hiero, for the Romans to make peace with Carthage. Carthage would retain its foothold in western Sicily, the continuation of the position of the last three centuries. But neither side had attempted to negotiate, nor did they do so until exhaustion stared Rome in the face.

158   *Diplomacy in the West*

It was Rome which insisted on going on fighting. Atilius Regulus' terms in 254 were unacceptable to Carthage, and he must have known it. Rome's main motivation for continuing for so long was for glory for its consular commanders, and the effect was to enhance the power of the Senate, which arrogated to itself the decision for peace and determined the terms of the treaty which ended the war. That the fighting was always outside Italy meant that the Romans could contemplate ravaging and looting foreign territory with greedy equanimity. Carthage more or less gave up the fight once Regulus' army was driven out from Africa and put more energy into expanding its control of the African interior than into fighting in Sicily, about which the city showed little concern. Hamilcar Barka's mission in Sicily was merely to keep the Romans busy, even though control of western Sicily had been the reason Carthage entered the war. Rome could have had peace at any time from 263 onwards but chose to go on fighting. There was no hope for diplomacy given that attitude.

## The Sardinian aftermath

Almost at once the peace was seen by Rome to be inadequate. Carthage descended into civil war between the citizens and the mercenaries whom the city had employed, and the soldiers in the garrison in Sardinia, a mixture of Italian, African, Spanish, and, no doubt, Sardinian mercenaries, took a leaf out of the Mamertines' book. They rebelled (or mutinied), seized control of the Carthaginian posts on the island, and then set about killing any Carthaginians they could find. When the fighting against the rebellious mercenaries in Africa died down, Carthage intended to recover control of Sardinia; the Sardinian rebels copied the Mamertines and appealed to Rome to take over. The first appeal was rejected, but the native Sardinians, exasperated by the mercenaries' violent conduct, rebelled against the rebels and drove them out. Some of them went to Italy and appealed again to Rome for assistance, this time to return them to their 'home'.[37] At that point Carthaginian envoys arrived at Rome to protest at possible Roman interference and to insist that Sardinia was Carthaginian.

By this time control of the island was thoroughly uncertain. Many Carthaginians had been killed by the rebel soldiers, who had themselves then been largely expelled by the Sardinians. The new Carthaginian expedition to recover the island could thus be said to be directed at an independent region. Sardinian independence, of course, would suit Rome very well but was unlikely to survive any Carthaginian expedition. The prospect of a victorious Carthaginian force established in Sardinian harbours was disquieting, and Rome decided to intervene. The Carthaginian envoys were informed that, according to the treaty of 241, Sardinia was one of the islands 'between Sicily and Italy' and that it should therefore be abandoned by Carthage. To reinforce the message war was formally declared, and a Roman expedition was sent to seize the island. Carthage, much damaged by the recent Mercenaries' War and probably unable to recruit more troops for the moment, was in no state to fight a new war against Rome; it necessarily succumbed to the Roman demands and agreed in a new treaty that the island should be Roman and to pay another indemnity.[38] (The original Roman indemnity of 1,000 talents had now grown to 3,200.) This is, of course, a classic exercise in power, taking advantage of an enemy *in extremis*. Polybios did not like it, but his opinion on Roman methods is erratic. One can see Rome's point of view and applaud the timing of its action, if not perhaps the brutality of the move.

Had Rome calculated the best way of ensuring Carthage's long-term hatred, however, it is difficult to think of an action more likely to achieve it. Directly after the Sardinian 'War' Hamilcar Barka went off to Spain to build a new Carthaginian empire – in order to collect funds to pay off the Roman indemnity, so he blandly claimed to a Roman envoy later.[39] The Sardinian crisis was solved by diplomatic browbeating, but it only engendered further warfare, first in Spain, then throughout the western Mediterranean.

In the long crisis between Rome and Carthage from 264 to 238, diplomacy figured as a serious element only at the beginning and the end. At the start Roman diplomacy was essentially a continuation of the various negotiations which had involved Rome, the Mamertines, Hiero, and Carthage since 270. In this process, the weaker participants, Hiero and the Mamertines, were sidelined into alliances with Rome, so that the problem became a war between the two great powers. After these early diplomatic passages neither side showed much interest in any diplomacy except in extreme circumstances. In the end even Rome was exhausted, while Carthage had successfully delayed defeat by the tactics employed by Hamilcar Barka until Rome could admit the need for a treaty. The agreement between Catulus and Hamilcar in 241, even when it had been modified by the Roman commissioners at the insistence of the Senate, was actually a compromise peace, though one in which Carthage had clearly suffered defeat.

Had Carthage been able to control its mercenaries, the issue of Sardinia would not have arisen, but once it came to Roman attention the Senate took the opportunity to expand the terms of the treaty of 241 to secure the island. It must have seemed, to those Romans familiar with Carthaginian methods in Sicily, to be a new threat. The island had fortified harbours which could be as tough to tackle as Lilybaion and Drepana. Roman methods, of course, were deeply unpleasant, especially to the victims, but to Rome they were manifestly very successful.[40]

## Notes

1. Polybios 3.25.2–5; Livy, *Per.* 13.
2. For these treaties before 279/278 see *CAH* (2) VII, part 2, 517–537; I am here concerned here with relations between the two cities in the Hellenistic period.
3. Pliny, *NH* 3.57–58 (from Kleitarchos, *FGrH* 137, F 31); Arrian, *Anabasis* 7.15.5–6; see A.B. Bosworth, *Conquest and Empire*, Cambridge 1988, 167, for a discussion of this embassy's likelihood.
4. Arrian, *Anabasis* 2.24.5.
5. Diodoros 22.7.5.
6. Plutarch, *Pyrrhos* 23.2.
7. Livy, *Per.* 14; Cassius Dio, fr. 43/Zonaras 8.2.
8. Plutarch, *Pyrrhos* 28.
9. See the summary in J.F. Lazenby, *The First Punic War*, London 1996, 1–10, for a succinct and clear consideration of this problem.
10. Diodoros 21.18.1–2.

160   *Diplomacy in the West*

11 Polybios 1.7.1-5; sources on the Mamertines are universally hostile; the story of their killing Messanans and appropriating their wives and property may be no more than an assumption; this was what was expected of mercenaries; it may thus be significant that nothing is ever heard of any suggestion of restoration.
12 Zonaras 8.6; B.D. Hoyos, 'The Rise of Hieron II: Chronology and Campaigns, 275-264 BC', *Antichthon* 19, 1985, 32-56.
13 Diodoros 22.13.7.
14 Polybios 1.9.8; Diodoros 22.13.2-4.
15 Diodoros 22.13.7-8.
16 Polybios 1.10.1.
17 Polybios 1.10.3-11.2.
18 Discussion of the Roman decision: J.W. Rich, *Declaring War in the Roman Republic in a Period of Transmarine Expansion*, Brussels 1976, 120-122; H.H. Scullard, *CAH*, vol. 7, 2nd ed., part 2, 540-543; W.V. Harris, *War and Imperialism in Republican Rome, 327-70 BC*, Oxford 1979, 182-190, for Roman purposes; A.M. Eckstein, *Senate and General*, California 1987, 74-93; Lazenby, *First Punic War*, ch 3; all these and other accounts, however, operate from the standpoint of Rome, or of source-criticism: the origin of the problem was in Messana, and this needs to be the starting point.
19 Polybios 1.11.4.
20 Polybios 1.11.2 and 4.
21 Unless this is a mere assumption by Polybios, based on Roman behaviour in his own time.
22 Polybios 1.11.7; Diodoros 23.1.2.
23 Eckstein, *Senate and General* 79, claims that Carthage's involvement was 'totally unexpected'. This cannot be right, given the Roman knowledge of the general situation, the city's joint history with both Carthage and Syracuse in the past, and, above all, the information which the Mamertine delegation brought on their appeal for Roman help. What was unexpected was that the result was a long war.
24 Polybios 1.11.9; Diodoros 23.2.1.
25 If Campania was the original home for many of the Mamertines it may be that some of them at least were Roman citizens; some were surely originally citizens of Campanian cities allied with Rome.
26 Polybios 1.11.10-12.3; Zonaras 8.9; Cassius Dio 11.12.
27 Polybios 1.16.1; Diodoros 23.4.1; Zonaras 8.9.
28 Diodoros 23.4.1.
29 Polybios 1.16.2; Diodoros 23.4.1.
30 Polybios 16.3; Diodoros 23.4; Pliny, *NH* 7.214; Eutropius 2.19.1.
31 Diodoros 23.4.1.
32 The contract between Rome and Hiero was renewed until his death; at that point conflict between the cities broke out again.
33 Diodoros 23.5.
34 Polybios 1.31.4-8.
35 Polybios 1.62.3-62.9.
36 Polybios 1.63.1-5.
37 Polybios 1.79.1-5.
38 Polybios 1.88.8-12.
39 Cassius Dio 12.48.
40 Polybios 1.1.8-12.

# 9 The diplomacy of Rome and Carthage – II

It seems reasonable to conclude from the material studied in the previous chapter that Roman diplomatic-military-naval priorities changed during the long first war with Carthage. That war, it is well to remember, lasted twenty-three years, long enough for a whole generation in Rome to come to maturity in its shadow and to believe that diplomatic problems were best solved militarily. This was clearly the reaction of the Senate in the Sardinian crisis, but by the end of the 230s diplomacy was being used again. As with Ap. Claudius Caudex in Messene, however, it was backed up by visible or implied armed force; this became the preferred Roman negotiating method, as demonstrated in two crises over Illyria, which resulted in the extension of Roman control over the Ionian Sea.

## The First Illyrian War

The First Romano-Illyrian War (228–228) has contradictory sources, Polybius and Appian, which makes it very difficult to follow what happened, but the result of the fighting was a negotiated treaty. One consul, A. Postumius, remained in Illyria after the main Roman forces had been withdrawn and organised several cities and tribes as Roman allies; these are listed as Kerkyra, Epidamnos, Apollonia, Pharos, Issa, the Parthini, and the Atintani; as part of the peace process the Illyrian queen Teuta, who had been the major enemy in the war, also became a Roman ally.[1]

This set of communities constituted a virtual Roman province. How actively the Romans governed the area is unclear, though officials were later stationed in some of the cities. The usual term used nowadays is that it was a 'protectorate', which seems more or less accurate. The whole affair had been as much a diplomatic campaign as a military, and the Romans had been concerned to gather local allies even more than to defeat Teuta's forces, suggesting that the campaign against her had been no more than an excuse to mount an expedition to the region. Further, Postumius sent envoys into Greece to announce the result of the campaign to the Aitolians and the Achaians, who had also been victims of Illyrian 'piracy'. Other envoys were sent by the Senate to convey the same information to Athens and Corinth.[2] All this makes the point of the new Roman presence and amounted to a warning to the Greeks to keep out of the region. There is no sign that the Aitolians and Achaians were annoyed at what might be seen as a Roman intrusion in their sphere of interest. They were probably relieved at not having to bother with the Illyrian threat any more.

The four Greek states were judiciously chosen: the two main leagues and the two greatest cities. The Roman expedition had come very close to Macedon while that kingdom was in the midst of a difficult succession crisis, and all four of the Greek states contacted by Postumius were in some way enemies of Macedon – Athens had just broken away and was huddling under the protection of Ptolemy by the time the Roman envoys arrived (see Chapter 6). It seems clear that Rome fully understood the diplomatic situation in Greece and that Macedon was already identified as a possible enemy, perhaps because it was feared that the kingdom might involve itself in the Illyrian campaign.

The strategic importance of Kerkyra, one of the elements of the new Roman region, had been clear for centuries, and in the last half-century the island city had been repeatedly seized by ambitious rulers whose policy had been to dominate the Ionian Sea. Kassandros, Demetrios, Agathokles, and Pyrrhos had all taken control of the island for shorter or longer periods – Rome was only the latest to do so. The string of islands south of Kerkyra – Kephallonia, Leukas, and so on – were also under contention, and the Aitolians had made attempts there. Since the Romans had fought Pyrrhos and their ships were evidently familiar with Kerkyra, it was clearly a sensitive place. The overall strategic result of this Illyrian war was to expand Roman control over the Ionian Sea coasts still further. After 228 only Syracuse and the eastern Sicilian coast and the Greek coast and islands south of Kerkyra were not under Roman control in one way or another, and Syracuse was an independent ally.

Most of this Roman expansion was accomplished by diplomacy, backed up by the large force sent in the ships, the same technique as that used at Messene by Caudex. This time it had a quick result and did not produce an interminable war. So the method could be used with success, given a skilful diplomat in command.

The Romans were also fortunate in their timing. The expanded Illyrian kingdom which the Romans had fought was allied with Macedon, making a potentially solid political block from the Adriatic coast to Thrace. However, in 229 King Demetrios II of Macedon was killed in battle; when the Roman expedition arrived off Illyria Macedon was in the midst of its succession crisis, for Demetrios' successor was his seven-year-old son Philip V. By the time the Macedonians had recovered their balance, the Romans had completed their war.

Postumius knew this, as did the Senate, and both were fully aware of the wider situation, as the messages to the Greeks show. So it was only to the Greek enemies of Macedon that the messages of the new Roman alliance, or protectorate, were sent. This helps to explain the apparently unnecessary size of the Roman expeditionary force, for it might have been necessary to fight Macedon as well as Illyria. Atintania, which controlled access to Macedon by the Aous Pass from the west, and which Teuta had secured from the Epeirotes, was included in this protectorate, thus separating these Balkan allies.

## Spain

The possibility of a Roman embassy being sent to interview Hamilcar Barka in Spain in 231 is now considered unlikely,[3] but only five years later an investigation of the extent of Carthaginian power in Spain was certainly made. By the early 220s both Carthage and Rome were advancing their frontiers, with far-reaching effects: the Roman conquest of northern Italy had stirred up the Gauls of that region and in southern Gaul; the Carthaginian conquests in southern and central Spain had had much the same effect in the rest of Spain. In combination these advances and conquests meant that from the Atlantic to the Alps and the Danube the peoples outside these empires were disturbed and apprehensive.

The Roman Senate apparently considered that both the Gauls and the Carthaginians were likely enemies. The city of Massalia in southern Gaul had long been on friendly terms with Rome; at some time in the third century it became a formal ally by treaty, and it may be through Massalia, which had several trading posts along the Spanish coast, that Rome was kept informed of Carthaginian progress in Spain. Hamilcar Barka died in 229, and his place was taken by his son-in-law Hasdrubal, who had been acclaimed as commander by the army and then confirmed in his command by the Carthaginian Senate. His position was thus even more independent of his home city than that of Hamilcar, and the Romans treated him very much as a near-independent ruler.

In about 226 a Roman delegation went to Spain, contacted Hasdrubal, and came back with a vague agreement that he would not cross a river which Polybios calls the Iber – probably the Ebro. Since he was by that time campaigning nowhere near the Ebro, Hasdrubal was no doubt happy to oblige the Romans,[4] but this cannot be regarded as a formal treaty. Such an agreement would need to be ratified by the Senates of both cities, and both either denied that this had happened or evaded discussing it. It was clearly deniable by both sides, though this does not remove its effectiveness at the time. The Romans later tended to refer to it as a treaty, but it was convenient for them to do so, since they could then claim that the Carthaginians were violating it; equally it was convenient for Carthage to deny that it had been ratified. At the time Rome could be reasonably confident that Hasdrubal had little interest in assisting the Gauls who were gearing up for an invasion of Roman Italy. (This came next year, 225, and was comprehensively defeated; contingents from beyond the Alps were present with the Cisalpine Gallic invaders.)

Whether the agreement can be seen as a treaty or not, it expired with Hasdrubal's death in 221, since it had been personal to him. By this time the Barkid family was effectively the hereditary rulers of Carthaginian Spain. Hasdrubal's successor, Hannibal, was Hamilcar's son, and he continued the Carthaginian campaigns, which by this time really were approaching the Ebro River. A major block on his progress was the city of Saguntum, controlling a substantial and fertile plain on the Mediterranean coast south of the Ebro. Being threatened, the city appealed to the one major power in the western Mediterranean who might help, Rome.[5]

This was the same reaction as the Mamertines and the Sardinian mutineers; it was presumably well understood by now that Rome would be sympathetic to any city volunteering to submit itself – as recently demonstrated also in Illyria. This contact involved a delegation of Saguntine envoys who travelled to Rome to appeal in person to the Senate, which sent its own delegation to interview Hannibal at Carthago Nova. This is presumably the first time Hannibal appreciated that the Saguntines had contacted Rome. When the Roman envoys interviewed him, Hannibal accused them of putting to death some leading citizens of Saguntum and claimed that at Carthage it was 'a hereditary trust . . . not to overlook any victim of injustice',[6] which was as specious a claim as any diplomat ever made. But one wonders if Hannibal had heard of a similar Roman claim in Illyria and was throwing it back in the envoys' faces.

The appeal to Rome by the Saguntines might indicate that some earlier alliance agreement had been made between the two cities. If the 'Ebro treaty' referred to the Ebro River, then Rome had in effect given the Carthaginians *carte blanche* to expand as far as that line – though how such an arrogant presumption was taken by Hasdrubal is not known – in which case Saguntum was in the Carthaginian sphere; but the Ebro treaty, if such it was, had expired with Hasdrubal's death, so that 'boundary agreement' no longer applied. If there was an alliance between Rome and Saguntum it was concluded either before 226 (the date of the Ebro treaty), and should therefore have been pointed out to the Carthaginians, or after Hasdrubal's death in 221. In either case it had been incumbent on Rome to notify Carthage and on the Carthaginians to inform Hasdrubal and Hannibal of its existence. In fact it is surely likely that both men knew of the alliance – if it existed. When Hannibal attacked the city, therefore, he assumed either that the alliance was defunct or that Rome would not react.

## Illyria again

In the meantime another crisis had developed in Illyria. One of those who had benefited from the Roman campaign in 229 was Demetrios of Pharos, who had been set up by the Romans in a principality of his own, no doubt with the aim of dividing Illyrian allegiances. He began to repeat Teuta's campaigns, which Rome interpreted as his having broken the peace treaty of 228, though that had been an agreement between Rome and Teuta, and since then she had either died or had abdicated. Demetrios had taken her place as regent for the child King Pinnes, so he was not bound by Teuta's treaty (unless the treaty was made in Pinnes' name, which seems unlikely). When he began raiding, the Romans had to slap him down, which they did by a relatively small expedition in 219.[7] It was the same situation as in Spain, where Hasdrubal's death in 221 ended whatever agreement he had made with Rome a few years before. Hence the new Roman embassy to his successor.

## Spain again, and the failure of diplomacy

Understanding the events in Spain is bedevilled by later Roman justifications and quite possibly by contemporary ignorance of Spanish geography. By muddling the geographical situation of Saguntum in relation to the Ebro River, a case can be made that Hannibal was breaking Hasdrubal's treaty, but this also draws attention to Roman deviousness. This interpretation was hardly necessary, since the treaty, if it was such, no longer applied, though it clearly suited Rome to claim that it did.

The muddle is not just in the sources but was probably part of the crisis as a whole, in that no one seems to have understood the precise status of Saguntum, nor the powers and status of Hannibal. As a young man newly assuming power, he had to demonstrate success in order to consolidate his position. Neither Rome nor Carthage wanted a new war, as is shown by their repeated attempts to create a settlement, but both cities were apprehensive that the other did. The confusion of power and motives made it impossible for any diplomatic efforts to succeed.

It seems probable that the Roman claim that Saguntum was under its protection was only revealed to Hannibal after he had begun his attack; and one must also have doubts as to the longevity of that protection. Further, whereas Hannibal may well have been attacking the city to prove himself, it was impossible for Carthage to disown him, and it seems evident that it was Rome's intention to stop any further Carthaginian advance in Spain.

Both principals appealed to Carthage, Hannibal for instructions, or perhaps to ensure the city's support,[8] and the Romans to complain or to warn. Roman envoys went to Spain to tell Hannibal that they regarded Saguntum as their ally. The Roman embassy to Carthage is poorly authenticated, but the situation really requires it, if only for the Romans to discover to what extent Hannibal had support at Carthage. There is a suggestion that the Carthaginian Senate was divided on the issue, which would not be surprising. Hannibal, in the midst of his siege, ignored the Roman warning and was supported by Carthage (which may not have been able to stop him). He eventually captured the city; Rome did nothing to assist its 'ally'.[9]

The Roman reaction was to take the problem back to Carthage, where a Roman delegation enquired as to whether Hannibal had authority from Carthage for what he was doing, a question designed to separate the city from its general. This was a distinct problem for the Carthaginians, since it was clear that for the past fifteen years at least they had exercised little control over what was going on in Spain, yet at the same time they could scarcely disavow Hannibal. He represented Carthage's best chance of building a land empire to replace that lost twenty years before and for gaining revenge on Rome, if that became Carthaginian policy – and this was surely the wish of a substantial number of Carthaginians. The answer from the Carthaginian Senate was therefore obfuscatingly ambiguous, which Rome could only assume was an attempt to delay any further action, so allowing Hannibal to make further gains.[10]

The whole episode is an example of diplomacy completely failing to deal with a complex situation. It cannot have helped that there were three well-separated authorities involved – four, if Saguntum counts – but the real problem was the general confusion and the contradictory understandings. It does seem that no amount of diplomacy could have solved the problem. The decisive event was not Hannibal in Spain but the visit of the Roman delegation to Carthage, which was clearly intended to provoke a Carthaginian response, either to deny that Hannibal was their agent or to confirm it. Once the Carthaginians – who were scarcely given the opportunity to consult with Hannibal – accepted responsibility for Hannibal's actions, the final Roman embassy declared war.[11]

## Hannibal's war

Hannibal seized the military initiative, but only by moving rather faster than the Romans, who appear to have assumed that the war would be easy.[12] Roman invasions of both Spain and Africa were planned, but Hannibal's march into southern Gaul compelled them to turn both armies about. His invasion of Italy was accompanied by a series of diplomatic initiatives which gradually widened the war into one which involved all the powers of the central and western Mediterranean. On his march into northern Italy he made contact with several of the Gallic tribes in the Po Valley which had recently been subjected to a Roman conquest and did not like it. They became his allies and provided him with troops.[13] This Gallic rising against Roman authority effectively returned the Cisalpine Gauls to independence. Hannibal marched into peninsular Italy, repeatedly defeating Roman armies, and in 215 he extended his diplomatic range into neighbouring states.[14]

The impressive series of victories by Hannibal's army convinced several states, in and out of Italy, that he was winning (just as in Sicily in 263 the Romans' victories convinced many Sicilian cities to join the winning side), and he was able to secure several more allies, so his victories led to the collapse of the Roman position in much of southern Italy.[15] The great Campanian city of Capua defected from the Roman alliance, moved into independence, and then made an alliance with Hannibal;[16] it was joined by Atella and Calatia, but not by other Campanian cities. He was also contacted by an envoy from Philip V of Macedon, with whom he made an alliance, though the capture of Philip's envoy meant that another envoy had to be sent to get a copy of the agreement.[17] Then he was contacted by the new regime at Syracuse, where the old pro-Roman King Hiero had died. His successor, his grandson Hieronymos, adopted an anti-Roman stance, in part by being reminded of the ambitions of Pyrrhos to build an Ionian Sea empire; with the disintegration of the Roman position in south Italy and the earlier break-up of the Epeirote kingdom, this may have seemed possible once more.

Hieronymos in fact had first contacted Carthage, and only then Hannibal, with the result that Hannibal's proposals undercut the negotiations in Carthage. Two Syracusan exiles in Hannibal's service were sent from Italy to Syracuse to propose that alliance.[18] In this case the proposal was less than successful in that Hieronymos was assassinated the next year.[19] The Roman reaction to the bids for independence by both Capua and Syracuse was to attack, and Hannibal's limitations were thus exposed, for he was quite unable to break either siege.

The Roman answer to the alliance between Philip and Hannibal was equally blunt and simple, though in this case the method was mainly diplomatic. When King Philip V of Macedon invaded Illyria (where he had friends) and came too near to success, a delegation went to Greece and successfully persuaded Philip's enemies there, notably the Aitolian League (already contacted after the First Illyrian War), to attack him.[20] Both sides, therefore, made carefully targeted diplomatic moves to widen the war. Major Roman armies were employed for two years in the sieges of Capua and Syracuse, and those armies were not available for service elsewhere in Italy, which was the main area of warfare – yet in Italy Hannibal was pinned down by still more Roman forces. A diplomatic initiative and the commitment of a few ships by Rome prevented Philip from mounting an intervention in Italy by first preventing his conquest of the ports in Illyria and then by distracting him into a new war in Greece. The prospect of a major Macedonian army operating alongside Hannibal's forces would have been very frightening to the Romans.

A mixture of fighting and diplomacy also marked the conduct of the war in Spain. Alliances were negotiated with a series of Spanish tribes, which meant doing to the Carthaginians in Spain what Hannibal was doing to Rome in Italy, since most of the relevant communities had been part of the Carthaginian sphere. However, only with the capture of the Carthaginian capital of Carthago Nova in 209 did a decisive shift in Spanish preferences come about. This happened among the Edetani and the Ilergetes to begin with,[21] then, after the victory of Scipio Africanus at Baecula, more tribes in the south joined the Roman side, by which time joining Rome was a sensible defensive move.[22] Since the Carthaginian army included recruits from Africa, Scipio extended his diplomacy there, visiting the Numidian King Syphax in his city, and made a useful contact.[23] (His visit coincided with that of the Carthaginian diplomat Hasdrubal Gisgo; since both men wanted Syphax's alliance, they refrained from attacking each other's ships in Syphax's harbour.) Scipio's immediate aim was to rouse the Numidian king against Carthage; in this he failed, but later he was able to use Syphax's rival Massinissa to overthrow him, which made Massinissa a firm ally when Scipio led the invasion of Africa in 205.

The diplomatic moves by both sides, therefore, had the overall effect of expanding the war geographically and extending it in time. Without support from his allies, it seems unlikely Hannibal would have lasted as long as he did in Italy, and Rome's allies in Spain and Greece prevented help reaching him in the crucial years when the military conflict in Italy was most precariously balanced. Hannibal's diplomatic moves came in two stages, first to detach Roman allies and subjects in Italy, then, when this was only partly successful, to extend the war to other regions (Greece, Sicily, Sardinia), though it is noticeable that the initiative of these extensions came not from Hannibal or Carthage, but from the others – Philip V, Hieronymos in Syracuse, the Sardinians. His own aim, of course, was to divide and distract the numerous Roman forces he faced – his recognition that he could not win the war without help. This was something he had realised from the start: Roman military strength in Italy was far too great. In effect Carthage was losing the war from 215 onwards, and the alliances which Hannibal's diplomats arranged only delayed the inevitable; those arranged by Roman envoys and officials were decisive in preventing Hannibal turning the stalemate into success.

It was Roman practice, at Messene in 264, in Illyria in 229 and 219, and in 218 in Spain and Africa, to use diplomacy both to investigate a situation and to threaten. When the moment for action arrived, overwhelming force was applied. This had worked at Messene and in Illyria, where in both cases the arrival of a large

Roman army had induced a number of smaller powers to join the Roman alliance quickly, so providing a firm geographic and political base from which to operate. But in both cases it had also provoked a wider confrontation. Had a small Roman force taken over in Messene in 264, just large enough to control the Mamertines and to suppress their raids, it is very probable that Hiero and Carthage would have been content, and the First Romano-Carthaginian War would not have happened. But the presence of twenty thousand Roman troops was clearly too great a force to simply establish control over the Mamertines – hence the quick alliances with the Greek cities, out of fear, including Syracuse, but hence also the immediate enmity of Carthage, whose presence in Sicily was thereby threatened by the potential defection of some of its cities.

Again, in Illyria, the rescue of Kerkyra and the other Greek cities did not require an armada and a double consular army. Teuta was well aware of Roman power, and she would no doubt have subsided had the cities merely received protective Roman garrisons. But 22,000 soldiers in two hundred ships was inappropriate to the Epeirote situation and meant that another target was probably in Rome's sights. It may have been Macedon, Teuta's ally, but in the first place it was aimed at the Illyrian kingdom. And so the Romans had to fight a difficult war in a difficult country and then make a compromise peace (and had to send another expedition ten years later). No doubt the Macedonians took due note; it is no accident that Philip V in his Roman war aimed first of all to gain control of Illyria and its ports; for him this was both a defensive and an offensive preparation. He took advantage of Rome's preoccupation with Hannibal's invasion, just as Rome took advantage of the Macedonian succession crisis in 229–228.

So the attempts to back up diplomacy with a great military force might solve the immediate problem, but it was likely that it would also lead on to greater wars. This was not how Romans saw it, and in 218 the same pattern was attempted, with two huge armies aimed squarely at the centres of Carthaginian power: 26,000 men for Africa and 24,000 for Spain. This followed up the usual diplomatic preparation, in both lands, and the use of local allies in Spain at Saguntum and the Massalian trading posts. But the combination failed again; the preparations only alerted the enemy to the threat, for, if Rome did not realise that the method was counter-productive, its victims certainly recognised the pattern. The Carthaginians made their counter-plans, and the arrival of Hannibal in Cisalpina turned the tables; his arrival prevented Scipio's large army from going to Spain (though part was sent on, to hover more or less uselessly in the north-east for several years); by his victories and his diplomacy he attracted allies, and his army destroyed Roman armies in battles. It was the reverse of the Roman method, but on a now-devastating scale.

## The appeal of Rome

It is worth noting here, since conditions changed later, that many of the Greek cities of Sicily and the Adriatic and Ionian Sea coasts quickly, even eagerly, accepted Roman protection. Partly this was because they were threatened by others – Syracuse, Carthage, the Illyrians, Macedon – but the Roman state was just as alien to these Greek city states as Carthage and the Illyrians, while Syracuse was a rich and renowned Greek city; also Rome was just as imperialistic as any of its competitors. It is worth wondering, therefore, why these Greek cities were so willing to put themselves under Roman power. (This willingness extended also into old Greece; by 200 Athens and Rhodes were keen to do the same, if for their own reasons, as were several cities along the Asia Minor coast.)

The answer must be that Rome appeared to be more sympathetic towards the life of Greek cities, including their insistence on autonomy, than its competitors. In Illyria the several cities which were gathered into the pseudo-province of Illyria all retained their autonomy, the right to coin money and collect their own taxes, and were subject to only the lightest of Roman supervision and control. (In other words, Rome was applying the century-old prescription laid out by Antigonos Monophthalamos at Tyre, which is summarised by the slogan 'the freedom of the Greeks' (Chapter 1), and which had been so honoured in the breach by him and his successor kings.) Similarly in Sicily, many of the cities which came into the Roman alliance in 263 retained their status as free and autonomous communities for centuries. This was in many ways the ideal of Greek civic freedom in the Hellenistic period: autonomy with protection. The system was instituted by diplomatic agreements between Rome and the individual cities. This had, of course, been Rome's method in developing its Italian 'commonwealth', and it proved to be applicable elsewhere. Few of these agreements are recorded, but it is clear that they existed, to such an extent that model agreements could be applied when new allies joined the system.

The reverse of the coin was the inimical attitude of many of the Italian communities, particularly in the south. These had long been under Greek political and cultural influence, and most of them had been conquered with some brutality by Rome – Lucanians, Samnites, Bruttians. These had taken the opportunity of Hannibal's victories to remove themselves from Roman control, and of course they suffered for it with Rome's eventual victory. Note also the similarly inimical behaviour of the major Greek cities of the south – Capua, Tarentum, and Syracuse all fought hard to avoid Roman control. The attitude of Roman subjects thus varied with their original treatment – those who volunteered stayed loyal, those who were conquered were liable to rebel. Diplomacy was thus more successful than force.

## The end of Hannibal's war

Diplomacy in the war last stages of the war was not a priority. With a Roman victory clearly likely after about 210 and a certainty after the defeat of Hannibal's brother Hasdrubal at the Metaurus River in 207, there was no need for Rome to look for compromise in its conquests. The defeated south Italians were crushed and their lands confiscated to the Roman state; Capua and Syracuse and Tarentum were conquered. Only at the end, in Greece and in Africa, were there meaningful negotiations to convert war into peace.

The failure of Roman forces to provide any serious help to their Aitolian ally in the war with Philip V led the Aitolians to open negotiations for peace in 206.

The Roman commander in Illyria, P. Sempronius Tuditanus, insisted that the terms of the alliance required that no separate peace was permissible, but the Aitolians rejected that interpretation. Only after the Aitolians and Philip had made peace did Rome send a major reinforcement to Illyria, and with that as backup Tuditanus himself made peace with Macedon, on the basis that Philip kept the territory he had conquered, which had been part of the Illyrian province before the war.[24]

The situation in Africa was not wholly dissimilar. The Senate had proved to be as reluctant to send an invasion force into Africa as it had been to reinforce the army in Illyria. The expedition commanded by P. Cornelius Scipio was therefore in part a private venture, the manpower consisting of his consular army reinforced by large numbers of volunteers. He had a hard fight of it, mixing negotiations with fighting, but only after the defeat of Hannibal's army at Zama were negotiations successful. Scipio had to cope with domestic opposition in Rome and faced the prospect of a long and difficult siege of Carthage, which would further stimulate that opposition. At the same time, it was clear to most in Carthage that such a siege would eventually succeed. A compromise peace, based on the Roman victory, was indicated. Carthage retained its autonomy, but lost control of its overseas territories, all of which had been conquered; it was to surrender Roman deserters, weapons, war elephants, and warships and pay an indemnity of 10,000 talents spread over 50 years. Despite opposition in both Rome (looking for harsher terms) and Carthage (looking to fight on) these terms were agreed by both Senates.[25] Their similarity to those of 241 is obvious.

## The end for Carthage

One result of Hannibal's War was Roman political paranoia concerning Carthage. Even in defeat, its empire stripped away, the African city remained a constant worry to the Roman Senate. Repeated Roman missions went to Africa over the next fifty years to investigate conditions there. These missions could hardly be called exercises in diplomacy; they were intended to interfere and intimidate, but this effect wore off as Carthage recovered. It was this paranoia at Rome which brought Carthage to destruction in 149–146.

The destruction of Carthage in some way was the Roman intention from the start in the third war, though the aim was originally to accomplish this by forceful diplomacy, intimidation, and deceit rather than by fighting; in the end, however, the old pattern asserted itself. The problem was seen to be the increase in Carthaginian wealth, the fundamental of power. The deadline was the year 151, when the last instalment of the indemnity imposed at the end of the second war was due to be paid. This would, at least in Carthaginian eyes, release the city from any political dependence on Rome. The spark which would set fire to the well-laid kindling was the continuing hostility between Carthage and its neighbour, the Numidian kingdom of King Massinissa, who was a firm ally of Rome. He had steadily chipped away at Carthage's territory for fifty years, and each time, when Carthage had appealed to Rome, Rome had taken Massinissa's side – he based his aggression on one of the terms of Scipio's treaty. No wonder Carthage seethed with resentment; it was all too reminiscent of the Sardinian crisis.[26]

Massinissa made a new demand on Carthage in 151, and this time Carthage resisted forcefully.[27] This was the decisive moment for Rome; diplomatic contacts with Carthage required the city to desist.[28] The Senate was not unanimous on the policy – it was never unanimous on any policy – but at least it accepted that neither Massinissa nor Carthage could be permitted to be victorious – since this would result in the unification of North Africa, forming a real threat to Roman power under whoever carried out the unification. An alliance was made with Utica, a member of the Carthaginian state (which was a federation rather like that of Rome in Italy); the city was also Carthage's competitor. Utica surrendered in timely fashion, presumably by pre-arrangement with Rome.[29]

A preliminary Roman threat persuaded the Carthaginian Senate to surrender three hundred hostages – young men, children largely of the senators themselves – who were housed at Rome. Then an army was sent, commanded by both consuls of the year, to present Rome's further demands. In discussion with the Carthaginian envoys these demands gradually escalated, undoubtedly by design. First, the envoys were intimidated by being forced to approach an audience with the consuls through the whole Roman army drawn up on parade, which produced a certain degree of submission; second, the city was disarmed by being forced to surrender all weapons and armour, and ships; then the crucial element was announced – the removal of the citizens to a new site or sites at least ten miles from the sea. The physical city of Carthage was to be destroyed, except for the temples and the necropolis; the dispersal of the population amounted to its political destruction as a community. The Carthaginian state was to be changed from a commercial city to a set of agricultural ones.[30]

The Roman consuls, who between them had little military, and no diplomatic, experience, in delivering these instructions had omitted one crucial detail – they might have disarmed the city but they had not secured its walls and gates. Carthaginian outrage at their terms translated into defiance; the gates were shut. The result was a war which lasted for three years. Once again forceful diplomacy, dominating and frightening the enemy, and the presence of a large and intimidatory army, had led Rome into an entirely unnecessary war.

Both sides employed diplomacy to advance their cases during the fighting, the Romans more successfully than their enemies. The city of Carthage was besieged, but for some time supplies could be brought in, mainly by sea, and diplomats were able to get out on their missions. Carthaginian envoys made contact with the king of the Mauri in modern Morocco, and with the insurgent, and temporary, king of Macedon, Andriskos (Philip VI), but neither would or could help.[31] Rome at first disdained help when Massinissa offered it, but after he died, in 148, Numidian forces were accepted;[32] at least one Hellenistic city, Side in Pamphylia, sent ships to help with the blockade;[33] perhaps others did as well. It was always possible for disillusioned Carthaginians to get out of the city, desert, and be accepted into the Roman forces. (At least nine hundred Roman soldiers went the other way.)

With a great deal of effort, Carthage was eventually stormed. And yet, even after all the fighting and the physical occupation of the city's ruins by Roman soldiers, the end eventually came not by a battle but by negotiation. It was clear that the

Roman forces could kill the last Carthaginians and were quite prepared to do so, and large parts of the city had already been destroyed in the fighting. Yet this final massacre would also inevitably cost a large number of Roman lives. The Carthaginian survivors negotiated surrender, which amounted to enslavement but not death.[34] Some refused even this, and the nine hundred deserters from the Roman forces, to whom no mercy would ever be shown, also defied Rome to the last; these either committed suicide or were killed in a final fight. Some Carthaginians had already surrendered before the end – these are termed, of course, deserters – and they were resettled outside the bounds of the old city, which really was destroyed physically, a curse being laid on any who later lived on the site. The territory which had been Carthage was annexed to the Roman Republic and was to be governed in future by a Roman praetor.

## Notes

1. Polybios 2.12.3; on this, and the Second Illyrian War, see S.I. Oost, *Roman Policy in Epirus and Acarnania in the Age of Roman Conquest*, Dallas, TX 1954.
2. Polybios 2.11.4 and 8.
3. Cassius Dio, frag. 48; H.H. Scullard, 'The Carthaginians in Spain', in *CAH*, vol. 8, 2nd ed., 17–43; Dexter Hoyos, *Hannibal's Dynasty*, London 2003, 55–97; Richard Miles, *Carthage Must Be Destroyed*, London 2010, 218–234; these, and others, rarely agree on many details.
4. Polybios 1.13.7.
5. Polybios 3.30.1; it is not known when this occurred.
6. Polybios 3.15.5–7.
7. Polybios 3.16.3–7; Appian, *Illyrian Wars* 8.
8. Polybios 3. Livy 21.6.1 and 12.5; Appian, *Spanish Wars* 2.10, 15.8.
9. Polybios 3.17.
10. Livy 21.10–11.
11. Polybios 3.20.6–21.8; Livy 21.17.4–6.
12. The quantity of studies on this war defy listing; I have used J.F. Lazenby, *Hannibal's War*, Warminster 1978, as a particularly level-headed account of events; see also those listing in note 3; all have good bibliographies; needless to say most modern accounts are fixated on military events, with diplomacy relegated well below.
13. Polybios 3.40.8–14; Livy 21.62.2.
14. Schmitt, *Staatsverträge* 519, 524, 525, 526, 527 are all treaties of alliance with Italians.
15. This is discussed in great detail by Michael P. Fronda, *Between Rome and Carthage, Southern Italy during the Second Punic War*, Oxford 2010; also Kathryn Lomas, *Rome and the Western Greeks*, London 1993.
16. Livy 23.6.5–7.12.
17. Livy 23.33.12–34.9 and 39.1–4; Polybios 7.9; Schmitt, *Staatsverträge* 528.
18. Livy 23.30.10–24.6; Polybios 7.1–4; Schmitt, *Staatsverträge* 529.
19. Polybios 7.7.3; Livy 24.21.1–3.
20. Livy 25.23.9 and 26.24.1; *SEG* XIII 382; F.M. Walbank, *Philip V of Macedon*, Cambridge 1940, 301–304.
21. Livy 26.51.10–14 and 27.17.9–11; Polybios 10.34.1–35.8 and 1.37.7–8.
22. Polybios 10.40.2–3.
23. Livy 28.18.6–8.
24. Livy 29.12.3–14; Schmitt, *Staatsverträge* 543.
25. Livy 30.16.1–12; Appian, *Libyan Wars* 32; Schmitt, *Staatsverträge* 548.

26 This is summarised well by Brian Caven, *The Punic Wars*, London 1980; it is of course also retailed in every history of the Roman Republic.
27 Appian, *Libyan Wars* 70–73.
28 Ibid. 74.
29 Ibid. 75.
30 Ibid. 76–81; this escalation process had earlier been applied in Spain, forcing the surrender of enemy cities; there was no excuse for the elementary mistakes made by the Roman 'negotiators'.
31 Ibid. 111.
32 Ibid. 107.
33 Ibid. 123.
34 Ibid. 130.

# Part IV
# The collision of East and West

# 10 The diplomacy of Antiochos III – II
## The Roman crisis

The Fifth Syrian War continued for seven years (202–195), though the major Syrian fighting was over by 199. Had Syria been the only matter in contention, peace could have been made then. Antiochos III, however, was determined to ensure actual possession of the many Ptolemaic posts along the Asia Minor coasts before the peace was agreed, and he spent the years 198 to 196 campaigning to secure these places. He had already spent several years of his reign securing control of cities in western Asia Minor, and in those endeavours he had repeatedly clashed with the Ptolemaic authorities in the coastal cities; in addition, several of those cities were important economic centres or were Ptolemaic naval bases. Removing these Ptolemaic posts was a sensible war aim to accomplish while he had the chance. This campaign included a large joint army-and-fleet expedition along the south coast of Asia Minor into the Aegean in 197.[1] Ptolemaic resistance was almost nil. Only after this campaign was completed, in 196, were peace negotiations held, apparently with the Rhodian Eukles leading for Antiochos.[2]

Philip V had captured some of the Ptolemaic places around the Aegean during a campaign in 201–200, but he was then defeated by Rome in the Second Romano-Macedonian War of 200–197, and his conquests mainly fell to Antiochos when he arrived in the west. The negotiation of the peace treaty with the Ptolemaic government was thus relatively simple: any territories captured by Antiochos thereby became his. In addition, as part of the peace process, a marriage was arranged between the King Ptolemy V and Antiochos' daughter Kleopatra, nicknamed Syra by the Egyptians as a result. The marriage took place at Raphia (of all places) in 195, and this event marked the ratification of the treaty.[3] The Ptolemaic kingdom was thus reduced to Egypt, Cyrenaica, and Cyprus. Antiochos had expanded his kingdom to acquire total supremacy in Asia Minor and the conquest of Phoenicia and Palestine. In all this there had been little scope for diplomacy, except in the final details.

The negotiations in 196–195 are wholly unknown; they took place at the same time as the negotiations between Romans and Greeks to end the Second Romano-Macedonian War. As a result of their simultaneous advances during previous years Rome and Antiochos steadily approached each other across Greece and Asia Minor, fighting different wars but well aware that the situation was becoming dangerous. In the end the two great powers did collide, but only after a long period of complex negotiations had almost succeeded in averting that conflict.

Contact between the two powers had perhaps been intended by Rome in 200 when three Roman legates set out to visit Egypt and Syria, probably in connection with the Roman intention to make war on Philip. (One of the Roman envoys, M. Aemilius Lepidus, went to see Philip and delivered an ambiguous message which Philip only later understood to be the Roman declaration of war.[4]) Since Ptolemy and Antiochos were at war with each other (and remained so until 195), the legates could be quite sure that neither would be likely, or able, to intervene in the war they knew was coming in Greece. Livy assumed that the delegation was intended to mediate between Antiochos and Ptolemy,[5] but there is no evidence for this, other than his interpretation; indeed, Rome was probably quite pleased to find two possible enemy great powers at each other's throats (in 200 the war in Syria was still unresolved). The envoys spent a long time in Greece, visiting several states, delaying at Rhodes, and then sending Lepidus to see Philip at Abydos. They were presumably intended as a fact-finding and ally-gathering mission, especially seeking to discover if either king was likely to intervene in Rome's own war with Macedon and to lay the ground diplomatically for that war.[6] It was the first of many such delegations who went to the east during the next half-century.

There is a story in Livy that Lepidus was invited in Egypt to become 'tutor' to the young Ptolemy V. This has become the basis for a theory that this embassy resulted in a condition of *amicitia* between Rome and Egypt, with attendant diplomatic consequences (though the precise meaning of *amicitia* is scarcely clear). The objections to the story are considerable: first, it seems to have been developed within the family of Lepidus, perhaps for mere prestige reasons; second, it seems unlikely that Lepidus, who went to meet Philip V at Abydos, ever reached Egypt; third, Livy's interpretation of the embassy as having a mediation role – the basis of the *amicitia* theory – is only his guess and is so highly unlikely that it may be dismissed. There is actually no direct evidence that the embassy went further east than Rhodes. If the mediation role is discarded as Livy's invention – it would have been rejected by Antiochos, if not by Ptolemy's government – then the main purpose of the embassy was fact-finding; at Rhodes they were well placed to discover the latest information about the Syrian War and had no reason to go further.

For the next two years both Rome and Antiochos were fully involved in their wars. Not until 198 was Antiochos free of fighting in Syria, after the conquest of Sidon in 199 and Gaza in 198; and that was the year Flamininus managed at last to transfer the fighting against Macedon away from the Macedonian defence of the Aous Pass and into Greece proper. That was the year the first authenticated diplomatic contact between the two took place, beginning a sequence of meetings and negotiations between Rome and the king over six years, until it became clear that no agreement could be reached between them. It is a diplomatic sequence which is in stark contrast with the contemporaneous events in Greece. The Roman war with Macedon came with scarcely any warning and by a process which transparently subverted Rome's own religious practices.[7] The discussions and movements of envoys between Antiochos and Rome, on the other hand, constitute one of the few clear and detailed examples of ongoing diplomatic negotiations in the Hellenistic period.

Flamininus was one of the Romans most closely involved in the discussions with Antiochos, even while he was organising the peace settlement in Greece; the public celebration at the Isthmia in 196 of the Roman withdrawal from Demetrias, Chalkis, and Corinth, the three cities called the 'Fetters of Greece', was in effect the Greek ratification of the peace – another restoration of the 'freedom of the Greeks'. It was, in effect, a dictated peace, and many in Greece were thoroughly dissatisfied, notably the Aitolian League; it began to unravel within two years, or even less, a factor with some effect on Antiochos' negotiations.

Rome and Antiochos exchanged several diplomatic messages while Flamininus was arranging Greek affairs, and he was involved in those discussions. After the visit of the legates to the east in 200 (potentially the first contact, initiated by Rome), the first direct contact (assuming the embassy of 200 did not go beyond Rhodes) came in 198 and was occasioned, it seems, by a complaint by Attalos of Pergamon that Antiochos' forces had encroached on his territory.[8] This excuse rapidly faded from view, implying that Antiochos had ordered his forces to withdraw.[9] It did, however, provoke the embassy from Rome to Antiochos. The encroachment occurred while Antiochos' army was moving west and was probably the result of a mere momentary error by a Seleukid subordinate commander. Attalos made use of it to encourage Roman support for his other projects, including support against Philip V. It is in fact a classic case of a weaker power attempting to induce a stronger ally to provide help for something the stronger was not interested in. Attalos' brief conquests in interior Asia Minor had been lost twenty years before, and he hoped to gain Roman support for their recovery. He also wanted an excuse to withdraw from the war in Greece and suggested that he be 'permitted' to do so in order to defend his territory against Antiochos' 'attack'; the Senate ignored this and sent an envoy to find out what was happening. The envoys will have discovered that, if an encroachment had actually taken place, it had ended almost at once.

The Roman delegates who went east (their names are not known) were probably on another investigative visit (rather than sent to upbraid Antiochos).[10] They met Antiochos, and when they returned to Rome they could report that Antiochos had in effect won his war with Ptolemy and now intended to mop up the Ptolemaic possessions in Asia Minor; they were accompanied on their return to the city by an envoy of the king. This had been accomplished by the time Antiochos was at Korakesion on his route west in early 197. There is no sign that they visited Attalos, and the meeting must have taken place in Syria to have been followed by a journey to Rome and a return visit to meet Antiochos by May 197.[11] The envoys' journeys were no doubt through Greece, and so Flamininus was probably well informed of Antiochos' movements. The Senate will also have been informed by Antiochos' envoys of the king's intentions – they were scarcely secret – and the senators responded by passing honorific decrees in the king's favour.[12] There was no conflict, and the implication of these little-known embassies is that the two 'sides' were actually exerting themselves to avoid one.

In the next year (196) Flamininus' negotiations for peace in Greece continued, and then the terms were announced at Corinth. Meanwhile Antiochos had reached western Asia Minor and was enforcing his authority over most of the cities there,

180    *The collision of East and West*

both those formerly Ptolemaic and those which had suffered from Philip's attentions.[13] This involved much careful diplomacy. Each city required to be persuaded to submit; only those, like Korakesion, with Ptolemaic garrisons resisted. Rhodes attempted to bluff him into stopping his advance, but the bluff was called, and an agreement was reached by which part of Karia was left to Rhodes.[14] In the course of his description of these events Livy reports the new diplomatic contact between Rome and Antiochos. Discussions may also have been held between Philip and Antiochos over the places (in Karia and on the Hellespont and Propontis) he had captured in the past few years. Once he had secured all the Ptolemaic places, Antiochos negotiated the peace treaty with Ptolemy V.

Two cities only had refused to submit to him, Lampsakos and Smyrna, and both of them appealed to Rome – in effect copying Athens' tactic in 200. To anyone familiar with Roman history – and there can have been few such people in Greece and Asia Minor and Syria at the time – this was also ominously reminiscent of the appeal of Saguntum which lead to the great war with Carthage, not to mention the appeals of the Mamertines and the Sardinian mutineers. It is doubtful, however, if the parallel was missed at Rome, though matters worked out somewhat differently.

Flamininus met two envoys from Antiochos, Hegesianax and Lysias, at the Isthmia.[15] Their purpose was, as before, to keep the Romans informed of Antiochos' intentions. Antiochos had carefully avoided treading on Roman toes by not putting any pressure on the cities which the Roman commissioners had freed from Philip's garrisons. Bargylia in Karia was one – a Ptolemaic post before Philip seized it – and Ainos and Maroneia in Thrace were others – these latter were especially sensitive since they had been controlled successively by Ptolemy and Philip, and Antiochos had begun campaigning in Thrace in their hinterland.

Flamininus' message to Antiochos through Hegesianax and Lysias is related by Livy in the form of Roman orders and reprimands, a tone which is unbelievable in the context[16] – his interpretation has all the hallmarks of Roman rewriting of history in justification of later conduct. The actual message was probably a report on the peace terms Flamininus had just announced at the Isthmia, since this clearly had an effect on Antiochos' intentions in Asia and Thrace. The meeting with the envoys probably also highlighted the potential problems which might grow into a conflict. The final message from Flamininus may thus have been a suggestion that a meeting between the king and some of the commissioners would be worthwhile, with the aim of clearing the air.[17] Alternatively Antiochos' envoys may have suggested it, and since Antiochos was the host of the meeting, this is perhaps more likely.

The meeting was to take place once the ten Roman commissioners for organising the peace terms in Macedon and Greece had done their work. This was a complex and elaborate diplomatic ballet. P. Cornelius Lentulus Caudinus went to Bargylia, and others to Ainos and Maroneia; two of the commissioners, P. Villius Tappulus and L. Terentius Massiliota, were not given specific tasks other than to attend the meeting with Antiochos; they waited at the island of Thasos for him to appear, for he was on campaign in Thrace for the whole summer. In addition, the Senate – which was presumably kept informed by Flamininus – nominated one of the commissioners, L. Cornelius Lentulus (Caudinus' cousin) to attend in its name.[18] The three months between the Isthmia in June and the meeting with the king in September were quite enough for senatorial instructions to reach Lentulus. It is obvious that no one was in any hurry, and the matter was not seen as urgent by either the Senate or the king.

Polybios claims that L. Lentulus' instructions from the Senate were that he should arrange a peace between Antiochos and Ptolemy.[19] This was a task which made little sense by this time, since it was clear that Antiochos had won the war, and peace negotiations were already under way. This Roman intervention certainly seems to have been mentioned at the meeting but was only one of several issues discussed, and one must assume that the source used by Polybios only picked out that one issue. L. Lentulus could, however, claim to be the senior envoy in the meeting because of his direct appointment by the Senate, though when he tried to pre-empt his colleagues by trying to reach the king first and alone, he was unsuccessful.

The meeting was delayed because Antiochos was pressing on with his aim of recovering control of all lands any of his ancestors had ruled or claimed, in this case Thrace.[20] His claim here was somewhat nebulous – the founder Seleukos I had been about to occupy it (and Macedon) when he was murdered outside the city of Lysimacheia; Antiochos II and Antiochos Hierax had both campaigned there, but neither had ever controlled all the land (and Hierax was of course a rebel, if a Seleukid). The Romans became steadily more concerned about what Antiochos was doing in the country as he became more successful, since by controlling Thrace he became a contiguous neighbour of Philip's Macedon. The two dynasties had frequently intermarried, and the two kings had concerted their dismemberment of Ptolemy's lands. An alliance of the two, and a sudden attack, could well dismantle all Roman authority west of the Adriatic. After the wars with the Cisalpine Gauls, Hannibal, and Philip, Rome was clearly paranoid about any strong neighbour.

The city of Lysimacheia, at the root of the Gallipoli peninsula, was named by Antiochos as the meeting place.[21] If the Romans knew that Seleukos I had been killed nearby, they might have understood it to be a significant choice, but there is no sign that they did know; Antiochos was in the process of refounding and rebuilding the city, which had been sacked by the Thracians, and this was a clear sign of Antiochos' determination to hold what he had and that the cities of the region were to be his (just as his choice of Seleukeia-in-Pieria for peace talks in 218 had been a sign of his determination to hold that city). The Roman delegates gathered there in the autumn of 196 before the king had emerged from his Thracian campaign. They were thus able to decide on their tactics and their priorities, and L. Lentulus, as the delegate with instructions from the Senate, took the lead. One of the preliminary arrangements they had made was to bring envoys of Lampsakos and Smyrna to the meeting, something supposedly not expected by Antiochos, though their presence in his own city was hardly unknown to him.

The conference lasted ten days, but the first days were occupied with informal meetings and talks, conducted in a friendly atmosphere, where areas of agreement

182    *The collision of East and West*

and disagreement were isolated and possible compromises identified.[22] Subjects would include implementing the peace terms in Greece; Antiochos' progress in Thrace, which Philip had already brought to Roman attention; and Antiochos' attitude to the Attalid kingdom, a Roman ally in the Greek war (Attalos I had now been succeeded by Eumenes II, with whom Antiochos did not have a treaty); the progress of his war against Ptolemy was also discussed.

These informal meetings were followed by a plenary session, which is Polybios' setting for competing speeches by Lentulus and Antiochos, composed by the historian, neither of which can be taken as reflecting the reality – though the speech he puts in Antiochos' mouth is well argued and convincing, while that given to Lentulus is blustering, irrelevant, rude – and wholly unbelievable in the context.[23] The one issue over which the two sides supposedly disagreed was the fate of Lampsakos and Smyrna. Lentulus introduced the envoys from the cities, but Antiochos refused to listen to their arguments – he had surely heard them already, and this was a conference between him and the Romans, not the Greek cities. He was also not unprepared, and announced that he was prepared to accept Rhodian arbitration on the status of these cities.[24]

This is too often portrayed as a confrontational meeting, with both sides springing surprises to confound the other, an interpretation which ignores the fact that the conference lasted for ten days.[25] A better interpretation sees it as a series of sensible discussions in a fairly relaxed atmosphere. Neither side was interested in war, nor was there any crisis, but there were certainly issues between them. The appearance of the delegates from the cities cannot have been a surprise to the king, nor was the proposed reference to Rhodes unexpected by the Romans, for it was exactly this sort of issue which would have been discussed in the preliminary private meetings.

Rhodes was a good choice as arbiter. Both Rome and the king were on good terms with it, and it had a reputation for advocating Greek cities' autonomy. The fact that the issue was aired publicly indicates that it was the one issue the two sides could not agree on; an arbitration by Rhodes was a way out for both. On the other hand, given Rhodes' known attitudes, it is likely that the city would come out in favour of the cities' autonomy, so Antiochos may well have been reconciled to never gaining control of them, but to have the disagreement decided by arbitration was a useful face-saver. If Rome had not been so determined never to submit to arbitration in any circumstances, it may well have found that Rhodes adjudged the cities to be in the Roman sphere – that is, 'free'; Antiochos, having suggested the procedure, would have been compelled to accept that result. But it is unlikely that Roman political and diplomatic imaginations were up to the concept, even though Rhodes was clearly aligned to them politically and internationally.[26]

The Roman delegation raised the issue of their own mediation to secure peace between Antiochos and Ptolemy. Antiochos pointed out that he had been in negotiations for some time over the peace treaty, but the instability of the government in Alexandria in recent years – hardly news to the Romans – was the main obstacle to reaching a conclusion. He stated that the talks were close to an agreement and that it would include the marriage of Ptolemy V with Antiochos' daughter.[27]

The Senate's inclusion of this in the agenda had an ulterior motive, for if Rome was the agent for arranging the peace, Ptolemy and Antiochos would both be placed under obligation. This would not be the case with Rhodes, since Rhodes was not powerful enough to enforce any such obligation. Rome certainly was, but neither Ptolemy nor Antiochos, the latter especially, had any wish to allow Rome any influence east of Greece and the Aegean. Antiochos' statement on the negotiations was thus neatly made, just as was his enlistment of Rhodes as arbiter. It seems clear that the Senate, and probably Flamininus, wanted to use these discussions as a means of intruding its influence into eastern political matters; Antiochos' skilful deflection and blocking foiled these moves, doing so in such a way as not to put any Roman noses out of joint.

The conference ended when a rumour arrived at Lysimacheia that Ptolemy V had died; it was not true, but Antiochos obviously had to return quickly to Syria – but he was delayed by a sailors' mutiny on the way, and then he was shipwrecked in Kilikia.[28] This was not a serious interruption to the talks, which had effectively been concluded by the time the rumour arrived. The Roman envoys returned to Greece, and Antiochos sent his own envoys across to Flamininus, still in Greece, when he stopped at Ephesos on his voyage east.[29] The Romans went on to Rome, but Antiochos' men were visiting Flamininus only. There is no indication of the subject of their discussions, but it must be assumed that Flamininus sent a reply, presumably a courteous note explaining the extension of Flamininus' *imperium* and thanking him for keeping him informed.[30] Antiochos sent a new message in the spring of 195, proposing an alliance between himself and Rome. This was answered by a visit to the king later in the year by P. Villius Tappulus.[31] This series of messages indicates once again that neither Rome nor the king was threatening one another; the messages were exchanges of information and tentative proposals for continued good relations. The sequence is a good example of two major powers delicately operating to ensure that no misunderstandings about their operations developed.

Both Flamininus and Antiochos were employed in wars in 195. Antiochos was busy once more in Thrace; Flamininus fought Nabis of Sparta. This exchange of messages let them inform each other of their plans and intentions, but the proposal for an alliance was not something Flamininus could deal with himself. This is the issue which brought about Villius' return visit to Antiochos. He came direct from Rome, where the Senate will have had to consider the idea. Villius no doubt deflated the whole alliance notion, for it now disappears. When he returned to Rome, as he had by the middle of 195,[32] he could report that Antiochos had at last made peace with Ptolemy, and the exchange of oaths and the betrothal of Antiochos' daughter with Ptolemy V had ratified the treaty. It was also a sign that Ptolemaic Egypt might be considered to be a subordinate kingdom of Antiochos' empire, just as Philip's Macedon was a subordinate kingdom of the Roman Republic, in both cases as a result of defeat in war and the conclusion of the subsequent treaty.

If it had not been obvious before, it was now clear that there were just two great powers left – Carthage, Macedon, and Egypt had been demoted. It may have been that which prompted the Senate to reject the idea of an alliance with Antiochos, but there was probably another reason, rooted in the mindset of the Roman politicians.

There seems to have been no concept of an alliance of equals in Roman thinking. Roman 'alliances' marked the subordination of the partner to Roman authority. Antiochos had a very similar attitude, but he was, as his suggestion implies, quite open to the idea of an alliance of equals. Since Rome could not envisage such a relationship, and perhaps feared that Antiochos would regard such an alliance as implying Roman subordination, it had to be refused. It is noticeable that by using the emollient Villius to deliver the message, the Senate was ensuring that feelings were not hurt, just as Antiochos had acted in the same way at the Lysimacheia conference.[33]

Antiochos' general imperial policy was 'restoration': he had 'restored' Phoenicia and Palestine to his family's kingdom, restored his position in Baktria, Parthia, 'India', and south Iran, recovered control over much of Asia Minor, was in the process of 'restoring' his dynasty's control of Thrace, and was physically restoring the city of Lysimacheia. He now nudged Eumenes II of Pergamon, offering him one of his daughters in marriage. Eumenes did not directly refuse, but he did ostentatiously help Flamininus in the war with Nabis, thereby indicating his choice of friend.[34] The Romano-Spartan War persuaded the Achaian League to join with Rome, and Rhodes did so as well. Diplomatically Flamininus' war on Sparta proved to be a point of decision for most of Greece, and most states chose to align with their protector rather than follow Nabis into a policy of independence.

The one Greek state Flamininus had been unable to bring with him was the Aitolian League. It seems unlikely that he made any serious attempt to do so, for with the rest of Greece – and Macedon – lined up as Roman allies, Rome had no need of an Aitolian alliance, or even its submission. Accordingly he felt able to recommend to the Senate, and the Senate to accept, the policy of evacuation of the Roman forces. During 194 they mostly returned to Italy, men and ships and commanders. This also meant that at that time the Senate saw no danger of a clash with Antiochos. In other words, their diplomatic exchanges between 200 and 195 successfully avoided any serious disagreements and solved some problems, and remaining issues were not seen by the Senate as being liable to cause any real trouble. The evacuation of Greece by Rome was a clear statement that relations with Antiochos were good, even as Antiochos campaigned again in Thrace.

However, Flamininus' policy was not unanimously accepted in Rome. In particular Scipio Africanus, consul for the second time in 194, the very year of the evacuation, was convinced that leaving Greece without a Roman garrison rendered it vulnerable both to internal disturbances and to external pressures. Nabis was still in power in Sparta, the Aitolians were publicly disgruntled, and Philip was still king in Macedon and might be supposed to wish for revenge and a release from the shackles Rome had placed on him. And just over the horizon was the army of Antiochos the great king, victorious against Ptolemy, in control of almost all Asia Minor, and now conquering all Thrace. Africanus had a very good argument to make, and by doing so he drove Flamininus into a position where he had to adopt a more hard-line approach to Antiochos than before.[35]

Antiochos sent two ambassadors to Rome late in 194. These were Hegesianax, originally from Alexandria Troas on the Hellespont and already known to

Flamininus, and Menippos, a Macedonian.[36] They reached Rome late in the year, saw the Senate, and were referred to a committee consisting of Flamininus and the ten commissioners who had worked in Greece to establish the peace terms. The envoys' task was to ask once again for a Roman alliance.[37] Such an agreement between the two remaining great powers of the region would be a defensive move for both, would institutionalise the diplomatic contacts and regular exchanges of envoys which the two powers had developed in the previous years, and would solidify the territorial results of their recent wars, leaving the world from Spain to India divided between the two of them. Implicitly it would leave Greece in the Roman sphere. To Antiochos it would be an adaptation of the treaty system he was familiar with among the monarchies, where a treaty remained in force while both principals remained alive. This could not work with a republic, whose chief officers were in office only a year, so a formal alliance would be a sensible alternative. It would also remove any threat he might feel that Rome intended an attack: otherwise he would find it necessary to concentrate much of his armed forces in Asia Minor, and perhaps he himself would need to live more or less permanently in Sardis or Ephesos. Rome was familiar with the idea of a lifetime treaty and had used the idea of a time-limited treaty itself, as with Hiero of Syracuse, for example, so there was no real difficulty in a formal sense. Such a treaty would last until Antiochos died and could then be renewed with his successor. This was the procedure when Philip V died (see Chapter 12), so the whole process was known to Rome. Antiochos had proposed something practicable, if the Senate and its committee could be brought to see it and if the fears voiced by Scipio Africanus had not infected the others. But such an alliance would have to be preceded by a settlement of all differences.

Livy has Menippos, in a contrived speech, define three types of treaty: one of terms imposed on a defeated enemy, one between equals in power after a war, and one between states who have never fought each other.[38] (It looks very much like a political science lecture, perhaps remembered by Livy from his school days, not something likely to be welcomed by the hard-headed committee members.) Flamininus brushed this aside – if indeed the distinction was ever made – insisting that a clear division be made between 'Roman Europe' and 'Seleukid Asia', as a preliminary to any alliance discussions. This would have a different effect than Antiochos' simple alliance; it would require him to evacuate Thrace (including Lysimacheia), and the issue of Lampsakos and Smyrna was revived as an issue, with Alexandria Troas now included; this was either to embarrass Hegesianax (whose home town it was) or by a misunderstanding. But the real issue was Thrace.[39] Flamininus, by his characterization of 'Europe' as 'Roman', was in fact demanding Antiochos' withdrawal from Thrace – but he was not offering to relinquish the three cities he claimed to be protecting in 'Seleukid Asia'. (There is no sign that Rhodes had made any move to arbitrate; it is not even known if the city had agreed to act as mediator.[40]) It also became clear that any treaty between Rome and Antiochos would not be regarded at Rome as one between equals but as one in which Rome would emerge as the superior. This was probably why Antiochos' earlier suggestion had been ruled out, but now his envoys seem to have finally understood the Roman position. This was hardly a position acceptable to Antiochos, the 'great king'.[41]

The talks went on for some time, though Livy's account once again compresses them into a single session. In the end, one of the commissioners, P. Sulpicius Galba, a man with a decade's experience of both war and diplomacy in Greece, demanded that the two envoys choose either to withdraw from Thrace or allow Rome to take the Asian cities into her 'protection' – not quite the position stated originally by Flamininus. Menippos replied that he had no authority to reduce Antiochos' kingdom – so maintaining his king's claim both to the cities in dispute and to Thrace. The envoys, to their surprise, found that the Roman Senate was in a threatening mood.[42]

The Senate decided to send two of its own envoys to Antiochos in reply to the embassy of Hegesianax and Menippos. The two envoys who were active on the Roman side in this embassy were P. Sulpicius Galba, who had intervened so effectively in the discussions in Rome, and P. Villius Tappulus, who must by now have been regarded at Rome as the Senate's Antiochos expert. (A third member is said to be P. Aelius Paetus, but he is never mentioned after the note of his appointment.[43]) They travelled east in the spring of 193, whereas Hegesianax and Menippos went home as soon as the conference ended, travelling in the winter of 194/193, an indication perhaps of their apprehensions after the meeting and the new Roman attitude.[44]

Diplomacy continued through that winter. Hegesianax stopped in Delphi on his way from Italy to Asia and was honoured there as *proxenos*. Delphi was effectively under Aitolian control, and Hegesianax will have met senior Aitolian politicians during his visit.[45] Meanwhile the Senate was making sure of Philip. Antiochos' successful conquest of Thrace had made him Philip's close neighbour, and this could be seen by Philip as a threat, as Rome had certainly come to see it, or as an opportunity to escape the Roman grasp. Philip was largely disarmed as part of the peace treaty, so his kingdom was vulnerable to a swift attack by Antiochos (or by Rome).[46] On the other hand, if Philip chose to join Antiochos with the aim of throwing off the restrictions imposed by Rome, he would open the way for Antiochos' forces to dominate all Greece and perhaps reach the Adriatic coast, where any Roman forces which were to campaign in the east had to land. We have no idea what talks went on between the two kings' representatives – there must surely have been some, since the situation demands it – but we do know something of what the Romans said to Philip. Three items emerge: Philip was given a strong hint that his son Demetrios, a hostage in Rome, might be released, and that the city of Demetrias might be returned to Macedonian control; an even more concrete inducement was the cancellation of the outstanding part of the tribute imposed on Macedon by the peace treaty.[47] So Rome offered a series of improvements in Philip's position, whereas Antiochos could only offer potentials and the possibility of a Seleukid takeover in Greece. In the event the restrictions on the size of Philip's army were also removed, and this may have been part of the original discussions as well; or perhaps Philip bargained that item into the agreement.

In the meeting of the Aitolian leaders with Hegesianax, presuming it took place, he could only encourage the former in their defiance of Rome, and in March 193 a meeting of the Aitolian Assembly decided to send envoys in search of allies: to Philip, Nabis in Sparta, and Antiochos.[48] Philip may have been tempted and was surely pleased at all the attention he was getting, but a long history of enmity towards the Aitolians, plus Rome's recent hints and concessions, lay between them.[49] The very reverse considerations operated at Sparta, where Nabis grasped at the very suggestion far too eagerly and, despite a warning from the Achaian League, he went to war almost at once to recover some of his lost lands.[50] This soon brought Roman forces back into Greece. The reply of Antiochos to the Aitolian envoy is not known. He certainly did not accept an alliance with the league, but the contact was clearly useful and bore fruit later.[51]

All this intense diplomacy had taken place before the Roman envoys Galba and Villius (and Paetus, maybe) reached Asia. None of it was definitive – except Nabis' premature move – for the participants were waiting on the issue of the talks between Antiochos and the Roman envoys. The Romans first saw Eumenes II at Pergamon, who made a clear declaration of 'loyalty' to Rome, though this was scarcely more than an alignment, not a definitive treaty of alliance.[52] Galba stayed on at Pergamon, having fallen ill – either genuinely or diplomatically – and Villius went on alone to see Antiochos on a courtesy visit. Villius was already known to Antiochos, and it may be that he went on, and Galba stayed back, because the two men had different diplomatic priorities; but Villius' visit must indicate a continuing wish by the Senate that peace be maintained.

Antiochos was campaigning in Pisidia, and he arranged a meeting of Villius and Galba at Ephesos with Minnio, his chief minister, where the real negotiations took place.[53] The sources we have on the meeting are brief and distorted, but they imply that a process of bargaining was going on, focussing particularly on the disputed cities, which are variously classified as 'Asian' or in 'Aiolis and Ionia'; Thrace is not referred to, for Antiochos' work there in the past three years had surely convinced the Romans that it was not negotiable. The slightest exercise of imagination would have told them this; its surrender would be like the Romans being asked to give up part of Cisalpine Gaul. The area of disagreement between the two great powers, at least in formal terms, had thus come down to the control of two or three cities on the coast of Asia Minor, though Flamininus' definition at Rome, referring to 'Roman Europe', and Galba's outburst show that Rome was apprehensive that Antiochos, by maintaining an army in Thrace, threatened the Roman position in Greece (which, of course, it did).

No decisions of any substance were reached at the Ephesos meeting. The area of disagreement between Antiochos and Rome remained exactly what it had been at Lysimacheia. The envoys returned to Rome with this message, but also reported on Nabis' actions, and said that they had seen no indication that Antiochos was making any special war preparations – this must be Villius, since Galba had not moved further than Ephesos. When they reported to the Senate, therefore, they made it clear that the only area where real trouble was likely was Sparta.[54] The Senate could see that the dispute over the cities was not to be easily resolved; this might be a pretext, or an excuse, for war, but it seems unlikely.

Unlike Nabis, the Aitolians were fully aware of Roman power from past encounters. They fully intended to overturn the Roman settlement of Greece contrived by Flamininus, but they could not do so alone, not even with Nabis' help. The only power which could do so now was Antiochos. Philip had shown his unwillingness to antagonise Rome; Nabis was hopeless. But an alliance of Aitolia and Antiochos might be powerful enough to entice other allies (even Philip) and so block or defeat any Roman riposte. After their envoy came back from Antiochos empty-handed, Thoas of Trichonos, a prominent politician, was sent to the king, presumably with concrete proposals for an alliance, though no details have survived. A return visit by Menippos to the Aitolian Assembly meeting of the Panaitolike in March 192 followed.[55] Meanwhile Antiochos had embarked on another Thracian campaign, thereby making it clear he was not at this point seriously interested in joining in a war in Greece.

The Aitolians, however, were apparently convinced that they could provoke a war and so bring in Antiochos to help and protect them once it had begun. (They were thus in their own way as impulsive as Nabis.) They adopted two resolutions at their meeting: one which asked King Antiochos to liberate Greece – by implication, from the Romans – and a second asking Antiochos to arbitrate the dispute between Aitolia and Rome,[56] which they surely knew would never be accepted by Rome. Meanwhile King Eumenes sent his brother Attalos to Rome to point out that Antiochos was again campaigning in Thrace.[57] Flamininus, invited to Aitolia by the league council (not by the assembly), did his best to calm the Aitolians down, with little success. They clearly believed that if Rome could be provoked, Antiochos would take a hand. Menippos described the wealth of armament Antiochos had.[58] This inevitably encouraged the Aitolians; since they rejected Flamininus' advice, we may assume from this message that Antiochos was not averse to a war in Greece.

The Roman settlement of Greece was breaking down only two years after the evacuation of the Roman forces; Nabis' antagonism could be ignored and dealt with, but that of the Aitolians was a different matter. A dispute developed over Demetrias, the city which the Romans had vaguely promised to return to Philip. An internal dispute between pro-Aitolian and pro-Roman groups in the city eventually provoked Flamininus to intervene and remove the pro-Aitolian head of state.[59] Such an action, by the man who had proclaimed the restoration of freedom to Greece, made it quite clear just what that 'freedom' meant in Roman eyes. No Greek state could consider itself 'free' in the circumstances. No doubt the Aitolians rushed to point this out to the rest of Greece.

The division in Demetrias between pro- and anti-Roman groups was replicated in other states. The Aitolians took the opportunity of reactions to the Demetrias crisis to launch a series of *coups*, aiming to seize control of Demetrias, Chalkis in Euboia, and Sparta, but they succeeded only at Demetrias, where Flamininus' man was overthrown.[60] This was the decisive move, an open challenge to the Roman system and to Flamininus personally. The Romans reacted by sending an army across the Adriatic, and persuaded Philip, finally compelled to make a decision – he must have been annoyed at events in Demetrias, but with a Roman army on his western doorstep he had no real choice – to give permission for it to march through his kingdom.

At the beginning, it was not clear who Rome's enemy would be, though Aitolia was the obvious choice at first. By this time, Antiochos had finished his campaign in Thrace and was back in Ephesos. From his point of view it looked very much as though Greece was disintegrating into an anarchic condition to which Rome, the author of the political system which was collapsing, had abandoned it. There seemed also to be a new opportunity to expand his kingdom. If the Aitolians were serious in their call for liberation he could replace the Roman system with one of his own. Late in 192 he took an army across the Aegean. It was so small a force that it could not possibly be regarded by the Romans as a serious threat to them but was large enough to persuade the local Greek states to join him.

No clear statement of Antiochos' purpose in this expedition has reached us. He had been invited into Greece by the Aitolians, who had largely botched their attempts to secure domination for themselves but who were also the only Greek state not part of the system set up by Flamininus in 196. The small size of Antiochos' expeditionary force – ten thousand men – suggests that he expected to work with the Aitolians in 'liberating' Greece and settling its affairs, replacing the failed Roman attempt – that is, the main activity was to be diplomatic. The main military force was to be Aitolian.

Antiochos' army landed near Demetrias, and Antiochos attended an Aitolian Council meeting at Lamia. He was elected *strategos* of the league, an honorary post, though it gave him a local position of importance. He was walking a careful path, aiming to settle Greece but hoping not to annoy Rome. However, his very arrival in Greece inflamed local political disputes; every Greek city now had to make a choice between Antiochos and Rome. The parties in power in most of Greece were pro-Roman groups, so their internal opponents were for Antiochos. The only way Antiochos was going to win the loyalty of the Greeks was if a series of local *coups d'etat* took place, with Antiochos' army providing the necessary backup – exactly what Flamininus had failed to do.

Whether Antiochos realised this when he sailed from Asia is unclear, but he soon got the message. He took a small force, composed half of his troops and half of Aitolians, to make another attempt to bring Chalkis in Euboia to his side. Argument failed. He left the talking to the Aitolian Thoas, so this is not surprising. The Chalkidian leaders sent for help, though no direct threats had been made against them and their city, and they appeared later at Aigion appealing to the Achaian League.[61]

After the Aitolians, the Achaian League was the strongest Greek state, and Antiochos also sent envoys to speak to the council. They found that Flamininus had come to put the Roman case. He arrived first, and the Achaians decided to align their league with Rome, assisted by the arrival of the delegation from Chalkis asking for help to maintain control of the city in the Roman interest; an envoy also arrived from Athens, where the same internal dispute was in progress.

Those who took the Roman side were much more ready to intervene in other cities to maintain support than was Antiochos. Both Flamininus and the Aitolians had shown their willingness to do this, but Antiochos had adopted a much softer approach, very deliberately taken no part in the arguments at Chalkis, and sent only a couple of envoys to the Achaian League meeting at Aigion. The result of that meeting was a clear diplomatic defeat for the king; the Achaians announced that they had an alliance with Rome, and Flamininus was able to send five hundred Roman troops (probably sent from the army landing in Epeiros or from the garrisons of the Illyrian cities) to help out in Athens and another five hundred to Chalkis.[62]

This was the moment when the stakes in the diplomatic game were raised further. The issue was control of Chalkis, one of the fortresses by which the Antigonid kings had in the past imposed their domination on Greece. On hearing that it was to be reinforced, Antiochos sent three thousand men to seize control of the mainland approach to the city at Salganeus. Some Achaian troops arrived first and seized the place, but the Roman contingent was intercepted and defeated in a scrappy fight at Delion. Having been forced into direct military action, Antiochos at last persuaded Chalkis to admit him, and the hostile forces, the Achaians and the surviving Romans, were allowed to depart by arrangement.[63]

The two sides had therefore carefully tested each other, though Rome and Achaia had rather suggested the weakness of their overall position by resorting to a deliberate challenge to Antiochos. Antiochos had obviously hoped to secure his supremacy in Greece by negotiation; Rome had been more concerned to bolster its existing position and to prevent defections. Neither had been keen to resort to fighting, but the use of Roman troops indicated that Rome was not averse to war. By late 192, the Roman army in Epeiros was available if needed, and the fight at Delion was enough to allow Rome to declare war, though it is probable that the Senate did not wait that long. Once the fighting had begun – and there had not been any until Delion – Antiochos could be rather more energetic in gathering support. But so could Rome, which had been almost as reluctant as Antiochos to become involved in the fighting. The small detachment sent to assist Chalkis had been as tentative and unthreatening as anything Antiochos had done.

The key to this situation, now that the two main powers of Greece (Aitolia and Achaia) were on opposite sides, was King Philip V of Macedon. His kingdom controlled the routes by which the Roman army would need to travel to reach Greece, or, alternatively, Antiochos' forces could reach the Roman landing places in Epeiros. The diplomatic tussle to secure Philip's allegiance is largely invisible, but Rome won the contest. (It must be assumed that Antiochos also made a serious attempt, but no record of it has survived.) The constraints imposed by the peace treaty of 197 were loosened further, and Philip was allowed to expand once more into Thessaly. Antiochos, offering, once more, the policy of 'the freedom of the Greeks', had not been able to offer Philip such an inducement, and the forces he had with him were not large enough to protect Philip against the Roman attack. So when Philip took the Roman side, the Roman army in Epeiros could reach Thessaly without much difficulty.[64]

Antiochos' diplomacy, however, did achieve some major successes. Gaining control of Chalkis had been crucial, as had, perhaps, his demonstration that he was prepared to use force. Almost at once the Boiotian League succumbed to his persuasions.[65] Envoys fanned out across central Greece; Phokis and Athamania, neighbours of Aitolia, joined him;[66] he allied with Elis and Messenia, neighbours of Achaia who might be able to neutralise its moves – Elis received a thousand soldiers to bolster its efforts.[67] An envoy went to Epeiros, which elicited a visit from the most prominent Epeirote politician, Charops, to the king. However, unless Antiochos could provide a large enough force to prevent the Romans from conquering Epeiros, Charops could hardly join him openly.[68]

This was the effective limit that diplomacy could accomplish. All the states which were not fully committed to Rome had by that time joined Antiochos. Antiochos and Rome had divided Greece between them; there were no neutrals of any importance left. The brief conflict at Delion had been the only fighting so far, but from now on this would take over. The key to the Roman advance lay in their forces' ability to march through Macedon and advance south through Thessaly. Antiochos' base in eastern Greece came under attack from the north, and defeat at Thermopylai compelled him to retire to Asia. The system of alliances he had built up in Greece disintegrated even more quickly than the Roman structure it had sought to replace.

During the war which followed, diplomacy continued. In order to have a large enough army to attack Antiochos, Scipio Africanus – though his brother was officially the Roman commander – negotiated a truce with Aitolia which let him take his army off into Asia. At the Hellespont he was met by an envoy from Antiochos suggesting peace but refused to negotiate. After the defeat of Antiochos' army at Magnesia, a truce was agreed, but the Roman commander Manlius Vulso conducted a cunning military-cum-diplomatic campaign among the cities and communities of western and central Asia Minor, skilfully detaching many of them from Antiochos' alliance; he ended by inflicting a solid defeat of the Galatians, who were still feared in the region, thereby suggesting that Roman power was worth having on your side.[69] Meanwhile a new consul turned the Aitolian truce into a new war and crushed the league. Antiochos was compelled to retire completely from Asia Minor and surrender a huge treasure and was forbidden to keep an elephant corps or a navy.[70] The exploitation of truces by the Roman commanders was at best unscrupulous, simultaneously masterly and deeply deceitful, and reminiscent of earlier senatorial exploitations of peace agreements to expand already negotiated peace terms in its favour. The Asia Minor spoils were divided in a conference at Apameia-Kelainai, pointedly held in the midst of Antiochos' former territories.

The contest between Rome and Antiochos was thus largely conducted through the practice of diplomacy, with active warfare occupying perhaps a year between the two much longer bouts of diplomatic campaigning. The approaches of the two combatants are well contrasted. The Seleukid method was generally the softer approach, with minimum backing by military force. This had become the normal method in the east, as in Antiochos' imposition of his power over the cities of western Asia Minor. The Roman method was to bring up a major armed force and use that as the main means of pressure – diplomacy conducted under imminent threat – though it had taken several years for the Senate to reach that point. This had been well learned in the diplomatic-military conflicts with men such as Alexander and Pyrrhos of Epeiros, and against Carthage.

Given that the Roman Empire eventually controlled all the Mediterranean basin, it might be assumed that this was the more effective method, if imperial expansion was the aim. The victims did not necessarily see that this was diplomacy's main or only task. Antiochos, after all, had been successful in expanding his kingdom, particularly in Asia Minor, by much less brutal methods, and his methods were inherited by the Attalid kings to whom Rome assigned much of Asia Minor in the Apameia treaty; and in the end, when Asia became Roman, it was the method Rome adopted in its control of that area.

## Notes

1. Hieronymos, *In Danielam* 11.15 (= Porphyry, *FGrH* 260 F 46; Livy 33.30.4–5); I have examined this campaign in my *The Roman War of Antiochos the Great*, Leiden 2002, 36–47; indeed that book is the basis for this chapter.
2. Hieronymos, *In Danielam* 11.17.
3. Ibid.
4. Polybios 16.27.5; Livy 31.18.1–5.
5. Livy 31.2.3.
6. Polybios 16.27.5; Livy 31.2.3–4; Appian, *Macedonian Wars* 4.2; Justin 30.3–31.1; Ager, *Interstate Arbitrations* 60, suggests, following M. Holleaux, *Rome, la Grece et les Monarchies Hellenistiques*, Paris 1935, 59, that Rome was quite willing to 'sacrifice Egypt' so long as Antiochos kept clear of the Macedonian War; also Walbank, *Commentary* 2.534 and id., *Philip V of Macedon*, Cambridge 1940, 316; it is not clear, however, in what way Rome had the capability of 'sacrificing' Egypt, nor what that meant – Rome showed no interest in assisting the Ptolemaic government at the time.
7. J.W. Rich, *Declaring War in the Roman Republic in the Period of Transmarine Expansion*, Brussels 1976; V. Warrior, *The Initiation of the Second Macedonian War*, Wiesbaden 1996.
8. Livy 32.8.9–16.
9. Antiochos was still in Syria at the time, so the encroachment into Attalos' lands was presumably the work of a subordinate commander; the absence of later comments on this suggests that it was quickly corrected. See my *Roman War*, 32–35, for a discussion.
10. Livy 32.8.15–16.
11. Livy 33.20.8.
12. Ibid.
13. John Ma, *Antiochos II and the Cities of Western Asia Minor*, Oxford 1999, 82–89.
14. Livy 33.20.1–6; Grainger, *Roman War*, 41–45; Ma, *Antiochos III*, 83–84.
15. Polybios 18.47.1–4; Livy 33.34.2.
16. Polybios 18.47.3; Livy 33.34.3–4.
17. Livy does not say such a message was sent to the king, but it is implicit in the decision to allot two commissioners to the meeting (33.35.1); it is inconceivable that they would simply turn up; Hegesianax and Lysias will have taken the message with them.
18. Polybios 18.50.1; Livy 33.39.1.
19. Polybios 18.49.3.
20. J.D. Grainger, 'Antiochos III in Thrace', *Historia* 15, 1996, 329–343.
21. Livy 33.38.12.
22. Polybios 18.50.4; Livy 33.39.3.
23. Polybios 18.50.5–9.
24. Polybios 18.52.1–5.

## Antiochos III – II: the Roman crisis 193

25 Modern discussions include E. Badian, 'Rome and Antiochos the Great, a Study in Cold War', in E. Badian (ed.), *Studies in Greek and Roman History*, Oxford 1964, 112–139, which has been influential until the modern Cold War faded away – see Errington in *CAH*; Will, *Histoire Politique*, 2.158–161; Erich M. Gruen, *The Hellenistic World and the Coming of Rome*, California 1984; recently Arthur M. Eckstein had been developing a new interpretation, as in *Mediterranean Anarchy, Interstate War and the Rise of Rome*, California 2006 (the conference is briefly discussed on 293–295); also Paul J. Burton, *Friendship and Empire: Roman Diplomacy and Imperialism in the Middle Republic (353–146 BC)*, Oxford 2011. Many of these discussions take as their starting point Rome's success, and their work is coloured by that. My version is in *Roman War*, ch 4.
26 Ager, *Interstate Arbitrations*, no 77.
27 Livy 33.40.1.
28 Livy 33.41.7–8; not on the way to Egypt, as Eckstein, *Rome Enters*, 146 and 310, claims – he 'made a descent on Alexandria' – nor to Cyprus, since he had already passed the latter, and was clearly aiming for Syria when wrecked.
29 Livy 33.41.6.
30 Grainger, *Roman War*, 102.
31 Livy 33.41.5; Grainger, *Roman War*, 102–106.
32 Livy 34.33.12.
33 Livy twice (32.8.13, 33.20.8) refers to Antiochos as *amicus populi Romani*. The earliest reference is in 198, which implies that the 'honour' was 'conferred' by the envoys who visited him in 200. This all seems highly unlikely. Why should Rome do this? Gruen, *Hellenistic Monarchies*, 622, suggests it was to bring him into diplomatic equality with Ptolemy; Eckstein, *Rome Enters*, 311, that it was connected with the Rome's prohibition on Antiochos invading Egypt – though Antiochos showed no signs of doing so and would clearly have rejected such an instruction. It is perhaps more probable that Livy made a mistake; he is notoriously careless in this section, particularly by distorting events to put Rome in a sympathetic light. He does not use the term later, when the alliance project is referred to; and if Antiochos was already 'a friend and ally of the Roman people', the alliance suggestion was not necessary.
34 Polybios 21.20.8; Livy 34.29.4; R.E. Allen, *The Attalid Kingdom: A Constitutional History*, Oxford 1983, 77.
35 Livy 34.42.3.
36 The term 'Macedonian' might mean a native of Macedon or a man of Macedonian descent. The term was also a description for those in the Seleukid kingdom descended from the original settlers; it was also a term, 'the Macedonian', in the royal titulature (as 'the Akhaimenian' had been for the Persian great kings).
37 Livy 34.57.6.
38 Livy 34.57.6–10.
39 Livy 34.58.1–3.
40 Ager, *Interstate Arbitrations* 77: 'neither the Hellenistic kings nor Rome was remarkable for willingness to submit to arbitration'. Indeed, thirty years later it was a Rhodian arbitration suggestion which brought down Roman wrath on the city.
41 Note that Antiochos' suggestion again implies that his status as 'friend and ally' did not exist, or was not of any importance.
42 Livy 34.59.1–2.
43 It was customary for the Senate to send three men on these missions, so Paetus may well have been a member; if so, we have no idea what he did.
44 Livy 34.59.6–8.
45 Dittenberger, *Sylloge* (3) 585, line 40; Grainger, *Roman War*, 147–150.
46 Antiochos could lay out a claim, thin though it was, to the Macedonian kingship, based on Seleukos I's conquest of Lysimachos, a Macedonian king, in 281; he had been on his way to take over in Macedon when he was murdered.

47 Livy 35.31.5; Diodoros 28.15.
48 Livy 35.12.1–6.
49 Livy 35.12.10–14.
50 Livy 35.12.7–9 and 13.1–3.
51 Livy 35.12.15–8.
52 Livy 35.13.6–9.
53 Nothing is known of Minnio: this is the only occasion he is even mentioned.
54 Livy 35.15.1–7.
55 Livy 35.32.1.
56 Livy 35.32.2–33.5; Ager, *Interstate Arbitrations* 84.
57 Livy 35.23.10.
58 Livy 35.32.1–33.6.
59 Livy 35.31.3–32.1.
60 Livy 35.34.4–11.
61 Livy 35.46.1–13; 50.8–10.
62 Livy 35.48–50.3.
63 Livy 35.50.3–51.9.
64 Livy 36.8.3–6 and 10.10; Appian, *Syrian Wars* 16.
65 Livy 36.6.1–5.
66 Livy 35.47.5–6.
67 Livy 36.5.2–3.
68 Livy 36.5.3–8; Polybios 20.3–4.
69 J.D. Grainger, 'The Campaign of Cn. Manlius Vulso in Asia Minor', *Anatolian Studies* 54, 1995, 23–42.
70 Livy 38.38.1–17.

# 11 The diplomacy of peacemaking (222–188)

Between 222 and 188 BC a dozen peace treaties were negotiated between the several major powers around the Mediterranean; since such activity is clearly one of the major functions of diplomacy it is worth considering how it was done. The Roman Republic was involved in half of them, and the others involved most of the other powers of the Greco-Macedonian world. Rome made peace with a long series of (former and future) enemies, and it was in part by these treaties that the city gained the commanding position of imperial power which was the effective foundation for its future empire. From 188 no rival state was able to block Roman expansion whenever the republic felt like it.

These treaties, therefore, while providing a discrete group which is reasonably well sourced, provide an opportunity for considering the differing approaches of the eastern monarchies and Rome. For example, the Roman approach steadily alters from a position of reasonableness and negotiation to one of dictation. Even so, Rome never ignored the possibilities of negotiation, and its initial dictatorial stance was usually modified by the practical need to discuss terms in order to actually bring about a condition of peace.

In a study of diplomacy, making peace at the end of a war is clearly one of the crucial elements. Diplomacy is, or should be, the primary means short of war of resolving international disputes, but at the end of a war, it was the primary means of ending the fighting. It may also have the aim of ensuring that no further wars occurred. This could be done by so crushing a defeated enemy that its revival as a military power was impossible or, alternatively, by making an agreement which solved all disputes between the two states.

The long negotiations between Rome and Antiochos III is a case of the latter type, where for several years both parties made a serious attempt to solve their mutual problems; the Greek settlement of T. Quinctius Flamininus may be seen as an example of the imposition of a peace on generally unwilling victims, one which was flawed from the beginning and soon failed;[1] an example of the 'crushing of a defeated enemy' would be the Third Romano-Macedonian War, to be discussed in the next chapter. Here is one major difference between the diplomatic processes of eastern and western states – no war in the east ended in such a 'crushing'. Alternatively both sides might realise that they were unable to prevail, and so make a peace which was in effect a truce; this was, of course, a guarantee of further disputes and wars. The treaties made between 222 and 188 show all these possibilities.

Not all of these treaties involved two great powers, but all involved at least one of them, and the processes are instructive. In theory a treaty between a great power and a lesser should have been fairly straightforward in that the great power should be able to dictate to the lesser, but this was not always the case.

## Sparta and the Symmachy, 222

At the end of the war between the Achaian League and Sparta in 222, the actual winner was King Antigonos Doson of Macedon, whose Greek alliance had been formally organised into a new Hellenic League (see Chapter 5). The army of the Achaian League had proved to be militarily incompetent in the face of the revived Spartan power of King Kleomenes III and had had to be rescued by Antigonos. For a time Sparta was almost capable of acting as a great power and certainly made a good fight against the Macedonian attack. The Macedonian king had prepared the way by bringing a large part of Greece into a super-league, the Symmachy, with himself as president and commander-in-chief. This he led to victory. Kleomenes escaped into a gilded internment in Egypt, and Antigonos dispensed his judgement in the city of Sparta, the first time the city had been captured by an enemy force.

There does not seem to have been any negotiation at the end of the war, nor a peace treaty as such. Kleomenes had been regarded as a dangerous revolutionary and had boosted Spartan power by reverting to what he thought was the ancestral Spartan constitution. With Kleomenes gone into exile and the other Spartan king (his brother Eukleidas – so much for reviving the ancestral constitution) dead in the final battle, there was actually no Spartan government with which to negotiate. Antigonos assumed power in the city and simply decreed an end to the more prominent and provocative of Kleomenes' revolutionary measures. The kingship was left vacant, but the oligarchic ephorate was revived; without the kings, the ephors were supreme; this was, according to Polybios, another 'return to the ancestral constitution'. Sparta became, in political terms, an oligarchy. Some of the Spartan borderlands were handed over to neighbours from whom Kleomenes had taken them or were made into independent states. A governor, Brachyllas of Thebes, was installed to see to all this, and Sparta was probably enrolled in the Symmachy which had been organised by Antigonos, more as a means of controlling the city than as a friendly and useful member.[2]

Since both kings had been killed or driven out, and the great majority of the Spartan citizens who had supported them had been killed in the battle and the preceding campaigns, Antigonos had a relatively easy task. There was no overt opposition to his measures, but that did not necessarily mean the Spartans were willing in the long run to accept this new reversion to the past – the immediate pre-Kleomenic past, that is – but given the city's exhaustion, Antigonos' measures were sufficient to control the city for the present.

No doubt it was all very satisfying to those who had suffered from Spartan attentions in the past – installing a Theban as *epistates* was a reminder that it was a Theban army a century and a half before which had brought Sparta low for the first time. The measures brought peace in the Peloponnese, but Sparta and Achaia fought another war in 207 (another Spartan defeat), the Romans fought the Spartans in 195 and again in 192–191, and in 188 the Achaian statesman Philopoimen compelled Sparta to become a member of the Achaian League, the Symmachy of Antigonos having disappeared. As a solution this last measure had a certain geographical merit, but it only internalised the Spartan problem within the league, and in the end it was continuing Spartan resentment at this Achaian domination which helped bring about the destruction of the Achaian League at Roman hands in 146.

The defeat of Sparta and the destruction of the Kleomenic regime in 222 was therefore no more than a superficial solution to what Peloponnesian politicians no doubt thought of as the 'Spartan problem'. The Spartans got the same treatment they had tended to deliver to their own defeated enemies, but tit-for-tat was not going to prevent them breaking out again. King Antigonos' peace was a purely temporary matter, despite his smashing and apparently decisive military victory, and he probably knew it – but then, all peace treaties were temporary arrangements.

## Naupaktos, 217: the Symmachy and the Aitolian League

After Sparta had been forcibly enrolled in the Symmachy only two major Greek states remained outside it, Athens and the Aitolian League. Athens was conspicuously under Ptolemaic protection and was clearly out of bounds unless Antigonos wanted yet another war, but the Aitolian League was a prime target, a power which had repeatedly annoyed both Achaia and Macedon in the past, as well as its other neighbours. It was now isolated, and, like Sparta under Kleomenes, it aspired to great power status.

The war which resulted began in 220 and is called the Social War, that is the War of the Allies, but a better name would be the Aitolian-Symmachic War. Antigonos was dead by the time it began, and by the time peace was being discussed the new king of Macedon, Philip V, was the Symmachy's leading power. Despite the array of enemies lined up against Aitolia, victory in the war had proved impossible: the Symmachy had become even more nakedly an instrument of Macedonian power, and many of the Greek states who had been keen to suppress Kleomenes' revolution were unenthusiastic about destroying Aitolia. Philip had meanwhile become convinced that a bigger opportunity for aggrandisement had opened up with the successes of Hannibal in Italy in 217 and set about negotiating an Aitolian peace so that his own hands would be free to take advantage of others' difficulties.

This therefore was a peace brought about by negotiation, not victory. Philip began the process by sending a prominent Aitolian prisoner, Kleonikos of Naupaktos, home to Aitolia with the suggestion of convening a peace conference. He brought his forces, land and sea, to Aigion, an Achaian city on the south coast of the Gulf of Corinth, only a short sail from Aitolia. While the Aitolians considered the proposal and Kleonikos moved back and forth with messages, Philip carried out a raid into the enemy territory in Elis. Exactly what messages Kleonikos delivered is not known, but from the speed with which matters were eventually arranged, they concerned the general terms of peace, with the details left for later discussion by the principals.

The Aitolians eventually proposed a face-to-face meeting. The main terms had apparently been agreed, and this was to be a ratification meeting. Philip agreed and sent out messages to his allies to come to join in. Since Philip was staying at Aigion, the nearest thing to a capital the Achaian League had, the Achaians at least had probably been kept informed and the others probably more distantly. Just to keep up the pressure Philip spent the time, while waiting for them to arrive, in capturing the island of Zakynthos, which had been a member of the Aitolian League.

When his allies arrived, Philip sent a selection of them across the Gulf to meet the Aitolians, who had gathered their forces – who were also their assembly – at Naupaktos. There were still items to be settled, and without Philip no agreement could be reached. Ratification must be by Philip, by the Aitolian Assembly, and by the Symmachy. The final negotiations therefore took place at one remove from all these authorities – by a committee of the Aitolian Assembly and by agents of the Symmachy. The allies returned to the king with an Aitolian delegation, which suggested that he take a force across the Gulf, presumably as a guarantee of Aitolian good faith. He established himself in a palisaded camp on Aitolian soil. The Aitolian Assembly arrived, without arms, and the final details were negotiated in effect between the assembly and Philip.

The general terms were that each side should keep what it held, and the detailed discussions sorted out what these were – Polybios could not be bothered to provide these details, which may suggest that, as an Achaian patriot, he was not pleased at the settlement. He provides a version of a speech by Agelaus of Naupaktos, who pointed to the 'cloud rising in the west', which could be either Rome or Carthage, or a reference to the war they were fighting.[3] This was a clever move since this was exactly what Philip was concerned to exploit; it suggests that the Aitolians knew full well why Philip was asking for a peace. Polybios claims that the Aitolians were anxious for peace but that they had haggled over the details of the terms, which also implies that they knew that their position was by no means weak. They understood Philip's new ambition, so they could hold out for better terms.[4]

The main interest in this peace process is that it demonstrates that there were definite stages in such negotiations: a beginning by which it was agreed to talk, detailed negotiations between delegates, and final ratifications by both sides. None of this is a surprise, but it is to be noted that the process was fully familiar to both parties; it was a process clearly widely understood.

The peace which resulted lasted for six years and might have lasted longer but for the actions of Philip, who so stirred up Roman enmity that they were able to persuade the Aitolians to restart the war. By this time the Symmachy had vanished, so Philip fought the new war on his own, but so did the Aitolians, for Roman participation. The enmity of Macedon and Aitolia ran deep – they had been in effect competing for hegemony in Greece for over a century – and it is likely that another war would have broken out sooner or later even without Roman interference, but the Aitolians certainly seized the opportunity provided by the promised Roman help. So the Peace of Naupaktos in 217 was ultimately a failure, in that the two sides fought each other again after a fairly brief interval – but then all peace treaties fail in the end.

## Seleukeia-in-Pieria 218 and Antioch 217, the Seleukid and Ptolemaic Kingdoms, Antiochos III and Ptolemy IV

Between the conquest of Sparta in 222 and the Peace of Naupaktos in 217 two other peace conferences were held, at Seleukeia-in-Pieria in Syria in 218 and at Antioch in 217. These have been discussed in some detail in Chapter 2 in the context of the pattern of the Syrian Wars, so here it will only be necessary to point out that the first meeting, in 218, was a delaying tactic by the Ptolemaic side to gain time in which to recruit and train a new army; the second meeting, which took place more or less simultaneously with that at Naupaktos, was the result of the great Seleukid military defeat at Raphia, and both sides aimed for the conference to succeed.

The 218 meeting at Seleukeia was one between powers which were equals; Antiochos III was the victor so far in the fighting, but the Ptolemaic government in its Egyptian fortress was by no means defeated strategically and still held large parts of the disputed territory. Antiochos III no doubt knew well enough that the Ptolemaic government was recruiting a new army, for the recruiting was on such a scale that it was impossible to keep it secret. Neither side expected peace to result from the meeting at Seleukeia; both used the meeting to advertise their cases.[5]

The 217 meeting followed the great defeat of Antiochos' army at Raphia, but the treaty which resulted could not be described as a Ptolemaic triumph. The only territory to change hands was Seleukeia-in-Pieria, which Antiochos had captured and which he now kept. That is, the Seleukid defeat had not altered in any serious way the relative strengths of the two states, and this was fully understood by both. The peace was easily agreed, and Ptolemy was content to give up Seleukeia and abandon his alliance with Akhaios in Asia Minor in exchange for peace.[6] The readiness of the Ptolemaic side to make peace suggests that the underlying geopolitical reality was fully understood and that Ptolemy knew he was in a basically weaker position than Antiochos; a peace made at that point would guarantee peace for the lifetime of one of the kings. Ptolemy was younger than Antiochos, while Antiochos was a warrior and Ptolemy less than bellicose; objectively it could be expected that Antiochos would die first, being the older and rasher. But human calculations of future events are usually wrong, as was this one, if it was made.

The meeting at Antioch, therefore, was a process of negotiation. It seems that Antiochos took part himself in the discussions, which will have speeded matters along and may well be the reason he was able to come out of the talks without losses. He kept the strategically important city of Seleukeia and succeeded in isolating his enemy Akhaios, whom he attacked in the next years without overt Ptolemaic interference. It may also be that the expense of the war significantly reduced the Ptolemaic kingdom's war-making capacity, so that its naval strength decayed – it

200  *The collision of East and West*

was also soon to be subjected to an increasingly difficult native Egyptian rebellion. When the next war came Ptolemaic power proved to have been hollowed out decisively. In the longer term, beyond the peace treaty, Antiochos was the winner.

## Rome and Syracuse, 211

The second war between Rome and Carthage also involved Syracuse, the kingdom which had been a Roman ally since the first war with Carthage. In 215 the city, now under Hieronymos, the grandson of King Hiero, made terms with Carthage and so incurred Roman enmity. This process therefore involved a treaty between Syracuse and Carthage, and eventually one between Syracuse and Rome. The achievement of the first of these treaties was a complicated affair, involving negotiations by the Syracusans with both the government in Carthage and with Hannibal in Italy. But neither Carthage nor Hannibal was interested in taking over Syracusan territory or imposing punitive terms; all they wanted was a Syracusan alliance and the city's participation in the war on their side. King Hieronymos was assassinated not long after concluding the treaty of alliance, and Hannibal's agents, Syracusan republican exiles, then seized control, abolished the monarchy, and kept the city in Carthage's alliance. There was a substantial element among the population which disagreed with this policy, and the alliance with Carthage inevitably brought Roman enmity.

Rome responded with a series of negotiations designed to break or prevent the Syracusan-Carthaginian alliance,[7] which were complicated by repeated upheavals in the city and by several changes in the Roman command; in the end the city was besieged and slowly conquered.[8] In the final negotiations the main obstacle was the demand by the Roman commander M. Claudius Marcellus for the surrender of Roman deserters who were fighting on the Syracusan side. The Syracusans let these men escape then asked for terms, offering the city in exchange for their own and their children's lives. To this Marcellus agreed, though he did permit the city to be sacked and looted, during which many who had their lives guaranteed were killed.[9]

This was a peace of surrender after military defeat. There was therefore no question of a new political settlement nor of a revival of the former Roman-Syracusan alliance. Syracuse was annexed to Rome. One might compare this with the conquest of Sparta by Antigonos III Doson eleven years before. The result at Sparta was the continued freedom of the defeated city, which used that freedom to go on making trouble for its neighbours, while Syracuse lost its independence but settled for a subordinated freedom and peace and prosperity.

## Arsamosata, 212, Baktra, 206, 'India' 206: Antiochos III and Kings Xerxes of Armenia, Euthydemos of Baktria and Sophagasenos of Paropamisadai

Antiochos III's eastern expedition involved making treaties with the Armenian King Xerxes and the Baktrian King Euthydemos; he also probably made agreements which amounted to treaties with the Parthian king and with Sophagasenos, the Indian ruler of the Paropamisadai. Of these we have a brief account of the agreement with Xerxes, even briefer remarks on that with Sophagasenos, nothing on a Parthian agreement, and a more detailed description of the negotiations with Euthydemos.[10]

The Armenian ruler Xerxes left his fortified town of Arsamosata while it was under siege by Antiochos; he was therefore able to operate to disrupt the siege when talks were proposed. According to Polybios, Antiochos 'sent for' Xerxes, but there must have been negotiations before that so that Xerxes would know he would be attending the meeting under a safe conduct. The terms we are told of were that Xerxes was 'forgiven' the outstanding tribute his father had failed to pay, but Xerxes himself was mulcted of a large contribution of cash, horses, and mules. In return he was given a female relative of Antiochos', Antiochis, as his wife. Antiochos was then able to march on without fearing trouble from Armenia. Antiochis murdered Xerxes not long after and returned to Antiochos,[11] but so far as we can see, the peace held.

The treaty with Euthydemos also followed an unsuccessful siege, said to have lasted for two years. Polybios' surviving account begins in the midst of the siege, when Teleas, an envoy of Antiochos, interviewed Euthydemos, who justified his occupation of the Baktrian throne. Teleas reported to Antiochos and was then sent back and forth between the kings conducting the negotiations (as did Kleonikos between Philip and the Aitolians).[12] Both kings had strong cards to play: Antiochos' siege was gripping Baktra and probably large parts of the kingdom; Euthydemos' resistance was detaining Antiochos at the extreme end of his kingdom for a long time, and he threatened to call in the nomads. When terms were agreed they were ratified at a meeting of Antiochos with Euthydemos' son Demetrios. Evidently as an extra inducement Demetrios was offered one of Antiochos' daughters as his wife, though there is no evidence that he accepted.[13] The terms agreed are not stated in detail, but Euthydemos kept his throne and surrendered his elephant stable. 'After making a written treaty containing other points and entering into a sworn alliance', the war ended. Antiochos had thus prevailed and had reduced Euthydemos to subordination.[14] The two kings were bound by oaths to keep the peace for the rest of their lives. They did not meet at any point during these events.

The visit to Sophagasenos went more smoothly. It seems there was no fighting. The 'alliance' between the two rulers was 'renewed' (but we do not know when the original agreement was made, if ever), and once again Antiochos confiscated Sophagasenos' elephants,[15] which could be regarded as the payment of tribute by a subordinate ruler to his suzerain. If the two were already in treaty relations before Antiochos arrived, as Polybios' mention of its 'renewal' implies, then it may be presumed that the terms of the new treaty were the same as the original, though nothing is known of the terms of either agreement.

These three treaties all have a similar pattern. Antiochos was apparently unwilling to administer the *coup de grace* to an enemy when he could reach an agreement which made his enemy a subordinate ally. The one enemy with whom he is not recorded as making a treaty was the Parthian king, for Polybios' surviving account breaks off in the middle of the fighting. The Parthian kingdom continued to exist but lost some territory; since it remained quiet after Antiochos marched off, an agreement had evidently been made; the terms therefore will have included the formal surrender of the conquered territory and the subordination of the Parthian king as a subject ally.

These treaties set up a sort of monarchic symmachy, with Antiochos presiding over a group of allied kings, a system which stayed in place until one of the kings died – which seems to have been Euthydemos in the 190s. Antiochos was on his way to the east again when he was killed in 187. All three of the subordinate kings were perhaps dead by then, so Antiochos was probably aiming to renew the system with their successors. Since the system operated and kept the peace for two decades, it may be regarded as a success.

## Macedon and Aitolia, 206

Philip V went to war with Rome in 215, to which Rome responded by forming an alliance with the Aitolian League, and from 211 the two were fighting Philip. The Aitolians soon found that Rome was not interested in much more than operating on the defensive in Greece, certainly while Hannibal was still active in Italy. By 207 it was clear that Philip was likely to be victorious in Greece, while Roman assistance to their ally was minimal.

In that year Philip raided deep into Aitolian territory and captured and sacked the federal sanctuary at Thermon. A group of four Greek neutral states intervened (not for the first time) to suggest negotiations.[16] The Aitolians agreed, even though this violated one of the terms of their alliance – that the two allied states would not make a separate peace. The Roman commander in Illyria, P. Sulpicius Galba, protested at what he could only regard as Aitolian perfidy and desertion, but he could not offer any concrete assistance to his desperate allies. The Aitolians in return regarded this refusal as also breaching the terms of the alliance; the two states were supposed to be fighting together, yet Rome was doing little or nothing in Greece and had lost control of some of its Illyrian territories. The league therefore made peace, despite Roman objections, probably on the same basis as in 217, that each should hold what it had gained. The resulting treaty included the allies of both Philip and the Aitolians in Greece, but it was the agreement between the two principals which counted; the rest simply fell into line. Livy says that the peace was concluded on Philip's terms, which in the circumstances is reasonable, since he was victorious, but he was not vindictive; some outlying parts of the league were lost.[17]

## Phoinike, 205: Rome and Macedon

The peace between Philip and Aitolia left Philip and the Romans facing each other in their battleground in Epeiros and Illyria. Rather late in the day the Romans sent a new army across the Adriatic to get the war going again, perhaps hoping that the Aitolians, having broken their Roman treaty, would be amenable to breaking their new Macedonian treaty – it was certainly suggested. The Aitolians had had enough; they could reasonably assume that, if they again succumbed to Roman blandishments, Rome would again leave them to fight alone.

The new Roman force, commanded by P. Sempronius Tuditanus, made no progress; Philip arrived to face the Roman attack but was equally unable to tackle the Roman forces.[18] Again a neutral Greek state, the Epeirotes, perilously close to the rival armies, intervened and suggested a peace conference. First they approached Tuditanus and got his agreement to the suggestion.[19] This was the crucial move, since only if the Roman commander had the authority to treat could talks even begin. Tuditanus had thus evidently been armed with such authority by the Senate before he left Rome, so he was not surprised at the approach. The new Roman army was clearly not intended to wage a major campaign – it was only eleven thousand strong, large enough to defend Roman territory but not enough for a serious campaign into Macedonia. In effect it was present to demonstrate that Rome was not making peace through necessity but by choice.

Philip was agreeable to talks and discussed the position with three Epeirote magistrates first, who will have been those who had seen Tuditanus. So these were exploratory discussions, aimed at discovering if the two sides' terms were in any way compatible. Philip then met Tuditanus at the Epeirote city of Phoinike and, with the neutral envoys and King Amynander of Athamania present, hammered out an agreement. Livy claims that 'Sempronius laid down the terms', but it is clear that the eventual result was a compromise.

This time there were detailed territorial adjustments to be agreed, but the net result was that, although Rome recovered some Illyrian territory, most of the disputed region was retained by Philip. Again a list of the allies of both sides was included in the treaty, but, as before, only the principals counted.[20] The treaty was speedily ratified by the Romans, and Tuditanus was elected consul for the next year, a rapid sequence which indicated clearly enough that Roman plans had been accomplished. Rome had lost territory by this war, not something Rome was accustomed to accept; the peace was unlikely to last.

Philip and Aitolia might both have been dissatisfied over their accomplishments in these wars, but both had clearly realised that further fighting between them would be pointless, at least under the circumstances of 206–205. Neither could be defeated without a long and expensive fight requiring more troops than either had on hand. To that extent the peace they made in 206 endured. On the other hand, that peace process built up a considerable head of resentment at Rome, and so the Peace of Phoinike was by no means definitive, even if Philip appears to have believed it was. In Rome the two treaties of 206 and 205 were regarded as marking defeats to be reversed as soon as possible.

## Rome and Carthage, 202/201

The peace treaty which resulted when Rome won its second Carthaginian war was very similar in its essentials to that which had ended the first of these wars in 241. Getting there, however, had been difficult. The Roman army which invaded Africa under P. Cornelius Scipio in 204 was not really large enough if it was intended to capture and destroy the city. For many Romans, this would be the most satisfactory conclusion to the war. Scipio was prepared to negotiate a peace, though it had to be based on a clear recognition of Roman victory; otherwise it would never be accepted by the Roman Senate. A first attempt to negotiate with the Carthaginian commander Hasdrubal and the Numidian King Syphax – a complex business – failed when the preliminary truce broke down.[21]

After further Carthaginian defeats serious negotiations between Scipio and a delegation of thirty Carthaginian senators produced a draft treaty which was sent to Rome for the Senate to consider. There was, as is only to be expected, considerable debate on whether to accept it; probably while the Senate was doing so, the Carthaginian armies in Italy (under Hannibal in Bruttium and his brother Mago in Liguria) were withdrawn to Africa. In the end it seems that the Senate ratified the treaty (though the matter is not certain).[22] In Carthage, however, the truce broke down. There was an attack on Roman envoys visiting the city to complain of earlier incidents who also brought the news of the Senate's ratification.[23]

A third attempt was supposedly made when Scipio and Hannibal are said to have talked before their armies met in battle at Zama, though this seems unlikely, unless one or other was prepared to give in; the presence of their armies implied otherwise.[24] The idea of such a meeting seems more likely to be a romance by inventive historians. After the Carthaginian defeat at Zama, a group of ten envoys from Carthage met Scipio at sea, and after a Roman naval demonstration before the city, he met another set of thirty envoys at his camp. These men were in effect asking for a truce and for a statement of Roman terms.[25]

Scipio gained a certain psychological advantage by his naval parade before the city and by having the envoys meet him amid his army, all of which emphasised the victory at Zama. He discussed the issue of terms with his war council. The chances of victory in a siege of the city were discussed, but its strength and large population were deterrents. Scipio also feared that he would be replaced by a new consul, who would make peace and so gain the glory.[26] Terms were worked out and presented to the Carthaginians; they were not greatly different from those which the Senate had already ratified. At Rome, there was a dispute over who should finally be responsible for ratification; by shifting the decision to the popular assembly, the peace was finally secured. Hannibal, convinced of the need for peace, is depicted as having the same sort of problem in Carthage.[27] The Carthaginians had gained a certain advantage by holding out long enough for the political pressure to tell on Scipio; it is not certain that they understood this, but it seems very probable.

By the terms Carthage lost all its overseas territories (which had been conquered anyway) and had to pay an indemnity spread over fifty years. There were various other minor terms, but it was these which were the most important.[28] The length of the indemnity period ensured that Carthage remained under Roman suzerainty for that time; this was reinforced by detaining a hundred Carthaginian hostages. It was a republican version of the lifetime treaties of the eastern monarchies, and as was the case with them, it was impossible to know what would happen at the end of that period. It is unlikely that anyone in 202/201 cared.[29]

## Gonnos, 197: Rome and Macedon

With the end of the war with Carthage, the Romans planned a new Macedonian war to rectify their earlier defeat. It was launched in 200, though without military success for two years. The last year of the war was punctuated by a series of peace conferences between King Philip and the Roman consul T. Quinctius Flamininus, first at the Aous Pass in June 198, then, after Flamininus had shifted his forces into central Greece, at Nikaia in Lokris in November, and finally, after Philip's defeat at Kynoskephalai, at Gonnos in Thessaly near the Tempe Pass. At each meeting the terms demanded by the Romans remained essentially the same: that Philip evacuate Greece. At the Aous meeting this was a ridiculous demand,[30] since the Roman forces had not yet even won a skirmish, but they became steadily more realistic as Flamininus' forces advanced towards Macedon.

At the meeting at Nikaia Roman demands had a greater plausibility, and a set of peace terms appears to have been worked out in a private meeting between the two principals. Philip sent a delegation to Rome for what he presumably expected would be ratification by the Senate, but the representatives sent by Flamininus raised a set of new demands.[31] This signals his later behaviour in unilaterally altering agreed peace terms even after they had been ratified. Not surprisingly, the war resumed. After his defeat at Kynoskephalai, Philip sent his herald to ask for permission to bury the dead of the battlefield, and the meeting at Gonnos was arranged. There, Philip announced that he would now accept the terms of the Nikaia meeting.[32]

Flamininus was under a certain constraint in all this, for his constant reiteration of the same terms indicates that these were the terms set by the Senate. Having gained revenge for the earlier defeat, the Senate was not prepared to countenance the destruction of the Macedonian kingdom, which might be the result if the more stringent terms produced at Rome after the Nikaia meeting were imposed. The Aitolian League would then be the most powerful Greek state, and the league was heartily disliked at Rome. The aim was evidently to achieve a Roman position as arbiter of Greek affairs without having to keep a garrison in the country, very much in the same way that the Carthaginian indemnity payment gave Rome a constant excuse to interfere in Africa. By accepting the Roman terms Philip was preserving his position, but he was also playing the Senate's game, though he may not have known it; not surprisingly the Senate now accepted the agreement.[33]

## Sparta, 195: Nabis and Flamininus

Flamininus revealed his unscrupulousness during his negotiations with Philip; the ruler of Sparta, Nabis, also suffered from this.[34] The settlement which was announced to great Greek joyfulness at Corinth in 196 included the withdrawal of Roman forces from the country and the liberation of the Greek cities. (This was not a treaty of peace, hence it is not considered here.) Nabis had occupied Argos and still held it after the general Greek 'liberation'. Fortunately, from Flamininus' point of view, neither Sparta nor Nabis evoked any sympathy among the rest of the Greeks, but Argos did. Using a combined Greek and Roman army Flamininus conducted an invasion of Sparta, which was, in fact, in formal terms, still a Roman ally. Nabis put up a good fight, but he faced overwhelming odds and quickly gave in when the enemy reached Lakonian territory.

Flamininus had a set of terms ready, but again they did not permit the destruction of the Spartan state. It was deprived of substantial tracts of territory but not of its independence and retained some disputed areas; Nabis remained in power. Roman intentions in the Peloponnesos were thus similar to those between Aitolia and Macedon: to foster a balancing power – Sparta – as against the potentially local power of the Achaian League. Despite Achaian wishes – Achaian forces had done much of the fighting – Sparta remained in existence with worthwhile power.[35]

This peace agreement did not work any better than that concluded with Antigonos Doson thirty years before. The drastic reduction in Spartan territory provoked the Spartans into repeated bouts of fighting. In 188 the Achaians forcibly brought the city into their league – which, of course, brought a continuing Spartan problem on their own heads. It also meant that the Roman purpose had been thwarted, though Sparta in the league was a source of weakness, not strength.

## Raphia, 195: Antiochos III and Ptolemy V

Antiochos III conducted a successful war against Ptolemy V between 202 and 195, conquering Koile Syria and the many Ptolemaic posts and cities along the south and east coasts of Asia Minor as far as Lysimacheia in the Gallipoli peninsula. Of the treaty which ended the war we know very little, other than that it was being negotiated during 196, when Antiochos met Roman commissioners at Lysimacheia; at the end of the meeting, which was held in September, he announced that peace had been concluded. The precise terms are unknown but are obvious from the result of the war. The lands conquered by Antiochos were formally transferred to him, and his daughter was given to Ptolemy in marriage.

A Rhodian, Eukles, is mentioned as an intermediary, either as a neutral arbitrator[36] – highly unlikely – or one of Antiochos' men. The negotiations probably began in 196, and according to Antiochos they were almost complete by September 196 when he stated this to the Romans at Lysimacheia. Since Antiochos had been campaigning in Thrace since June, the talks had obviously been conducted by one of his agents – Eukles, presumably – but we do not know where. (I use 'Raphia' as the identifier because the marriage of Kleopatra Syra and Ptolemy V took place there, and this event was the effective ratification of the treaty; it would not have taken place unless all the terms were already in place.)

The scale of the dowry is not known, and this has provoked a theory that it consisted of the conquered lands of Palestine and Phoenicia, or perhaps the revenues therefrom which were assigned to Kleopatra, but to believe that Antiochos would surrender any part of a land, or any of his rights over it, that his family had fought repeatedly to gain for the past century is nonsense. The negotiations cannot have been difficult: the terms, after such a comprehensive defeat, were obvious (see Chapter 6).[37]

## Apameia, 188: Rome and Antiochos III

The war between Rome and Antiochos III in 192–188 produced a radical reversal of fortune for the king; he was defeated at Thermopylai in Greece, at sea, and at Magnesia in Asia Minor.[38] After Magnesia he appears to have decided at once that it was not worth fighting on, though he still had large forces at his command, and he could have gathered another army during the next winter as large as that which had been defeated. But he had been left to fight alone both in Greece and in Asia (except for some assistance from Ariarathes of Kappadokia). The Aitolians had made a truce which allowed the Romans to bring their full strength against him. (It must have seemed, at least to the Romans, to be a characteristic of the Aitolians to desert an alliance when things were not going well – see next section on the treaty of Ambrakia.)

The process of negotiation is detailed in both Livy and Polybios. Antiochos retreated to Apameia-Kelainai in Phrygia, where he decided that the fight could not be resumed. He sent a herald, Mousaios (named, for once) to see the consul, then Zeuxis, governor of Asia Minor, and Antipater, the king's 'nephew' (who had performed the same service after Raphia twenty-seven years before), were sent to discuss the truce terms.[39] These men were the equivalent of the consul as negotiators, and both sets of negotiations were subject to ratification, by the Roman Senate and the king.

The Romans therefore had two treaties to negotiate, with the Aitolians (see the next section) and with Antiochos. Antiochos was given a truce, on payment of five hundred talents, which was in effect his war chest; he was thus partly paralysed.[40] A set of more or less onerous peace terms were laid out, agreed to, and sent to Rome for ratification. The Roman army stayed in occupation in western Asia Minor, and a new consul, Cn. Manlius Vulso, was assigned Asia as his province. He conducted a most cunning campaign through Asia Minor, marching carefully to avoid any of Antiochos' remaining positions or allies but at the same time leaving them isolated amidst a series of new Roman allies. He capped his expedition by a great defeat of the Galatians, who, after a century, were still a live menace to the non-Galatian inhabitants of Asia Minor.[41]

Vulso having established a dominating Roman position in Asia Minor, the terms of peace were ratified at Rome. Antiochos was to evacuate Asia Minor and Thrace, give up his war elephants and his warships, surrender five named Roman enemies, and pay a huge indemnity of 15,000 talents over the next ten years, with an initial payment of 2,500 talents – which would probably drain his treasury in the short term and severely damage his military capacity after that. Vulso's campaign having left Antiochos no political position in Asia Minor, he accepted.[42] There had been, in effect, no negotiations. A Roman commission of ten senators arrived to divide the spoils up between Rome's allies in a conference. This was the meeting, at Apameia-Kelainai in Phrygia, which gives its name to the treaty; but the peace treaty with the king had clearly been concluded well before the meeting took place; Apameia was only the division of the spoils, not the place of the treaty.

The terms were ratified by the Senate and the oath was administered to Antiochos by Q. Minucius Thermus and L. Manlius Vulso, after the delivery of the first, large, instalment of the indemnity.[43] It is clear from later items, however, that the terms were not fully implemented, and Rome did not insist. Of the former enemies to be surrendered to Rome, at least two, Hannibal and Thoas the Aitolian, were still at liberty later (though Rome hunted Hannibal down when he was under less sympathetic protection in Bithynia); the payment of the indemnity stopped when Antiochos died; after another fifteen years Antiochos' son, Antiochos IV, made the contemptuous gesture of handing over what he said was the outstanding balance – though it was probably much less than that. Many of Antiochos' ships were certainly burnt, but by the Romans, and there is some doubt that those under Antiochos' control were ever destroyed; it is highly unlikely that the war elephants were killed; no Roman inspection team went to Syria to check. This is the obvious reason for Seleukid non-compliance, but Rome's failure to agree to a new treaty with the new king indicates that the Senate understood and accepted this lifetime-limited practice of the eastern kingdoms.

## Ambrakia, 188: Rome and Aitolia

The Roman-Aitolian truce agreed in 191 was supposed to allow final peace terms to be negotiated. The Senate, after the experience of the past thirty years of working with the Aitolians, was in no mood to be generous. An Aitolian delegation met the Senate and was presented with two alternatives: unconditional surrender – what the Romans called *deditio* – or pay an indemnity of a thousand talents and accept a Roman alliance, which, of course, meant handing over control of Aitolian foreign policy to Rome. The Aitolians rejected both; the war revived.[44]

This was awkward for the Roman expeditionary force in Asia; the driving force there, Scipio Africanus, quickly arranged a new six-month truce. A new Aitolian delegation went off to Rome to find out if the Senate would offer better terms.[45] The Roman ploy served its purpose; the 'negotiations' took long enough for the Asian expedition to defeat Antiochos before the truce expired. The end of the truce then produced another Aitolian complication, and they fell into a dispute with King Philip. When the new Roman commander, M. Fulvius Nobilior, approached in the spring of 189, the Aitolians found themselves at war on three separate fronts, but once again they refused any terms which subordinated them to Rome.

After more fighting, Nikandros of Trichonion, the Aitolian commander facing Nobilior, approached him for new terms. Nobilior had captured the city of Ambrakia after a long and difficult siege, which seems to have convinced both sides to consider peace more constructively. Nobilior responded with an offer to reduce the indemnity, the surrender of any cities taken by Rome, and the usual surrender of deserters.[46] He had a personal motive, having his eye on some easier victims than the Aitolians. The Senate did insist on imposing an alliance on the league but otherwise accepted Nobilior terms. (He had presumably been given discretion to modify the Senate's original terms.)[47]

## Conclusion

This set of treaties negotiated in various places and between several states indicates that all parties accepted a series of conventions when it came to concluding peace. The idea that Rome imposed its requirements on defeated opponents is not credible in this period. In no case was a peace concluded without negotiation. The example of the Aitolians in 189–188 is notable and instructive. Repeatedly they refused to accept the Roman formulation and so succeeded in escaping the *deditio* and reducing the indemnity they had to pay. Similarly, the Roman treaty with Antiochos III was never fully enforced.

The process was always the same; a truce ended the fighting, the terms of peace were discussed by agents of the principals, agreement was reached, then ratification took place, usually at some distance from the place of negotiation. All too often Rome tried to ratchet up the terms, though not always successfully – the expedition of Vulso through Asia Minor was clearly an action of this type. Rome also clearly understood – note the cases of Syracuse and the Seleukid kingdom – that if and when a king died, his obligation ceased. Not only that, but the terms might well be unenforceable even if the king lived on. Several parts of the treaty with Antiochos III were ignored by the Seleukid government even while Antiochos was alive. It was also not unknown for later Roman governors and officials to vary the peace terms unilaterally – Flamininus in Greece was a prime case, but not the only one. (Also note that Carthage had supposedly surrendered its warships but sent six vessels to join the Roman naval campaign against Antiochos in 191.)

Rome may well have felt itself different from the other states of the Mediterranean, but it behaved in much the same way, at least in negotiating with them; the deviousness of such men as Scipio Africanus and Flamininus showed a strong contrast between Roman behaviour and that of the Hellenistic kings. Aitolia was also different, in its serial breaking of engagements. It is thus not a question of Rome against the rest, but of kings against republics. Clearly kings took much more care to observe the terms of their oaths than their republican neighbours, who could always cite an overturning vote in Senate or assembly as justification for their treaty-breaking. Treaties with kings, however, died with them, and revival would require re-negotiation with their heirs. But it was clearly more comfortable to be linked with a king in a treaty than with a republic – and still more dangerous if the republic was, like Aitolia, a democracy.

## Notes

1 It is also, however, a peace in the tradition of the Greek *koine eirene* – common peace – which has been traced back for several centuries; but they did not work either; see T.T.B. Ryder, *Koine Eirene, General Peace and Local Independence in Ancient Greece*, Oxford 1965, dealing with examples in the fourth century BC.
2 Polybios 2.70.1; 4.22.4–5; 24.7–8; Plutarch, *Kleomenes* 30.1; Paul Cartledge and Anthony Spawforth, *Hellenistic and Roman Sparta*, London 1989, 57–58.
3 Polybios 5.10 4.1–11; the authenticity of the speech has been impugned, but that can be done with every such composed speech in the ancient world; the sense may well be authentic even if the precise words are not; see C. Champion, 'The Nature of

## 210    The collision of East and West

Authoritative Evidence in Polybius and Agelaus' Speech at Naupactus', *Transactions of the American Philosophical Association* 127, 1997, 111–128.
4  Polybios 101.5–105.2; F.W. Walbank, *Philip V of Macedon*, Cambridge 1940 (reprinted 1967), 64–67.
5  Polybios 5.67.1–68.1.
6  Polybios 5.87.1–8; not included in Schmitt, *Staatsverträge*.
7  Note, in reference to treaties and the deaths of kings, that the propraetor Ap. Claudius Pulcher (governor of the Roman part of Sicily) first approached Hieronymos to request a renewal of the treaty with Hiero, which had lapsed with the death of the old king (Polybius 7.2.3; Livy 24.6.2).
8  Livy 24.23.1–31.5; Richard J. Evans, *Syracuse in Antiquity, History and Topography*, Pretoria 2009, 100–104.
9  Livy 25.28.1–31.11; Plutarch, *Marcellus* 19.
10  None of these treaties is included in Schmitt, *Staatsverträge*.
11  Polybios 8.23.1–5.
12  Actually it is not clear if Teleas was Euthydemos' or Antiochos' man; it scarcely matters for the discussion.
13  Again it is uncertain whether Antiochos had a daughter of marriageable age; married in 221, his eldest possible child could only be 14 by 206; his first child was a son, so any daughter was still well below marriageable age.
14  Polybios 11.39.1–10; for a discussion of the general background see Rachel Mairs, *The Hellenistic Far East*, California 2014, ch. 4.
15  Polybios 11.39.11–12.
16  Ager, *Interstate Arbitrations* 57.
17  Appian, *Macedonian Wars* 3; Livy 29.12.1; Walbank, *Philip V*, 99–101; J.D. Grainger, *The League of the Aitolians*, Leiden 1999, 334–336; not listed in Schmitt, *Staastsvertrage*.
18  Livy 29.12.2–10.
19  Livy 29.12.11–12.
20  Appian, *Macedonian Wars* 3; Livy 29.12.13–15; Walbank, *Philip V*, 102–103; Schmitt, *Staatsverträge* 543; the list of the other participants is controversial but hardly affects the actual peace treaty.
21  Polybios 14.1–14; Livy 30.3.4–7; Appian, *Libyan Wars* 17; Cassius Dio 17.72.
22  Livy 30.16.10–11, 21.11–23.8; Polybios 15.1.3–4; Appian, *Libyan Wars* 31–32; Cassius Dio 17.74.
23  Livy 30.24.5–7, 25.3; Polybios 15.1.1–2.15; Appian, *Libyan Wars* 34.
24  Polybios 15.6.3–8.1.
25  Livy 30.36.10.
26  J.F. Lazenby, *Hannibal's War*, Warminster 1976, 228.
27  Polybios 15.19.2–9; Livy 30.40.7–10.
28  Livy 30.36–37.
29  Polybios 15.18.1; Livy 30.37.1; Appian, *Libyan Wars* 54; Cassius Dio, frag 57; the terms in the preliminary agreements are in Schmitt, *Staatsverträge*, 548.
30  Livy 32.10.1–8.
31  Polybios 10.1–12; Livy 32.32.9–37.6; Plutarch, *Flamininus* 5.6; Appian, *Macedonian Wars* 8.
32  Polybios 18.36–39; Livy 33.11–13; Plutarch, *Flamininus* 9; Appian, *Macedonian Wars* 9.2; Walbank, *Philip V*, 172–178.
33  Livy 33.24.3–6; for a discussion of the issues, see A. Eckstein, *Senate and General, Individual Decision-Making and Roman Foreign Relations 264–194 BC*, California 1987, 285–294.
34  As did Antiochos III when attempts to settle his disputes with Rome shifted to the city and Flamininus was under closer senatorial scrutiny.

35 Livy 38.38.2–17; Plutarch, *Flamininus* 12.
36 The fact that Eukles was a Rhodian does not mean Rhodes itself was involved; the Seleukids and the Ptolemies regularly employed expatriate Greeks in high positions – the Aitolians Theodotos and Skopas, commanding in Koile Syria, are further prominent examples.
37 Livy 33.39.1–40.6 and 35.13.4; Gunther Holbl, *The History of the Ptolemaic Empire*, London 2000, 155–156; J.D. Grainger, *The Syrian Wars*, Leiden 2010, 268–271.
38 Grainger, *Roman War*, ch. 15: for sources and discussion.
39 Livy 37.44.4–45.18; Polybios 21.16.1–17.8; Justin 31.8.8; Diodoros 29.10.
40 Livy 37.45.11–18; Polybios 21.17.1–8.
41 J.D. Grainger, 'The Campaign of Cn. Manlius Vulso in Asia Minor', *Anatolian Studies* 45, 1995, 23–42.
42 Livy 38.38.2–17.
43 Livy 38.39.1–6.
44 Livy 37.1.1–6; Polybios 21.2.4–6.
45 Livy 37.7.4–6; Polybius 21.5.7–12.
46 Livy 38.9.6–11; Polybios 21.29.14–15 and 30.8–9.
47 Livy 38.19.1–10.

# 12  Rome and Greece (188 – *c*.120)

After the distribution of the spoils at Apameia – Kelainai in 188, Rome once more withdrew its forces from the lands east of the Adriatic Sea, though not entirely. It had already controlled the Adriatic and Ionian coasts and cities and islands, from Issa to Kerkyra, for the previous forty years, and these remained part of its dominions. So the city was able, without much effort, to keep itself informed about events in the east and had some forces available in the area at need – the small forces which Flamininus could deploy against Antiochos III in 192 may have come from that area.

The various arrangements, peace treaties, awards of territory, and benefactions which Rome arranged between the peace with Macedon in 197 and the distribution of the spoils of war with Antiochos III in 188 left every state from Illyria to the Taurus Mountains indebted in one way or another to Rome. This was not a condition of control, nor yet a condition of independence. The best term is perhaps one adopted from the nineteenth-century British Empire, another weird conglomeration of disparate territories: it was Rome's 'informal empire' – Greece, Asia Minor, North Africa. For half a century Rome struggled to avoid imposing direct control; for that same half-century the states of the region struggled to cope with Rome's non-system. In the end two wars brought the system to an end. After 146 Greece (and Carthage) were a part of the empire unambiguously; then the problem shifted into Asia Minor.

So this chapter will consider that informal empire in the half-century or less after its inception. During that time Rome made an attempt to implant the ideas promulgated, however imperfectly, by Flamininus in his pronouncement in 196 that the Roman army would be withdrawn from Greece and that 'the Greeks were freed'. The political vacuum this created tempted Antiochos III to fill it, but he was driven out. After that the region included several sizeable kingdoms, the Macedonian and Attalid states, Bithynia and Kappadokia, one major league, the Achaian, and a series of cities of various sizes. Having created the system, Rome had to supervise it, for any problems which arose naturally landed on its doorstep. The means of supervision were, that is, mainly diplomatic, at least in intention.

Major problems had to be dealt with at Rome, which usually did so by sending an embassy to attend to the matter on the spot. Minor problems could be dealt with by a well-established local Greek system of arbitration which Rome generally adopted.[1] This was a method of problem solving which had occurred with every imperial power in the region, from the Akhaimenid Empire on – Persia, Athens, Sparta, Thebes, Macedon, and the Hellenistic kingdoms, and now Rome. All of them allowed, even encouraged, the local disputes to be settled locally if possible, so that only the major issues reached the imperial metropolis.

At least that seems to have been the general idea. It did not always work, as some of the local disputes continued for so long that they became major issues. Further, Rome was distinctly unenthusiastic about becoming involved in many petty (as it saw it) disputes. Even in major issues, such as wars between kingdoms, the Senate was inclined to let the disputants sort the problem out for themselves. On the other hand, a clear victory for one side in a war (and so an increase in the victor's power) was not a welcome outcome, and intervention might then follow.

Much of this has been well studied already, and it would be redundant to recapitulate the work of Gruen on Roman relations with Greece,[2] or Ager on arbitrations,[3] or Kallet-Marx on the spread of direct Roman control over the east after 148.[4] But there are three major wars in the half-century after Flamininus which cast light on the new diplomatic processes as developed under the Roman 'informal empire', and they deserve to be considered in some detail – the Third and Fourth Macedonian Wars, and the Akhaian War, of which the last virtually abolished the informal system, at least in Greece. In addition there is the process of the Roman takeover of the Attalid kingdom in 133–129 and the subsequent application of a modified 'informal empire' scheme in Asia Minor which may be considered briefly.

## The diplomacy of the Third Macedonian War, 188–171

This, the best documented of these wars, will occupy the larger part of this chapter. It is also a case study in diplomatic practice as applied by one of the more arrogant Roman Republican generations – and one of the least competent. The few Romans who demonstrated diplomatic abilities therefore stand out well clear of the rest. It will also form a stark contrast with earlier Roman methods and those of their Hellenistic contemporaries.

The preliminaries of this war between Rome and Macedon, the war itself, and its aftermath between 171 and 167 exhibit the full range of Hellenistic diplomatic practices – negotiations, marriage alliances, threats, alliances, spies, conspiracies, retributions, loyalties, disloyalties, lies, betrayals, and so on, but as usual the sources show all this particularly as operating from the aspect of Rome. This is a situation which we can study because of those particularly good, if biased, sources: Polybios' account, while not complete, is important because he was a contemporary and at times an active participant in events; he knew just about everyone of importance involved; his account underlies that of Livy which, while even more biased, is more or less complete; there are also alternative accounts and fragments of information in Cassius Dio, Justin, Diodoros, and Appian, if brief, a biography by Plutarch, and some helpful inscriptions.

Relations between Macedon and Rome had been unfriendly since Philip V made his alliance with Hannibal at the height of the latter's successes in 215. Philip had assisted Rome against Antiochos III and Aitolia, but such gains as he had made, in Thessaly and in Thrace, had been removed by Rome in the years of peace which followed, by a variety of decisions of the Senate in responding to complaints by Philip's neighbours.[5] Philip carefully avoided giving any real excuse for Roman concern, knowing he was very precariously situated, while at the same time building up the strength of his kingdom in population and wealth and exercising his army in campaigns against his northern barbarians, campaigns which Rome was happy to see him undertake.

Philip died in 179 and was succeeded by his son Perseus.[6] Almost the first action Perseus took was to report his father's death and his own accession to Rome, and at the same time he asked that the treaty agreed with his father be 'renewed', as Polybios puts it.[7] That is, the same terms were agreed between the two states, though, given the usual difficulties any new king faced at his accession it was clearly in Rome's power to have imposed new restrictions on Perseus had the Senate wished. It is apparent that no change was required. By making the request, of course, Perseus was putting himself in a subordinate position with regard to Rome but was also receiving a guarantee of his position as king and a guarantee of peace – unless a breakdown in relations between them took place.

The difficulty was that such relations were not entirely under either Perseus' or Rome's control. Another circumstance which had not changed from Philip's time was the practice of third parties playing on Roman fears and preconceptions to further their own interests, and a series of incidents brought Roman-Macedonian relations to the breaking point. In 174, for example, King Massinissa of Numidia claimed to some Roman envoys that envoys from King Perseus had been in Carthage and that Carthage had sent an embassy in return.[8] This was, of course, hearsay, possibly invented by Massinissa, but he was playing very skilfully on Roman fears, since Carthage and Macedon were still considerable powers against whom Rome had fought very difficult wars in the relatively recent past. The combination of the two could still be a Roman nightmare. The Senate sent an embassy of three men to Macedon to enquire into this.

Soon afterwards, coincidentally, another embassy was sent to investigate troubles in Aitolia. The two sets of envoys returned in the spring of 173, apparently at more or less the same time. Aitolia was reported to be in a hopeless condition of *stasis*. The envoys to Macedon claimed that Perseus had evaded an interview with them[9] but did report that he was making extensive preparations for war. Since Perseus had continued his father's policy of military domination in Thrace, this, at least, is likely to be true, though Livy implies that the envoys accused him of preparing a new Roman war – but not to his face, only in the Senate.

The envoys said that the king had given two separate excuses for refusing to see them: that he was on campaign or that he was ill. Both were claimed to be false, but it seems unlikely that Perseus would deliberately evade a meeting with a group of Roman envoys and even more unlikely that he would give such excuses if they were not true. So the most acceptable explanation is that these reasons were actually correct. Maybe the envoys made a weak attempt to see him and, being put off once, did not bother again. Altogether this is a strange matter but resulted in increased Roman suspicions. Livy comments that as a result 'a Macedonian war was in prospect'.[10] If this is a reflection of the Roman conclusions as early as 173, and not just a Livian editorial comment, the subsequent events must be seen as deliberate Roman preparations for war or even provocations.

During the summer M. Claudius Marcellus was sent to Aitolia to try again to sort out that league's internal problems where earlier Roman attempts had failed. He then visited Achaia, where in a speech to the assembly he made Roman dislike of Perseus – Livy's term is 'hate' – very clear.[11] This may be Marcellus going his own way, but it looks more like a semi-official test of Greek responses to Perseus' kingship. This very public statement was followed by a gathering of ambassadors at Rome later in the year. King Eumenes of Pergamon addressed the Senate on the subject of Perseus' supposed preparations for war,[12] but, not surprisingly, without noting his own interests. By a pair of marriages Perseus had tended to box Eumenes in, at least diplomatically: Perseus himself had married the daughter of King Seleukos IV, and his sister Apama was married to King Prusias II of Bithynia (another sister was married to a Thracian king).[13] Both of these states could be regarded as Eumenes' enemies – as indeed could Perseus himself, who was Eumenes' neighbour in Thrace. On the other hand, these marriages brought Perseus no assistance in the war which soon began; as usual marriage alliances were not actual political or military alliances.

Perseus' envoy at Rome, Harpalos, answered Eumenes, but he could do little more than deny that his king was preparing for a war with Rome.[14] Perseus was trapped by this series of complaints and comments and reports, and soon by a series of Greek envoys as well. Some complaints had come even earlier from Thessaly, though this seems to have been aimed mainly at getting Roman help in sorting out internal Thessalian problems, the Thessalians realising that the only way of getting Roman attention was by complaining about Perseus. Harpalos could hardly refute Eumenes' accusations detail by detail, since it would necessarily be unconvincing – and quite likely a good deal of them were invented in the first place, so Harpalos would be unable even to discuss them. The Senate was pleased to hear all this, of course, but the Rhodian envoy spoiled the party by accusing Eumenes himself of interfering in their own affairs.[15]

Various accusations against Perseus continued to reach the Senate: from Eumenes' claim of an assassination plot organised by Perseus during a visit to Delphi;[16] from a citizen of Brundisium who claimed that Perseus proposed to poison Romans passing through the port.[17] All this, though dubious in every case, succeeded in bringing the Senate to the point of decision – which may have been the purpose of the accusations. The Roman garrisons in the cities along the Illyrian coast were reinforced.[18] Perseus had actually given no excuse for a war, despite considerable goading and provocation.

Such incidents, if they really were instigated by Perseus, or if they were calculated inventions on the Roman side, were part of the underside of diplomacy which is rarely mentioned in the ancient accounts. Most likely they were accidents or inventions or misinterpretations, but they certainly succeeded in increasing the tension between Rome and Macedon. Harpalos travelled as quickly as possible back to Macedon to report to Perseus,[19] who was therefore confirmed in his expectation of a Roman war. He must have realised it had become increasingly likely ever since Marcellus' speech to the Achaians; another embassy went from Rome to Eumenes to congratulate him on his survival of the assassination plot.[20]

How far all this was a deliberate campaign by Perseus' enemies, how far it was encouraged by the Roman Senate, and how far the Senate was collectively duped into going to war are issues impossible to decide at this distance, but the combination of issues reinforced mutual enmity and suspicion. One of the most telling elements was probably the realisation by Rome – confirmed by more than one embassy – that Philip and Perseus were in fact well-armed, which made Perseus dangerous. A certain paranoia existed at Rome, evident in much of Livy for this period,[21] and any non-Roman power with any strength at all was liable to be seen as an enemy.

By late 173 it is clear that Rome had determined on war. Next year envoys arrived in Rome from three Thracian peoples, the Maedi, Ceprati, and Asti. They were welcomed by senators, an alliance was agreed, and the envoys were given presents.[22] Thrace was an area where Perseus had campaigned; these peoples had perhaps been alerted to the possibilities of the situation by Eumenes, whose territory in the Gallipoli Peninsula made him their neighbour; or they had heard of the Roman anti-Perseus propaganda initiated by Marcellus. The initial contact may have come from Rome, in the knowledge that, as Livy puts it, they lived in the 'rear' of Perseus' territories.

The intervention of Rhodes with its complaints about Eumenes indicated that not all the Greek states were on board the Roman diplomatic raft as yet. Investigations by Roman envoys among the Aitolians and the Thessalians had suggested that it was the ruling groups in the Greek states which were on the Roman side in the developing quarrel and that the poorer classes had sympathy for Perseus. He had forgiven Macedonian debtors early in his reign and had provided a refuge for runaway slaves,[23] some of whom had presumably fallen into slavery through debt. In 174 he campaigned to bring his Dolopian subjects under control; some of them had wanted to appeal to Rome over an internal dispute, which was the usual way of getting Rome to detach a land from Macedonian rule.[24] By definition it was the wealthy classes which wanted this separation, presumably in some cases to be able to oppress the poor more determinedly. This class conflict afflicted Aitolia and Thessaly as well, and Perseus' action in Dolopia seemed to favour the poor. He had marched home through Thessaly, sending envoys and letters in advance and conspicuously not looting the lands he passed through. He had therefore much political support amongst the poor, but such people had little or no actual power; those with power and wealth generally favoured Rome; Rome was as conspicuous in giving them support in class conflicts as Perseus in appealing to the poor.[25]

The Rhodians were disputing control of parts of Lykia and Karia with Eumenes, and, while Rome preferred to be allied with Eumenes, Rhodes' enmity would not be pleasant, particularly in view of its naval capability. Ti. Claudius Nero and

C. Decimius were sent to Rhodes and Crete on an investigatory mission, with authority to renew the old Roman-Rhodian friendship treaty should that be thought worthwhile – that is, if the Rhodians seemed likely to be hostile, for the friendship treaty would be a means of exerting Roman control.[26]

The year 172 was therefore spent by both Rome and Perseus in intense diplomacy. Rome had a head start, having already decided during the previous year that war was probable; the war, that is, was intended by the Senate. The exchange of embassies in the early part of the year was followed by the decisive Roman move: the praetor Cn. Sicinius was ordered to collect a force of five thousand infantry and three hundred cavalry – a legion, in other words – and move them across the Adriatic[27] to secure landing places in Illyria for the arrival of a larger army later.

Along with these forces Roman envoys were sent all over Greece and Illyria to secure local help, in addition to the Thracian alliances and the envoys to Rhodes and Crete. Nero and Decimius went on to check on the attitudes of the eastern kings, Antiochos IV, the regents for the Ptolemies, and Eumenes.[28] Presumably these extra tasks had been added after the envoys had left for Greece, since the original mission was simply to Rhodes and Crete; this suggests a step change in the Roman pace of preparation, which is also indicated by the gathering and transport of Sicinius' forces. They found that Perseus had already contacted the eastern kings. While this was in preparation, yet more envoys went to Perseus, where his supposed derelictions were listed and 'reparations' were demanded; this was in effect a declaration of war, though it does not seem that Perseus fully appreciated it. (It is in a way a repetition of the incomprehension of his father when Lepidus provided an indistinct declaration of war on him at Abydos – it begins to seem a deliberately obfuscatory Roman delaying tactic.)

Livy has an account of the meeting in which both sides lost their tempers, but the essential point is that Rome's demands were in effect an ultimatum, and Perseus' refusal to comply, or his rejection of the Roman demands, was an acceptance of the coming war.[29] Rome's method, of course, was designed to cast the blame for the war on the enemy. Its envoys could claim that Roman requests were reasonable, but Perseus was obdurate – the tactics of the blackmailer and the terrorist.

The Roman envoys who went to the eastern kingdoms found that Perseus' contacts with the kings had no result – in Livy's patronising phrase, the kings were 'loyal' – but only Eumenes showed interest in helping Rome, supported by his ally Ariarathes V of Kappadokia;[30] but neither could have much effect on the war. King Kotys of the Thracian Odrysai supported Perseus, which effectively neutralised the Roman alliances with the other Thracians; Prusias of Bithynia relapsed into neutrality; Rhodes offered little support because of Rome's alliance with Eumenes.[31]

In Greece the lead in whipping up support was taken by one of the Senate's Greek experts, Q. Marcius Philippus, whose father had been a guest-friend of Perseus' father. The Achaians were annoyed by a blundering Roman appeal which put them on the same level as their disliked neighbours and were lukewarm.[32] In Thessaly, on the other hand, where Perseus' power was close, Marcius had an enthusiastic reception from those in power.[33] He had to operate with some brutality

218   *The collision of East and West*

in Boiotia in order to break up the league and remove from power those men who tended towards supporting Perseus.[34] He persuaded the Achaians to send a thousand soldiers to occupy the fortress of Chalkis, and this maintained the Roman orientation of its Boiotian neighbours, but this was the limit of the help the Achaian League would provide. It cleverly inveigled Achaia onto the Roman side while also controlling Boiotia. On the whole, it cannot be said that Marcius had much success in gathering worthwhile support.

While in Thessaly, Marcius received envoys from King Perseus. Perseus was now clear about Roman intentions; even if the odd business of the demand for 'reparations' had not convinced him, the arrival of Roman forces in Illyria close to his western border did. He asked for a meeting with his father's guest-friend. Marcius agreed, though it took a good deal of discussion and posturing before the meeting took place. They put their respective cases, encapsulated by Livy into the traditional pair of rival speeches composed by himself. A truce was agreed so that Perseus could send envoys to Rome to discuss terms; quite possibly this had been Marcius' aim all along, to gain time to secure Greek allies.[35]

Perseus, however, also used the time of the truce, not only to send his envoys to Rome but to canvass for allies among the same states in Greece and the Aegean where Philippus was holding meetings; in particular he looked to Rhodes. The Rhodians emphasised their friendship with Rome but were less than keen on the war.[36] The Macedonian envoys called in at Boiotia on their way home and gained some response at two of the cities, Koroneia and Haliartos, but to become Perseus' allies they required to be protected by a strong Macedonian forces, and this Perseus could not afford. He gave as the reason that he had agreed to a truce, but he was never going to waste good troops on such inconstant and isolated allies.[37]

At Rome the king's envoys were received in the temple of Bellona, outside the city's official boundary, because a state of war existed (which may well have been news to the Macedonians). The evidence of warlike preparations they must have encountered on their journey through Illyria and southern Italy made their mission pointless, and in the event they were also ambushed in the meeting. They put the case for peace and protested that their king had never had any intention of attacking Rome, but Perseus was then accused of attacking and capturing a group of Thessalian cities during his march through Thessaly a couple of years earlier. This had never before been mentioned. The Romans based it on a Thessalian accusation, probably invented – Perseus had been extra careful on that march – so as to provide an excuse to end the talks. This was another declaration of war. The envoys were given thirty days to leave Italy, and an order was made for all Macedonians in Italy to leave.[38]

Roman diplomatic tactics in this preparation for war were marked by a degree of unscrupulousness, hostility, lies, and deceit which would do credit to any twentieth-century totalitarian dictator, but not to any contemporary Hellenistic king; these kings valued their honour and their oaths too highly to conduct their international relations in Rome's way. The decision for war had been taken, it seems, by late 173, when M. Claudius Marcellus railed against Perseus to the Achaian Assembly, but no fighting took place until 171. In the interval Rome did its best to assemble a set of allies who could encircle Macedon, with little real success. King Eumenes was keen, but then he had his own reasons for hostility to Perseus. Even after numerous Roman envoys travelled throughout Greece and the Aegean, not one state volunteered to join the Roman alliance, though some joined in response to Roman threats. Rhodes and Achaia, the two most important Greek states at this time, expressed friendship towards Rome, but between them no more than a thousand soldiers were produced, and those only to form a garrison at Chalkis, not to take part actively. Thessaly was persuaded to join the Roman effort without much difficulty, but, like Eumenes, its rulers had their own reasons to fear Perseus and seem to have provided no troops; the Boiotian League had to be broken up to ensure that it did not join Perseus. The Thracian tribes which allied with Rome were quickly neutralised once Kotys of the Odrysai joined Perseus.

The reasons for this lack of enthusiasm are partly because for a Greek state to come out against Perseus might well produce internal troubles and partly that none of them, except perhaps Thessaly, saw Perseus as a threat. (Indeed, it is difficult to see Perseus as a threat to Rome, though that is clearly what Rome understood.) It must also be in part because of Rome's brutal diplomatic methods. Rome's decision for war had surely been obvious by early 172, if not from the time of Marcellus' speech in 173. If that was so, and if no Greek state had any real dispute with Perseus, the Greek attitude was to let the Romans get on with it themselves. As the methods of the Roman envoys became clear, no doubt an element of dislike entered Greek reactions. Marcius' treatment of the Boiotian League was surely observed by Greeks with fear and distaste. Lack of concern, fear of internal reactions, and Rome's unpleasantness were all good reasons to explain the general Greek reluctance to become involved. Even at Rome the methods Marcius used towards his guest-friend Perseus were disliked.[39]

## War diplomacy, 171–167

The war finally began in 171 and exhibits the essential integration of diplomacy and fighting in an unusually clear way. The Roman transport of a consular army to Greece stimulated some Greek assistance, but only Eumenes provided a force of substantial size. Several cities supplied ships, but the naval commander made a point of deliberately requesting Rhodian help; eventually six ships were sent, only to be told that they were not needed and dismissed – as were all the other allied vessels provided. The whole process was presumably a test to see if Rhodes' earlier indecision could be resolved and to see who was on Rome's side, but the clumsy method produced much Rhodian resentment.[40]

Early fighting involved one Roman army holding Epeiros while the major Roman force was sent into Thessaly, but Perseus' forces held off all Roman attacks until late 170, when Q. Marcius Philippus was given the command. Two legates, M. Popillius Laenas and Cn. Octavius, were sent around southern Greece to calm down the allies, who were annoyed by the arrogant and rapacious behaviour of the unsuccessful Roman commanders and soldiers. The legates made serious efforts to win over the 'moderates' in the cities they visited, men who were neither violently pro-Macedonian nor strongly pro-Roman, aiming to display a care for local opinion and local sensibilities without imposing any serious obligations. A request for garrisons made by the pro-Roman Akarnanians (probably to back up a purge of their opponents) was deflected;[41] when the praetor C. Claudius Centho in Illyria asked for Achaian reinforcements, the request was referred to Marcius, who blocked it.[42] The two legates displayed considerable diplomatic expertise, even delicacy. Marcius' previous experience in Greece suggests his influence was behind this diplomatic process. (The later behaviour of both envoys was such that they would hardly be anyone's first choice to be diplomatic and conciliatory.)

Marcius successfully entangled Rhodes. Envoys from the city went to him and to Rome to repair relations, particularly once it was seen that Marcius had a better military and diplomatic grip on the situation than his predecessors and therefore that Rome was likely to win fairly soon. Marcius suggested that a Rhodian effort at mediation might be useful; he did not mean it, and the Rhodians should have realised this, but they had to follow up on the suggestion. Rome never accepted third-party mediation, since, as some Rhodians argued at the time, it implied Roman weakness. The offer to mediate peace only provoked Roman scorn, anger, and a powerful refusal; it was another mark against Rhodes in the Roman book.[43]

Centho in Illyria had to cope with the Epeirote Confederacy, which broke apart over the issue of the war: the Molossi joined Perseus, the other tribes joined the Romans. He also had to cope with King Genthius of the Illyrians, who was not trusted by either side. During 169 Genthius was at last persuaded to join Perseus by the promise of a bribe.[44] This could have been serious, but Centho held his own. Since only the initial deposit of Perseus' bribe was paid, no doubt Genthius' interest in helping him rapidly faded. Perseus could be as unscrupulous as his Roman opponents, but Genthius fell into his own trap.

Marcius meanwhile succeeded in making the first breach in Perseus' defences in the mountains around Mount Olympus. The Macedonian forces retreated in good order and adopted another powerful defensive position. Roman diplomacy during 169 therefore succeeded in holding the ring in Greece, Illyria, and the Aegean while Marcius at last made the crucial military advance. With access into Macedon gained it merely remained for the Roman forces to finish the fighting. Effective commanders were deployed for 168: the consul M. Aemilius Paullus carried the land war into Macedon, the naval praetor Cn. Octavius put some vigour and discipline into the naval forces, M. Acilius Gallus finished off Genthius. Between them they completed the war by the middle of 168.

The Senate decided that Macedon should no longer pose any sort of a threat to Italy or Greece, and the kingdom was broken up into four republics. The Greek states, friends, enemies, or neutrals, were crushed diplomatically: a massacre of anti-Roman Aitolians put the pro-Roman dictator Lykiskos firmly in power; a thousand Achaians, moderates, neutrals, and anti-Romans, were carried off to Italy, theoretically for trial, actually just to get them into exile; Rhodes was ordered out of the mainland possessions awarded to it by Rome twenty years earlier. The Roman army was turned loose to ravage the Molossian lands, carrying off 150,000 people into slavery. The aim was to render Greece docile, so that, once again, the Roman forces could be withdrawn.

Roman diplomacy in the 170s had been an almost naked preparation for war, and during the actual fighting, diplomacy was resorted to when it was necessary to quieten Greek distractions in order that the troops could win the victory. The Roman aim was to destroy Macedon, something clear at least by the start of the fighting. Greek unwillingness to be involved only earned retribution in the form of purges, massacres, and punishments afterwards. The use to which Rome put its diplomacy was therefore purely in pursuit of its own power, not in search of agreed solutions to problems, which was more usually seen as the purpose of diplomacy amongst the Hellenistic monarchies. This ruthlessness was, of course, one of the reasons Rome repeatedly expanded its power and empire, but it was a very different process than that understood in the Greek or Macedonian states east of the Adriatic. It was also very unpleasant for those caught by the Roman methods.

## Between wars

The evacuation of Roman forces from Greece in 167 left the assertion of Roman power to the exercise of diplomacy once again. This meant the Senate fending off repeated Achaian requests for the return of its arrested hostages and Roman arbitration of a series of inter-Greek disputes. Rome was also driven reluctantly to involvement in the affairs in Asia Minor. For two decades Rome's post-167 system worked reasonably well, at least from Rome's point of view. The Senate had little or nothing to do to assert its authority: arbitration and occasional embassies were sufficient; in the end, however, the 'lesson' of the destruction of Macedon faded.

The Achaian League was the most awkward Greek state, as it attempted to maintain some sort of control over the whole of the Peloponnese in the face of resistance from some of its elements. Sparta's membership in the league did not prevent it from attempting to reclaim lost lands at the expense of other members, and it appealed for Roman arbitration more than once, without success. Rome took the view that this was an internal Achaian League matter.[45] Similarly Roman intervention in a dispute between Athens and Delos was more in the nature of conciliation than diplomatic action.[46]

Some Greeks states were quite willing, however, to take military action on their own. Rhodes, for example, succeeded in recovering its old Roman alliance in 164[47] but paid no attention to Rome when it began to campaign against Cretan piracy. Rhodes was so weakened by the Roman retribution in 167 that it was in danger of being defeated and appealed for help to the Achaians; but it was outmanoeuvred by the Cretans, who sent an envoy of their own to Achaia who persuaded the league to take no action without Roman approval. Rhodes moved on to Rome and secured the appointment of a Roman arbitrator. The result of his work – and even his name, except for his *praenomen* 'Quintus' – is not known;[48] probably, as Gruen suggests, the war simply petered out.[49] This Roman intervention was a diplomatic action as much as an arbitration, or at least an attempted one.

Rome did nothing about the Rhodian-Cretan War until the issue was brought to its attention, though the Senate no doubt already knew about it. Rome had therefore deliberately refrained from involving itself, just as it did with Sparta. In Asia Minor, after the withdrawal of the forces in 167, both King Eumenes the Attalid and King Prousias of Bithynia attempted to enlist Roman help in their mutual disputes, but again the Senate failed to respond except by sending mediators, who achieved nothing.[50]

Eumenes, like Rhodes, was active diplomatically and militarily, notably in combatting the Galatians of the interior, still a menace to their neighbours. After he defeated them, they appealed to Rome; the Senate sent a commission to investigate, then decreed that they should be autonomous, which would presumably protect Eumenes' lands from further attacks.[51] Prousias attempted the same ploy, repeatedly appealing to Rome against what he claimed were encroachments or attacks by Eumenes. The Senate sent out investigating commissions but did nothing concrete to end the argument,[52] probably in large part because Prousias was judged to be lying. Yet Eumenes was not given any conspicuous assistance, despite his long supposed friendship with Rome. Eumenes' agent in all this was usually his brother and eventual successor Attalos, who appears to have understood Roman indifference. That indifference, however, had a limit. When Prousias campaigned against the Attalids after Eumenes' death in 159, he seems to have assumed that Roman indifference to his charges and raids was actually an unwillingness to act. He launched a war, invading and ravaging Attalos' territories.

The Senate had been sceptical at the first news of Prousias' attack, being assured by Prousias' envoys that nothing of the sort had happened;[53] this was quickly contradicted by new information and then by the arrival of an envoy from Attalos accompanied by one of its own envoys, P. Cornelius Lentulus, who had been sent out earlier to attempt to end the fighting.[54] A new pair of envoys, L. Apuleius and C. Petronius, was sent out after the confirmation;[55] with Lentulus' news another delegation was sent, headed by C. Claudius Centho, with L. Hortensius and C. Aurunculeius.[56] The envoys organised a meeting of the two kings, each to be attended by 'only' a thousand men, at which Roman conciliation and royal reconciliation would take place. Prousias turned up with his whole army and drove Attalos, his guard, and the Roman envoys helter-skelter to take refuge in Pergamon. Hortensius and Aurunculeius forthwith returned to Rome to report this, while Centho (presumably) stayed with Attalos.[57] The Senate was annoyed but still did not leap to Centho's and Attalos' defence.[58] Yet another delegation went east, ten strong this time, headed by L. Anicius.[59]

Arriving at Pergamon, they confronted Prousias, whom they threatened in some way. He began negotiations, accepting some of the Roman demands, rejecting others, but the envoys were not prepared to discuss matters, and when Prousias failed to accept their terms in full they declared that he was no longer a friend and ally of Rome and left the meeting. At last Prousias realised his peril; he trailed after the envoys, who were unwilling to make any concessions. They braced up Attalos, who had gathered his forces, then scattered to persuade Attalos' allies and friends to support him; some headed back to Rome to report.

A joint naval force of Attalos' and allied ships raided along the Bithynian coast, distracting Prousias from any further attacks or raids he might be contemplating.[60] The message to Rome stimulated the Senate to send another group of envoys, three men headed by Centho's brother, Caius. These had instructions 'to put an end to the war', but it was the mobilisation of Attalos' allies which had the real effect on Prousias, for the same instructions had been given to every previous set of Roman envoys. A treaty was arranged, the combatants returned to their original boundaries, and Prousias agreed to pay damages.[61]

The succession of senatorial delegations to sort out this quarrel can seem ludicrous, and it may be, as Gruen has argued,[62] that Rome was largely indifferent; yet the Senate did in the end bring about a peace settlement. It sent five successive sets of envoys so that the participants could use them to negotiate a treaty, as they eventually did; the Senate's envoys were thus mediators, not arbitrators. Only when Rome was defied and the war got out of hand was the set of ten envoys sent; the number was clearly a sign of Roman seriousness. The threat to renounce Roman friendship with Prousias was potent because it was simultaneously a threat of war. The Senate was, quite rightly, extremely reluctant to go so far, but its envoys were able to organise the local forces to compel Prousias to come to terms – and those terms were relatively lenient.

## Attalid conspiracies

The Attalid kings developed a tradition of meddling in their neighbouring kingdoms' affairs after their great expansion of territory in 188. This is, of course, a type of diplomacy, but the Attalid version was to begin with a plot, then let the person leading the plot proceed on his own. In 175, in the first of these cases, the Seleukid prince Antiochos IV was decked out in royal robes at Pergamon by the whole Attalid family of four brothers, headed by Eumenes II, and escorted to the Seleukid boundary by Pergamene troops, who probably took him on to Antioch, where he was able to overthrow the regime of the regent-minister Heliodoros and seize power.[63]

The trick was tried again in 159 when Alexander Balas was 'recognised' as a bastard son of Antiochos IV and promoted as a candidate to displace Demetrios I. This time the plot took much longer to come to fruition and required decisive naval and financial and military support from Ptolemy VI to achieve success. Eumenes II could take credit for originating the plot, but Attalos II pushed it through, and it was Ptolemy who did the real work.[64] (See Chapter 13).

One of the elements in this plot was to send Alexander and his sister Laodike to Rome to impress the Senate. This was not difficult to do since the Senate was already annoyed with Demetrios. Attalos appears to have been adept at using Rome, or at least the name of Rome, to further his policies.[65] When the Kappadokian King Ariarathes V was driven from his throne by his brother Orophernes, Attalos could cite earlier Roman approval of Ariarathes and Roman dislike of Orophernes' sponsor Demetrios I as his justification for a military intervention to restore the rightful king.[66] Similarly, in 149, when Prousias II of Bithynia was subject to a plot organised by his son Nikomedes, it turned out that Nikomedes had been encouraged and favoured and financed by Attalos. When he rose against his father he received decisive military help from Attalos, whose forces invaded Bithynia. This was despite the presence of a Roman embassy charged with reconciling father and son and despite the earlier peace treaty between the kings.[67]

Attalos' most brazen and curious plot came with a pretender to the Macedonian throne, a mercenary soldier called Andriskos who bore a resemblance to the Macedonian King Perseus. Probably for a lark he was promoted as pretender by a friend. At Antioch, Perseus' former wife Laodike was King Demetrios' wife, and Andriskos attempted to get her endorsement but was thrown out by an exasperated Demetrios – one of a long series of lucky moments in the story, for Laodike would surely have denounced him; she was hardly likely to recognise or accept one of her former husband's bastards.

Andriskos went on to the Attalid kingdom, where a number of Macedonians had taken refuge after the Third Romano-Macedonian War and where he was accepted as a viable pretender. Members of the royal family – again – provided him with the necessary regal outfit. (He was also accepted by the Thracian King Teres, who was married to Perseus' sister.) Probably to the surprise of all his sponsors, Andriskos then successfully invaded Macedon and was accepted as 'King Philip VI'. He thereby overthrew with revealing ease the Roman disposition of 167.[68] But we must ask what Attalos was thinking of in encouraging Andriskos in his adventure? Andriskos actually dealt with Attalos' brother Athenaios, and his wife, Kallippa, a former courtesan of Perseus', but Attalos presumably knew what was going on. Perhaps he was simply intoxicated with previous successful conspiracies and could not resist trying for an even greater prize. At least Attalos had the sense to provide a Pergamene fleet to assist the Roman forces in suppressing Andriskos when the first Roman military reaction was defeated by Andriskos' Macedonian forces. (What Andriskos thought of this reversal and betrayal is not recorded.) The result was the replacement of the four weak Macedonian republics by a single Roman province, governed by a Roman magistrate and garrisoned by a Roman army. This would obviously severely cramp Attalid style from now on; one might suggest that it served them right.

Diplomacy takes curious forms. Attalos was clearly a past master at international plotting, successfully installing proteges on neighbouring thrones – Alexander Balas, Ariarathes, Nikomedes, even Andriskos – and avoiding any retribution. By claiming to be acting as Rome's agent he was able to promote his own policies. He and his predecessor Eumenes had depended in the beginning on Roman support, though it might take a long time to become effective. Roman diplomacy was very limited in its effects, by design; Rome clearly expected its friends and allies to act for themselves in minor matters.

## The Achaian War

Achaian troops assisted in the destruction of Andriskos, but meanwhile a crisis developed within the league. A Spartan delegation went to Rome in 149 to argue once more for the city's separation from the league, but the Senate ignored it. In Achaia this appeal was regarded as illegal under the league's constitution (correctly, and this had been the basis for earlier senatorial refusals to hear Spartan complaints). An Achaian army invaded Lakonia to assert the league's authority. Diaios, the Achaian *strategos*, demanded that a group of dissident Spartan politicians be exiled; this backfired, for they at once went to Rome to lay their new complaint before the Senate.[69]

The Senate was much more concerned about the wars it was fighting in Macedonia, Africa, and Spain. The Spartan issue seemed trivial by comparison. An Achaian delegation, led by the senior pro-Roman politician Kallikrates, left for Rome to counter the Spartans' complaints, but he died on the way; Diaios took the lead, a change which was regarded by Polybios and by later historians as crucial. The Senate's eventual response was sufficiently ambiguous to be misunderstood by both sets of Greeks; in Sparta it was taken as 'permission' to secede; in Achaia the opposite. A Roman embassy was organised to sort matters out, though given the record of Roman embassies in the last two decades it could be assumed that it would do little.[70] In Macedon, the conqueror of Andriskos, Q. Caecilius Metellus, received a different delegation which was on its way to Asia to see Prousias. When he heard that the Achaians had invaded Sparta again, he persuaded the envoys to visit Achaia as well. They gave a warning to the Achaian commander Damokritos, who had refrained from inflicting much damage in Lakonia. In Achaia this restraint was seen as treason; Damokritos was driven into exile.

Diaios gathered an army for yet another invasion of Lakonia but was deterred by a stern message from Metellus, who was now a successful commander with the Roman army at his command. Diaios occupied parts of the Lakonian borderlands then agreed to a truce. This was the situation – a frozen crisis – when at last the Roman embassy ordered in 149 arrived. The three men reached Corinth in the summer of 147. The leader was L. Aurelius Orestes, a man familiar with Greece – his cognomen implies Greek origin or sympathies. His delayed arrival probably allowed the Senate to gain a better understanding of the 'Spartan problem'; meanwhile the war in Macedon had been won, and that in Africa was on its way to victory – the delay may not have been mere senatorial lethargy.[71]

This time for consideration, however, led to the conclusion that Rome could no longer tolerate the existence of the Achaian League. Orestes did his best to prepare the Achaian leaders for the blow, meeting Diaios and other elected officials informally before the assembly. He told them that the Senate had decided in favour of Sparta, which would be permitted to secede from the league, but then he added that four other cities would also be detached – Herakleia-by-Oeta to the north (which seems to have recently joined), Orchomenos, Argos, and Corinth.[72]

Diaios spread this news through Corinth, which produced an anti-Spartan riot. Orestes was threatened, and perhaps roughed up. He returned to Rome, where he reported his rough treatment.[73] A new Achaian envoy, Thearidas, set off to attempt to persuade the Senate to reverse itself, but he met a new Roman envoy, Sex. Julius Caesar, on the way, and they returned to Achaia together. Caesar was conciliatory, concentrating on persuading the Achaians to let Sparta go, but he said nothing about the other cities, so it was clear that the Senate's decision stood. He got nowhere in his non-negotiations, not surprisingly, and when he felt he was being hoodwinked by Diaios and deliberately delayed and distracted, he left as angrily as Orestes.[74]

The Achaians organised for war against Sparta. From Macedon Metellus sent four of his officers to attempt to persuade the Achaians to be 'sensible'. They were shouted down in the assembly.[75] The Achaian *strategos* Kritolaos conducted his own diplomatic campaign, gathering allies in Boiotia, in Lokris, and Chalkis in Euboia.[76] None of this was secret, and the Senate was well informed of what was happening. None of its attempts to persuade the Achaians to agree to Roman terms had succeeded, not those sent by the Senate nor those from Metellus. The Achaians were now organising an alliance clearly intended to be hostile to Rome. The Achaian army was used against Herakleia-by-Oeta, which had accepted its own detachment from the league at Rome's behest quite willingly. From the perspective of Macedon, Metellus must have feared a junction of all Greece against him; he sent a force south.[77] The assembly which had insulted Metellus' officers had also declared war on Sparta, which had in effect been placed under Roman protection earlier; this was an action which was regarded by Polybios as an effective declaration of war against Rome.[78]

The Senate now had no choice but to declare war on Achaia. With two Roman armies approaching, that of Metellus from Macedon and that of the consul L. Mummius from Italy, the Achaians had probably no chance of surviving, but at least they made a fight of it. (Metellus' four officers scattered to Athens and Sparta and Naupaktos as his agents, no doubt to bolster the courage of Rome's allies.) The war ended with the destruction of Corinth – where Roman magistrates and officers had been mocked and insulted – and in the dissolution of the Achaian League.[79]

Diplomacy had failed in this affair, but, given the terms Rome sought to impose, it probably never had a chance. There is no doubt that the Senate had made a serious attempt to avoid war, and equally no doubt that the Achaians eventually decided they had no choice but to challenge Roman supremacy if they were to be able to administer their own affairs. The unexpected and shocking decision to break up the league compelled the Achaians into a direct challenge. This was not in fact diplomacy but dictation, but only after the diplomacy had failed.

## The annexation of Asia

The Senate's old policy of not interfering clearly changed during the generation after the war with Perseus, driven by the unwillingness of the Greek states to involve themselves in Roman policies. The willingness manifested in Asian affairs to mediate rather than dictate, apparent in the 150s, gave way to the deliberate destruction of the Achaian League and the annexation of Macedon (and Africa) in the 140s. The unwillingness of Rome to extend its direct territorial control had evidently ended. But these changes simply shifted the problem from Greece to Asia.

It came as a surprise in Rome that Attalos III, who died in 133, had bequeathed his wealth and estates to the city.[80] His motives are not recorded, but may have been similar to those of Ptolemy VIII, who made a will leaving his kingdom of Kyrene to Rome, being concerned to block plots and threats against him. To be effective such a will would need to have been less than secret, and it does not seem that anyone knew of Attalos' intentions.[81]

Attalos' bequest sparked interest in Rome but only at first in terms of the wealth which was implied, when Ti. Sempronius Gracchus proposed to use it to fund his plan to settle colonists.[82] Rome was preoccupied with the crisis this issue produced during 133 and 132 (just as wars in Spain and Africa and Macedon had preoccupied it at the time of the Achaian crisis in 146), with the result that it was only in 132 that a senatorial commission of five was sent to sort out the details.[83]

By then the Senate knew that it faced a difficult situation in Asia. The provisions of the will gave the city of Pergamon its freedom and may have made the same provision for other cities. What it did not do was deal with the royal succession, though handing his own wealth and his estates to Rome did imply that Attalos' kingdom was to be liquidated. This ambiguity opened the way for his half-brother Aristonikos to make a bid for the apparently vacant kingship, proclaiming himself as Eumenes III.[84] He was resisted by some of the cities, who sent envoys to Rome to make their case for their own freedom being recognised.[85]

The delay in Rome was caused by the slow transmission of the news and by the political complications in the city; Aristonikos therefore had a head start and succeeded in gaining control over much of the kingdom. The Roman commissioners were evidently ignorant of these realities in Asia when they set out, since they were provided with no military backup. Their purpose was thus presumably to investigate rather than decide. But their arrival was, relatively quickly, followed by the dispatch of a consul and a consular army to suppress Aristonikos.

The Senate had therefore dithered over whether and how to accept Attalos' legacy, probably because it was not clear what it consisted of.[86] The arrival of the cities' envoys helped the Senate to clarify the situation, and the reports from the five senatorial commissioners will have indicated what needed to be done and the scope for Roman action. When the army arrived, under the command of the consul P. Licinius Crassus, Aristonikos had already been defeated at sea by the Ephesian fleet and had retired inland[87] – and the arrival of a full Roman army indicated clearly that the decision of Rome was for annexation.

The cities who sent envoys to Rome had clearly been anxious to assert their freedom, or their entitlement to it. By doing so they obviously assumed that Rome would accept the bequest, while also understanding that the details – such as the freedom of the cities – would need to be decided. Among other neighbours of the Attalid kingdom, similarly, the kings of Bithynia, Pontus, Kappadokia, and others saw the possibilities inherent in the situation, above all in the rising of Aristonikos, and intervened militarily against him. When the five commissioners arrived in Asia, therefore, all these enemies of Aristonikos had already emerged and taken action.

When Crassus arrived, therefore, he found the materials for an anti-Aristonikos alliance ready to hand – the Greek cities, the peripheral kingdoms, and Rome. He evidently spent some time organising the alliance, including the need to coordinate all participants' actions, for it was not until late in the year that he moved to attack Aristonikos' forces. His defeat and death at the hands of Aristonikos' forces scarcely affected the situation, and his successor M. Perperna (who had already been assigned the province of Asia) finished off Aristonikos' main forces without

## 228  *The collision of East and West*

difficulty.[88] He also died in office, so the completion of the conquest was left to yet another consul, M. Aquillius, who then spent three years, assisted by the usual senatorial commission of ten, in organising the new province. This involved distributing spoils to the kings and confirming the status of the cities – a repetition of the procedure at Apameia-Kelainai sixty years before.[89]

The opportunities for diplomacy were not great in this crisis. Events on the ground in Asia were quickly out of Roman control, and the activities were largely in Asian hands until the formalisation of the alliance, which was presumably carried out by Crassus. When that was done it was only the successive deaths of the consuls which delayed the end. There was presumably some diplomacy involved in Aquillius' distribution of lands and territories – bribery was suggested – but this would be less than difficult to achieve. It is probable that the various kings had already seized their prizes during the fighting.

The Roman conduct in this crisis was very reminiscent of the activity of the envoys in the preceding crisis in Asia between Prousias II and Attalos II, in that much of the fighting was left to the local powers, and Rome's role was mainly an organising one. Diplomacy thus had become a practice which was hardly relevant. The extension of Rome's empire had acquired a clear momentum of its own, so that relatively minor military expeditions and dictatorial 'diplomacy' was all that was required from now on.

## Notes

1 Listed in Ager, *Interstate Arbitrations*, e.g. 100, 105, 120, and others.
2 E.S. Gruen, *The Hellenistic Monarchies and the Coming of Rome*, California 1984, chapters 11 to 16.
3 Ager, *Interstate Arbitrations*.
4 Robert Kallet-Marx, *Hegemony to Empire: The Development of the Roman Imperium in the East from 148 to 62* BC, California 1995.
5 N.G.L. Hammond and F.W. Walbank, *A History of Macedonia*, vol. 3, Oxford 1988, 454–456.
6 Sometimes said to be 'illegitimate', but this is probably not so.
7 Polybios 40.58.8; this was the same action as that taken by Ap. Claudius Pulcher when Hiero of Syracuse died but from the 'opposite' direction, so to speak.
8 Livy 41.23.1–3; this is, in fact, a repeat of a Roman rumour that Perseus' father had sent a Macedonian contingent to assist Hannibal at the battle of Zama (Livy 30.26.3–4). Rome had called up Carthaginian warships to fight against Antiochos III in 191 despite prohibiting the city from possessing such ships in the treaty of 202 (Livy 36.42).
9 Livy 41.23.3, 24.6, 27.4, and 42.2.1–2.
10 Livy 42.2.5.
11 Livy 42.6.1–2.
12 Livy 42.11–13; Gruen, *Hellenistic Monarchies*, 501 (note), casts doubt on Marcellus' speech at Aigion because Livy connects it with Eumenes' visit to Rome later; but he does not say anything more than that it was one of the origins of that visit – which rather authenticates the speech.
13 Polybios 25.4.8; Livy 42.12.3–4; Appian, *Macedonian Wars* 2.
14 Livy 42.14.2–3.
15 Livy 42.14.6–9.
16 Livy 42.15.3–16.5.

Rome and Greece   229

17  Livy 42.17.2–9.
18  Livy 42.18.3.
19  Livy 52, 15.1.
20  Livy 42.18.4–5.
21  As exhibited also in Cato the Censor's constant complaints about Carthage.
22  Livy 42.19.6–7.
23  Polybios 25.3.1–3.
24  Livy 41.22.4 and 41.13.8; Appian, *Macedonian Wars* 9.6.
25  Alexander Fuks, 'Social Revolution in Greece in the Hellenistic Age', *La Parola del Passato* 111, 1966, 437–448; E.S. Gruen, 'Class Conflict and the Third Macedonian War', *American Journal of Ancient History* 1, 1976, 29–66; G.E.M. de Ste Croix, *Class Struggle in the Ancient Greek World*, London 1981, 524, 659–660; the issue is bedevilled by modern ideologies, but fortunately it is not central to the diplomacy issue.
26  Livy 42.19.8.
27  Livy 42.18.3.
28  Livy 42.19.7–8 and 26.7–7.
29  Livy 42.25.1–14.
30  Livy 42.29.9 and 12.
31  Livy 42.46.7.
32  Livy 42.37.7–38.7.
33  Livy 42.38.8–43.3.
34  Livy 42.43.4–10; Polybios 27.1–2.
35  Livy 42.38.3–43.3.
36  Livy 42.46.1–6.
37  Livy 42.46.7–10; Polybios 27.5.
38  Livy 42.36.18; also 48.2–3; Polybios 27.6; Appian, *Macedonian Wars* 11.5–9.
39  Livy 42.47.4.
40  Polybios 27.7.1–16.
41  Livy 43.17.6–9.
42  Polybios 28.13.
43  Polybios 29.10; Appian, *Macedonian Wars* 17.
44  Polybios 29.2.7; Livy 44.27.8–12; Appian, *Macedonian Wars* 18.1.
45  Paul Cartledge and Antony Spawforth, *Hellenistic and Roman Sparta, a Tale of Two Cities*, London 1989, 81–83.
46  Polybios 32.7.1–2; Ager, *Interstate Arbitrations* 140.
47  Gruen, *Hellenistic Monarchies*, 572.
48  Diodoros 31.38 and 43, Polybios 33.15.3–16.1; Ager, *Interstate Arbitrations* 144.
49  Gruen, *Hellenistic Monarchies*, 578–579.
50  Polybios 30.1 and 18; Ager, *Interstate Arbitrations* 134.
51  Livy 45.34.10–14; Polybios 30.19, 28; Diodoros 31.12; Polyainos 4.8.1.
52  Livy 45.34.10.
53  Maybe they did not know of their king's intentions, or maybe, in the classic formulation of Sir Henry Wotton, they had been 'sent to lie abroad for the good of their country'.
54  Polybios 32.16.1–5 and 33.1.1.
55  Polybios 32.16.5.
56  Polybios 33.1.1–2.
57  Polybios 32.15., 33.7.1–2; Appian, *Mithradatic Wars* 3; Diodoros 31.35; for explanations of Prousias' policy at this point see L. Robert, *Etudes Anatoliennes*, Paris 1937, 111–18, Gruen, *Hellenistic Monarchies*, 587–588, F.W. Walbank, *A Historical Commentary on Polybios*, vol III, Oxford 1979, 536–542.
58  Senatorial indignation at the mistreatment of its envoys was episodic and clearly based not on the dignity of its members but on the needs of the wider situation. Centho and his colleagues were not avenged, other than in the general result of the crisis in Asia;

in Achaia L. Aurelius Orestes and even four officers sent by Caecilius Metellus, when roughed up in the assembly, were factors in the Roman declaration of war.
59 Polybios 33.7.3–4; 12.2.
60 Polybios 33.12.5–13.3.
61 Polybios 33.13.4–10; Appian, *Mithradatic Wars* 3; *OGIS* 327; the sources are collected in Ager, *Interstate Arbitrations* 142.
62 This is the running argument throughout the chapters on Greece and Asia Minor in *Hellenistic Monarchies*.
63 J.D. Grainger, *Syrian Wars*, Leiden 2010, 284–285; O. Morkholm, *Antiochos IV of Syria*, Copenhagen 1966; Will, *Histoire Politique*, 2.303–305.
64 Diodoros 31.32a; Polybios 33.15.1–2, 18.6–12; Grainger, *Syrian Wars*, 328–331.
65 Gruen, *Hellenistic Monarchies*, 196–197, 589–592.
66 Polybios 32.12.
67 Polybios 36.15; Appian, *Mithradatic Wars* 4–7; Doodoros 32.21; Justin 34.4.2–5.
68 Livy 45.18 and Epitome 48–50; Diodoros 31.40a and 32.15. 9a, 9b; Zonaras 9.28; Polybios 36.10 and 12; J.M. Helliesen, 'Andriscus and the Revolt of the Macedonians, 149–148 BC', in *Ancient Macedonia*, vol. 4, Thessaloniki 1986, 307–314; I have detailed the whole story in *Rome, Parthia, India*, Barnsley 2013, ch. 3.
69 Pausanias 7.12.3–7; Cartledge and Spawforth, *Hellenistic and Roman Sparta*, 88–89.
70 Pausanias 7.12.4.
71 Pausanias 7.13.1–4; Gruen, *Hellenistic Monarchies*, 520, claims the Senate 'dallied' in sending the envoys; Pausanias is slightly less censorious: 'rather slow'.
72 Pausanias 7.14.1–3; Livy, *Epitome* 51, Polybios 38.9; Justin 34.1.
73 Polybios 38.9.1–2; Polybios claims he exaggerated the hurt caused.
74 Pausanias 7.14.2–4; Polybios 38.9–11; Diodoros 32.26.3–4.
75 Polybios 28.12.1–4.
76 Pausanias 7.14.4–15.2; Polybios 14.2.
77 Pausanias 7.15.2–3.
78 Polybios 38.13.6.
79 Polybios 38.15.1–18.12 and 39.2.
80 Plutarch, *Ti. Gracchus* 14.1; Livy, *Per.* 58–59; Strabo 13.4.2; Appian, *Mithradatic Wars* 62; Justin 36.4.3; Pliny *NH* 33.148, and other minor references; it is to be noted that none of these sources is less than a century later than the events, and collectively they are uncertain as to the full contents of the bequest.
81 This episode is interpreted in a wide variety of ways, largely due, as usual, to poor source material. See A.N. Sherwin-White, *Roman Foreign Policy in the East*, Oklahoma 1984, 80–88; Kallet-Marx, *Hegemony to Empire*, 99–122, Gruen, *Hellenistic Monarchies*, 592–608; Will, *Histoire Politique*, 2.416–425, for a sample of the variety.
82 Plutarch, *Ti. Gracchus* 14.2.
83 Strabo 14.1.38.
84 See note 80; J. Hopp, *Untersuchungen zur Geschichte der letzten Attaliden*, Munich 1977; K.J. Rigsby, 'Provincia Asia', *Transactions of the American Philosophical Association* 118, 1988, 123–153.
85 Kallet-Marx, *Hegemony to Empire*, 102–104.
86 This is Kallet-Marx's interpretation, which seems convincing.
87 Strabo 14.1.38.
88 Ibid.; Justin 36.4.8–10; Livy, *Per.* 59.
89 Kallet-Marx, *Hegemony to Empire*, 109–122.

# 13 The later Syrian Wars (195 – c.140)

The conditions in which the later wars for Syria were fought – after Antiochos III's conquest of Koile Syria – were very different from those of the first five. First, the cession of Syria to Antiochos III in 195 meant that the onus for aggression now lay with the Ptolemies; second, and this followed from the first, the Ptolemaic dynasty was grievously weakened by the great rebellion of the native Egyptians which lasted for over twenty years, between 207 and 186, and which was liable to erupt at times in various places over the next century; it was also weakened, of course, by the loss of the territory which it hoped to recover.

## Peacemaking, 168

The two dynasties did in fact fight each other four more times after the death of Antiochos III in 187, but both eventually fell into periods of confusion and civil war. This makes it less easy than in the previous century to be clear that the practices of diplomacy as they had evolved in the century after the establishment of these great dynasties still operated in the same way. The Sixth Syrian War (170–168) does seem, however, to show much the same pattern as earlier. The war began with a threatened invasion of Palestine by the Egyptian regents, Lenaios and Eulaios, who were acting for the child King Ptolemy VI. They were pre-empted in their preparations by Antiochos IV's own invasion of Egypt.[1]

Neither king (for the regents operated in the name of Ptolemy) was restrained by any previous treaty, since both had come to their thrones since the last treaty had been signed, that of 195. The end of the war came in 168 when Antiochos was rescued from the possibility of having to besiege Alexandria by the intervention of a Roman diplomat, C. Popillius Laenas, who insisted on a peace being made.[2] Antiochos retained Palestine and Phoenicia, but he evacuated Egypt and had to give up Cyprus, which he had conquered.

This event is, of course, portrayed by Livy as a major Roman triumph, in which a single Roman diplomat dictated terms of peace to two obstreperous Hellenistic monarchies, humiliating one of the kings into the bargain. In fact, it was a bit more complicated than that, but above all, Laenas' intervention played directly into Antiochos' hands; he had no wish to become involved in a siege of Alexandria, which was by then the only thing left he could attempt to bring the war to an end. The Roman delegation (not just Laenas) had waited for some time in Greece before moving from Alexandria to meet Antiochos, until, that is, they knew that the Ptolemaic government was desperate enough to accept almost any terms; it is quite probable that Laenas had already been in contact with Antiochos and knew that he would be happy to make peace – for Antiochos' actions all along during this campaign had clearly been aimed at bringing the Ptolemaic regime to terms. Once Laenas knew that the government (another set of regents) was sufficiently beaten down, he could finally meet with Antiochos. The circle in the sand was pure theatricality.[3]

Livy's interpretation emphasises Roman power, and he expected it to be wielded; in fact Laenas was no more than a mediator waiting for an opportunity to intervene. Despite the presence of a Roman army in Greece and its progress in the war there against Macedon, no-one in the Hellenistic east could believe that this force posed a serious military threat to Antiochos, either in Egypt or in Syria.

Repeated attempts by Greek states had been made to arbitrate or mediate in the conflict. All of these, almost without exception, had been instigated by Rome, and a Roman, T. Numisius Tarquiniensis, had even been appointed to mediate by the Senate.[4] Rhodes may have been urged to mediate by Q. Marcius Philippus;[5] 'Ptolemy' – that is, the regents – had asked envoys from Athens, the Achaian League, Miletos, and Klazomenai to act as a joint delegation, but since they acted for Ptolemy they merely ended hearing Antiochos' exposition of his aims and purposes, with emphasis on his 'rights'.[6] A second Rhodian embassy achieved nothing;[7] an Achaian embassy was planned, instigated again by Rome, but was overtaken by the Roman mission of Laenas.[8]

Such attempts at mediation between great powers never succeeded. Only the application of a distinct threat would ever work, since the mediators needed to be able to insist on their decisions being implemented. This was surely understood at Rome, and Marcius was well experienced in the ways of diplomacy amongst the Greeks. The several embassies instigated by Rome from the Greek states never had a chance of bringing the war in Egypt to an end. Similarly the embassy of Numisius can scarcely have been expected to succeed given that he was virtually unknown and of no obvious status even at Rome. The fact that Laenas waited not only until the Ptolemies were on their knees and thus at last willing to accept terms but that he delayed until the Roman war with Perseus was won suggests that the Romans were basically unwilling to see Antiochos, in particular, free to intervene on behalf of Perseus, his brother-in-law. The dispatch of a sequence of powerless mediators can only be seen as a public relations exercise in delaying tactics.

The one item in Antiochos' repertory of peace terms which was not part of Laenas' package was the king's position *in loco parentis* which he held toward Ptolemy VI for a time. Holding such a position would have put him in a strong moral position and perhaps have given him a powerful political influence over the Ptolemaic government. He was the uncle for all three of the children and was their closest blood relative, so he had a good claim, in personal terms at least, to be their tutor. On the other hand, he had murdered, or had caused to be murdered, his stepson, which was one of the reasons the regents had given for launching their war. It may well be to avoid such a tutorship that the Ptolemaic government was so obdurate in resisting agreeing to peace terms. To have the Seleukid king supervising their every action would be intolerable – as it would be to Rome as well. Such a position would also have been extremely awkward for Antiochos and would have prevented the further adventures he was contemplating. Here is another element to be weighed with respect to his acceptance of Roman mediation: it released him from an obligation he no longer wished to hold.

As a result of the conclusion of this treaty – technically between Antiochos IV and the Ptolemaic King Ptolemy VI – Antiochos believed himself safe from any possible Ptolemaic attack. During the next years, just like Antiochos III in 212 and 187, he set off on an eastern expedition in an attempt to repeat or revive the dynastic empire in the east.

## Dynastic weakness

Of the two kingdoms the Ptolemaic was now much the weaker. Only if the lost province of Koile Syria was recovered would it become a truly great power once again. So, just as the Seleukid kings had worked hard for a century to gain control of the region from the Ptolemies, now the Ptolemaic kings were just as determined to attempt to recover it, and this ambition can be traced through the several Syrian-Egyptian political crises until both dynasties were effectively powerless after about 100 BC. For several decades the Ptolemaic dynasty was hamstrung by a series of royal minorities and native Egyptian rebellions. Minorities meant rule by regents, who were quarrelsome, greedy, and never conducted a stable government – and were succeeded by a king who needed to establish himself in power before attempting any foreign policy adventures.

The Seleukids had their own dynastic troubles, with every king from 175 to the end of the dynasty being in one way or another an usurper, while most of them also died by violence, assassinated or murdered or killed in battle; two were taken into Parthian captivity; there were also rebellions, interventions from non-Seleukids, dynastic minorities, and foreign invasions. With all this mayhem in both kingdoms the diplomacy of the events which can still be called Syrian Wars is difficult to discern – not helped, of course, by the fragmentary and discontinuous nature of the sources.

The treaty brokered by the Roman intervention in 168 lasted until 164, when Antiochos IV died in Iran. Ptolemy VI was entangled in his own dynastic quarrel with his brother Ptolemy VIII – who reduced the kingdom once more by taking on the rule of Cyrenaica – and by a long series of campaigns within Egypt to put down minor rebellions. He was in no position to mount a new Syrian War until the early 150s. In addition he and Demetrios I, who seized the Seleukid throne in 162, were acquainted[9] and perhaps saw themselves as friends, which may also have restrained Ptolemy.

Ptolemy VI was hampered by a variety of considerations in any attempt to recover his lost provinces, but the diplomatic conditions for a new war were propitious from about 160. In the end it came because the accession of Demetrios to the

Seleukid kingship had created a new diplomatic alignment in the whole eastern Mediterranean region.

## The misbehaviour of Cn. Octavius

Changes in the Seleukid kingdom were of interest to the Roman Senate. It was mainly concerned in seeing the kingdom weakened by internal disputes, or at least by regency governments. Lysias, the regent for Antiochos IV's son Antiochos V, faced one attempt to displace him by violence, and at least two major Roman diplomatic missions went to Syria to investigate the position. One, led by Ti. Sempronius Gracchus,[10] visited Antiochos IV but saw nothing to worry about, especially since Antiochos was clearly intending to campaign in the east. The second embassy arrived while Lysias was regent.

The visit of this second set of diplomats produced an incident well known, even notorious, among historians of the Hellenistic period, but it is one which is more usually retailed than explained. Cn. Octavius had been a diplomat under Q. Marcius Philippus in Greece during the Third Macedonian War and, as praetor in 167, had commanded the Roman naval forces in the Aegean; he was elected consul in 163, and next year he was sent by the Senate on an investigatory mission to the countries of the eastern Mediterranean. His companions were Sp. Lucretius and L. Aurelius Cotta, who were from families which, unlike Octavius', had reached the consulship in the previous century, but the men themselves were not consular: Lucretius had been praetor in 172 (four years before Octavius), but Cotta had not yet reached that office. It was a reasonably balanced group, in other words, a mixture of a new high flier and two perhaps more conservative lesser men. Octavius spoke Greek, knowing the language well enough to act as an interpreter, and was habituated to Greek customs, as his fatal visit to baths at Laodikeia-ad-Mare, which were in the gymnasium, attest. He clearly was the main man, and the others seem to have had no independent role; Octavius, a rising man in Roman politics, was also evidently a domineering type. Eventually they reached Syria.

We know little of what was said during any meetings with Lysias, but Octavius was able to get around a good deal. Suddenly in discussions with Lysias he referred to the terms of the peace between Rome and Antiochos III in 188. He pointed to two clauses in particular, one that Antiochos III must reduce his navy to no more than ten triremes and second that he must cease to maintain a stable of war elephants. He pointed out to Lysias that the Seleukid army in 162 still had such a stable of elephants and insisted that the animals be killed and that any surplus warships be destroyed.

This process certainly began, because the screams of the animals – the killing was done by hamstringing them, and letting them die of pain and starvation – infuriated the Seleukid citizens who heard them. The elephant stables were at (Syrian) Apameia, but some of the beasts were kept at Antioch, where they were used for display in parades and festivals. The warships were at Seleukeia-in-Pieria, and probably at other ports, including Laodikeia and Ptolemais-Ake. In other words, a considerable proportion of the Syrian urban population became aware of what was happening, and, no doubt, why. Hence their anger. Octavius visited Laodikeia-ad-Mare, and there, in the public baths, he was murdered by a man called Leptines after a local orator-philosopher called Isokrates had conducted a public campaign against both Rome and Octavius.[11]

Shortly after the murder Demetrios I escaped from Roman detention in Italy, reached Syria, and made himself king, ordering the murder of Lysias and Antiochos V in the process. Perhaps as a species of atonement for having left Italy without formal permission, one of Demetrios' first acts as king was to arrest Leptines, who had been boasting of his deed, and send him to Rome, along with Isokrates. Leptines was no less forthcoming and proud in meeting the Senate – but the Senate did nothing.[12] We then lose sight of the two men; presumably they went home.

The Senate's non-reaction is the oddest element in this affair, though not the only one. It may go back to the original instructions under which Octavius and his colleagues operated. They were to make a tour of the eastern lands, first Macedonia, where they were to reconcile discordant factions, then Galatia and Kappadokia. Syria was next, and they were then to go on to Alexandria in Egypt, again to reconcile disputatious kings. The Syrian episode was the only part of their mission which was not designed to calm things down. There the instructions were the 'to manage the affairs of the kingdom as the Senate determined'. Polybios adds that this involved burning the kingdom's warships and hamstringing the elephants.[13]

In fact, Polybios' account of the Senate's instructions is somewhat disorganised. He states the Senate's instructions, with the explanation that it was all aimed at dominating Lysias and Antiochos V while the Seleukid government was weak. He sends the commissioners on their way, and only then adds that they had instructions to see to the burning of the ships and the killing of the elephants. Finally, he adds the information that the men had to visit the other places – Macedon, Asia Minor, Egypt. This awkward structure looks as if it is the result of a lack of later revision and that the note about the ships and the elephants was added later, after the event, possibly even interpolated by a later hand. That is, the Senate's instructions were probably couched in the deliberately vague way Polybios states at the beginning, and Octavius and his colleagues were expected to act on their own initiative. They were evidently provided with a copy of the Apameian peace terms, which is not something one would expect them to have to hand – or Lysias to provide. Octavius' use of his initiative turned out to be the attacks on the ships and the elephants, so it is possible that Polybios, or another, added that note later, assuming that this was part of the Senate's instructions – but such detailed instructions do not fit with the vague and *carte blanche* tenor of the original wording.

Furthermore, the instructions quoted by Polybios are unusual in that they expected more activism by the envoys than was normal for these long-range Roman embassies. There had been several of them since about 200, when a group of envoys may have visited Egypt and Syria. In that case one of the envoys, M. Aemilius Lepidus, the junior member of the embassy, was detached to confront Philip V at the siege of Abydos.[14] One result was Rome's second war with Macedon, but another was the beginning of the lengthy series of exchanges of envoys between Rome and Antiochos III which eventually ended in Rome's war with that king, though only after much to-and-fro negotiation (see Chapter 10). Later groups of envoys in the east were normally observatory rather than pro-active, reporting on local conditions back to Rome. This had been the role of the most recent embassy in the east, that led by Gracchus, in 166.[15] Since then things in the east had changed, so perhaps the Senate had now decided that a more intimidatory approach would be best; Cn. Octavius was certainly likely to be intimidating, and Lysias more likely to be intimidated than Antiochos IV. Octavius had been a colleague of Laenas in Greece, and shared his abrupt and brutal approach when he could deploy it. In Greece he had been restrained by Q. Marcius Philippus, and so emollient. He was clearly a man able to adjust his approach to circumstances yet, like Laenas, was all too likely to ignore polite convention and display his Roman arrogance.[16]

It is a pity that no source other than Polybios provides much information about the mission's purposes. Appian and Dio/Zonaras link the mission with the fact that the Seleukid kingdom was now ruled by a regent, but all the sources highlight different elements in the situation. Polybios thought an opportunity was being taken to weaken the Seleukid state; Dio assumed that the commissioners were sent to act as guardians of the child king, Antiochos V; Appian assumed that the Senate's purpose was to deny the kingdom to Demetrios. Neither Dio nor Appian claims that the purpose was to disarm the Seleukid government. In other words, all these historians have imposed their own interpretations on events. The greatest weight must be given to the contemporary Polybios, with reservations in view of the disorganisation of his account. The Senate's original instructions may thus have been deliberately vague; any subsequent supplementary instructions remained secret. No later information was apparently available, even to Polybios, except what the commission actually did – which is not necessarily what they were supposed to do. The instructions were certainly supplemented, for messages were sent after the envoys while they were on their travels.

The three commissioners had travelled without haste, spending time, as instructed, in Macedon, in Galatia, and in Kappadokia, so the mission to Syria was not urgent. They probably knew that Lysias faced a challenge from another would-be regent, Philip, who had been left in command of the main Seleukid field army in Iran when Antiochos IV died and was advancing westwards with the intention of replacing Lysias. They presumably also knew that Lysias was attending to the Jewish rebellion in Palestine. The greater the pressures on the regent the more malleable he would be, so their journey appears to have been timed to reach Syria when Lysias was at his most vulnerable.

In fact, if this really was their intention, they mistimed it. Lysias conducted a swift campaign into Judaea, suppressed the rebellion there, then returned to Antioch, which had been occupied in his absence by Philip. But Lysias had taken Antiochos V to Judaea with him, so he held the trump card; he had little difficulty in suppressing Philip.[17] The Roman embassy was informed of events by King Ariarathes in Kappadokia, who offered them a bodyguard in view of the 'unsettled state of the kingdom'.[18] They refused it, and when the commission reached Syria, Lysias had surmounted his recent difficulties, only to succumb to Octavius' demands on the ships and the elephants.

There was no serious possibility of Rome attacking Syria if Lysias refused. The only source of pressure Octavius could apply was Demetrios, who was detained in Italy, though he had asked more than once to be allowed to return to Syria and had been refused each time. If Demetrios, whom many must have seen as the rightful king, was to arrive in Syria, the best Lysias could hope for was another civil war; the worst was his own death – and perhaps that of his ward, the boy Antiochos V. Probably to fend off Demetrios, therefore, whose release Octavius could threaten, even though it may have been a bluff, Lysias complied with Octavius' demands.

Lysias and his government had no doubt protested and prevaricated at Octavius' demands; Octavius clearly insisted, perhaps threatened. In order to see that his demands were met we must assume that he and his colleagues visited the shipyards and the elephant stables – which would mean visits to Seleukeia-in-Pieria, the main port of the kingdom, and to Apameia, where the elephants were. He will have met Lysias at Antioch, the government centre, and he was at Laodikeia-ad-Mare when he was killed. He evidently spent a good deal of time in Syria, which rather suggests that Lysias' reluctance to comply slowed things down considerably, though he clearly felt unable to defy the Romans. And, of course, Octavius was still in Syria, at Laodikeia, when he was killed.

It is worth being clear about this: Octavius was wrong in his demands. The treaty of Apameia only said that Antiochos III must reduce his ships to ten and must get rid of the elephants. It did not lay that obligation on his successors. Octavius did not have the authority to insist on the destruction; this must have been at least part of Lysias' case in answering him, and the fact that he began the killing and the burning means that Octavius was able to use a most credible threat. The only one which Lysias feared was Demetrios' release. Octavius, like Laenas at Alexandria five years before, was thus using the most brutal diplomacy to get his way. That he was not only wrong but had exceeded his instructions is a mark of his arrogant brutality. All this must be part of the explanation for the Senate's lack of reaction when his murderer was presented to it: the senators were embarrassed.

After Octavius' murder, Demetrios really did arrive, following his escape from Italy. His first order was that Lysias and King Antiochos be killed, and soon he sent Leptines the assassin and his inspirer Isokrates to Rome for judgement. They were accompanied by a gift of ten thousand gold pieces as a sweetener – or perhaps as a sign of Demetrios' gratitude at being allowed to leave Italy. The Senate deliberated and finally took the money but dismissed the two men without inflicting punishment. The probable stated reason for not acting against them was that the crime was committed in Syria and that it was therefore up to the Syrian authorities to punish the perpetrators. And so, of course, if they were returned to Syria unpunished, Demetrios would have to do something – either punish these popular men or let them continue their anti-Roman agitating. The Senate's decision may well therefore have been another attempt to destabilise the Seleukid state.

This episode bristles with problems and puzzles, largely ignored by most historians. The absence of the other two Roman commissioners in the accounts is noteworthy, and one wonders what their attitudes were. They were, as it turned out, at the ends of their careers, though not in quite so drastic a way as Octavius. Neither reached higher office, despite their relatively exalted birth and good prospects. The Senate's failure to react to the murder might suggest shame at its envoy's behaviour, though shame is not a reaction expected of Roman senators. The Senate, if it had ordered the execution of Leptines, would have been fully understood then and later and might have sent a salutary message to others who might threaten Roman envoys – but he was let off.

The most obvious conclusion is that Octavius was acting on his own initiative, and that by failing to act in any way against Leptines the Senate was indicating that Octavius was in the wrong. This may be taken, if in a convoluted way, as confirmation of the theory advanced in this study that the treaties made with kings lasted only so long as they lived and that the death of a king invalidated the treaty unless it was specifically renewed – as Perseus renewed that of Philip V with Rome when he succeeded to the kingdom and as the regents for Ptolemy V wanted Antiochos III to do in 205/204. So the war fleet and the war elephants in Syria were not violations of the treaty of Apameia, which had expired, and the Senate, if not Octavius, knew it. Lysias' decision to succumb to Octavius' pressure was therefore due to the threat Octavius could bring against him, namely the release of Demetrios.

It cannot be believed, however, that Octavius was ignorant of such a basic element of contemporary diplomatic practice. He had sufficient experience of diplomacy in Greece, and under Marcius' mentorship, to allow us to assume he knew it well enough. Therefore his action in Syria was deliberate and personal, not a matter of suddenly discovering the Seleukid transgression of an old, defunct, treaty. He had learned his diplomatic practice in a place and time where the Roman consuls – Marcius Philippus and Aemilius Paullus – following the lead of earlier envoys and of the Senate as a whole, were stretching the bounds of diplomatic practice, where diplomacy was being used to mislead and lie and cheat on a large scale. Octavius and Laenas had operated in this way in Greece in order to calm down Greek unease at Roman military incompetence and arrogance – Laenas acted in as arrogant a way as any Roman ever did with Antiochos IV in Egypt; this only highlights the softer approach of both men in Greece, and unease was expressed at this sort of diplomatic behaviour in the Senate even as the Third Macedonian War was ending.

Octavius was therefore one of the group which was using Roman power to browbeat and bully perceived opponents, preferably the weakest and those who could not react or resist. Another set of Roman envoys tried at about the same time to browbeat Ptolemy VI, who outfoxed two envoys, and ten years later he simply ignored the 'orders' of a group of five commissioners, each travelling in his own quinquereme, as arrogant and intimidatory behaviour as can be imagined.[19] (See the next section of this chapter.) Lysias was in a much weaker position in Syria and could be forced into compliance.

There is another aspect here of rather wider significance than relations between Rome and the Seleukid kingdom. The murder of Octavius is one of a series of insults to Roman envoys in the mid-second century, many of which were also ignored by the Senate. Several were noted in the last chapter, during the wars between Attalos II and Prousias II and during the crisis over the future of the

Achaian League. The insult to Aurelius Orestes in the Achaian Assembly did occasion anger in the Senate, but the only action which followed was to despatch yet another envoy, Sex. Julius Caesar, who was distracted and hoodwinked by Diaios until he left in anger. Neither of these was the occasion for the Roman military reply which eventually followed. In Asia the gross mistreatment of the ten envoys, who attempted to bring the two kings to a meeting and were then chased in undignified fashion to refuge in Pergamon city, was also followed by the despatch of a new set of envoys.

So the refusal of the Senate to take action in the case of the murder of Octavius fits into a pattern of senatorial refusals in other, if less extreme, cases. It must be concluded that either the Senate did not feel itself able to take any effective action – though the punishment of Leptines and Isokrates was surely possible – or that the senators did not care, though they surely felt it was necessary to deter future insults. The answer may well be that it was seen as incumbent on the hosts to protect the lives and persons of the envoys and that the replacement and execution of Lysias by Demetrios, or the punishment of Prousias by the Roman-organised alliance which defeated him, was enough. The destruction of the Achaian League which followed the insults to Orestes and Caesar and the envoys of Metellus could also be seen as sufficient. The problem there, of course, is that the punishment was sufficiently detached from the crime as not to be consequential; there was no direct lesson administered.

## Rome and the two Ptolemies

Following the peace treaty with Antiochos IV, the Ptolemaic government for four years operated under the joint management of Ptolemy VI, his sister Kleopatra II, and his brother Ptolemy VIII. By 164, however, Ptolemy VIII had ousted his brother, who went to Rome to appeal for assistance to the Senate. The Senate was obligated to assist them because of its intervention in securing the peace treaty, but, as usual in this period, it was willing only to send envoys, who had no obvious effect.

For several years the brothers bickered, and at irregular intervals one or the other would appeal for Roman assistance, which was forthcoming only to the extent of envoys being sent or resolutions passed, none of which had any effect on the situation in the Ptolemaic kingdom. In 163 Ptolemy VI took matters into his own hands, went to Cyprus, and from there organised the ouster of his brother from Alexandria. Ptolemy VIII then was assigned Cyrenaica, by agreement between the two brothers. He appealed to the Senate. There were Roman envoys in Alexandria at the time of the agreement, and they may well have been involved. The Senate's decision was that Ptolemy VIII should also have Cyprus as his kingdom.

An embassy was appointed to supervise the transmission, but when Ptolemy VIII began recruiting an army to achieve his aim by force he was dissuaded, on the promise that the Roman envoys would negotiate with Ptolemy VI for his installation in Cyprus. They failed in this; Ptolemy VIII suffered a rebellion in Cyrenaica, and meanwhile Ptolemy VI made it clear that he intended to abide by the original

240    *The collision of East and West*

agreement of partition. In effect, he was denying the competence of the Senate's envoys to intervene.

Ptolemy VIII appealed again to the Senate, which once more accepted his appeal and 'ordered' his installation in Cyprus; Ptolemy VI ignored this. The Senate was not prepared to exert any sort of force to back up its decision. Its decision was unenforceable without a major military expedition to invade and conquer Egypt. Ptolemy VI had operated very cleverly within Egypt and had gained substantial local support, while Ptolemy VIII had managed to make himself thoroughly unpopular when he ruled in Alexandria in 164/163. The Senate was helpless.

The issue recurred at least twice more, with similar results. Even sending five Roman envoys, each in a quinquereme, had no effect. Ptolemy VI understood perfectly clearly that Rome was never going to be willing to exert itself militarily at such a distance from Italy, and so he could ignore any senatorial resolution or decision. Rome's diplomatic clout in the mid-second century was thus restricted to its near neighbours.

## The diplomacy of Demetrios I

Demetrios I, once he was king in 162, could not be intimidated as easily as the insecure Lysias. He was faced by a rebellion led by the viceroy of the eastern satrapies, Timarchos, who was 'recognised' by the Roman Senate.[20] This action was clearly intended to contribute to any confusion in the kingdom produced by the rebellion. Demetrios simply ignored the Roman message and defeated and killed Timarchos.[21] Both he and Ptolemy therefore showed that the Senate's authority was so limited that its 'orders' were irrelevant. The 'new diplomacy', hostile and threatening, of which the older senators had complained, associated with Marcius Philippus and his followers Octavius and Popillius Laenas, was ineffective in the face of men who paid no attention and in the absence of military backing.

Having gained his rightful throne and survived the initial difficulties and challenges during 162–160, Demetrios then conducted such inept diplomacy that he alienated all the neighbouring powers. Perhaps because he was brought up largely in Italy and among Roman senators, he was clumsy in his international relations and tended to prefer underhanded methods and conspiracies to open contacts (his version, perhaps, of the current Roman methods, and perhaps also a consequence of his conspiratorial escape from Italy). One result was that he himself fell before a successful conspiracy. Antiochos IV's good relations with the Attalid kings were changed by Demetrios' defiance of Rome and were then further damaged by an unsuccessful attempt to interfere in the succession to the Kappadokian kingship.[22]

More serious was Demetrios' attempt to gain control of Cyprus, a Ptolemaic province under the rule of Ptolemy VI. This was a long-standing ambition of the Seleukids, and Antiochos IV had actually succeeded during the Sixth Syrian War, until Popillius Laenas had insisted that the island be returned to Ptolemy VI as part of the terms agreed at Eleusis. Demetrios contacted the governor, Archias, and offered him a bribe of five hundred talents for the island. He accepted but was discovered (fairly extensive preparations would obviously be needed) and then committed suicide.[23] So Demetrios did not gain Cyprus, but he did gain the enmity of Ptolemy, and this was the decisive moment in another conspiracy, whose target was Demetrios himself.

The killing of the rebel Timarchos alienated his brother, Herakleides, who had been a prominent minister of Antiochos IV. Herakleides sought out two children who were said to be of Antiochos IV and promoted the boy, Alexander, as an alternative king. He interested Attalos II of Pergamon, Antiochos' ally, who felt politically put out by Demetrios' success and was later angered by Demetrios' interference in Kappadokian affairs, an activity Attalos felt was his prerogative. Attalos professed to recognise Alexander as king and installed him in the Taurus Mountains, on the undefined border between his and Demetrios' kingdom, with a bandit chief called Zenodoros, as a permanent threat to Demetrios.[24]

Alexander and his sister's parentage is nowhere stated. It is assumed that he was the son of Antiochos IV by a courtesan called Antiochis (or perhaps she was his sister – all the names are of the restricted royal type). When he had assigned the tax revenues of two Kilikian cities for her maintenance, those cities complained vigorously but unsuccessfully, and it was surely the memory of this which induced Attalos to place Alexander in the nearby mountain lair of Zenodoros.[25]

This took place soon after the defeat and death of Timarchos, after which Herakleides conducted a personal odyssey of diplomacy, visiting Egypt and Rome in his quest for support. He made no real progress other than to alert these powers to the existence of Alexander and his sister, Laodike, and thus interest them in the potentialities of assisting and using them. At Rome they were presented to the Senate, without any concrete result, though the Senate did nothing to stop Herakleides' *sub-rosa* diplomacy.[26] The Senate's reaction was in fact very similar to its 'recognition' of Timarchos several years before. Demetrios' unsuccessful intrigue aimed at stealing Cyprus annoyed Ptolemy VI sufficiently for him to take up Alexander's cause; needless to say, Ptolemy had an agenda of his own in this, apart from following Herakleides' script.

With Egyptian money and ships behind him, Alexander was at last able to make serious progress, though it took time. The problem of Cyprus blew up in 154, but it was not for two more years that the plot against Demetrios emerged into the open. How much of it was visible to Demetrios at any time is not known. He was surely aware of Alexander at Zenodoros' castle, so he was probably not wholly surprised. In 152 Alexander landed in Ptolemais-Ake with some soldiers.[27] There are no details of their strength, but it is reasonable to assume that the ships had been provided by Ptolemy and perhaps by Attalos, and that they must also have provided the money to hire the mercenaries. The Seleukid commander in Ptolemais-Ake surrendered to Alexander at once, along with his troops, so he had been suborned in advance. This was exactly what Demetrios had been attempting in Cyprus, so Ptolemy no doubt felt justified and well revenged.

This plot was as much an example of diplomatic practice as Demetrios' attempt to gain Cyprus or his intervention in Kappadokia. Negotiations led by Herakleides involved the kings of the Attalid and Ptolemaic dynasties, a chieftain in the Taurus Mountains who was clearly essentially an independent ruler, the Roman

Senate, and the garrison commander of Ptolemais-Ake. The whole process, from the emergence of Alexander as pretender in 159 to the landing at Ptolemais, took seven years, and Rome was irrelevant in the whole matter. Only when Ptolemy VI was seriously annoyed by Demetrios I was real strength put behind the plot – but once Ptolemy really was engaged he very largely managed the affair. For the Attalids this returned the diplomatic situation of Antiochos IV's time, with a king on the Seleukid throne beholden to Attalos II, though he had done little enough to promote Alexander other than make some diplomatic gestures.

After a war lasting two years Alexander defeated and killed Demetrios in battle but was then confronted by the standing threat of an attack by Demetrios I's son, Demetrios II, who had been sent out of the kingdom for safety when the war began. Demetrios II returned to Syria with a mercenary army, which had been the product of diplomatic negotiations, and made sufficient progress so that Ptolemy VI intervened to assist his protege. He did so first by giving his daughter Kleopatra Thea to Alexander in marriage – a mark of his recognition as king – and later by marching his army through Palestine and Phoenicia, thereby occupying those provinces. His forces remained there for some months, and it seems reasonable to suppose that this was the price he had demanded for rendering his assistance to Alexander. It was a reversal of the verdict of the Fifth Syrian War.[28]

But then in a complicated fight both Ptolemy and Alexander died. Ptolemy's army rapidly retreated back to Egypt, leaving Demetrios II as the sole Seleukid king and having recovered the (briefly) lost province. There may or may not have followed a peace treaty between Demetrios II and the new King Ptolemy VIII, who had rapidly moved in to take his brother's place in Egypt, but not necessarily, since these two had not actually been at war. A treaty, in the event, was scarcely necessary. Demetrios was quickly involved in a new civil war aggravated by an invasion of his eastern territories by the Parthians, and he was therefore no threat to Ptolemy. Meanwhile Ptolemy VIII had his own problems in Egypt; indeed, never in his reign during the next thirty years did he show any interest in extending his dominions.

## The new diplomacy

It is evident that the practices of diplomacy during these later Syrian Wars (195–145) had changed. Roman diplomacy in Greece in the war against Perseus had the deliberate aim of preparing for war and had been so far lacking in success that the war was followed by a brutal Roman crackdown which the weak Greek states could not resist. This tough diplomacy was applied also to the kingdoms in the eastern Mediterranean, and it worked where there was a political weakness to exploit, as with Lysias, but failed, as with Ptolemy VI and Demetrios I, where the kings were firmly seated in power. It was, when attempted beyond Greece, no more than a bluff, with no strength behind it, since it was obvious to all that Rome had no intention of intervening militarily east of Greece; within Greece, of course, Roman brutality was backed up by the presence or proximity of a victorious army; the memory of invasions by Roman armies three times in a generation (200, 191, 171) inevitably concentrated Greek minds.

In the relations between the eastern kingdoms, two levels of diplomacy would seem to have been engaged. On the surface there were the usual courteous contacts, though little is known of these, since they only come to light where conflict is involved. Below that surface there were repeated intrigues designed to gain political advantage – the installation of Antiochos IV as king, the interventions of Demetrios I in Kappadokia and Cyprus, the lengthy plotting of Herakleides to overthrow Demetrios I, the ambitions of Andriskos. Such intrigues had happened before, though earlier they were aimed at gaining relatively minor advantages before a future war rather than overthrowing a regime. This may have been a result of the new Roman brutality affecting the older practices in the east. Roman diplomatic practice was always aimed at overwhelming a perceived enemy by preparing for war (as at Messene in 264), whereas, in the kingdoms of the east, the aim of diplomacy was usually to gain advantage in the intervals between wars, or to solve problems in order to avoid war, or to make peace at the end of a war, but not to destroy an enemy.

## Roman envoys' grand tours

The envoys and embassies sent out from Rome were of four types. Many were mediators or arbitrators, often requested by the parties involved, to deal with a dispute between a pair of Greek islands or cities or between rival claimants to a foreign throne. Another large set were sent as messengers of the Senate to deliver its counsel, or a warning, or a declaration of war, to a particular foreign state, tasks which might include visiting other states in the local region; the successive embassies to Greece before and during the Third Macedonian War, or those to the Achaian League before that league's destruction, are examples; there were others to Spanish tribes, to North Africa between 200 and 150, and to various tribes to the north of Italy. In a way the sets of commissioners sent out to settle the precise terms of peace after a major war were also envoys, though little negotiation was involved, more dictation than diplomacy.

The fourth group are relatively few but have occasioned some fairly extravagant claims. These embassies went on what are sometimes described as diplomatic 'grand tours'. There were five of them, all between 200 and 144 BC, and all were headed by particularly distinguished Romans, with in each case two colleagues who were clearly subordinate but who were also capable of acting alone. The first of these embassies were sent in 200, evidently in advance of the Roman attack on Macedon which began later in that year, and supposedly to visit Antiochos III and Ptolemy V.[29] The presence as envoys of C. Claudius Nero, the victor of the Metaurus battle, and P. Sempronius Tuditanus, the long-term commander against Philip in the Illyrian region, would imply that the envoys were chosen particularly for their martial achievements. The third of the envoys, the young M. Aemilius Lepidus, was detached when they reached Rhodes to confront Philip in his siege of Abydos and deliver a disguised declaration of war.

Other sources than Livy – Appian and Justin – say that the object of this embassy was actually to contact Antiochos III and Ptolemy V with a view to mediating their

244   *The collision of East and West*

conflict, the Fifth Syrian War. Given that war on Philip had been decided, and that Philip was associated with Antiochos in the war against Ptolemy, it is more likely that they were charged with investigating that possible alliance and maybe to ensure that the Seleukid-Ptolemaic war continued so that Antiochos would not be able to intervene in the Roman-Macedonian War. Lepidus' dispatch from Rhodes rather implies that the envoys had quickly realised the impossibility of the Seleukid intervention and so went ahead with their ambiguous declaration of war. It is possible that the envoys went on to Syria and Egypt. There is no record of this, but it does seem likely that they established contact with both kings while they had the chance. They could not bring about peace between the kings, and indeed it was in the Roman interest to see that the war went on so that neither king had the opportunity to intervene in Macedon.

The purpose of the embassy was thus not to bring about peace in Syria but to investigate the general situation. They stopped at Rhodes, which was a good news centre, perhaps contacted the kings, and learned the details of the Syrian war. Having got so far it seems unlikely that they would pass up the chance of going all the way to Syria and Egypt to investigate on the spot, perhaps separating to do so. There was a tradition in the Aemilius family that Lepidus had become some sort of guardian of Ptolemy V. This is hardly to be accepted, but there must be some foundation to the story, and a visit by Lepidus to Egypt would thus seem to be likely. The 'grand tour' was thus less an exercise in active diplomacy and more an investigation into the general political situation.

The basic motivation of the second of these tours, headed by Ti. Sempronius Gracchus in 166, was perhaps the same, to investigate conditions following the upheavals of the Third Romano-Macedonian War and the Sixth Syrian War.[30] There was no conflict in the region to give an excuse for Livy or others to claim that Rome was acting as a peacemaker, so this embassy was probably, once again, only investigatory. Antiochos IV had made a great display of his military might in his grand parade at Daphne near Antioch during 166, and it would be reasonable for Rome to investigate whether Antiochos intended to use his power in some way against Rome. Gracchus returned with the reassuring news that Antiochos intended to use his army in an eastern expedition.

Gracchus and his colleagues visited Greece, King Eumenes in Pergamon, and the kingdom of Kappadokia before reaching Antiochos in Antioch. Only in Syria is Gracchus recorded as having done anything in the way of diplomacy, where he was charmed and flattered by the king. On his return to Rome he reported that none of the objects of his investigation posed any threat; in this he was clearly perfectly correct. He is, however, reported to have been coddled by all whom he visited. This is taken as a criticism, despite the correctness of his conclusions.

The embassy of Octavius and his colleagues, discussed earlier in this chapter, visited much the same region two or three years later, when the political conditions had changed: Antiochos was dead and the kingdom was ruled by the regent Lysias, there was a near-civil war in Egypt, and Kappadokia was disturbed. As noted earlier in this chapter the embassy had instructions to conciliate the various disputes, though the instructions for the Seleukid visit were different. Octavius waited until he was clear that Lysias had survived the initial troubles before actually visiting Syria. His activities there would suggest that he was intent on reducing the military and naval power of the kingdom, even if he did not have specific instructions for that. One of his colleagues went off to Kappadokia, whose King Ariarathes V had his own quarrel with Lysias, whom he blamed for not having safeguarded his mother and sister when they visited Antioch and had been killed.[31] We do not know what report Octavius' surviving colleagues made when they reached Rome again, but not long afterwards Demetrios escaped from Roman detention and made himself king in Syria. Yet another embassy then went from Rome to investigate the situation in the Seleukid kingdom – the third in four years. The leader of the embassy was once again Ti. Sempronius Gracchus.

This embassy was to look first at affairs in Greece, then the Attalid kingdom, where it was to mediate between Eumenes and the Galatians, who had made complaints.[32] Gracchus went on to Kappadokia as before, where he was contacted by an envoy from Demetrios. His instructions were to 'await the results of Demetrios' action'. That is, just as Octavius had waited to see if Lysias survived, so Gracchus was doing the same with Demetrios. Most of Gracchus' work in this embassy was therefore to observe and investigate. The only active diplomatic action he took was in promoting peace between Eumenes and the Galatians. He did not even go to Syria, for after Demetrios' envoy returned from visiting him in Kappadokia, Demetrios had to send to Pamphylia and then to Rhodes to contact him. It had become apparent that Demetrios was firmly seated, and he was encouraged to send envoys direct to Rome.

The fifth of these grand tour embassies was sent out, probably in 144 BC, under the leadership of Scipio Aemilianus.[33] He followed the precedent set by the previous four, all essentially investigatory. Scipio visited all the powers of the east: Greece, where he could report on the condition of the region after the Macedonian rebellion and the destruction of the Achaian League; Asia, where Attalos II was now at peace with Bithynia; interior Asia Minor; Syria, where the country was in turmoil after Demetrios II's seizure of the throne; Egypt, where he humiliated the fat and ungainly Ptolemy VIII in public. He is said to have been sent to settle the affairs of the kings, but he did nothing of the sort. In no case can any trace be found of him taking any action, diplomatic or otherwise. It has been suggested that one of the reasons he was sent on the embassy was to get him away from Rome, where his renown was too great for the rest of the senators. If so, his instructions on the embassy cannot have been any more than, once again, to report on conditions in the east.

(It may be that the group of commissioners headed by P. Cornelius Scipio Serapio, which went to Asia in 132, might be counted as an investigatory mission after the death of Attalos III. We know so little about it, however, that it is difficult to make a decision. The fact that the senators had no military backup does imply that their function was investigatory, not an intervention.)

These embassies were undoubtedly useful for Rome in maintaining some sort of contact with the various rulers in the east and in gathering information on the conditions of the countries there and on their powers. On occasion the envoys could take mediating action, as when Gracchus mediated between Eumenes and the Galatians. But this stands out as the only occasion in which one of these ambassadors took any action at all – except Octavius, of course. These embassies were not active Roman interventions in the east; they were passive investigations of local possibilities.

## Diplomacy after Demetrios and Ptolemy VI

The failure of source material from about 150 BC renders it impossible to discuss diplomatic actions during the next century, and by the time that period has passed the issue is the exercise of Roman power. There are records of a dozen or so mediations and arbitrations by Rome and Greek states, but the record on interstate diplomacy is meagre;[34] for this late period every case is based on epigraphic material, often fragmentary, and the standard collection of the cases has only two after 100 BC.

The Syrian Wars of 126–123 and 103–101 do show kings and queens active in diplomacy, but their actions do not show any clearer evidence of diplomatic practice than are revealed by earlier wars and conflicts.[35] The sources for these events are even more difficult than for the earlier: the last Syrian War, in 103–101, has papyri, epigraphic, and written sources, none of which connect at all clearly. Until better source material emerges, it is best to leave these late wars out of the account.

## Notes

1 Porphyry *FGrH* 260 F 49a.
2 This is the 'day of Eleusis': Livy 44.19.13–15; Polybios 9.27.5.
3 For interpretations not necessarily identical to this one see O. Morkholm, *Antiochos IV of Syria*, Copenhagen 1966, W. Gwyn Morgan, 'The Perils of Schematism: Polybios, Antiochos Epiphanes and the "Day of Eleusis" ', *Historia* 59, 1990, 37–76; Gruen, *Hellenistic Monarchies*, 114–115 and 658–660; Ager, *Interstate Arbitrations* 122.
4 Polybios 29.25.1; Livy 45.17.3.
5 Polybios 28.17.13–15.
6 Polybios 28.19.1–7, 20.13; this curious list came about in fact because delegations from the cities were in Alexandria for a different purpose.
7 Polybios 28.23.1–5.
8 Polybios 29.24.10, 25.1–2, 6.
9 They had met in Rome in 164: Diodoros 31.18.
10 Polybios 30.27.1; Diodoros 31.17.
11 Polybios 31.2.9–11; Appian, *Syrian Wars* 46; Zonaras 9.25.
12 Polybios 32.3.1–3.13.
13 Polybios 31.2.9–11.
14 Polybios 16.34.1; Livy 31.18.1; Appian, *Macedonian Wars* 4.1.
15 Polybios 30.27.1; Diodoros 31.17.
16 A.J. Toynbee, *Hannibal's Legacy*, vol. 2, Oxford 1965, 608–645, compiled a list of the misdemeanours of Roman envoys and others overseas (and in Italy) in the second century; Octavius' exploit in Syria is not included but clearly fits in with the other items listed.
17 J.D. Grainger, *The Syrian Wars*, Leiden 2010, 317.

## The later Syrian Wars  247

18 Polybios 31.8.5–8; Ariarathes had his own reason to be annoyed with Lysias, so his offer was hardly meant to safeguard the Romans and more to denigrate Lysias.
19 Polybios 33.11.4–7.
20 Diodoros 31.27a, 28–29; Polybios 31.33 and 32.2–3.
21 Appian, *Syrian Wars* 47; Trogus, *Prologue* 34.
22 Appian, *Syrian Wars* 47–48; Diodoros 31.32, 32a; this, of course (see Chapter 12), was resolved when Attalos II re-enthroned Ariarathes V.
23 Polybios 33.15 and 18.6–14
24 Diodoros 31.32a.
25 II *Maccabees* 4.30; see also on all this Grainger, *Syrian Wars*, 328–332.
26 Polybios 33.15 and 18.6–14.
27 II *Maccabees* 10.1.
28 Grainger, *Syrian Wars*, 331–346.
29 Polybios 16.23.1–7; Livy 31.1.1–4; 18.1–7; Doodoros 28.6.
30 Polybios 30.27.1–31.3; Livy, *Per.* 46; Diodoros 31.17 ad 28.
31 Polybios 31.7.2–4.
32 Polybios 31.15.9–10; 32.3, 33.1–4; Diodoros 31.28.
33 The embassy's date is disputed: A.E. Astin, *Scipio Aemilianus*, Oxford 1967, accepted the traditional dating of 140–139, but H. Mattingly, 'Scipio Aemilianus' Eastern Embassy', *Classical Quarterly* 36, 1986, 491–495, made a better case for 144–143.
34 Ager, *Interstate Arbitrations*, 156–171.
35 Grainger, *Syrian Wars*, 369–402.

# Conclusion

The purpose of this book has been to draw attention to the element in ancient international relations which we can characterise as diplomacy. This was an essential lubricant to relations between states, then as now, and was vital when there were several states, as there were in the Hellenistic age in the eastern Mediterranean. Each such state-system tends to develop its own methods and procedures in diplomacy. That of the Hellenistic system developed during the contest for power following the death of Alexander the Great and continued in use for a century and a half. It was eventually disrupted and overturned by the dominating methods employed by the Roman Republic, which emerged from a more testing and brutal system in the western Mediterranean.

The diplomacy of the eastern Mediterranean states was based on the diplomatic methods which had emerged among the several kings after Alexander's death. The kings' authority was based above all on control of an army and on the political inheritance from Macedon, from whose aristocratic society the first kings all originated. The system is distinctive – that is, it is different from other comparable diplomatic systems – in that it relied on the kings keeping their oath-sworn word, so that an agreement between two kings lasted until one of them died. This was an inheritance from their Macedonian origins. From one point of view, this produced frequent wars, but it also often freed kings from apprehensions of attack and produced regular periods of guaranteed peace.

Within that overall accepted set of conditions, the kings were able to engage in peacetime contests – proxy wars, intrigues, espionage – in which they deliberately restricted themselves to activities well short of open warfare; they could also concentrate on minor wars and conquests, on recovering their authority within their kingdoms after rebellions, and on developing their resources without the constant fear of attack. So, for example, there may have been six Syrian Wars between the Seleukid and Ptolemaic kingdoms between 301 and 152, but during that period (150 years) only 28 years were consumed in those wars, and therefore, to put it the other way around, over 120 were years of peace. This was clearly one of the reasons for the considerable economic growth of the Hellenistic period.

The institutions of diplomacy, in so far as they existed, were less obviously distinctive. The fact that there was no word for 'diplomacy' in either Greek or Latin indicates that as a political practice it was not recognised; this does not mean it did not exist. Such practices as were used were largely inherited from Greece of the preceding period of the city states. Negotiations – the primary diplomatic activity – consisted, as before, of heralds and envoys travelling to meet and talk with other envoys or with the kings, who were the only elements in the state-system with any authority and who had to ratify any agreements. The apparent significance of royal intermarriage turns out, on examination, to be minimal: no royal marriages can be counted as an 'alliance' beyond the immediate period of the wedding, and in no case can it be shown that the kings allowed the marriage of a son or daughter to influence their diplomacy or international conduct.

This Hellenistic diplomatic system can be traced in use for a century and a half, if not more, in the eastern Mediterranean. The three great powers who originated the methods successfully used them also in their relations with the many minor kingdoms – in Asia Minor, Kyrene, Baktria, even India – during that time. The arrival of Roman power in the eastern Mediterranean at first did not change the system. Rome evidently accepted its norms, as can be seen in its early relations with Syracuse and Macedon between 264 and, say, 180. But Roman military power was so brutally overwhelming that the city was able to impose its own interpretation of the practices on the rest. This was applied in Greece and Macedon from the 170s and in Asia Minor fifty years later. In the remnants of the Hellenistic world in the eastern Mediterranean, the old system was can be seen to operate still into the 120s, but after that it seems to have finally broken down amid the disintegration of the major kingdoms.

The main Roman diplomatic methods were based on a dictatorial mindset. These became first evident in the treatment of Macedon and Greece after 167, though there were earlier indications in the dictated peace settlements of 196 and 188. During the preparations for the Third Macedonian War in the 170s Rome found that its techniques of diplomatic persuasion did not bring the assistance it expected from its Greek clients, most of whom were unwilling to involve themselves in the new war. As a result Rome, having won the war, turned its brutality onto its Greek allies; twenty years later that brutality brought the final destruction of any pretence of independence of the Greek cities.

That is to say, the Roman use of Hellenistic diplomatic methods was adapted to imperial conquest. Twice, in 200 and 172, Rome had attacked Macedon without just excuse, in violation of the oaths sworn by its representatives in previous peace agreements and in violation of its own religious practices – in 179, Rome had accepted that the peace agreed with Perseus' father in 197 should continue yet deliberately engineered a new war only a few years later. The Hellenistic system was not one in which aggressive wars such as this were permitted, notwithstanding annexations of disputed provinces. (The oaths of kings lasted until their deaths, but once one party was dead, a new war was expected, as, for example, the envoys of Ptolemy V's regents in 205–203 understood.) But the republican system of government permitted a state such as Rome to disregard previous commitments and agreements if the governing group considered advantage could be gained thereby. (This was also the practice in the Greek republican states, such as Aitolia and Achaia.) This attitude could not be accommodated within the Hellenistic system; it could be coped with if the aberrant state was relatively small and/or weak – Aitolia, for example; but the clear military power of Rome inevitably broke through the Hellenistic inhibitions.

The end result was, of course, the Roman Empire, already in process of formation after 146. A long period of peace followed from the reign of Augustus to that of the Severans, punctuated by occasional civil wars. But to get from the ordered and predictable working of the Hellenistic diplomatic system to the peace of the Roman Empire, the Hellenistic world had to go through the fire of Roman conquest, destruction, and extortion, a fate which the Hellenistic system of diplomacy had been, at least in part, designed to avoid. In the end, of course, Greece took its conqueror captive, and the Roman emperors much resembled Hellenistic kings, though their need for diplomacy was much reduced. Nevertheless, relations between Rome and the surviving Hellenistic kingdom, Parthia, were very much in the Hellenistic pattern.

# Bibliography

Adcock, Sir Frank, and D.J. Mosley, *Diplomacy in Ancient Greece*, London 1975.
Ager, Sheila M., 'Familiarity Breeds: Incest in the Ptolemaic Family', *Journal of Hellenic Studies* 125, 2005, 1–34.
Allen, Charles, *Ashoka: The Search for India's Lost Emperor*, London 2012.
Allen, R.E., *The Attalid Kingdom: A Constitutional History*, Oxford 1983.
Astin, A.E., *Scipio Aemilianus*, Oxford 1967.
Badian, E., 'Rome and Antiochos the Great, a Study in Cold War', in E. Badian (ed.), *Studies in Greek and Roman History*, Oxford 1964, 112–139.
Basch, L. 'The *Isis* of Ptolemy II Philadelphus', *Mariner's Mirror* 71, 1985, 129–137.
Bevan, E.R., *The House of Seleucus*, London 1902.
Billows, Richard A., *Antigonos the One-Eyed and the Creation of the Hellenistic State*, California 1990.
Billows, Richard A., *Kings and Colonists: Aspects of Macedonian Imperialism*, Leiden 1995.
Bosworth, A.B., *Conquest and Empire*, Cambridge 1988.
Burstein, S.M., 'Arsinoe II Philadelphus, a Revisionist View', in E. Borza (ed.), *Philip II, Alexander the Great, and the Macedonian Heritage*, Washington, DC 1982, 197–212.
Burton, Paul J., *Friendship and Empire: Roman Diplomacy and Imperialism in the Middle Republic (353–146 BC)*, Oxford 2011.
Cartledge, Paul, and Antony Spawforth, *Hellenistic and Roman Sparta*, London 1989.
Caven, Brian, *The Punic Wars*, London 1980.
Cawkwell, George, *Philip of Macedon*, London 1976.
Cohen, Getzel M., *Hellenistic Settlements in Europe, the Islands, and Asia Minor*, California 1995.
Cohen, Getzel M., *The Hellenistic Settlements in the East from Armenia and Mesopotamia to Bactria and India*, California 2013.
Cohen, Raymond, and Raymond Westbrook (eds.), *Amarna Diplomacy: The Beginnings of International Relations*, Baltimore 2000.
Colledge, Malcolm A.R., *The Parthians*, London 1977.
Cook, J.M., *The Troad*, Oxford 1973.
Delorme, J., *Le Monde hellénistique, 323–133 avant J.-C.*, Paris 1975.
Dmitriev, Sviatoslav, *City Government in Hellenistic and Roman Asia Minor*, Oxford 2005.
Eckstein, A.M., *Senate and General*, California 1987.
Eckstein, A.M., *Rome Enters the Greek East*, Oxford 2008.
Eckstein, Arthur M., *Mediterranean Anarchy, Interstate War, and the Rise of Rome*, California 2006.

Ellis, J.R., *Philip II and Macedonian Imperialism*, London 1976.
Errington, R.M., *A History of the Hellenistic World, 323–30 BC*, Oxford 2008.
Ferrary, J.L., and P. Gauthier, 'Le Traite entre le roi Antiochos et Lysimacheia', *Journal des Savants* 1981, 327–345.
Fraser, P.M., *The Rhodian Peraea and Islands*, Oxford 1954.
Fraser, P.M., *Ptolemaic Alexandria*, Oxford 1972.
Fraser, P.M., *Cities of Alexander the Great*, Oxford 1996.
Fronda, Michael P., *Between Rome and Carthage, Southern Italy during the Second Punic War*, Oxford 2010.
Fuks, Alexander, 'Social Revolution in Greece in the Hellenistic Age', *La Parola del Passato* 111, 1966, 437–448.
Gera, D. 'Ptolemy Son of Thraseas and the Fifth Syrian War', *Ancient Society* 18, 198763–73.
Grainger, J.D., *The Cities of Seleukid Syria*, Oxford 1990.
Grainger, J.D., *Seleukos Nikator: Constructing a Hellenistic Kingdom*, London 1990.
Grainger, J.D., *Hellenistic Phoenicia*, Oxford 1991.
Grainger, J.D., 'The Campaign of Cn. Manlius Vulso in Asia Minor', *Anatolian Studies* 54, 1995, 23–42.
Grainger, J.D., 'Antiochos III in Thrace', *Historia* 15, 1996, 329–343.
Grainger, J.D., *The League of the Aitolians*, Leiden 1999.
Grainger, J.D., *The Roman War of Antiochos the Great*, Leiden 2002.
Grainger, J.D., *The Cities of Pamphylia*, Oxford 2009.
Grainger, J.D., *The Syrian Wars*, Leiden 2010.
Grainger, J.D., *Rome, Parthia, India*, Barnsley 2013.
Grant, Michael, *The Hellenistic Greeks from Alexander to Cleopatra*, London 1982.
Green, Peter, *Alexander to Actium*, London 1990.
Gruen, Erich S., 'Class Conflict and the Third Macedonian War', *American Journal of Ancient History* 1, 1976, 29–66.
Gruen, Erich S., *The Hellenistic World and the Coming of Rome*, California 1984.
Habicht, Christian, *Athens from Alexander to Antony*, Cambridge, MA 1997.
Hammond, N.G.L., and G.T. Griffith, *A History of Macedonia*, 3 vols, Oxford 1979–1988.
Harris, W.V., *War and Imperialism in Republican Rome, 327–70 BC*, Oxford 1979.
Hauben, H., 'Rhodes, Alexander and the Diadochi from 333–332 to 304', *Historia* 26, 1977, 307–309.
Hauben, H., 'Philocles, King of the Sidonians and General of the Ptolemies', *Studia Phoenicia* 5, 1987, 413–427.
Helliesen, J.M., 'Andriscus and the Revolt of the Macedonians, 149–148 BC', in *Ancient Macedonia*, vol. 4, Thessaloniki 1986, 307–314.
Herrmann, P., 'Antiochos III und Teos', *Anadolu* 9, 1965, 29–159.
Holleaux, M., *Rome, la Grece et les monarchies Hellenistique au IIIe siecle avant J-C*, Paris 1935.
Holt, Frank L., *Thundering Zeus*, California 1999.
Hopp, A.J., *Untersuchungen zur Geschichte der letzten Attaliden*, Munich 1977.
Hoyos, B.D., 'The Rise of Hieron II: Chronology and Campaigns, 275–264 BC', *Antichthon* 19, 1985, 32–50.
Hoyos, B.D., *Hannibal's Dynasty*, London 2003.
Huss, W., 'Die Beziehungen zwischen Karthago und Ägypten in hellenistischer Zeit', *Ancient Society* 10, 1979, 119–137.

Huss, W., 'Eine ptolemäische Expedition nach Kleinasien', *Ancient Society* 8, 1977, 32–56.
Jones, C.P., and C. Habicht, 'A Hellenistic Inscription from Arsinoe in Cilicia', *Phoenix* 43, 1989, 317–346.
Kallet-Marx, Robert, *Hegemony to Empire: The Development of the Roman Imperium in the East from 148 to 62 BC*, California 1995.
Karttunen, Klaus, *India and the Hellenistic World*, Helsinki 1997.
Kosmin, Paul J., *The Land of the Elephant King*, Cambridge, MA 2014.
Larsen, J.A.O., *Greek Federal States*, Oxford 1968.
Lazenby, J.F., *Hannibal's War*, Warminster 1978.
Lazenby, J.F., *The First Punic War*, London 1996.
Leveque, Pierre, *Le monde hellenistique*, Paris 1969.
Lomas, Kathryn, *Rome and the Western Greeks*, London 1993.
Lund, Helen S., *Lysimachus*, London 1986.
Ma, J., P. Derow, and A. Meadows, 'RC 38 (Amyzon) Reconsidered', *ZPE* 10, 1995, 71–80.
Mairs, Rachel, *The Hellenistic Far East*, California 2014.
Mattingly, Garrett, *Renaissance Diplomacy*, London 1955.
Mattingly, H., 'Scipio Aemilianus' Eastern Embassy', *Classical Quarterly* 36, 1986, 491–495.
McShane, Roger B., The *Foreign Policy of the Attalids of Pergamon*, Urbana, IL 1964.
Migotte, L., *Les souscriptions publiques dans les cites grecques*, Quebec 1992.
Miles, Richard, *Carthage Must Be Destroyed*, London 2010.
Morgan, W. Gwyn, 'The Perils of Schematism: Polybios, Antiochos Epiphanes and the "Day of Eleusis"', *Historia* 59, 1990, 37–76.
Morkholm, O., *Antiochos IV of Syria*, Copenhagen 1966.
Narain, A.K., *The Indo-Greeks*, Cambridge 1957.
Ogden, D., *Polygamy, Prostitutes and Death*, London 1999.
Oost, S.I., *Roman Policy in Epirus and Acarnania in the Age of Roman Conquest*, Dallas, TX 1954.
Peremans, W., 'Les Revolutions Egyptiennes sous les Lagides', in H. Maehler and V.M. Strocka (eds.), *Das Ptolemäische Ägypten*, Mainz 1978, 39–50.
Piejko, F., 'Antiochos III and Teos Reconsidered', *Belleten* 1991, 13–69.
Podary, Amanda, *Brotherhood of Kings: How International Relations Shaped the Ancient Near East*, Oxford 2010.
Preaux, Claire, *Le Monde Hellenistique, La Grece et l'Orient 323–146 av J.-C.*, 2 vols, 2nd ed., Paris 1987–1988.
Rawlings, H.R., 'Antiochos the Great and Rhodes', *American Journal of Ancient History* 1, 1976, 2–28.
Reger, Gary, 'The Political History of the Kyklades, 260–220 BC', *Historia* 43, 1994, 32–69.
Rich, J.W., *Declaring War in the Roman Republic in the Period of Transmarine Expansion*, Brussels 1976.
Rigsby, K.J., 'Provincia Asia', *Transactions of the American Philosophical Association*, 118, 1988, 123–153.
Robert, L., *Etudes Anatoliennes*, Paris 1937.
Schmitt, H.H., *Untersuchungen zur Geschichte Antiochos des Grossen und seiner Zeit*, Wiesbaden 1964.
Shear, T.L., *Kallias of Sphettos and the Revolt of Athens in 286 BC, Hesperia* Supplement 17, Princeton, NJ 1978.
Sherwin-White, A.N., *Roman Foreign Policy in the East*, Oklahoma 1984.

## Bibliography

Shipley, Graham, *The Greek World after Alexander, 323–30* BC, London 2000.
Siebert, J., *Historische Beiträge zu den dynastischen Verbindungen in hellenistischer Zeit*, Wiesbaden 1967.
Seibert, J., 'Philokles Sohn des Apollodorus, König von Sidoner', *Historia* 19, 1970, 337–351.
Tarn, W.W., *Antigonos Gonatas*, Oxford 1913.
Tarn, W.W., *The Greeks in Baktria and India*, 2nd ed., Cambridge 1966.
Tarn, W.W., revised by G.T. Griffith, *Hellenistic Civilisation*, 3rd ed., London 1952.
Tillyard, H.J.W., *Agathocles*, Cambridge 1908.
Toynbee, A.J., *Hannibal's Legacy*, vol. 2, Oxford 1965.
van Oppen de Reiter, B.E., 'Argaeus, an Illegitimate Son of Alexander the Great?', *ZPE* 287, 2013, 206–210.
Veisse, A.E., *Les 'revoltes egyptiennes': recherches sous les troubles interieures en Egypte du Regne de Ptolemee III a la conquete romaine*, Paris 2004.
Walbank, F.W., *Philip V of Macedon*, Cambridge 1940 (reprinted 1967).
Walbank, F.W., *The Hellenistic Age*, London 1981.
Warrior, V., *The Initiation of the Second Macedonian War*, Wiesbaden 1996.
Welles, C.B., *Alexander and the Hellenistic World*, Toronto 1970.
Whitehorne, John, *Cleopatras*, London 1994.
Wiemer, H.U., 'Karien am Vorabend des 2 makedonischen Krieges: Bemerkunden zu einer neuen Inschrift aus Bargylia', *Epigraphica Anatolica* 33, 2001, 1–14.
Will, E., 'Les premiers annees du regne d'Antiochos III (223–219 av. J-C)', *Revue des etudes grecques* 75, 1962, 72–129.
Worrle, M., 'Epigraphische Forschungen zur Geschichte Lykiens, II: Ptolemaios II und Telmessos', *Chiron* 8, 1978, 83–111.

# Index

Abydos 178, 217, 235, 243
Achaian League 1, 11, 57, 88–93, 96–8, 100, 116, 117, 161–2, 184, 187, 189–90, 196–8, 206, 212, 215, 218–21, 224–6, 232, 239, 243, 245
Adea-Eurydike, wife of Philip III 35, 37
Adriatic Sea 3, 11, 130, 132, 168, 186, 212, 217, 221
Aegates Islands, battle 157
Aegean Sea 41, 57–9, 87, 117, 118, 177, 183, 189, 234
Aelius, C., Roman commander 134
Aelius Paetus, P. 186
Aemilius Barbula, L. 135, 137–8
Aemilius Lepidus, M., Roman envoy 70, 178, 217, 235, 243, 244
Aemilius Paullus, M. 220, 238
Aetna, Mount 154
Africa (north) 125, 127, 130, 140, 156, 166–8, 169–71, 203, 212, 225, 226, 243
Agathokles, grandson of Agathokles 133
Agathokles, Ptolemaic regent 105, 113–16
Agathokles, Syracusan king 37, 39, 125–8, 130, 132–3, 136, 140, 141, 143, 148, 162
Agelaos of Naupaktos 198
Agesilaos, envoy 20
Agis, Paeonian king 16
Agis, Spartan king 92, 96
Agis of Taras 137–8
Aigina 96, 100
Aigion 189, 197–8
Ainos 180
Aitolian League 1, 3, 11, 23, 26, 27, 57, 69, 70, 88, 89, 92–3, 96, 100, 106, 161–2, 166, 169–70, 179, 184, 197–9, 202–3, 205, 207–8, 213, 216, 220; and Antiochos III 186–91
Akarnanians 220
Akhaimenid Empire 1, 17, 55, 65, 212

Akhaios (I) 45
Akhaios (II), king in Asia Minor, Seleukid rebel 44–5, 59, 60, 68, 104–5, 106–9, 110, 113, 199
Akragas 126, 127, 129, 132, 139, 147
Akrotatos, Spartan prince 129–32
Alchimachos, envoy 18
Alexander, son of Krateros 89–90
Alexander, son of Pyrrhos 141
Alexander I Balas (Seleukid) 46–7, 49, 223, 241
Alexander II, Epeirote king 34, 35, 36, 37, 132; and Taras 128–9, 131, 138, 140, 143
Alexander III, the Great, king of Macedon 1, 2, 11, 15, 17, 18, 29, 36, 38, 56, 60, 112, 126, 128, 143, 248; marriages of 35
Alexander IV, king of Macedon 24, 35, 40
Alexander V, king of Macedon 136
Alexander Isios, Aitolian envoy 69
Alexandria-by-Egypt 2, 13, 46, 88, 99, 100, 113, 115, 117, 182, 231, 235, 237, 239
Alexandria Ilios (or Troas) 62, 185
Alinda 61
Ambrakia 136, 208
Amestris, wife of Lysimachos 37
Amphilochia 136
Amyntas, Macedonian pretender 35
Amyntas III, king of Macedon 16, 34
Amyzon 60, 61–2, 69
Andriskos, Macedonian pretender ('Philip VI') 171, 224
Andromachos, father of Akhaios II 44–5, 107, 108
Andros 56, 84
Androsthenes of Kyzikos, Seleukid commander 112
Anicius, L. 222
Antigone, wife of Pyrrhos 39, 136

# 256  Index

Antigonid dynasty/kingdom 1, 41, 50, 56, 84, 90–3
Antigonos I Monophthalamos, king 2, 11, 14, 15, 17, 18, 19–28, 30, 36, 53, 63, 64, 69, 75–6, 84; and 'freedom of the Greeks' 20, 22, 27, 57, 169
Antigonos II Gonatas, king of Macedon 41, 57, 81, 85, 87–8, 89–96, 137; marriage of 40, 42, 43, 49, 78
Antigonos III Doson, king of Macedon 50, 60, 92, 94, 97–100, 196–7, 200, 206
Antioch 2, 48, 104, 106, 111, 199, 223, 224, 234, 236, 237, 244, 245
Antioch-in-Persis 5
Antiochis, daughter of 45
Antiochis, daughter of Antiochos III 45, 48
Antiochis, daughter of Seleukos II 48–9, 110
Antiochis, Seleukid courtesan 241
Antiochos I 12–13, 14, 30, 38–9, 40, 41, 42, 43, 49, 58, 66, 67, 68, 75, 77–9, 86, 137
Antiochos II 13, 14, 41, 43, 49, 58, 66, 67, 77, 79–81, 87, 181
Antiochos III 3, 4, 13–14, 15, 17, 44, 47, 49, 59–63, 67–8, 69, 79, 95, 103–16, 177–8, 200–2, 206, 209, 231, 233–4; and Aitolians 186–8; diplomatic methods 105, 108; marriages of 36, 44, 67; and Ptolemaic partition treaty 117–18, 139, 238; and Rome 178–92, 195, 207, 212, 243; *see also* Fourth and Fifth Syrian Wars and Romano-Seleukid War
Antiochos IV 15, 47, 68, 70, 208, 217, 223, 231–6, 238, 239, 240, 244
Antiochos V 234, 237
Antiochos VII 47, 49
Antiochos Hierax, king in Asia Minor 44, 45, 50, 67, 181
Antiochos 'the Young King', son of Antiochos III 47, 49, 65, 68, 109
Antipater, Macedonian regent 17, 18–19, 29, 40, 68; daughters' marriages 36–7, 41–2
Antipater, 'nephew' of Antiochos III 106, 117, 207
Antony, Mark 51
Aous Pass 162, 205
Apama, wife of Seleukos I 38, 43
Apameia, Syria 234, 237
Apameia-Kelainai, Asia Minor, Treaty of 63, 70–1, 191–2, 207, 212, 228, 235, 237–8
Apollonia, Illyria 130, 132, 161

Apulia 128–32, 139
Apulieus, L. 222
Aquilius, M. 228
Arachosia 109, 110, 112–13
Arados, Syria 79
Aratos, son of Aratos 97
Aratos of Sikyon 88–94, 96–100, 117, 145; methods 91, 96, 100
Archagathos, son of Agathokles
Archelaos, Ptolemaic king 51
Archias, Ptolemaic governor 240–1
Archidamos, Spartan king 128, 129
Areia 109, 110
Areus, Spartan king 85–6
Argos 89–91, 100, 144, 205–6, 225
Ariarathes III, king in Kappadokia 44, 48, 66
Ariarathes IV, king in Kappadokia 45, 48, 49, 207
Ariarathes V, king in Kappadokia 48, 217, 223, 232, 245
Aristippos II, tyrant of Argos 91, 96
Aristodemos of Miletos, envoy 20, 21, 23, 69
Aristomachos I, tyrant of Argos 89–91
Aristomachos II, tyrant of Argos 96
Aristonikos, Pergamene pronce ('Eumenes III') 227
Arkadia 91, 96
Armenia 15, 27, 200
Arsamosata 200–1
Arsinoe II, daughter of Ptolemy I 37, 40, 45, 85
Arsinoe IV, wife of Ptolemy IV 45, 113
Artabarzanes, Atropatenian king 110
Artaxerxes Ochos, Akhaimenid king 35
Artaxias, Armenian king 68
Artemidoros, envoy 18
Asia Minor 11, 12, 15, 28, 30, 44, 56, 59, 67, 75, 77, 85, 103, 108, 115, 117, 137, 169, 177, 179, 185, 191–2, 206, 207, 212, 221, 226–8, 235, 249
Asoka, Indian emperor 113
Aspendos 60
Asti, Thracian tribe 216
Atella 166
Athamania 191
Athenaios, Attalid prince 224
Athens 1, 3, 18, 23, 26, 27, 28, 38, 56–7, 62, 76, 84, 85–6, 89–91, 117, 118, 126–38, 161, 212; 'neutrality' of 92–6, 99, 101, 197; and Rome 180, 189, 221, 226, 232
Atilius Regulus, M. 64, 156–7, 158

Atintania 161, 162
Attalid dynasty/kingdom 4, 36, 45, 46, 50, 62, 67–8, 182, 192, 213
Attalos, Macedonian noble 33–4
Attalos I, Pergamene king 45, 61, 68, 95, 104, 108, 112, 179
Attalos II, Pergamene king 50, 88, 222–4, 228, 238, 241–2, 245
Attalos III, Pergamene king 226–7, 245
Attika 86, 89, 91–4, 98
Audata, wife of Philip II 33–4
Audoleon, Paeonian king 39
Aurelius Cotta, L. 234
Aurelius Orestes, L. 225, 239
Aurunculeius, C. 222

Babylon 1, 6, 11, 22, 28, 143
Babylonia 19, 21, 27, 75, 82, 109
Baecula, battle 167
Baktra 109–10, 111, 201
Baktria 11, 35, 67, 68, 109–11, 113, 184, 200–2, 249
Bardylis, Illyrian king 16, 33, 39
Bargylia 180
Barsine, concubine of Alexander III 35, 40
Barsine, wife of Alexander III 35
Basilicata 128
Bekaa Valley, Phoenicia 104, 105
Berenike, daughter of Ptolemy II, wife of Antiochos II 13, 43, 44, 46, 49, 80–1
Berenike, daughter of Magas, wife of Ptolemy III 42–3, 45, 49, 82
Berenike, wife of Ptolemy I 37–8, 43
Berenike V, Ptolemaic queen 50–1
Bikenna, wife of Pyrrhos 39
Bithynia 44, 45, 65, 66–7, 68, 77, 208, 212, 222–3, 227, 245
Black Sea 11, 85
Boiotia 23, 27, 89, 90, 218, 226; League of 89, 191, 219
Bosporan kingdom 78, 81, 87
Bosporos 78
Brachyllas of Thebes, Spartan governor 196–7
Brundisium 215
Bruttians 128–31, 132–3, 138–9, 169, 204
Byzantion 81, 85–6, 87, 106

Caecilius Metellus, Q. 225–6, 239
Calabria 128
Calatia 166
Campania 130, 138–9, 140, 145–6, 148, 150, 166

Capua 166–7, 169
Carthage 2, 3, 4, 38, 60, 63, 78, 86, 95, 115, 119, 125–8, 133–4, 137, 168–9, 180, 183, 198, 213; diplomatic contacts with Rome 127, 140–1, 143, 165–6, 170; Mercenaries' War 158; and Messene 145–54; and Pyrrhos 139–40, 143–4; and Sardinia 158–9; and Spain 163–4, 165; *see also* Wars
Carthago Nova 164, 167
Caspian Sea 109
Caudine Forks, battle 130
Central Asia 30, 39
Ceprati 216
Chaeroneia, battle 18
Chalkidian League 55
Chalkis, Euboia 90, 179, 188–90, 218, 219, 226
Chandragupta Maurya, Indian Emperor 22
Charops of Epeiros 181
China 7
Chryseis, wife of Demetrios II and Antigonos III 98
Cisalpine Gaul 131, 145, 163, 166, 168, 181, 187
Cities, relations with kings 55–63
Claudius Caecus, Ap. 139
Claudius Caudex, Ap. 149–54, 161, 162
Claudius Centho, C. 220, 222–3
Claudius Marcellus, M. (I) 200; (II) 215, 216, 218
Claudius Nero, Ti. 216–17, 243
Corinth 28, 57, 60, 70, 76, 86, 88, 89, 90–3, 97, 98, 100, 161, 178, 179, 205, 225, 226; League of 24, 26–7
Corinth, Gulf of 197–8
Cornelius Lentulus, L. 181, 192
Cornelius Lentulus, P. 222
Cornelius Lentulus Caudinus, P. 180–1
Cornelius Scipio Aemilianus, P. 245
Cornelius Scipio Africanus, P. 167, 170, 184, 185, 191, 203–4, 208, 209
Cornelius Scipio Serapio, P. 245
Crete, Cretans 24, 58, 81, 95, 109, 217, 221–2
Crimea 78, 81, 87
Cyprus 20, 23–5, 28, 42, 57, 76, 114, 231, 239, 243
Cyrenaica 11, 42–3, 49, 65, 66, 77, 82, 108, 117, 125–6, 128, 177, 233, 239

Damokritos, Aitolian commander 225
Darius III, Akhaimenid king 17, 35

## 258  Index

Decimius, C. 217
Deidameia, wife of Demetrios I 37
Deinokrates, Syracusan politician 127
Delion, battle 190, 191
Delos 56, 59, 87, 90, 221
Delphi 5, 87–8, 186, 215
Demetrias 179, 186, 188–9
Demetrios, son of Philip V 186
Demetrios I, Baktrian king 67, 112, 113, 201
Demetrios I (Seleukid) 3, 48, 223, 224, 233–7, 239–42
Demetrios I Poliorketes (Antigonid) 21, 23–7, 28–30, 42, 56, 57, 63, 64–70, 75, 78, 84, 99, 135, 162; marriages of 36, 37, 38–9, 133, 137
Demetrios II (Antigonid) 41, 48, 50, 90, 93, 96, 162
Demetrios II (Seleukid) 46–7, 48, 49, 242, 245
Demetrios of Phaleron 85, 100
Demetrios of Pharos 164
Demetrios 'the Fair' 42–3, 117
Diaios, Achaian politician 225, 239
Diodotos I, Baktrian governor 67
Diodotos II, Baktrian king 67
Diogenes, Macedonian commander 93
Diognetos, Seleukid envoy 41–2, 44, 104
Dionysiac Association of Artists 5
Dionysios I, lord of Sicily 125
Dionysios II, lord of Sicily 125
Diplomacy 248–50; Hellenistic period 2; 'new' 242–3; origins of Hellenistic 2, 11–31; process 106–7; Roman methods 154–9; secrecy 3, 117–18
Diplomats, lack of professional 4, 12; methods 105
Dodona 87–8, 89
Dolopia 216
Drangiana 110
Drepana

Ebro, River 163, 164
Editani 167
Egypt 1, 5, 6, 13, 15, 20, 24, 25, 28, 41, 43, 70, 76, 82, 88, 105, 107, 177, 178, 196; rebellions in 68, 95, 113, 116, 117–18, 200, 231, 233
Ekregma 20, 21, 22, 23, 64
Eleusis, Egypt 240
Elimiotis 33–4
Elis 91, 191, 197
Elymais 68

Envoys 69–71; in marriage negotiations 41–2
Epameinondas of Thebes 37–8
Epeiros 3, 34, 69, 70, 129, 134, 136–41, 162, 166, 168, 190–1, 203, 219–20
Ephesos 58, 60, 79–81, 85, 87, 183, 185, 187, 188, 227
Epidamnos 161
Epidauros 91
Erythrai 79
Eryx 140
Etruria 138
Etruscans 126–8, 143
Euboia, wife of Antiochos III 36
Eukleides, Spartan king 196
Eukles of Rhodes, Seleukid envoy 41, 42, 177, 206
Eulaios, Ptolemaic regent 231
Eumenes I, Pergamene ruler 68
Eumenes II, Pergamene king 36, 48, 50, 182, 184, 187, 188, 215–17, 219, 222, 223, 244, 245, 246
Eumenes of Kardia 19
European Union 7
Eurydike, daughter of Antipater 36, 37–8
Eurydike of Athens, wife of Demetrios I 37–8, 126
Euthydemos I, Baktrian king 67, 111–12, 113, 200–1

Fabricius Luscinus, C. 134, 138–9
Florence 7
France 7
Fulvius Nobilior, M. 208

Galatians 12, 44, 45, 50, 58, 66, 68, 77, 85, 139, 141, 191, 207, 222, 235, 236, 245, 246
Gallipoli peninsula 87, 181, 206, 216
Gaul, Gauls 69, 163, 166
Gaza 21, 29, 75, 105
Gedrosia 110
Genthius, Illyrian king 220
Getai 33–4
Glaukias, Illyrian king 130
Glaukias, king of the Taulantanii 17
Gonnos 205
Greece 1, 27, 28, 56, 57, 85, 87, 106, 115–16, 125; and Rome 161, 167–9, 178–9, 182–3, 202, 212, 219, 221, 232

Hadranon 154
Haliartos 218
Halikarnassos 56, 59

Halikyai 156
Hamilcar Barka 157–9, 163
Hannibal 141, 163–4, 165–6, 169–70, 181, 197, 200, 202, 204, 208
Harpalos, Macedonian envoy 215–16
Hasdrubal, Carthaginian commander 204
Hasdrubal, son-in-law of Hamilkar 163–5
Hasdrubal, son of Hamilkar 169
Hasdrubal Gisco 167
Hasmonaean kingdom/dynasty 65; see also Judaea
Hegesianax, Seleukid envoy 180, 184, 186
Hegesias of Lampsakos, envoy 69
Hekataios, envoy 18, 41–2, 69
Helenos, son of Pyrrhos 141
Heliodoros, Seleukid regent 223
Hellenic Symmachy 99–100, 196–9
Hellespont 20, 22, 64, 78, 180–91
Hellespontine Phrygia 18
Herakleia, Magna Graecia 129, 138
Herakleia-by-Oeta 225–6
Herakleia-Pontike 37
Herakleides, Seleukid conspirator 241
Herakles, son of Alexander III 35, 40
Hermeias, Seleukid minister 61, 69, 104–5
Hermione 96
Hiero, Syracusan king 145, 147–53; ally of Rome 155–7, 159, 166, 185, 200
Hieronymos, Syracusan king 166, 167, 200
Hindu Kush mountains 112
Hippomedon of Sparta, Plolemaic governor 59
Hipponion 133
Hitler, Adolf 7, 14
Hittites 6
Hortensius, L. 222
Hyrkania 109

Iapygii 132
Iber, River 163
Idomeneus, envoy 20, 24
Ilergetes 167
Ilion 60
Illyria 2, 17, 33–4, 39, 132, 161–2, 164, 166–70, 202–3, 212, 215, 217, 218, 220, 243
India 2, 3, 7, 11, 22, 60, 109, 112, 113, 143, 184, 249
Ionia 58, 86
Ionian Sea 125, 129, 131, 140, 141, 149, 161–2, 168, 212
Ipsos, battle 28, 29, 64
Iran 21, 27, 28, 67, 109, 184, 233, 236

Island League 56, 58, 85, 90
Isokrates, Seleukid orator 235, 237, 239
Issa 161, 212
Italy 1, 2, 7, 89, 125, 130, 136–8, 141, 143, 156, 158, 163, 166–7, 184, 197, 200, 202, 218, 237, 240, 243
Itanos, Crete, Ptolemaic naval base 58, 81, 84

Jason of Pherae 33–4, 40
Judaea 65, 236; see also Hasmonaean
Julius Caesar, C. 51
Julius Caesar, Sex. 225, 239

Kallias of Sphettos, Ptolemaic envoy 56–67, 59, 69, 85
Kallikrates, Achaian politician 223
Kallippa, wife of Athenaios 224
Kappadokia 49, 66, 67, 75–6, 212, 227, 235, 236, 240, 241, 243, 244
Karia 58, 97, 180, 216
Karmania 109, 110, 113
Kassandros, king of Macedon 14, 17, 19, 20–2, 23, 24, 25–6, 29, 30, 64–5, 75, 132, 136, 162; marriage of 40
Kastor of Alexandria, Ptolemaic envoy 99
Katyai 92
Kenturipa 154
Kephallonia 162
Kerkidas of megalopolis 97–98
Kerkyra 38, 39, 131–3, 136–7, 140, 161–2, 212
Khremonides, Athenian politician, Ptolemaic commander 85, 100
Khyber Pass 109
Kilikia 18, 19, 24, 28, 29, 30, 38, 57, 63, 76, 80, 117, 183, 241
Kineas of Thessaly, envoy 137–41
Kings, self-proclamation of 24
Klazomenai 232
Kleomenes II, Spartan king 129
Kleomenes III, Spartan king 96–100, 117
Kleonikos, Aitolian envoy 197–8, 201
Kleonymos, Spartan prince 131–2, 138, 143
Kleopatra, daughter of Philip II 34, 35, 36, 37
Kleopatra, wife of Philip II 33–4, 35
Kleopatra II, daughter of Ptolemy V 45, 46, 47, 239
Kleopatra III, daughter of Ptolemy VIII 50
Kleopatra VII, Ptolemaic ruler 51

## Index

Kleopatra Syra, daughter of Antiochos III, wife of Ptolemy V 13, 41, 44, 45–6, 177, 182, 206
Kleopatra Thea, daughter of Ptolemy VI, wife of Alexander Balas, Demetrios II, Antiochos VII 46–7, 292
Kleoptolemos of Chalkis 37
Koile Syria 12, 13, 106, 107, 108, 109, 117, 231, 233
Korakesion 59, 179
Koroneia 218
Kotys, Thracian king 217, 219
Krateros, Macedonian commander 18, 36, 37, 89
Kritolaos, Achaian politician 226
Kroton 132–3, 138
Kyklades Islands 84; see also Island League
Kynnane, daughter of Philip II 35
Kynoskephalai, battle 205
Kyrene 37, 77, 125, 226, 249
Kyzikos 36

Lacinian Cape 131, 132, 134
Lakonia 206, 225
Lamia 189
Lampsakos 62, 160, 181, 182, 185
Lanassa, daughter of Agathokles 37–8, 39, 132, 133, 136–7
Laodike, daughter of Antiochos II 44
Laodike, daughter of Antiochos III 47
Laodike, daughter of Seleukos IV 47–8, 49, 224
Laodike, sister of Alexander Balas 223, 241
Laodike, wife of Akhaios 44
Laodike, wife of Antiochos III 41, 44, 61, 104
Laodike, wife of Antiochos II 43, 44, 80
Laodike, wife of Mithridates III 46
Laodike, wife of Seleukos II 44
Laodikeia-ad-Mare 234–5, 237
Latium 139
Laurion 94
Lenaios, Ptolemaic regent 231
Leonnatos, Macedonian commander 18, 36, 37, 41, 69
Leontinoi 139
Leptines, Seleukid assassin 235, 237–8, 239
Leukas 162
Libya 77
Licinius Crassus, P. 227
Liguria 204

Lilybaion 140, 157, 159
Lipari Islands 132, 147, 151, 155, 157
Lokris 226
Lokroi 138
Longanos, River, battle 147, 148, 152
Louis XIV, king of France 7
Lucanians 128–31, 133, 134, 138–9, 169
Lucretius, Sp. 234
Lutatius Catulus, Q. 64, 157, 159
Lutatius Cerco, Q. 157
Lydiadas, tyrant of Megalopolis 91, 92, 96
Lykia 58, 59, 84, 216
Lykiskos, Aitolian tyrant 220
Lyppeios, Paeonian king 16
Lysias, Seleukid envoy 180
Lysias, Seleukid regent 234–8, 239, 240, 244–5
Lysimacheia 14, 79, 118, 184, 185, 206; conference at 181, 183, 184, 187, 226
Lysimachos, king 2, 14, 17, 19, 21, 25, 27–8, 30, 57, 59, 64–5, 66, 67, 75–6, 137; marriages of 37, 39, 40
Lyttos, Crete 81, 105

Maccabees, revolt of 68–9; see also Hasmonaean; Judaea
Macedon 3, 4, 11, 13, 14, 21, 26, 28, 34, 37, 55–6, 64, 77–8, 84, 85–6, 88, 93, 95, 129, 137, 181, 183, 212–21; and Greece 18, 96; and Illyrian Wars 16–17;and Rome 162, 168, 178–80, 190–1, 212–19, 224, 235, 236, 243; see also Wars
Maedi 216
Magas, king of Cyrene 11, 42, 49, 66, 77–8, 82, 108
Magnesia, battle 63, 191, 207
Mago, Carthaginian commander 140
Mago, son of Hamilkar 204
Makella 155
Mamertines 134, 140, 145–8, 150, 152–5, 158, 163, 168, 180
Mandonion 128
Manlius Vulso, C. 48, 191, 207, 209
Manlius Vulso, L. 208
Mantineia 92
Marcius Philippus Q. 217–18, 219–20, 232, 234, 236, 238, 240
Maroneia 59, 180
Marriage, royal 3, 4, 111; purposes of 33–54
Massilia 163, 168
Massinissa, Numidian king 167, 170–1, 213
Mauri 171

Mauryan Empire 112
Meda, wife of Philip II 33–4
Media 19, 21, 104
Media Atropatene 65, 109
Megalopolis 90, 91–2, 96
Megara 91, 100
Memnon, Persian commander 35
Memphis, Egypt 106
Menander, Greco-Indian king 60
Menestratos of Phokaia, Seleukid official 61
Menippos, Seleukid envoy 185–6, 188
Meno of Segesta, assassin 133
Mentor, Persian commander 35
Mesopotamia 64
Messapians 129, 131
Messene, Greece 191
Messene, Sicily 134, 140, 144, 147–56, 162, 167–8, 243
Metapontum 131
Metaurus river, battle 169, 243
Methana, Argolis, Ptolemaic naval base 58, 85
Metrodoros, envoy 61
Milan 7
Miletos 5, 58–9, 79, 81, 87, 232
Milo, Epeirote commander 137–8, 144
Miltiades of Athens 38
Minnio, Seleukid minister 187
Minucius Thermus Q. 208
Mitanni 6
Mithradates II, king of Pontos 41, 44, 48, 66, 104
Mithradates II, Parthian king 47
Mithradates VI, king of Pontos 51
Molon, Seleukid rebel 104, 105, 109, 110
Molossi 33–4, 136, 220
Morocco 171
Moschion of Thera, envoy 20, 24
Mousiaos, Seleukid envoy 207
Mummius, L. 226

Nabataea 65
Nabis, Spartan tyrant 183, 184, 187–8, 205–6
Naples 7
Napoleon, French emperor 7
Naupaktos 198, 226
Nikaia, daughter of Antipater 36, 37
Nikaia, Lokris 205
Nikaia, wife of Alexander of Corinth 90
Nikandros of Trichonos, Aitolian commander 208

Nikanor of Stageira, envoy 18
Nikesipolis, wife of Philip II 33–4, 40
Nikomedeia 66
Nikomedes 61
Nikomedes I, Bithynian king 68
Nikomedes II, Bithynian king 223
Nikophanes of Megalopolis 97–8
Numidia 1, 167, 170
Numisius Tarquiniensis, T. 232
Nysa, daughter of Antiochos the Young king 47, 48

Oaths in treaty making 14–15, 21, 28, 208, 209
Octavius, Cn. 219, 234–9, 240, 244–5
Odrysai 217, 219
Olympias, wife of Philip II 33–4, 35, 36
Olympos, Mount 220
Olynthos 55
Ophellas, governor of Cyrene 37, 38, 125–7
Opis 38
Orchomenos 92, 225
Orophernes, Kappadokian pretender 223
Orphon, Syracusan envoy 125–6
Oscan 145
Ostia 140, 148
Otacilius Crassus, M'. 154
Oxyartes 35
Oxythemis, Antigonid envoy 133

Paeonia 16, 39
Paestum 127
Paiones 136
Palestine 12, 13, 28, 75, 105, 106, 109, 117, 177, 184, 226, 231, 242
Pallene 92
Pamphylia 245
Panormos 140
Pantaleon, Aitolian envoy 92
Paropamisadai, India 110, 112–13, 200
Parthia 1, 47, 67, 109–11, 113, 184, 200–2, 233, 242
Parthini 161
Parysatis, wife of Alexander III 35
Pataliputra, India 60
Patroklos, Ptolemaic commander 85
Peace treaties 3, 4, 80–1, 115, 195–209
Peiraios 88, 90, 92, 93, 94
Pella 2
Pelopidas of Thebes 18
Peloponnese 20, 86, 88–91, 96–9, 116, 197, 206, 221

## 262  Index

Pelops son of Pelops, Ptolemaic envoy 114–15, 117
Perdikkas, Macedonian regent 18, 19, 29, 36, 37
Perdikkas III, king of Macedon 16
Pergamon 2, 44, 67, 95, 187, 222, 227
Perperna, M. 227–8
Perseus, King of Macedon 48, 49, 50, 213–21, 232, 238, 242
Persian Empire 11; *see also* Akhaimenid empire
Persis 68, 110, 113
Petronius, C. 222
Pharnakes I, king of Pontos 47
Phaselis 59
Pherae 33
Phila, daughter of Antipater 26; wife of Demetrios I 29, 37–8, 39
Phila, daughter of Seleukos I, wife of Antigonos II 40, 41, 42, 49, 78, 85
Phila, wife of Philip II 33–4
Philetairos, lord of Pergamon 67–8
Philinna, wife of Philip II 33–4
Philip, Seleukid pretender 236
Philip II, king of Macedon 2, 16, 17–18, 23, 27, 30, 55–6, 99; marriages of 33–4, 35, 36–7, 39
Philip III Arrhidaios, king of Macedon 35, 37
Philip V, king of Macedon 4, 14, 50, 59, 60, 70, 95, 98, 103, 113, 115–17; and Aitolia 197; and Ptolemaic partition agreement 117–18; and Rome 119, 162, 166–7, 169–70, 177–9, 171–83, 185–6, 187, 190
Philocharis, Tatentine politician 134–5
Philotera, daughter of Ptolemy I 40
Phlius 96
Phoenicia 12, 13, 24, 28, 57, 75, 104, 106, 177, 184, 206, 242
Phoenike 203
Phokis 191
Phrygia 70
Pindos Mountains 140
Pinnes, Illyrian king 164
Pisidia 187
Po, River 166
Polyperchon, Macedonian regent 20, 40
Pontos 44, 65, 227
Pope 7
Popillius Laenas, M. 219, 231–2, 236, 238, 240
Postumius, A. 161–2
Postumius Megellus, L. 135

Prepelaos, son of Antipater 21, 28–9, 64–5
Propontis 59, 117, 180
Prousa 66
Prousias II, Bithynian king 215, 217, 222–4, 228, 238, 239
Prytanis of Karystos, Ptolemaic envoy 94
Ptolemaic dynasty/kingdom 1, 15, 37, 41, 42, 60, 62, 65, 84–5, 117, 177–9, 231–3, 248; marriage policy 42–6
Ptolemais, daughter of Ptolemy I 37, 42
Ptolemais-Ake 234, 241–2
Ptolemy, son of Agesarchos, Ptolemaic envoy 115–16
Ptolemy, son of Lysimachos, lord of Telmessos 80
Ptolemy, son of Sosibios, Ptolemaic envoy 115
Ptolemy I 2, 11, 12–13, 14, 15, 17, 19–23, 24–6, 27–30, 39, 42, 56–8, 59, 64, 65, 66, 75–7, 80, 84, 126, 132–3, 136; and 'freedom of the Greeks' 20, 22; marriages of 36, 40
Ptolemy II 2, 12, 42, 43, 50, 56–8, 66, 77–81, 85–7, 88–9, 100; marriages of 40, 41, 45
Ptolemy III 13, 15, 45, 49, 82, 87, 91, 93–4, 96–8, 99–101, 103–4, 105, 108
Ptolemy IV 13, 15, 45, 95, 105–7, 108, 111, 112, 113, 114, 115, 199
Ptolemy V 13, 14, 15, 41, 44, 45–6, 49, 112, 114, 177–8, 180, 182–3, 206, 238, 244
Ptolemy VI 45, 46–7, 49, 84, 223, 231–3, 238–43
Ptolemy VIII 45, 226, 233, 239–40, 242, 245
Ptolemy XIII 51
Ptolemy Keraunos, king of Macedon 39, 40, 41, 77, 137
Ptolemy of Aloros, Macedonian regent 16
Ptolemy 'the Son' 58, 79
Pyrrhos, Epeirote king 36, 37, 38, 64, 70, 78, 86, 89, 192; marriages of 39–40, 132, 136–7; and the West 125, 132, 135–41, 143, 147, 154, 162, 166
Python of Byzantion, envoy 18

Quinctius Flamininus T. 179–80, 183–4, 187–90, 195, 205, 209, 212

Raphia 177; battle 18, 106, 107, 108, 111, 113, 199, 207; peace of 206
recognition of new kingdoms 65–9

Rhegion 133, 138, 139, 143, 147, 148, 150–2, 154
Rhodes 20, 23–6, 29, 30, 60, 62, 64, 70, 80, 84, 95, 106, 118, 135, 178, 179, 180, 182–5, 215, 216–20, 221–2, 243–4, 245
Rhosos 28, 38, 64
Roman Empire 1, 4, 65
Rome 2, 3, 4, 12, 13, 18, 48, 59, 69, 78, 86, 89; and Antiochos III 15, 36, 68, 103, 178–92, 207; and Athens 95, 180; diplomatic contacts with Carthage 127, 140–1, 143, 165–6, 170; and Egypt 113, 115; and Greek cities 168–9; and Macedon 118, 177; and Magna Graecia 126, 129, 131–6; and Messene 148–54; and Pyrrhos 137–41, 143–4; and Sardinian 'war' 158–9; Senate of, as ratificatory agency 63–4, 157; *see also* Wars
Roxane, wife of Alexander III 35
Russia 7

Saguntum 163–4, 165, 168, 180
Salganeus 190
Sallentini 131
Samaria 28
Samnites 129, 130, 135, 138–9, 141, 169
Samos 58, 79, 85, 95
Sardinia 158–9, 161, 163, 167, 170, 180
Sardis 36, 60, 61, 62, 108, 185
Scythians 33–4
Segesta 155
Seleukeia-in-Pieria 82, 105, 106, 108, 109, 111, 181, 199, 234
Seleukid dynasty/kingdom 1, 11, 15, 37, 41, 62, 84, 233, 248; cities of 56, 59; marriage policy 47
Seleukos I 2, 11, 12, 15, 17, 19, 21–3, 27–30, 41, 64–5, 66, 68, 75–7, 85, 103, 113, 137, 181; marriages of 38–9
Seleukos II 13, 44, 67, 82, 91, 103
Seleukos III 103
Seleukos IV 47, 48, 215
Sellasia, battle 100
Sempronius Gracchus, Ti (I) 227; (II) 234, 236, 244, 246
Sempronius Tuditanus, P. 170, 203, 243
Sicily 1, 3, 11, 39, 119, 125–8, 129–30, 139–41, 143–5, 149, 153–8, 166, 167–8
Sicinius, Cn. 217
Side 171
Sidon 28, 76
Sikyon 88–9, 97
Sinai 76

Siris, River, battle 138
Skepsis 21
Skopas, Ptolemaic commander 116
Smyrna 60, 62, 180, 181, 182, 185
Sogdiana 38, 109, 111
Sophagasenos, Indian king 110, 112, 113, 200–1
Sosibios, Ptolemaic minister and regent 99, 105–7, 109, 113, 116
Sostratos of Knidos, Ptolemaic envoy 56
Spain 7, 159, 163–8, 227, 243
Sparta 1, 3, 57, 62, 69, 85–6, 92, 96, 100, 200, 212, 221; and Rome 183, 184, 187, 188–9, 196–7, 205–6, 224–5; and Sicily 129–30, 140; and Taras 128, 131, 134
Spitamenes 38
Strait of Messina 149
Stratonike, daughter of Antiochos II 44, 66
Stratonike, daughter of Ariarathes IV 50
Stratonike, daughter of Demetrios I, wife of Seleukos I and Antiochos I 28, 29, 30, 38–9, 40, 42, 64, 77, 85
Stratonike, daughter of Seleukos IV, wife of Demetrios II 41, 48, 50, 90
Stratonike, wife of Antigonos I 28
Stratonike of Kyzikos, wife of Eumenes I 36
Sulpicius Galba, P. 186, 187, 202
'Summit meetings', 21, 29, 63–5, 111
Syphax, Numidian king 167, 204
Syracuse 86, 125–8, 145–7, 153–6, 162, 166–9, 200, 209; civil war 133–4; and Pyrrhos 139–40
Syria 19, 23, 27, 28, 29, 38, 49, 65, 75, 77–8, 80, 82, 84, 87, 104, 107, 118, 177, 178, 183, 208, 234

Tainaron, Cape 131
Taranto, Bay of 131
Taras (Tarentum) 89, 128–34; and Pyrrhos 137–8, 144, 148; and Rome 130, 131–2, 134–6, 156, 169
Tarentine 131, 132, 134; Roman-Spartan 184; Roman-Syracusan 156, 200
Tarquinii 126
Taurus Mountains 65, 76, 212, 241
Tegea 92
Teleas, envoy 201
Telmessos 59, 80
Tempe Pass 205
Teos 61–2
Terentius Massiliota, L. 180
Teres, Thracian king 124

Teuta, Illyrian Queen 162, 162, 164, 168
Thasos 180
Thearidas, Achaian politician 225
Thebes 18, 56, 57, 60, 113
Theodotos, Aitolian mercenary commander, Ptolemaic governor 109, 105, 109, 116
Theodotos Hemiolios, Seleukid commander and envoy 106, 107
Theoxene, daughter of Ptolemy I, wife of Agathokles
Thera, Ptolemaic naval base 58, 86
Thermon 88
Thermopylai, battle 191
Thessalonike, daughter of Philip II 40
Thessaly 16, 33–4, 35, 190–1, 213, 215, 216, 218
Thoas of Trichonos, Aitolian politician 188, 189, 208
Thourioi 129, 133–6
Thrace 14, 21, 27, 180–3, 185, 187–289, 206, 213, 215
Timarchos, Aitolian adventurer 58, 79–80
Timarchos, Seleukid rebel 69, 240–1
Timosthenes of Rhodes, Ptolemaic ship commander 78
Tiridates, Parthian king 112
Tlepolemos, Ptolemaic regent 116
Treaties, duration of 13–14; of Apameia 63, 70, 191; lack of enforcement 209; of Naupaktos 197–9; oaths of ratification 14–15; of Phoinike 202–3; process of 195, 198, 204, 209; purpose of 12; ratification of 64–5, 70–1; Roman-Carthaginian 64, 170; Roman-Spartan 184; Roman-Syracusan 156, 200; Roman-Tarentine 131, 132, 134
Troizen 91
Tunis, Tunisia 126
Tyndaris 155
Tyre 28, 47, 57, 76, 143, 169

Utica 171

Valerius Laevinus, P. 138
Valerius Maximus, M. 154
Venetia 131
Venice 7
Venusia 130, 132, 133, 134, 138, 139

Wars: 'Brothers' 44, 93; Khremonidean 41, 81, 85–7; Lamian 18, 41–2; Roman-Achaian 213, 224–6; Roman-Carthaginian (Punic) (First 78–9, 125, 144–58, 168, 200; Second ('Hannibalic') 115, 166–8, 203–4; Third 170–2); Roman-Illyrian (First 161–2, 166; Second 164); Roman-Macedonian (First 59, 198, 202–3; Second 177–80, 205; Third 4, 195, 213–21, 234, 238, 243, 244, 249; Fourth 213); Roman-Samnite 130–1, 147; Roman-Seleukid 45, 62, 70–1, 191–2, 207; Roman-Spartan 183, 184, 187–8, 205–6; 'Social' 137–9; Sparta-Macedonian 99–100; Syrian 12, 58, 75–82, 246 (First 12–13, 14, 42, 58, 66; Second 13, 41, 79–81, 86; Third 13, 43, 81–2, 87, 91; Fourth 13, 103–4, 115; Fifth 13, 14, 41, 95, 100–7, 113, 177–80, 199–200, 242, 244; Sixth 15, 231, 242, 244; Seventh 46)
Wotton, Sir Henry 7

Xanthos 80
Xerxes, Armenian king 49, 110–11, 200–1

Zakynthos 198
Zama, battle 170, 204
Zenodoros, Kilikian chieftain 241
Zeuxis, Seleukid viceroy 61, 109, 207
Ziaelas, Bithynian king 44, 45
Zipoetes, Bithynian king 66